MATERIALS FOR ARCHITECTS AND BUILDERS
AN INTRODUCTION

ARTHUR LYONS

*MA (Cantab) MSc (Warwick) PhD (Leicester) DipArchCons (Leics) Hon LRSA
Principal Lecturer in Building Materials and Computer Aided Design, School of the
Built Environment, De Montfort University, Leicester, UK*

BUTTERWORTH
HEINEMANN

OXFORD   AMSTERDAM   BOSTON   LONDON   NEW YORK   PARIS
SAN DIEGO   SAN FRANCISCO   SINGAPORE   SYDNEY   TOKYO

Butterworth-Heinemann
An imprint of Elsevier Science
Linacre House, Jordan Hill, Oxford OX2 8DP
225 Wildwood Avenue, Woburn MA 01801-2041

First published 1997
Transferred to digital printing 2002

British Library Cataloguing in Publication Data
A catalogue record for this book is available from the British Library

ISBN 0 340 64556 3

For information on all Butterworth-Heinemann publications
visit our website at www.bh.com

Printed and bound in Great Britain by Antony Rowe Ltd, Eastbourne

CONTENTS

—

LIST OF COLOUR PLATES

—

ABOUT THE AUTHOR

—

Dr Arthur Lyons is principal lecturer in building materials and computer aided design within the School of the Built Environment, De Montfort University, Leicester, UK. He was educated at Trinity Hall, Cambridge; Warwick and Leicester Universities in the fields of natural sciences and polymer science and has a diploma in architectural building conservation. He has been a lecturer in building materials within schools of architecture, surveying and the built environment for over 20 years. Dr Lyons was recently honoured with life membership of the Leicestershire and Rutland Society of Architects in recognition of his services to architects and architecture.

PREFACE

—

Materials for Architects and Builders is written as an introductory text to inform students at undergraduate degree and national diploma level of relevant visual and physical properties of the standard building materials. There are 15 chapters covering the wide range of materials under traditional headings. Each section describes the manufacture, salient properties and typical uses of the various materials, with the aim of ensuring their appropriate application. Key materials are also illustrated by their use within buildings of architectural merit.

European Standards have been incorporated alongside the former British Standards, and comparisons are made to update readers who are more familiar with the earlier data and terminology. Where names of materials or their spellings have already been affected by European rationalisation, the new terms have been explained and used. For example: 'stress grading' for timber becomes 'strength grading'; 'sulphate-resisting' becomes 'sulfate-resisting' for cement; and grade 43A steel is now designated as S275. However, despite rapid changes in relation to the designations for timber, concrete and steel, some materials of construction have yet to be significantly affected by European legislation.

New materials where they are becoming well integrated into standard building processes are described; older materials no longer in use are generally disregarded. The use of chemical terminology is kept to the minimum required to understand each subject area, and is only significantly used within the context of the structure of plastics. Tabulated data are restricted to an informative level appropriate to student use. An extensive bibliography and listed sources of technical information are provided at the end of each chapter to facilitate direct reference where necessary.

The text is well illustrated with over 150 line drawings and photographs, showing the production, appearance and appropriate use of materials, but it is not intended to describe construction details as these are well illustrated in the standard texts on building construction. Environmental concerns, including energy-conscious design, and the effects of fire, are automatically considered as part of the broader understanding of the various key materials.

The text is essential reading for degree, BTEC and advanced GNVQ students of architecture, building, surveying and construction, and those studying within the broad range of built environment subjects who wish to understand the principles relating to the appropriate use of construction materials.

Arthur Lyons
October 1996

ACKNOWLEDGEMENTS

—

I wish to acknowledge the assistance of my colleagues in the School of the Built Environment of De Montfort University, Leicester, and in particular, Professor Peter Swallow, for reviewing the various chapters of this book. I wish to thank my wife, Susan, for her participation and support during the production of this work, also my daughters Claire and Elizabeth for their constant encouragement. I am indebted to the numerous manufacturers of building materials for their trade literature and for permissions to reproduce their published data and diagrams. I am grateful to building owners, architectural practices and their photographers for the inclusion of the colour photographs; to Her Majesty's Stationery Office, the Building Research Establishment, the British Standards Institution and trade associations for the inclusion of their material.

I should like to thank the following organisations for giving permission to use illustrations:

ANMAC Ltd. (Fig. 11.2); Baggeridge Brick Plc. (Fig. 1.13); BDC Concrete Products Ltd. (Fig. 2.11); the British Cement Association (Figs. 3.4, 3.5, 3.8 and 3.17–3.19); British Steel Plc. (Figs. 5.1–5.5 and 5.9); Cem-FIL International Ltd. (Fig. 11.4); the Copper Development Association (Fig. 5.13); Hanson Brick Ltd. (Fig. 1.3); James & Son Ltd. (Fig. 11.6); KME UK Ltd. (Figs. 5.12 and 5.13); the Lead Sheet Association (Fig. 5.14); the Metal Cladding and Roofing Manufacturers Association (Fig. 5.11); Natural Stone Products Ltd. (Fig. 9.4); NedZinc BV (Fig. 5.15); Pilkington Glass Ltd. (Figs. 5.7, 7.5, 7.7, 7.8 and 7.16); Pyrobel (Fig. 7.11); Redland Plc. (Fig. 1.8); the Securiglass Company Ltd. (Fig. 7.10); the Steel Construction Institute (Figs. 5.5 and 5.8); the Stone Federation of Great Britain (Fig. 9.2); Tarmac Masonry Products Ltd. (Fig. 2.6); TRADA Technology Ltd. (Figs. 4.10 and 4.11); and the Zinc Development Association (Fig. 5.15).

INFORMATION SOURCES

—

Specific information relating to the materials described in each chapter is given at the end of the appropriate section; however, the following are sources of general information relating to construction materials.

- Building Regulations 1991, 1995 and Approved Documents
- Specification (published annually)
- RIBA Office Library and Barbour Index (updated regularly)
- Building Research Establishment (BRE) publications
- Trade association publications
- Trade literature and journals
- British Board of Agrément certificates
- British and European Standards updated in the quarterly *BSI News*
- Eurocodes:
     Eurocode 1 Basis of design and actions on structures (1995)
     Eurocode 2 Design of concrete structures (1992)
     Eurocode 3 Design of steel structures (1992)
     Eurocode 4 Design of composite steel and concrete structures (1994)
     Eurocode 5 Design of timber structures (1994)
     Eurocode 6 Design of masonry structures (ENV 1995)
     Eurocode 7 Geotechnical design (1995)
     Eurocode 8 Design provisions for earthquake resistance of structures (1996)
     Eurocode 9 Design of aluminium alloy structures (expected 1997).

The Eurocodes establish standards for the design of structures across the European Union. To date,

Eurocodes 1 to 5, 7 and 8 including concrete, steel, composite and timber, have been published; the others are in preparation. The British Cement Association, the Steel Construction Institute and the Timber Research and Development Association have published guidance on their respective Eurocodes published to date. The Brick Development Association is participating in the development of Eurocode 6.

European Standards (EN) have been published for a wide range of materials. A full European Standard, known in the UK as BS EN, is mandatory and over-rules any conflicting previous British Standard, which must be withdrawn. Prior to full publication, the Draft European Standards are coded prEN. Prospective standards, where documentation is in preparation, are published as European pre-standards (ENV). These are similar to the previous British Drafts for Development (DD) and would normally be converted to full European Standards (EN) after the three-year experimental period, when any conflicting national standards would have to be withdrawn. The BRE Digest 397 (1995) gives guidance on the harmonisation of standards within Europe and BRE Digest 408 (1995) outlines the attestation of conformity and ' CE ' marking for construction products within the single European market.

The Building Research Establishment (BRE) publishes informative and authoritative material on a wide range of subjects relating to construction. Trade associations produce advisory and promotional literature relating to their particular area of interest within the building industry.

Information for this text has been obtained from a wide selection of sources to produce a student text with an overview of the production, nature and properties of a diverse range of building materials. New individual products and modifications to existing products frequently enter the market; some materials become unavailable. Detailed information, and particularly current technical data relating to any specific product for specification purposes, must therefore be obtained directly from the manufacturers or suppliers and cross-checked against current standards and regulations.

ABBREVIATIONS

GENERAL

ABS	acrylonitrile butadiene system
APP	atactic polypropylene
ASR	alkali–silica reaction
CFCs	chlorofluorocarbons
CPE	chlorinated polyethylene
CPVC	chlorinated polyvinyl chloride
CSPE	chlorosulfonated polyethylene
DD	draft for development
DPC	damp-proof course
DPM	damp-proof membrane
EN	Euronorm
ENV	Euronorm pre-standard
EPDM	ethylene propylene diene monomer
EPR	ethylene propylene rubber
EVA	ethylene vinyl acetate
FPA	flexible polypropylene alloy
GGBS	ground granulated blastfurnace slag
GRC	glass-fibre reinforced cement
GRG	glass-fibre reinforced gypsum
GRP	glass-fibre reinforced polyester
HCFCs	hydrochlorofluorocarbons
HDPE	high-density polythene
LDP	low-density polythene
MAF	movement accommodation factor
MDF	medium-density fibreboard
MDFMR	medium-density fibreboard, mositure resistant
ODP	ozone depletion potential
OPC	ordinary Portland cement
OSB	oriented strand board
PBAC	polystyrene-bead aggregate cement
PFA	pulverised fuel ash
PHA	partially halogenated alkane
PIB	polyisobutylene
PIR	polyisocyanurate foam
PMMA	polymethyl methacrylate
PTFE	polytetrafluoroethylene
PUR	rigid polyurethane foam
PVA	polyvinyl acetate
PVC	polyvinyl chloride (plasticised)
PVC-U	polyvinyl chloride (unplasticised)
SBS	styrene butadiene styrene
Sg	specific gravity
THF	tetrahydrofuran
UF	urea-formaldehyde
VET	vinyl ethylene terpolymer

UNITS

dB	decibel
µm	micrometre, or micron (10^{-6} m)
nm	nanometre (10^{-9} m)

CHEMICAL SYMBOLS

Al	aluminium
C	carbon
Ca	calcium
Cl	chlorine
Cr	chromium
F	fluorine
Fe	iron
Mn	manganese
Mo	molybdenum
N	nitrogen
Ni	nickel
O	oxygen
S	sulfur
Si	silicon
Sn	tin
Zn	zinc

CEMENT NOTATION

C_2S	dicalcium sicilate
C_3S	tricalcium silicate
C_3A	tricalcium aluminate
C_4AF	tetracalciumaluminoferrite

BRICKS AND BRICKWORK

Introduction

Originally, bricks were hand moulded from moist clay and then sun baked, as is still the current practice in certain arid climates. The firing of clay bricks dates back well over 5000 years, and is now a sophisticated and highly controlled manufacturing process; yet the principle of burning clay, to convert it from its natural plastic state into a dimensionally stable, durable, low-maintenance ceramic material, remains unchanged.

Clay bricks

The wide range of clays suitable for brick making in the UK gives a diversity to the products available. This variety is further increased by the effects of blending clays, the various forming processes, the application of surface finishes and the adjustment of firing conditions. Earlier this century most areas had their own brickworks with characteristic products; however, ease of road transportation and continuing amalgamations within the industry have left a reduced number of major producers and only a few small independent works.

The main constituents of brick-making clays are silica (sand) and alumina, but with varying quantities of chalk, lime, iron oxide and other minor constituents, e.g. fireclay, according to their source. The largest UK manufacturer uses the Lower Oxford clays of Bedfordshire, Buckinghamshire and Cambridgeshire to produce the *Fletton* brick. This clay has some carbonaceous content that reduces the amount of fuel required to burn the bricks, reducing cost and producing a rather porous structure. Other particularly characteristic bricks are the strongly coloured *Staffordshire Blues* and *Accrington Reds* from clays containing high iron content and the yellow *London Stocks* from the Essex and Kent chalky clays with lower iron content.

SIZE

The standard metric brick is $215 \times 102.5 \times 65$ mm, weighing between 2 and 4 kg, and is easily held in one hand. The length of a brick (215 mm) is equal to twice its width (102.5 mm) plus one standard 10 mm joint and three times its height (65 mm) plus two standard joints (Fig. 1.1).

The building industry modular co-ordination is based on multiples of 300 mm (British Standard BS 6750: 1986); thus four courses of 65 mm brickwork with joints give a vertical height of 300 mm, and four stretchers with joints co-ordinate to 900 mm. The British Standard (BS 3921: 1985) lays down maximum and minimum dimensions for the cumulative length, width and height of a random sample of 24 bricks as shown in Table 1.1. No individual brick may have any dimension exceeding the appropriate co-ordinating size. The standard allows for a significant range of size, which may cause problems on site in carefully detailed brickwork, for example, when all the bricks are well to the lower end of the permitted range. The European Standard (EN 771) will determine acceptable tolerance limits on clay brick sizes in relation to the square root of the mean work size measured for ten bricks.

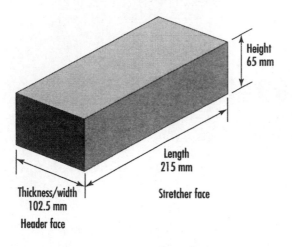

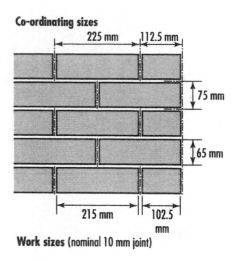

Work sizes (nominal 10 mm joint)

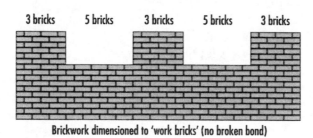

Brickwork dimensioned to 'work bricks' (no broken bond)

Fig. 1.1 Brick and co-ordinating sizes

Table 1.1 Tolerances on 24 bricks to BS 3921: 1985

	Brick dimensions	Limiting overall measurements for 24 bricks (mm)			
		Standard	Maximum	Minimum	Difference
Length	215	5160	5235	5085	150
Width	102.5	2460	2505	2415	90
Height	65	1560	1605	1515	90

The metric standard evolved from the slightly larger Imperial sizes, typically 9 × 4⅞ × 2⅞ in (229 × 111 × 73 mm). Some manufacturers offer a limited range of bricks to full Imperial dimensions, or alternatively to a depth of 73 mm, for bonding in to Imperial brickwork for restoration and conservation work.

The 1970s saw the introduction of metric modular bricks with co-ordination sizes of either 200 or 300 mm in length, 100 mm wide and either 75 or 100 mm in height. The popularity of these bricks has now declined, but they did give the architect opportunities for increasing or reducing horizontal emphasis and scale within the context of traditional brickwork. The British Standard BS 6649: 1985 now only refers to the 200 × 100 × 75 mm modular co-ordinating format.

MANUFACTURE OF CLAY BRICKS

There are five main processes in the manufacture of clay bricks:

- extraction of the raw material;
- forming processes;
- drying;
- firing;
- packing and distribution.

Extraction of the raw material

The process begins with the extraction of the raw material from the quarry and its transportation to the works, by conveyor belt or road transport. Topsoil and unsuitable overburden are removed first and used for site reclamation after the usable clay is removed.

The raw material is screened to remove any rocks, then ground into fine powder by a series of crushers and rollers, with further screening to remove any oversize particles. Small quantities of pigments or other clays may be blended in at this stage to produce various colour effects; for example, manganese dioxide will produce an almost black brick and fireclay gives a teak brown effect. Occasionally, coke breeze is added into the clay as a source of fuel for the firing process. Finally, depending on the subsequent brick forming process, up to 25% water may be added to give the required plasticity.

Forming processes

Handmade bricks

The handmade process involves the throwing of a suitably sized clot of wet clay into a wooden mould on a bench. The surplus clay is struck off with a framed wire and the green brick removed. The bricks produced are irregular in shape with soft arrises or edges and interestingly folded surfaces. Two variations of the process are pallet moulding and slop moulding.

In pallet moulding, a stock board, the size of the bed face of the brick, is fixed to the bench. The mould fits loosely over the stock board, and is adjusted in height to give the appropriate thickness to the green brick. The mould and board are sanded to ease removal of the green brick, which is produced with a *frog* or depression on one face. With slop moulding, the stock mould is placed directly on the bench, and is usually wetted rather than sanded to allow removal of the green brick, which, unlike the pallet-moulded brick, is smooth on both bed faces (Fig. 1.2).

Soft mud process

The handmade process has now largely been automated, with the clay being mechanically thrown into pre-sanded moulds; the excess clay is then removed and the bricks released from the mould. These *soft mud* process bricks retain much of the individuality associated with true handmade bricks, but at a lower cost.

Pressed bricks

In the *semi-dry* process used for *Fletton* bricks the appropriate quantity of clay is subjected to a sequence of four pressings within steel moulds to produce the green brick. These bricks usually have a deep frog on

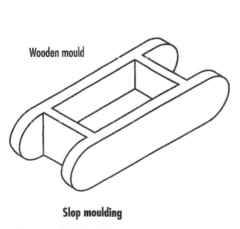

Slop moulding

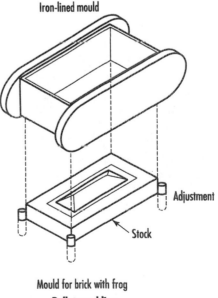

Mould for brick with frog
Pallet moulding

Fig. 1.2 Moulds for handmade bricks

one bed face. For facing bricks, texturing on both headers and one stretcher may be applied by a series of rollers. A water spray to moisten the surface, followed by a blast of a sand/pigment mixture, produces the sand-faced finish.

With clays that require a slightly higher water content for moulding, the *stiff plastic* process is used in which brick-size clots of clay are forced into the moulds. A single press is then required to form the brick. Engineering bricks made by this process often have shallow frogs on both bed faces. In all cases the size of the mould is calculated to allow for the anticipated drying and firing shrinkage.

Extruded wire cut bricks

In this process clay with a water content of up to 25% is fed into a screw extruder which consolidates the clay and extracts the air. The clay is forced through a die and forms a continuous column with dimensions equal to the length and width of a green brick (Fig. 1.3). The surface may then be textured or sanded, before the clay column is cut into brick units by a series of wires. The bed faces of wire cut bricks often show the drag marks where the wires have cut through the extruded clay. Perforated wire cut bricks are produced by the incorporation of rods or tines between the screw extruder and the die. The perforations save clay and allow for a more uniform drying and firing of the bricks without significant loss of strength. Thermal performance is not significantly improved by the incorporation of such voids.

Fig. 1.3 Extruding wire cut bricks

Drying

To prevent cracking and distortion during the firing process, green bricks produced from wet clays must be allowed to dry out and shrink. Shrinkage is typically 10% on each dimension, depending upon the moisture content. The green bricks, laid in an open chequerwork pattern to ensure a uniform loss of moisture, are stacked in, or passed through, drying chambers which are warmed with the waste heat from the firing process. Drying temperatures and humidity levels are carefully controlled to ensure shrinkage without distortion.

Firing

Both intermittent and continuous kilns are used for firing bricks. The former are used in a batch process in which the single kiln is loaded, fired, cooled and unloaded. In continuous kilns, the firing process is always active; either the green bricks are moved through a fixed firing zone, or the fire is gradually moved around a series of interconnecting chambers to the unfired bricks. Both continuous systems are more energy efficient than the intermittent processes. Generally, for large-scale production, the continuous tunnel kiln (Fig. 1.4) and the Hoffman kiln (Fig. 1.5) are used. Down-draught kilns, clamps and intermittent gas-fired kilns are used for the more specialised products. Dependent on the composition of the clay and the nature of the desired product, firing temperatures are set to sinter or vitrify the clay. Colour variations called *kiss-marks* occur where bricks were in contact with each other within the kiln and are particularly noticeable on *Flettons*.

Tunnel kiln

In the tunnel kiln process the bricks are loaded 10 to 14 high on kiln cars which are moved progressively through the preheating, firing and cooling zones. A carefully controlled temperature profile within the kiln and an appropriate kiln car speed ensures that the green bricks are correctly fired with the minimum use of fuel, usually natural gas. The maximum firing temperature within the range 940°C to 1200°C depends upon the clay, but is normally around 1050°C, with an average kiln time of three days. The oxygen content within the atmosphere of the kiln will affect the colour of the brick products. Typically a high temperature and low oxygen content

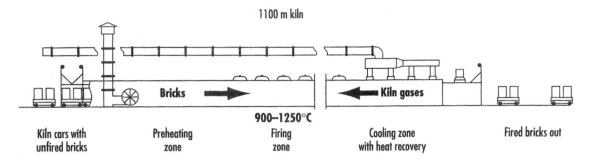

Fig. 1.4 Tunnel kiln

are used in the manufacture of blue bricks. A higher oxygen content will turn any iron oxide within the clay red.

Hoffman kiln

Introduced in 1858, the Hoffman kiln is a continuous kiln in which the fire is transferred around a series of chambers which can be interconnected by the opening of dampers. There may be 12, 16 or 24 chambers, although 16 is usual. The chambers are filled with typically 100 000 green bricks. The chambers in front of the fire, as it moves around, are preheated, then firing takes place (at 960–1000°C), followed by cooling, unloading and resetting of the next load. The sequence moves on one chamber per day, with three days of burning. The usual fuel is low-grade coal, although natural gas and land-fill methane are used by some manufacturers.

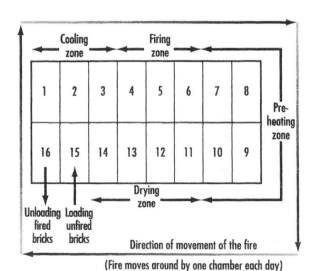

Fig. 1.5 Hoffman kiln plan

Intermittent gas-fired kilns

Intermittent gas-fired kilns are frequently used for firing smaller loads, particularly *specials*. In one system, green bricks are stacked onto a concrete base and a mobile kiln is lowered over the bricks for the firing process. The firing conditions can be accurately controlled to match those within continuous kilns.

Clamps

The basis of clamp firing is the inclusion of coke breeze in the clay, which then acts as the major source of energy during the firing process. In the traditional process, alternate layers of unfired bricks and additional coke breeze are stacked up and then sealed over with waste bricks and clay. The clamp is then ignited with kindling material and allowed to burn for two to five weeks. After firing, the bricks are hand selected because of their variable finish from under- to over-fired. More recently, gas-fired clamps have been developed which give a fully controlled firing process but which still produce bricks with the characteristic dark patches on their surfaces caused by the burnt breeze content.

Down-draught kilns

Down-draught kilns are used for high-temperature firing, especially of engineering bricks, in an intermittent process. Fuel is burnt around the perimeter of the kiln, which is stacked with green bricks. The hot gases rise towards the domed roof, forcing down the cooler gases through a perforated floor and out to the chimney. Thus the heat is retained and the very high temperatures needed for hard-burnt bricks are achieved.

Packaging and distribution

Damaged or cracked bricks are removed prior to packing. Most bricks are now banded and shrink-wrapped into packs of between 300 and 500, for easy transport by fork-lift truck and specialist road vehicles. Special shapes are frequently shrink-wrapped onto wooden pallets.

SPECIFICATION OF CLAY BRICKS

To specify a particular brick it is necessary to define certain key criteria, which relate to form, durability and appearance. The British Standard BS 3921: 1985 gives a performance specification based on size, frost resistance, soluble-salt content, compressive strength and visual appearance, but these criteria alone are insufficient to specify a particular brick.

Within the building industry the classification is based on a combination of several traditional descriptions:

- place of origin and particular name (e.g. Staffordshire smooth blue);
- clay composition (e.g. Gault, Weald or Lower Oxford Clay, Etruria Marl, Keuper Marl (Mercian Mudstones) or shale);
- variety – typical use (e.g. Class A engineering, common or facing);
- type – form and manufacturing process (e.g. solid, frogged, wire cut);
- appearance – colour and surface texture (e.g. coral red rustic);
- durability (e.g. specified frost resistance and soluble-salt content);
- physical properties (e.g. strength if a figure greater than 5 N/mm^2 is required).

Variety

Bricks may be described as common, facing or engineering.

Common bricks

Common bricks have no visual finish and are therefore usually used for general building work, especially where the brickwork is to be rendered or plastered, or will be unseen in the finished work.

Facing bricks

Facing bricks are manufactured and selected to give an attractive finish. The particular colour, which may be uniform or multicoloured, results from the blend of clay used, and the firing conditions. Additionally, the surface may be smooth, textured or sand-faced as required. Facing bricks are used for most visual brickwork where a pleasing and durable finish is required.

Engineering bricks

Engineering bricks are dense and vitreous, with specific loadbearing characteristics and defined low water absorption. The two classes (A and B) in the British Standard BS 3921: 1985 are defined according to their minimum average crushing strengths and water absorption (Table 1.2). Engineering bricks are used to support heavy loads, and also in positions where the effects of impact damage, water absorption or chemical attack need to be minimised. They are generally *reds* or *blues* and are more expensive than other machine-made facing bricks, because of their higher firing temperature.

Type

Type refers to the form of the brick and defines whether it is solid, frogged, cellular, perforated, or of a special shape (Figs. 1.6 and 1.7). By definition (BS 3921: 1985), frogged bricks may have depressions on one or both bed faces but the total volume of frog should not exceed 20% of that of the whole brick. Perforated bricks may have holes up to 25% of the gross volume of the brick but with no hole more than 10% of the volume and with a 30% minimum total thickness of material measured across the brick from the stretcher face. Cellular bricks have cavities closed at one end. Keyed bricks are used to give a good bond to plaster or cement rendering.

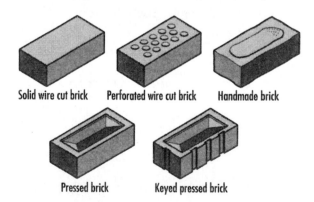

Fig. 1.6 Brick types

Solid wire cut brick　Perforated wire cut brick　Handmade brick

Pressed brick　Keyed pressed brick

For maximum strength, weather resistance and sound insulation, bricks should be laid with the frogs uppermost, so that the frogs are completely filled with mortar; with double-frogged bricks the deeper frog should be uppermost. Manufacturers normally quote compressive strengths on the basis of fully

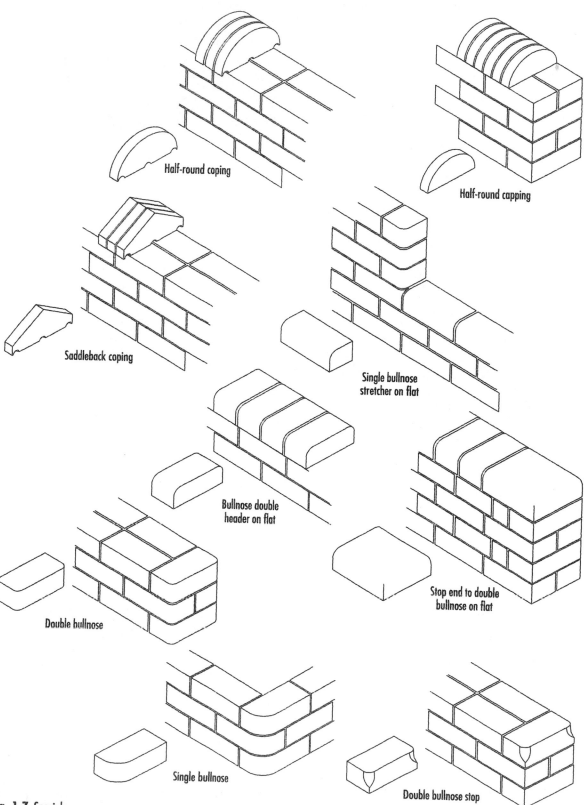

Half-round coping

Half-round capping

Saddleback coping

Single bullnose
stretcher on flat

Bullnose double
header on flat

Double bullnose

Stop end to double
bullnose on flat

Single bullnose

Double bullnose stop

Fig. 1.7 Specials

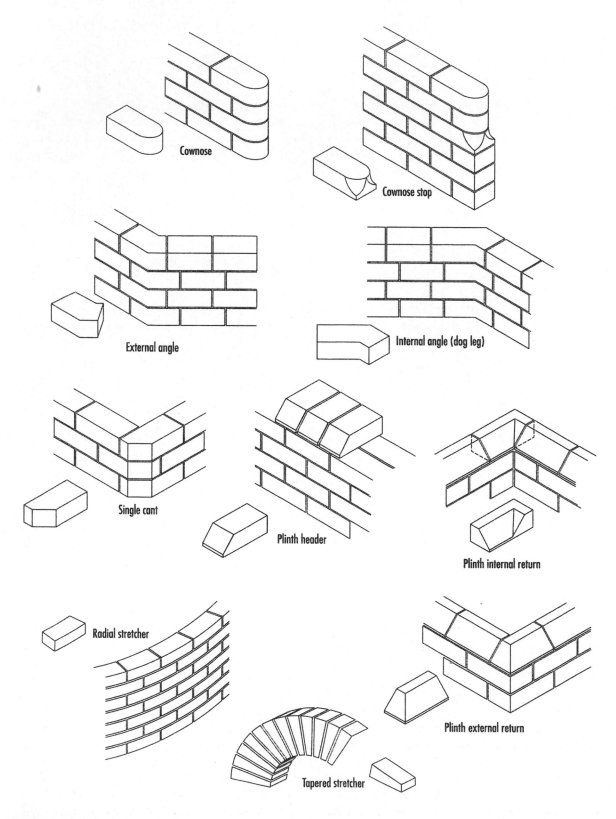

Cownose

Cownose stop

External angle

Internal angle (dog leg)

Single cant

Plinth header

Plinth internal return

Radial stretcher

Plinth external return

Tapered stretcher

Fig. 1.7 (continued)

filled frogs; however, for cheapness, speed and possibly to minimise the dead weight of construction, frogged bricks are frequently laid frog-down. Inevitably this leads to a resultant reduction in their loadbearing capacity.

Standard specials

Increasingly, *specials* (special shapes) are being used to enhance the architectural quality of brickwork. British Standard BS 4729: 1990 illustrates the range of standard specials, which normally can be made to order to match standard bricks (Fig. 1.7). Manufacturers also frequently make purpose-made specials (*special specials*) to the particular requirements of the architect or builder. Inevitably, delivery of specials takes longer than for ordinary bricks, and their separate firing frequently leads to some colour variation between the specials and the standard bricks, even where the clay used is identical. The more complex specials are handmade, usually in specially shaped stock moulds, although some can be made by modifying standard bricks before firing. The range of shapes includes copings and cappings (for parapets and freestanding walls), bullnose (for corner details, e.g. window and door reveals), plinths (for corbelling details and cills), cants (for turning angles), arches and brick slips (to mask reinforced concrete lintels, etc.). Special bricks are also manufactured by cutting standard bricks, then, if necessary, bonding the pieces with epoxy resins. This has the advantage of ensuring an exact colour match to the standard bricks. Many brick slips and arch voussoirs sets (bricks to create an arch) are produced by this method.

APPEARANCE

The colour range of bricks manufactured in the UK is extensive. The colours range from light buffs, greys and yellows through pastel pink to strong reds, blues, browns and deep blue/black, depending mainly upon the clay and the firing conditions, but also on the addition of pigments to the clay or the application of a sand facing. Colours may be uniform, varied over the surface of individual bricks or varied from brick to brick. The brick forms vary from precise to those with rounded arrises; textures range from smooth and sanded to textured and deeply folded, depending upon the forming process (Fig. 1.8).

In view of the variability of bricks from batch to batch it is essential that they should be well mixed, preferably at the factory before palleting, or, failing this, on site. If this is not done sufficiently, accidental colour banding will appear as the brickwork proceeds. Sand-faced bricks are liable to surface damage on handling, which exposes the underlying colour of the brick. Chipping of the arrises on bricks with *through colour* is visually less detrimental. Where rainwater run-off is an important factor, e.g. on cills and copings, smooth rather than heavily rusticated bricks should be used, as the latter would saturate and stain. Handmade bricks with deep surface folds should be laid frog-up so that the creases or *smiles* tend to shed the rainwater from the face of the brickwork.

Imported glazed bricks, which are available in a wide range of intense colours, are sometimes used for their strong aesthetic effect or resistance to graffiti. They are commonly manufactured in a two-stage process, which involves the initial firing of the green brick to the *biscuit* stage, followed by the application of a *slip* glaze and a second firing. In an alternative one-stage process a clear slip glaze is applied before firing to allow the natural colour of the brick to show through.

The visual acceptability of facing bricks and the quality of the bricklaying would normally be assessed on site by the construction of a reference panel to an agreed standard, using at least 100 randomly selected bricks with examples of any colour banding, the proposed bonding, mortar and jointing. All subsequent brick deliveries and constructed brickwork should then be checked against the reference panel.

DURABILITY

Frost resistance

Bricks are classified within BS 3921: 1985 into one of three categories: frost-resistant (F), moderately frost-resistant (M) or not frost-resistant (O) (Table 1.3). Only category F is totally resistant to repeated freezing and thawing when in a saturated condition. Category M bricks are durable except when subjected to repeated freezing and thawing under saturated conditions. Therefore, they should not be used in highly exposed situations, such as below damp-proof courses, for parapets or brick-on-edge copings, but are suitable for external walls which are protected from saturation by appropriate

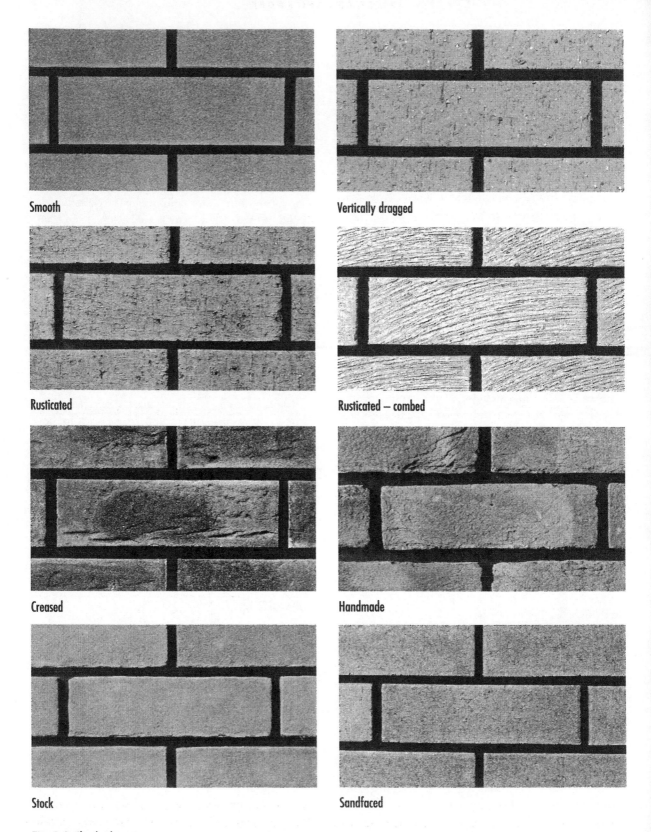

Smooth

Vertically dragged

Rusticated

Rusticated – combed

Creased

Handmade

Stock

Sandfaced

Fig. 1.8 Clay brick textures

details. Category O bricks need to be protected by cladding or used internally.

Soluble-salt content

The soluble-salt content of bricks is defined by two categories: low (L) and normal (N) (Table 1.3), of which only the low category has defined maximum limits. The soluble salts derive from the original clay or from the products of combustion during the firing process. Soluble salts can cause efflorescence: soluble sulfates may migrate from the bricks into the mortar or any rendering, causing it to expand and deteriorate by sulfate attack. If used in an exposed situation, N category bricks should be bonded with sulfate-resisting cement mortar.

Table 1.2 Compressive strengths and water absorption for clay bricks

Designation	Compressive strength	Water absorption
Engineering class A	not less than 70 N/mm²	not more than 4.5%
Engineering class B	not less than 50 N/mm²	not more than 7.0%
Damp-proof course (buildings) — DPC1	not less than 5 N/mm²	not more than 4.5%
Damp-proof course (external works) — DPC2	not less than 5 N/mm²	not more than 7.0%
All other bricks	not less than 5 N/mm²	no limits

Efflorescence

Efflorescence sometimes appears as a white deposit on the surface of new brickwork. It is caused by moisture carrying salts from inside the bricks and mortar to the surface, where the water evaporates leaving the crystalline salts. Under most conditions efflorescence disappears without deleterious effect within one year. In exposed brickwork that is constantly subjected to a cycle of wetting and drying, efflorescence can occur at any time; further, a build-up and expansion of crystalline salts under the surface (*crypto-efflorescence*) may cause the face of the brickwork to crumble or spall. The four categories of efflorescence are defined according to the percentage cover of salt deposit: nil (no deposit of salts), slight (10% maximum), moderate (10–50%) and heavy (over 50%).

Staining

The surface of brickwork may be stained by cement during the building process, or by lime leaching out

Table 1.3 Designation of frost resistance and soluble-salt content for clay bricks

Designation	Frost resistance	Soluble-salt content
FL	frost resistant	low salt content
FN	frost resistant	normal salt content
ML	moderate frost resistance	low salt content
MN	moderate frost resistance	normal salt content
OL	not frost resistant	low salt content
ON	not frost resistant	normal salt content

of the fresh mortar. In either case the excess should be brushed and washed off, without saturating the brickwork.

PHYSICAL PROPERTIES

Compressive strength

Clay bricks are available with a range of compressive strengths from the minimum specification of 5 N/mm² to well over 100 N/mm². The criteria for general use, damp-proof courses and engineering use are set out in Table 1.2.

When crushing strength is being assessed, because of the natural variability of the product, a random sample of 10 bricks should be tested, with all frogs filled with mortar and an average value determined.

Water absorption and suction

The level of water absorption is critical when bricks are to be used for damp-proof courses, or as engineering bricks. Appropriate limits are shown in Table 1.2, although generally absorption ranges from 1% to 35%. Suction rates are now quoted by most brick manufacturers, as high values can adversely affect the bricklaying process. Bricks with high suction rates absorb water rapidly from the mortar, making it insufficiently plastic to allow for repositioning of the bricks as the work proceeds. Generally, low or medium suction rates (1.0–2.0 kg/m² per min) are advantageous. In warm weather, high-suction-rate bricks may be wetted in clean water before laying, but any excess water will cause the brick to float on the mortar bed and also increase the risk of subsequent efflorescence and staining.

Moisture and thermal movement

After the firing process, bricks absorb moisture from the atmosphere and expand irreversibly, up to a maximum of 0.1%. It is therefore recommended that bricks should not be used for at least two weeks after firing (although it is now recognised that this irreversible process may continue at a decreasing rate for 20 years). Subsequent moisture and thermal movements are largely reversible and movement joints allowing for a 1 mm movement per 1 m of brickwork should be allowed, typically at 10–12 m centres and at a maximum of 15 m, in restrained walls. Unrestrained or lightly restrained walls should have movement joints at 7–8 m centres. Horizontal joints should be at approximately 12 m intervals, as the vertical movement is of the same order as movement in the horizontal direction.

For many buildings, the necessary movement joints can be made inconspicuous by careful detailing or can be featured as part of the design. Appropriate locations for movement joints would be where differing structural forms adjoin, such as abutments between walls and columns or where the height or thickness of a wall changes; alternatively, movement joints can be placed at design details such as brickwork returns, re-entrant corners, or the recesses for downpipes. In expansion joints, fillers such as cellular polythene, polyurethane or foam rubber should be used, as these are easily compressible. Pointing should be with a flexible sealing compound, such as two-part polysulfide.

> Typical reversible moisture movement = 0.02%
> Typical reversible thermal movement = 0.03%
> Thermal movement = $4-8 \times 10^{-6}$ deg C^{-1}

Thermal conductivity

The thermal conductivity of brickwork is dependent upon its density and moisture content but generally clay bricks are poor thermal insulators. Brick manufacturers quote thermal conductivities at a standard 5% moisture content for exposed brickwork, and may also give the 1% moisture content figure for protected brickwork.

Using bricks with a typical thermal conductivity of 0.96 W/m K, it is possible to achieve a U-value of 0.45 W/m^2 K, for double-skin brickwork with 50 mm polyurethane or polyisocyanurate board cavity insulation.

The thermal conductivity of clay bricks at 5% moisture content typically ranges between 0.65 and 1.95 W/m K.

Fire resistance

Clay brickwork generally offers excellent fire resistance by retaining its loadbearing capacity, integrity and insulating properties. British Standard BS 5628 Part 3: 1985 indicates that 100 mm and 200 mm of loadbearing clay-brick masonry will give 120 minutes and 6 hours of fire resistance, respectively.

Acoustic properties

Good-quality brickwork is an effective barrier to airborne sound, provided that there are no voids through the mortar for the passage of sound. The average sound insulation value over the normal frequency range (100–3150 Hz) for a half-brick wall is 42 dB, while that for a single brick wall plastered on both sides is 50 dB. Sound absorption by brickwork over the normal frequency range is fairly low and is further decreased by the application of normal plaster or paint. However, the application of acoustic plasters or the provision of gaps in facing brickwork backed by absorbent material will reduce sound reflection.

QUALITY CONTROL

To meet the consistent standards of quality required by clients, many brick manufacturers are now operating quality-assurance systems. These require manufacturers to document all their operational procedures and set out standards to which products must adhere. Quality is controlled by a combination of an internal self-monitoring system and two to four independent spot-check reviews per year. Both the content of the technical literature and the products themselves are subjected to this scrutiny.

Brickwork

CLAY BRICKWORK

The bonding, mortar colour and joint profile have a significant visual effect on brickwork. The overall effect can be to emphasise as a feature or reduce to a minimum the impact of the bonding mortar on the bricks. Additionally the use of polychromatic brickwork with complementary or contrasting colours for quoins, reveals, banding and even graphic designs can have a dramatic effect on the appearance of a building.

The three-dimensional effects of decorative dentil courses and projecting corbelled features offer the designer further opportunities to exploit the effects of light and shade. Normally, a projection of 10–15 mm is sufficient for the visual effect without causing increased susceptibility to staining or frost damage. Curved brickwork constructed in stretcher bond shows faceting and the overhang effect, which is particularly accentuated in oblique light. With small-radii curvatures, the necessary change of bonding pattern to header bond can also be a visual feature, as an alternative to the use of curved-radius bricks.

The *Gothic Revival* exterior of the Queens Building, De Montfort University, Leicester (cover illustration), shows the visual effects of polychromatic brickwork and voussoir specials. This energy-efficient building maximises use of natural lighting, heating and ventilation, using massive masonry walls to reduce peak temperatures. The mortar, which matches the external coral-red brickwork, reduces the visual impact of the individual bricks, giving the effect of planes rather than walls. This is relieved by the colour and shadow effects of the polychromatic and corbelled features, which are incorporated in the ventilation grilles and towers. The special bricks, cill details and banding are picked out in a deeper cadmium red and silver buff to contrast with the characteristic Leicestershire red-brick colouring.

Mortars

The mortar in brickwork is required to give a bearing for the bricks and to act as a sealant between them. Mortars should be weaker than the individual bricks, to ensure that any subsequent movement does not cause visible cracking of the bricks, although too weak a mix would adversely affect the durability of the brickwork. Mortar mixes are based on blends of either cement/lime/sand, masonry cement/sand or cement/sand with plasticiser. When the mix is gauged by volume an allowance has to be made for bulking of damp sand. The five mix designations are shown in Table 1.4. A typical 1:1:6 (cement:lime:sand) mix (designation (iii)) would generally be appropriate and durable for low-rise construction, but for calculated structural brickwork or for increased resistance to frost in exposed situations a greater-strength mortar (designation (i) or (ii)) may be required. In the repointing of old brick-

Table 1.4 Mortar mix designations

Designation	Cement:lime:sand	Masonry cement: sand	Cement:sand with plasticiser
(i)	1:0:3–1:¼:3		
(ii)	1:½:4–1:½:4½	1:2½–1:3½	1:3–1:4
(iii)	1:1:5–1:1:6	1:4–1:5	1:5–1:6
(iv)	1:2:8–1:2:9	1:5½–1:6½	1:7–1:8
(v)	1:3:10–1:3:12	1:6½–1:7	1:8

work it is particularly important to match the porosity of the brick to the water-retention characteristics of the mortar. This prevents excessive loss of water from the mortar before hydration occurs, which may then cause the pointing to crumble.

Sands for mortars are normally graded to BS 1200: 1976, which designates two grades, type S and type G. Type G has more fine material (300, 150 and 75 microns) and therefore requires more cement to achieve the same strength and durability as the equivalent mortar mixed with a type S graded sand.

Ideally, brickwork should be designed to ensure the minimal cutting of bricks, and should be built with a uniform joint width and vertical alignment of the joints (perpends). During construction, brickwork should be kept clean and protected from rain and frost. This reduces the risk of frost damage, patchiness and efflorescence. Brickwork may be rendered externally or plastered internally if sufficient mechanical key is provided by appropriate jointing or the use of keyed bricks. For repointing existing brickwork, it is necessary to match carefully the mortar sand, and to use lime mortar where it was used in the original construction.

Bonding

Figure 1.9 illustrates the effects of bonding. The stretcher bond is standard for cavity walls and normally a half-lap bond is used, but an increase in horizontal emphasis can be achieved by the less standard quarter or third bond. In conservation work it may be necessary to use half bricks (snap headers) to match the appearance of bonding in solid brick walls. For one-brick-thick walls more variations are possible; most typical are the English and Flemish bonds. The equivalent English and Flemish garden wall bonds, which have more stretchers, are primarily used for one-brick-thick walls, where the reduced number of headers makes it easier to build

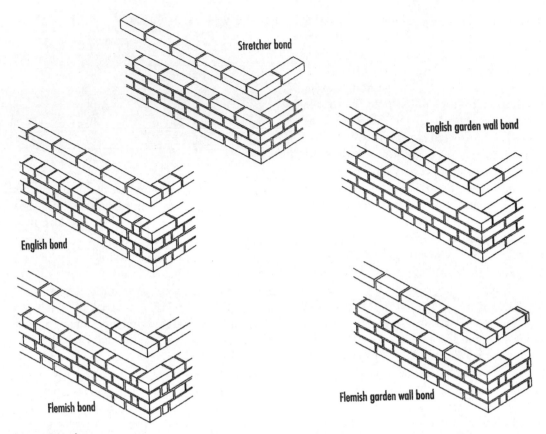

Stretcher bond

English garden wall bond

English bond

Flemish bond

Flemish garden wall bond

Fig. 1.9 Brick bonding

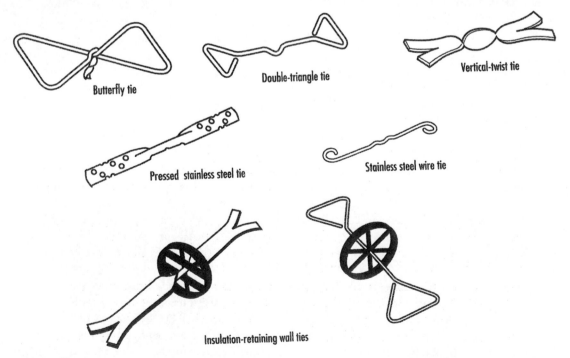

Butterfly tie

Double-triangle tie

Vertical-twist tie

Pressed stainless steel tie

Stainless steel wire tie

Insulation-retaining wall ties

Fig. 1.10 Wall ties

both sides fairfaced. Panels of herringbone brickwork (raking bond), or dog-tooth and dentil courses, as in Victorian brickwork, can generate interesting features.

In all cavity brickwork, wall ties to BS 1243: 1978, manufactured from galvanised steel wire or thin stainless steel strip (Fig. 1.10), should be incorporated according to BS 5628 Part 3: 1985. They should be laid drip down and level or sloping down towards the outer leaf. In partially filled cavities, the wall ties should clip the insulation cavity batts to the inner leaf. In all cases the cavity, insulation and ties should be kept clear of mortar droppings and other residues by using a protective board.

Coloured mortars

Mortar colour has a profound effect on the overall appearance of the brickwork, since with stretcher bond and a standard 10 mm joint, the mortar accounts for 17% of the brickwork surface area. A wide range of light-fast coloured mortars are available which can be used to match or contrast with the bricks, thus highlighting the bricks as units, or creating a unity within the brickwork. The coloured mortars contain inert pigments, which are factory-blended to a tight specification to ensure close colour matching between batches. Occasionally, black mortars may bloom owing to lime migration to the surface. Coloured mortars can be used creatively to enhance the visual impact of the brickwork and even to create designs on sections of otherwise monochromatic brickwork. The quantity of pigment should not exceed 10% by weight of the cement.

Mortar colours may also be modified by the use of stains after curing; however, such applications only penetrate 2 mm into the surface, and therefore tend to be used more for remedial work. Through-body colours are generally more durable than surface applications.

Joint profiles

The standard range of joint profiles is illustrated in Fig. 1.11. It is important that the main criteria should be the shedding of water to prevent excessive saturation of the masonry, which could then deteriorate. Normally the brickwork is jointed as the construction proceeds. This is the cheapest and best method, as it gives the least disturbance to the mortar bed. Pointing involves the raking out of the *green* mortar to a depth of 13–20 mm, followed by refilling of the joint with fresh mortar. This is only appropriate when the desired visual effect cannot be obtained directly by jointing; for example, when a complex pattern of coloured mortar joints is required for aesthetic reasons.

The square recessed (raked) joints articulate the brickwork by featuring the joint, but these should only be used with durable, (FL) high-absorption bricks under sheltered conditions; furthermore, the recess should be limited to a maximum depth of 6 mm. The struck or weathered joint also accentuates the light and shade of the brickwork, while, as a tooled joint, offering good weather resistance in all grades of exposure. If the visual effect of the joint is to be diminished, the flush joint may be used, but the curved recessed (bucket-handle) joint, which is compressed by tooling, offers better appearance and weathering properties. No mortar should be allowed to smear the brickwork, as it is difficult to remove subsequently without the use of dilute acid or pressure jets of water.

Reinforced brickwork

Reinforcement may be introduced vertically or horizontally into brickwork (Fig. 1.12). Bed-joint reinforcement, usually austenitic stainless steel, should be completely surrounded by mortar with a

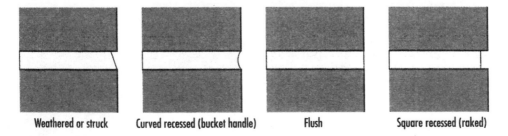

| Weathered or struck | Curved recessed (bucket handle) | Flush | Square recessed (raked) |

Fig. 1.11 Joint profiles

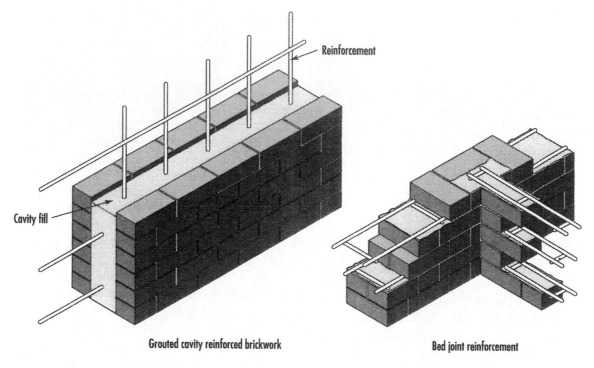

Grouted cavity reinforced brickwork   Bed joint reinforcement

Fig. 1.12 Reinforced brickwork

minimum cover of 15 mm. For continuity in long walls, sections of reinforcement should be sufficiently end lapped. Vertical reinforcement is possible in cavity or in pocket-type walls, where the void spaces are formed in the brickwork, then reinforcement and concrete are introduced after the masonry is completed. Care should be taken when using vibrators to compact the concrete within new masonry.

Decorative brickwork

Plaques, motifs, murals and sophisticated sculptures (Fig. 1.13) can be manufactured to individual designs both for new buildings and for the renovation or refurbishment of Victorian red *terracotta*. The designs are carved as a bas-relief in soft solid through-colour brickwork or moulded in the unfired clay in relatively small units and joined on site with a matching mortar. For repetitive units, the clay is shaped in an appropriate wooden mould. Relief depths of 10–30 mm give shadow and contrast sufficient for most sculptural effects to be seen, although the viewing distances and angles must be considered. For large brickwork sculptures, the whole unit may be built in green bricks, with allowances made for the mortar

joints and drying contraction. The design is then carved, numbered, dismantled, fired and reassembled on site.

Fig. 1.13 Decorative carved brickwork

Preassembled brickwork

The use of preassembled brickwork supported on reinforced concrete or steel frames offers the builder a potentially higher level of quality control and increased speed of construction on site. It also offers the scope to create complex details, and forms such as long, low arches, that would be expensive or impossible in traditional brick construction. Specialist manufacturers produce large complete brick-clad precast-concrete panels. Typically the rear faces of brick slips are drilled at an angle, then stainless steel rods inserted and fixed with resin adhesive. The brick slips are laid out with spacers within the panel mould, prior to the addition of steel reinforcement and concrete. Finally the brick slips are pointed up, giving the appearance of normal brickwork.

CLAY BRICK PAVING

Many clay brick manufacturers produce a range of plain and chamfered paving bricks together with a matching range of paver accessories. Bricks are usually nibbed to set the spacing correctly. The material offers a human scale to large areas of hard landscape, especially if creative use is made of pattern and colour. Typical patterns (Fig. 1.14) include herringbone, running bond, stack bond, basket-weave and the use of borders and bands. Profiled brick designs include decorative diamond and chocolate-bar patterns, and pedestrian-management texturing. The paving bricks may be laid on a hard base with mortar joints or alternatively on a flexible base with fine sand brushed between the pavers. Edge restraint is necessary to prevent lateral spread of the units.

Pavers are classified as PA for pedestrians, motor cars and light vans and PB for, additionally, public transport and commercial vehicles. Table 1.5 shows the standard sizes. Clay pavers are frost resistant and with a high transverse strength as determined by the British Standard three-point loading test (BS 6677: 1986). Wet skid resistance, determined by the British Standard test (BS 6677: 1986), is necessarily high to ensure safe pedestrian use.

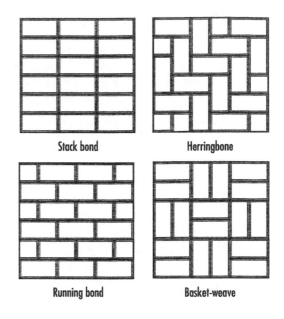

Stack bond   Herringbone

Running bond   Basket-weave

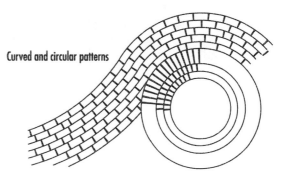

Curved and circular patterns

Fig. 1.14 Paver designs

Table 1.5 Standard work sizes for pavers

Length (mm)	Width (mm)	Thickness (mm)
215	102.5	50
215	102.5	65
210	105	50
210	105	65
200	100	50
200	100	65
200	133	65*
300	200	65*

* (produced by some manufacturers)

Calcium silicate bricks

Calcium silicate bricks, also known as sandlime or flintlime bricks, were first produced commercially in Germany in 1894, and then in the UK in 1905. Initially their use was confined to common brick applications, but in the 1950s their durability for foundations was exploited. Research into mix design and the development of improved manufacturing processes subsequently led to the production of a full range of loadbearing-strength classes and attractive facings. Calcium silicate bricks are competitively priced and have about 3% of the UK brick market.

SIZE

The work size for calcium silicate bricks is 215 × 102.5 × 65 mm, the same as for clay bricks, with a co-ordinating size of 225 × 112.5 × 75 mm, allowing for 10 mm mortar joints. Generally, calcium silicate bricks are more accurate in form and size than fired clay bricks, which inevitably distort in the manufacturing process.

MANUFACTURE OF CALCIUM SILICATE BRICKS (SANDLIME AND FLINTLIME BRICKS)

The raw materials of calcium silicate bricks are silica sand (approximately 90%), hydrated lime, crushed flint, colouring pigments and water. (If quicklime is used, it is fully hydrated before the bricks are pressed, to prevent expansion under the steam treatment.) A mixture of sand, lime and water is used to manufacture the natural white sandlime brick. The addition of colouring pigments or crushed-flint aggregate to the standard components or the application of texturing to the brick surface gives the wider product range.

The appropriately proportioned blend is pressed into brick units, stacked on bogies, moved into the autoclave and subjected to steam pressure (0.8–1.3 N/mm²) for 4 to 15 hours at 180°C (Fig. 1.15). This causes the hydrated lime to react chemically with the surface of the sand particles, enveloping them with hydrated calcium silicates which fill many of the void spaces between the sand particles. Subsequently the calcium silicates react slowly with carbon dioxide from the atmosphere to produce calcium carbonate, with a gradual increase in the strength of the bricks.

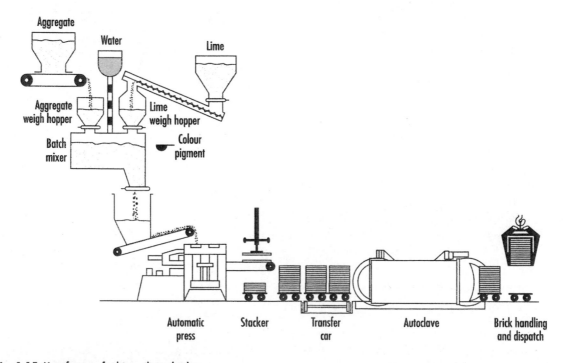

Fig. 1.15 Manufacture of calcium silicate bricks

APPEARANCE

The manufacturing process results in accurate shapes and dimensions, and, with untextured calcium silicate bricks, a smooth finish. The colour range is extensive: from white and pastel shades through to deep reds, blues, browns, greens and yellows. The visual effect of the brickwork tends to be that of precision. The bricks tend to be more brittle than clay bricks and are therefore more susceptible to damage on their arrises.

SPECIFICATION OF CALCIUM SILICATE BRICKS

Types

Both solid and frogged calcium silicate bricks are available. Manufacturers produce a wide range of matching specials to BS 4729: 1990; special specials to clients' requirements and brick slips for facing reinforced concrete.

DURABILITY

Calcium silicate bricks have good frost resistance, but should not be exposed repeatedly to either strong salt solutions, acids or industrial effluent containing magnesium or ammonium sulfates. The bricks have a negligible salt content and therefore efflorescence, and sulfate attack on the mortar, cannot arise from within the bricks. The bricks are themselves resistant to sulfate attack and can therefore be used below ground with a suitable sulfate-resisting cement mortar. However, calcium silicate bricks should not be used as pavers where winter salting can be expected.

PHYSICAL PROPERTIES

Compressive strength

The British Standard BS 187: 1978 defines a range of five classes according to compressive strength, as shown in Table 1.6.

Weight

Calcium silicate bricks weigh between 2.4 and 3.0 kg, depending upon their class.

Water absorption

Water absorption is usually in the range 8–15% by weight as defined by BS 3921: 1985.

Table 1.6 Minimum compressive strength for calcium silicate bricks

Class	Minimum mean compressive strength (N/mm^2)
3	20.5
4	27.5
5	34.5
6	41.5
7	48.5

Moisture and thermal movement

Unlike clay bricks, which expand after firing, calcium silicate bricks contract. This shrinkage is increased if the bricks become wet before use, and therefore site protection of brick stacks from saturation is essential. Similarly, unfinished brickwork should be protected from both saturation and freezing during construction. Reversible moisture movement for calcium silicate bricks is greater than for clay bricks, so expansion joints must be provided at intervals between 7.5 and 9.0 m. Such movement joints should not be bridged by rigid materials. Generally, a weak mortar mix should be used (e.g. 1:2:9 cement:lime:sand), except below damp-proof course level (DPC) and for copings, to prevent visible cracking of either the mortar or the bricks.

Typical reversible moisture movement = ± 0.05%
Typical reversible thermal movement = ± 0.05%
Thermal movement = $8–14 \times 10^{-6}$ deg C^{-1}

Thermal conductivity

The thermal conductivities are equivalent to those of clay bricks of similar densities.

The thermal conductivity of calcium silicate brick ranges from 0.6 W/m K (class 3) to 1.3 W/m K (class 6).

Fire resistance

The fire resistance of calcium silicate bricks is similar to that of clay bricks, with 100 mm giving 120 minutes' and 200 mm giving 6 hours' fire resistance, according to BS 5628 Part 3: 1985. The Building Regulations make no distinction between calcium silicate and other bricks in respect of fire resistance.

Acoustic properties

Acoustic properties are related to mass and are therefore the same as for clay bricks of equivalent density.

Calcium silicate bricks fulfil the Building Regulations: 1985 (England and Wales) for resistance to air-borne sound between dwellings for both 215 mm solid and double 102.5 mm/50 mm cavity walls, provided that all frogs and joints are filled, and the appropriate plastering applied.

CALCIUM SILICATE BRICKWORK

Most design considerations are the same for either clay or calcium silicate brick. However, calcium silicate bricks are particularly popular for their light-reflecting properties, for example in light wells or atria. Their smooth crisp appearance with a non-abrasive surface is particularly appropriate for some interior finishes and also forms an appropriate base for painted finishes. The use of complementary coloured mortars enhances the aesthetic effect of strongly coloured bricks. Their dimensional accuracy gives some advantage in the bricklaying process, and cost is comparable to that of the equivalent clay bricks.

The interior of the Queens Building of De Montfort University, Leicester (Plate 1) illustrates the effective use of calcium silicate brickwork in creating a light internal space. Incorporated within the ivory Flemish-bond brickwork are restrained bands of polychromatic features and robust articulation of obtuse-angle quoins. The accuracy of the brickwork emphasises the clarity of the internal form, reflecting the disciplines of engineering that the building houses.

Concrete bricks

Recent developments in the use of iron oxide pigments have produced a wide range of colour-stable quality concrete-brick products. Currently concrete bricks are competitively priced and hold approximately 10% of the total brick market share.

SIZE

The standard-size of concrete bricks is 215 × 103 × 65 mm, as for clay bricks, but because of their manufacturing process, concrete bricks can be made to close tolerances, so accurate alignment is easy to achieve on site. Half-brick walls can readily be built fairfaced on both sides. Other sizes, as shown in Table 1.7, are listed in BS 6073: 1981.

Table 1.7 Standard and modular sizes for concrete bricks

	Length (mm)	Width (mm)	Height (mm)
Standard	215	103	65
Modular	290	90	90
	190	90	90
	190	90	65

MANUFACTURE OF CONCRETE BRICKS

Concrete bricks are manufactured from blended dense aggregates (e.g. crushed limestone and sand), together with cement under high pressure in steel moulds. Up to 8% of appropriately blended iron oxide pigments (BS 1014: 1985), depending on the tone and depth of colour required, are added to coat the cement particles which will then form the solid matrix with the aggregate. The use of coloured aggregates also increases the colour range. The accurate manufacturing process produces bricks that have clean arrises.

APPEARANCE

A wide range of colours, including multicolours, is available, from red, buff and yellow to green and black. Surfaces range from smooth to simulated natural stone, including those characteristic of handmade and textured clay bricks. Because of the wide range of pigments used in the manufacturing process, it is possible to match effectively new concrete bricks to old and weathered clay bricks for the refurbishment or extension of old buildings.

SPECIFICATION OF CONCRETE BRICKS

Types

Concrete bricks may be solid, perforated or frogged, according to the manufacturer.

Three categories are defined: common, facing and engineering. The latter can be manufactured with a range of strengths and densities to specific requirements. A normal range of specials to BS 4729: 1990 is produced, although, as with clay and calcium silicate bricks, a longer delivery time must be expected.

It is a requirement of BS 6073: 1981 that the manufacturer's reference, the crushing strength, the dimensions and the brick type are clearly identified with each package of concrete bricks. Engineering-quality concrete bricks should be used below ground where sulfates to Class 3 levels (BS 5628) are present.

DURABILITY

Concrete bricks are resistant to frost and are therefore usable in all normal levels of exposure. Like all concrete products, they harden and increase in strength with age. As with calcium silicate bricks, they can be made free of soluble salts and thus free from efflorescence. Concrete bricks should not be used where industrial effluents or acids are present.

PHYSICAL PROPERTIES

Weight and compressive strength

The standard concrete brick weighs approximately 3.2 kg and has a minimum crushing strength of 7.0 N/mm², although 20–40 N/mm² is the typical range. Engineering bricks have a strength of 40 N/mm² with a sulfate-resisting Portland or equivalent cement content of 350 kg/m³ (BS 6073: 1981).

Water absorption

Water absorption is typically 8%, but engineering-quality bricks average less than 7% water absorption after 24 hours' cold immersion, and are suitable for aggressive conditions such as retaining walls, below damp-proof course level and for inspection chambers.

Moisture and thermal movement

Concrete bricks have a typical drying shrinkage of 0.04%, although 0.06% is allowed by BS 6073 Part 1: 1981. Moisture and thermal movements are greater than for calcium silicate bricks and movement joints should be at 5–6 m centres. Because of their moisture movement, prior to laying, concrete bricks should not be wetted to overcome excessive suction, but the water retentivity of the mortar should be adjusted accordingly. Brick stacks should be protected on site from rain, frost and snow.

Thermal conductivity

The thermal conductivities of concrete bricks are equivalent to those of clay and calcium silicate bricks of similar densities. Partially filled cavities, maintaining a clear cavity, are recommended to prevent water penetration to the inner leaf.

The thermal conductivity of concrete bricks ranges between 1.4 and 1.8 W/m K.

The requirements of the Building Regulations Approved Document Part L 1995 Edition for exposed walls can be achieved using concrete bricks with appropriate insulation. A typical partial cavity fill system is:

103 mm concrete facing brick;
50 mm cavity air space;
35 mm aluminium foil faced polyisocyanurate foam;
103 mm concrete common brick;
13 mm lightweight plaster;

giving a U-value of 0.45 W/m² K.

Fire resistance

The fire resistance of concrete bricks is of the same order as that of clay and calcium silicate bricks.

Acoustic properties

Dense concrete bricks are suitable for the reduction of air-borne sound transmission. On a weight basis, they are equivalent to clay and calcium silicate bricks..

CONCRETE BRICKWORK

With the wide range of colour and texture options now offered by concrete-brick manufacturers, it is frequently difficult to distinguish visually, except at close quarters, between concrete and clay brickwork. The visual effects of using coloured mortars and various jointing details are as for clay bricks, but for exposed situations the use of raked joints is not recommended.

References

FURTHER READING

Brick Development Association. 1994: *The BDA guide to successful brickwork*. London: Edward Arnold.
Brunskill, R.W. 1990: *Brick building in Britain*. London: Victor Gollancz.
Lynch, G. 1994: *Brickwork: History, technology and practice*, vol. 1. London: Donhead Publishing.
Lynch, G. 1994: *Brickwork: History, technology and practice*, vol. 2. London: Donhead Publishing.
Nash, W.G. 1983: *Brickwork 1*, 3rd ed. Cheltenham: Stanley Thornes.

Thomas, K. 1996: *Masonry walls – Specification and design*. Oxford: Butterworth-Heinemann.

STANDARDS

BS 187: 1978. Specification for calcium silicate (sandlime and flintlime) bricks.

BS 743: 1970. Materials for damp-proof courses.

BS 1014: 1985. Pigments for Portland cement and Portland cement products.

BS 1200: 1976. Sands for mortar for plain and reinforced brickwork, blockwalling and masonry.

BS 1243: 1978. Specification for metal ties for cavity wall construction.

BS 3921: 1985. Specification for clay bricks.

BS 4729: 1990. Dimensions of bricks of special shapes and sizes.

BS 5628. Code of practice for use of masonry:
    Part 1: 1992. Structural use of unreinforced masonry.
    Part 2: 1995. Structural use of reinforced and pre-stressed masonry.
    Part 3: 1985. Materials and components, design and workmanship.

BS 6073. Precast concrete masonry units:
    Part 1: 1981. Specification for precast concrete masonry units.
    Part 2: 1981. Method for specifying precast concrete masonry units.

BS 6100. Glossary of building and civil engineering terms:
    Part 5. Masonry.
    Sec. 5.1: 1992. Terms common to masonry.
    Sec. 5.3: 1992. Bricks and blocks.

BS 6270. Code of practice for cleaning and surface repair of buildings:
    Part 1: 1982. Natural stone, cast stone and clay and calcium silicate brick masonry.

BS 6477: 1992. Specification for water repellents for masonry surfaces.

BS 6649: 1985. Specification for clay and calcium silicate modular bricks.

BS 6676: Thermal insulation of cavity walls using man-made mineral fibre batts (slabs):
    Part 1: 1986. Specification for man-made mineral fibre batts (slabs).
    Part 2: 1986. Code of practice for installation of batts (slabs) filling the cavity.

BS 6677. Clay and calcium silicate pavers for flexible pavements:
    Part 1: 1986. Specification for pavers.
    Part 2: 1986. Code of practice for design of lightly trafficked pavements.
    Part 3: 1986. Method of construction of pavements.

BS 6750: 1986. Specification for modular co-ordination in building.

BS 8000. Workmanship on building sites:
    Part 3: 1989. Code of practice for masonry.

BS 8103. Structural design of low-rise buildings.
    Part 2: 1996. Code of practice for masonry walls for housing.

BS 8208. Guide to assessment of suitability of external cavity walls for filling with thermal insulation:
    Part 1: 1985. Existing traditional cavity construction.

BS 8215: 1991. Code of practice for design and installation of damp-proof courses in masonry construction.

CP 111: 1970. Structural recommendations for loadbearing walls.

DD 34: 1974. Clay bricks with modular dimensions.

DD 59: 1978. Draft for development for calcium silicate bricks with modular dimensions.

DD 140. Wall ties:
    Part 1: 1986. Method of test for mortar joint and timber frame connections.
    Part 2: 1987. Recommendations for design of wall ties.

DD 155: 1986. Method for determination of polished paver value of pavers.

EN 771. Specification for masonry units:
    Part 1. Clay.
    Part 2. Calcium silicate.
    Part 3. Aggregate concrete.
    Part 4. Autoclaved aerated concrete.
    Part 5. Manufactured stone.
    Part 6. Natural stone.

EN 772. Testing of masonry units.

EN 845:
    Part 1. Ancillary components – tiles, straps, hangers and support angles.
    Part 2. Lintels.
    Part 3. Prefabricated bed-joint reinforcement.

EN 846. Test methods.

EN 998:
    Part 1. Rendering mortar.
    Part 2. Masonry mortar.

EN 1015. Mortar tests.

EN 1745. Determination of designed and declared thermal values.

DD ENV 1991. Eurocode 1: Basis of design and actions on structures.
    Part 1: 1996. Basis of design.
    Part 2.2: 1996. Actions on structures exposed to fire.

DD ENV 1996-1-1. Eurocode 6: Design of masonry structures:
    Part 1.1: Rules for reinforced and unreinforced masonry – crack and deflection control.
    Part 1.2: Design of masonry structures – supplementary rules for structural fire design.

BUILDING RESEARCH ESTABLISHMENT PUBLICATIONS

BRE Digests

BRE Digest 157: 1992. Calcium silicate (sandlime, flintlime) brickwork.
BRE Digest 245: 1986. Rising damp in walls: diagnosis and treatment.
BRE Digest 246: 1981. Strength of brickwork and block-work walls: design for vertical load.
BRE Digest 273: 1983. Perforated clay bricks.
BRE Digest 280: 1983. Cleaning external surfaces of buildings.
BRE Digest 329: 1993. Installing wall ties in existing con-struction.
BRE Digest 359: 1991. Repairing brick and block masonry.
BRE Digest 360: 1991. Testing bond strength of masonry.
BRE Digest 361: 1991. Why do buildings crack?
BRE Digest 362: 1991. Building mortar.
BRE Digest 380: 1993. Damp-proof courses.
BRE Digest 401: 1995. Replacing wall ties.

BRE Defect Action Sheets

BRE DAS 115: 1989. External masonry cavity walls – selection and specification.
BRE DAS 116: 1989. External masonry cavity walls: wall ties – installation.
BRE DAS 128: 1990. Brickwork: prevention of sulphate attack.
BRE DAS 129: 1990. Freestanding masonry boundary walls: stability and movement.
BRE DAS 130: 1990. Freestanding masonry boundary walls: materials and construction.

BRE Good Building Guides

BRE GBG 14: 1992. Building simple plan brick or block-work freestanding walls.
BRE GBG 17: 1993. Freestanding brick walls – repairs to copings and cappings.
BRE GBG 19: 1994. Building reinforced, diaphragm and wide plan freestanding walls.

BRE Information Papers

BRE IP 6/86. The spacing of wall ties in cavity walls.
BRE IP 16/88. Ties for cavity walls: new developments.
BRE IP 12/90. Corrosion of steel wall ties: history of occurrence, background and treatment.
BRE IP 13/90. Corrosion of steel wall ties: recognition and inspection.
BRE IP 10/93. Avoiding latent mortar defects in masonry.

BRE Report

BR 117: 1988. Rain penetration through masonry walls: diagnosis and remedial details.

BRICK DEVELOPMENT ASSOCIATION PUBLICATIONS

Design Notes

DN 3: 1988. Brickwork dimensions tables.
DN 7: 1986. Brickwork durability. J.R. Hardy and R.A. Smith.
DN 8: 1988. Rigid paving with clay pavers. M. Hammett and R.A. Smith.
DN 9: 1988. Flexible paving with clay pavers. R.A. Smith.
DN 10: 1988. Designing for movement in brickwork. J. Morton.
DN 11: 1990. Improved standards of insulation in cavity walls with outer leaf of facing brickwork. R.W. Ford and W.A. Durose.
DN 12: 1991. The design of curved brickwork. M. Hammett and J. Morton.
DN 13: 1993. The use of bricks of special shape.
DN 15: 1992. Brick cladding to timber frame construction.

Building Notes

BN 1: 1991. Brickwork – Good site practice.

Technical Information Paper

TIP 8: 1988. A basic guide to brickwork mortars.

Technical Papers

Hammett, M. (1988) The repair and maintenance of brickwork. *Building Technical Note* 20.
Lilley, A.A. (1990) Flexible brick paving: application and design. *Highways & Transportation* **10**(37).

TRADE ASSOCIATIONS

Brick Development Association, Woodside House, Winkfield, Windsor, Berks. SL4 2DX (01344 885651).
British Wall Tie Association, PO Box 22, Goring, Reading, Berks. RG8 9YX (01734 842674).
Calcium Silicate Brick Association, 24 Fearnley Road, Welwyn Garden City, Herts. AL8 6HW (01707 324538).
Concrete Brick Manufacturers Association, 60 Charles Street, Leicester LE1 1FB (0116 2514568).
Mortar Producers Association Ltd., PO Box 143, Wokingham, Berks. RG40 3YS (01344 761661).

2

BLOCKS AND BLOCKWORK

Introduction

The variety of commercially available concrete blocks is extensive, from dense through to lightweight, offering a range of loadbearing-strength and sound and thermal insulation properties. Where visual blockwork is required either internally or externally, fairfaced blocks offer a selection of textures and colours to a different visual scale compared with that associated with traditional brickwork. Externally, visual concrete blockwork weathers well, provided that adequate attention is given to the quality of the material and rainwater run-off detailing. Blockwork has considerable economic advantages over brickwork in terms of speed of construction, particularly as the lightweight blocks can be lifted in one hand.

While clay blocks are used extensively for masonry construction in continental Europe, there is no demand from the building industry within the UK and they are not commercially available. The use of clay blocks for floor construction has been superseded by the use of reinforced concrete inverted T-beams with concrete infill blocks.

Concrete paving blocks, which offer opportunities for creative hard landscaping with their diversity of form and colour, are widely used for town pedestrian precincts and individual house driveways.

Concrete blocks

TYPES AND SIZES

Concrete blocks are defined as solid, cellular or hollow, as illustrated in Fig. 2.1.

Concrete blocks are manufactured to various workface dimensions in an extensive range of thicknesses, offering a wide choice of loadbearing capacity and level of insulation. The standard workface size, which co-ordinates to three courses of metric brickwork allowing for 10 mm mortar joints, is 440 × 215 mm (Fig. 2.2), but the other sizes in Table 2.1 are allowed within the British Standard BS 6073: 1981 for aesthetic and constructional reasons. For example, narrow bands of a different colour may be used as visual features within fairfaced blockwork and certain specialist foundation or party wall blocks are normally laid flat. Blocks up to 620 mm in length offer speedier construction.

MANUFACTURE

Dense concrete blocks, which may be hollow, cellular or solid in form, are manufactured from natural dense aggregates, including crushed granite, limestone and gravel. Medium and lightweight concrete blocks are manufactured incorporating a wide range of aggregates, including expanded clay, expanded blastfurnace slag, sintered ash and pumice. Concrete is cast into moulds, vibrated and cured. Most aerated blocks are formed by the addition of aluminium powder to a fine mix of sand, lime, fly ash (pulverised fuel ash) and Portland cement. The hydrogen gas generated by the dissolution of the metal powder produces a non-interconnecting cellular structure. The process is accelerated by pressure steam curing in an autoclave (Fig. 2.3). For some products, additional insulation is provided by filling the voids in the cellular blocks or by bonding on a layer of extruded polystyrene, polyurethane or foil-faced

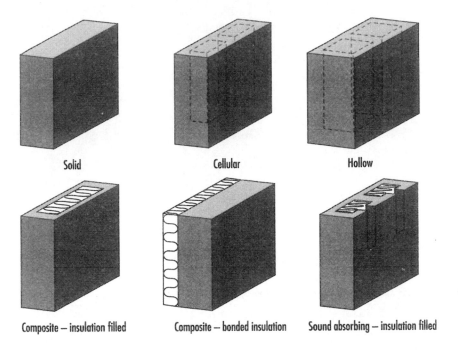

Solid   Cellular   Hollow

Composite – insulation filled   Composite – bonded insulation   Sound absorbing – insulation filled

Fig. 2.1 Types of concrete blocks

phenolic foam (Fig. 2.1). Standard blocks, typically natural grey or buff in colour, are usually shrink-wrapped for delivery.

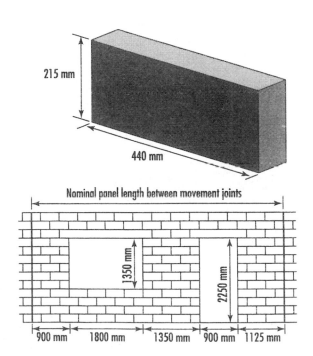

Fig. 2.2 Co-ordinating sizes for blockwork

Table 2.1 Work and co-ordination sizes for concrete blocks

Work size		Co-ordination size		Availability
Length (mm)	Height (mm)	Length (mm)	Height (mm)	
390	190	400	200	widely available
440	215	450	225	most common size
620	215	630	225	limited availability

A selection of thicknesses is produced by most manufacturers from the range 50, 60, 70, 75, 90, 100, 115, 125, 130, 135, 140, 150, 175, 190, 200, 215, 230, 250, 275 and 300 mm.
Coursing blocks to workface heights of 65 mm are usually available.

PROPERTIES

Density and strength

Concrete blocks range in compressive strength from 2.8 N/mm² to 30 N/mm², with associated densities of 420 to 2200 kg/m³ and thermal conductivities from 0.10 to 1.5 W/m K at 3% moisture content (Table 2.2). Blocks of up to 20 kg, (e.g. 440 × 215 × 100 mm at 2000 kg/m³) may be manually handled on site within current health and safety regulations. Drying shrinkages must comply with BS 6073 Part 1: 1981 and are typically in the range 0.03–0.05%.

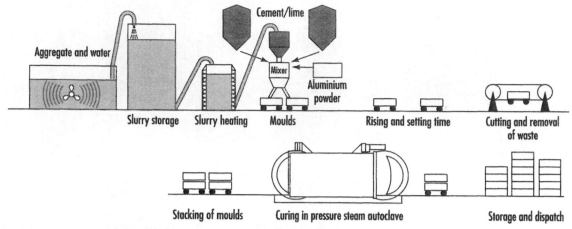

Fig. 2.3 Manufacture of aerated blocks

Table 2.2 Typical relationship between density and thermal conductivity for concrete blocks

Nominal density (kg/m³)	2200	2000	1800	1600	1400	1200	1000	900	800	700	600	500	420
Typical thermal conductivity (W/m K)	1.5	1.10	0.83	0.63	0.47	0.36	0.27	0.24	0.20	0.17	0.15	0.12	0.10

(Blocks of differing compositions will vary from these average figures)

Durability

Dense concrete blocks and certain aerated lightweight blocks are resistant to freeze/thaw conditions below damp-proof course (DPC) level. However, some lightweight concrete blocks, below 7 N/mm² crushing strength, should not be used below DPC level, except for the inner skin of cavity construction.

Fixability

Aerated and lightweight concrete blocks offer a good background for fixings. For light loads, cut nails to a depth of 50 mm are sufficient. For heavier loads, wall plugs and proprietary fixings are necessary. Fixings should avoid the edges of the blocks.

Thermal insulation

The Building Regulations Approved Document Part L 1995 edition set a standard U-value of 0.45 W/m² K for exposed walls. Typically this can be achieved with fairfaced brickwork, a 50 mm cavity, 40–50 mm extruded polystyrene or mineral wool, 100 mm lightweight blocks and gypsum plaster to the interior or the equivalent system with full cavity fill (Fig. 2.4). Similarly, the U-value target of 0.45 W/m² K can be achieved with 100 mm external

fairfaced blockwork as an alternative to fairfaced brickwork, provided that the necessary additional thermal resistance is given by slightly increased cavity insulation or the use of lightweight plaster.

Fire resistance

Concrete block construction offers good fire resistance. Solid unplastered 90 mm blocks can give up to 60 minutes' fire protection when used as load-bearing walls; certain 150 mm and most 215 mm solid blocks can achieve 6 hours' protection.

Sound insulation

The Building Regulations 1991 Approved Document E provides guidance on minimum standards of acoustic insulation for party walls between houses. The passage of air-borne sound depends upon the density and porosity of the material. The following three systems would perform to the required standard.

A A solid 195 or 215 mm wall made from dense concrete blocks of 1950 kg/m³ density, laid flat and plastered to 12.5 mm on both sides, giving an overall weight of at least 415 kg/m².

B Two leaves of 100 mm dense concrete blocks of 1950 kg/m³ density, with a 50 mm cavity and

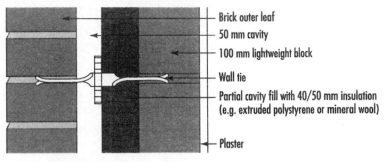

Brick and cavity wall – partial fill system

- Brick outer leaf
- 50 mm cavity
- 100 mm lightweight block
- Wall tie
- Partial cavity fill with 40/50 mm insulation (e.g. extruded polystyrene or mineral wool)
- Plaster

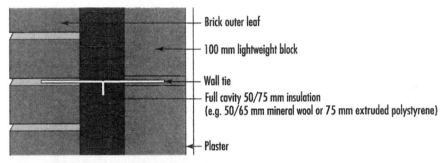

Brick and block cavity wall – full fill system

- Brick outer leaf
- 100 mm lightweight block
- Wall tie
- Full cavity 50/75 mm insulation (e.g. 50/65 mm mineral wool or 75 mm extruded polystyrene)
- Plaster

Fig. 2.4 Typical blockwork cavity construction achieving U-values of at least 0.45 W/m² K

plastered to 12.5 mm on both exposed faces, giving an overall weight of at least 415 kg/m².

C Two leaves of 100 mm lightweight concrete blocks of 1400 kg/m³ density, with a 75 mm cavity and plastered to 12.5 mm on both exposed faces, giving an overall weight of at least 250 kg/m².

These systems will perform to the required standard provided that there are no air leaks within the construction, all joints are filled, and there is no serious loss of thickness caused by chasing out on opposite sides of a single-leaf construction. Vertical chases should, in any case, not be deeper than one third of the block thickness. Horizontal chases should be restricted to not more than one sixth of the block thickness, because of the potential loss of structural strength.

Sound absorption

The majority of standard concrete blocks with hard surfaces are highly reflective to sound, thus creating long reverberation times within building enclosures. Acoustic absorbing concrete blocks are manufactured with a slot on the exposed face which admits sound into the central cavity. Since the void space is lined with sound-absorbing fibrous filler, incident sound is dissipated rather than reflected, significantly reducing reverberation effects. Acoustic control blocks in fairfaced concrete are suitable for use in swimming pools, sports halls, industrial buildings and auditoria.

SPECIALS

Most manufacturers of blocks produce a range of *specials* to match their standard ranges. Quoins, cavity closers, splayed cills, flush or projecting copings, lintel units, bullnose ends and radius blocks are generally available, and other specials can be made to order (Fig. 2.5). The use of specials in fairfaced blockwork can greatly enhance visual qualities. Matching full-length lintels may incorporate dummy joints and should bear onto full, not cut, blocks.

FAIRFACED BLOCKS

Fairfaced concrete blocks are available in a wide range of colours from white, through buff, sandstone,

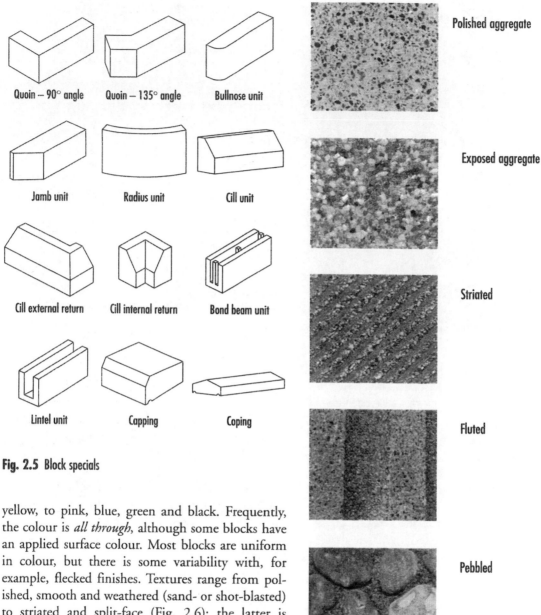

Quoin – 90° angle   Quoin – 135° angle   Bullnose unit

Jamb unit   Radius unit   Cill unit

Cill external return   Cill internal return   Bond beam unit

Lintel unit   Capping   Coping

Fig. 2.5 Block specials

Polished aggregate

Exposed aggregate

Striated

Fluted

Pebbled

Fig. 2.6 Architectural masonry finishes

yellow, to pink, blue, green and black. Frequently, the colour is *all through*, although some blocks have an applied surface colour. Most blocks are uniform in colour, but there is some variability with, for example, flecked finishes. Textures range from polished, smooth and weathered (sand- or shot-blasted) to striated and split-face (Fig. 2.6); the latter is intended to give a random variability associated more with natural stone.

Glazed masonry units are manufactured by the application of a thermosetting material to one or more faces of lightweight concrete blocks which are then heat-treated to cure the finish. The glazed blocks are available in an extensive range of durable bright colours and are suitable for interior or exterior use. Where required, profiled blocks to individual designs can be glazed by this system. Most manufacturers produce a range of specials to co-ordinate with their standard fairfaced blocks, although, as

with special bricks, these specials may be manufactured from a different batch of mix, and this may give rise to slight variations. In specific cases, such as individual lintel blocks, specials are made by cutting standard blocks to ensure exact colour matching.

Blockwork

FAIRFACED BLOCKWORK

With fairfaced blockwork, an appropriate choice of size is important for both co-ordination and visual scale. While blocks can be cut with a masonry cutter, the addition of small pieces of block, or the widening of perpends over the 10 mm standard, is unacceptable. The insertion of a thin *jumper* course at floor or lintel height can be a useful way of adjusting the coursing. Curved blockwork can be constructed from standard blocks, the permissible curvature being dependent upon the block size. The oversail between alternate courses should not normally exceed 4 mm in fairfaced work. If the internal radius is exposed, then the perpends or vertical joints can be maintained at 10 mm with uncut blocks, but if the external radius is exposed, the blocks will require cutting on an angle or splay. For tighter curves *specials* will be required.

BOND

A running half-block bond is standard, but this may be reduced to a quarter bond for aesthetic reasons. Blockwork may incorporate banding of concrete bricks, but because of differences in thermal and moisture movement it is inadvisable to mix clay bricks with concrete blocks. Horizontal and vertical stack bond and more sophisticated variations such as basket-weave bond, can be used for infill panels within framed structures (Fig. 2.7). Such panels will require reinforcement within alternate horizontal bed joints, to compensate for the lack of normal bonding.

REINFORCEMENT

Blockwork will require bed-joint reinforcement above and below openings where it is inappropriate to divide the blockwork up into panels, with movement joints at the ends of the lintels. Bed-joint reinforcement would be inserted into two bed joints above and below such openings (Fig. 2.8). Cover to bed reinforcement should be at least 25 mm on the external faces and 13 mm on the internal faces. Combined vertical and horizontal reinforcement may be incorporated into hollow blockwork in accordance with BS 5628 Part 2: 1985, where

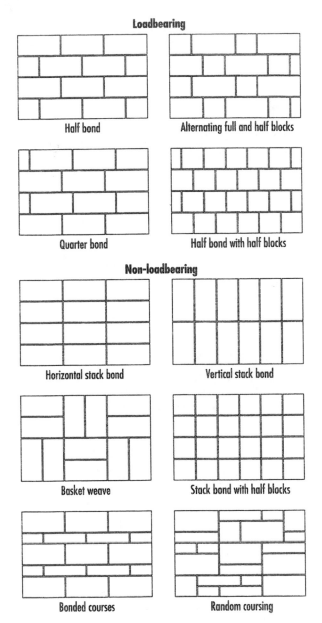

Fig. 2.7 A selection of bonding patterns for visual blockwork

demanded by the calculated stresses. Typical situations would be within retaining basement walls, and with large infill panels to a framed structure.

MOVEMENT CONTROL

Concrete blockwork is subject to greater movements than equivalent brickwork masonry. Therefore the location and form of the movement joints requires greater design-detail consideration, to ensure that inevitable movements are directed to the required locations and do not cause unsightly stepped cracking or fracture of individual blocks. Blockwork walls over 6 m in length must be separated into a series of panels with movement-control joints at approximately 6 m centres. Ideally, such movement joints should be located at intersecting walls, or at other points of structural discontinuity, such as columns. Additionally, movement joints are needed at changes in thickness, height or loading of walls, above and below wall openings, and adjacent to movement joints in the adjoining structure (Fig. 2.9). Wall ties

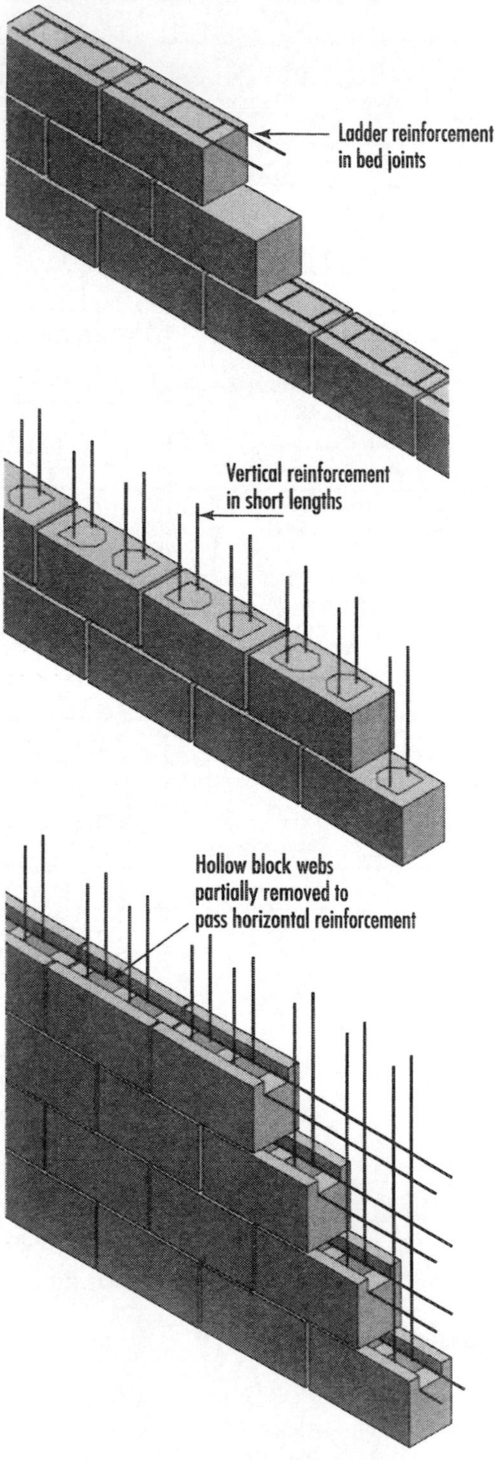

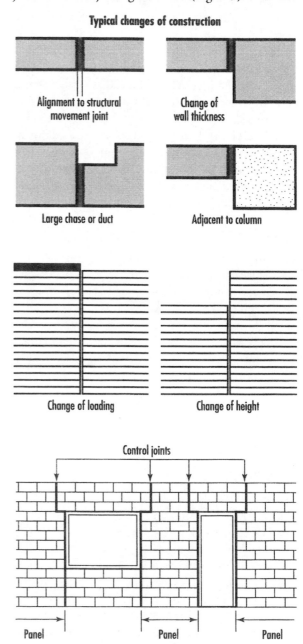

Typical changes of construction

Alignment to structural movement joint

Change of wall thickness

Large chase or duct

Adjacent to column

Change of loading

Change of height

Control joints

Panel   Panel   Panel

Fig. 2.8 Reinforced blockwork

Ladder reinforcement in bed joints

Vertical reinforcement in short lengths

Hollow block webs partially removed to pass horizontal reinforcement

Fig. 2.9 Blockwork movement joints

should allow for differential movement between the leaves in cavity construction and should be spaced at 900 mm horizontally and 450 mm vertically, for 50–75 mm cavities.

MORTARS

The mortar must always be weaker than the blocks to allow for movement. The usual mixes, are by volume:

cement/lime/sand	1:1:5 to 1:1:6
cement/sand + plasticiser	1:5 to 1:6
masonry cement/sand	1:4 to 1:5

Where high-strength blockwork is required, then stronger mortars may be necessary. Mortar joints should be slightly concave, rather than flush. Bucket-handle and weathered or struck joints are suitable for external use, but recessed joints should only be used internally. Coloured mortars should be ready mixed or carefully gauged to prevent colour variations. Contraction joints should be finished with a bond breaker of polythene tape and flexible sealant. For expansion joints, a flexible filler is required, e.g. bitumen-impregnated fibreboard with a polythene-foam strip and flexible sealant. Where blockwork is to be rendered, the mortar should be raked back to a depth of 10 mm for additional key.

FINISHES

Internal finishes

Plaster should be applied normally in two coats to 13 mm. Blocks intended for plastering have a textured surface to give a good key. Dry lining can be fixed with battens or directly with adhesive to the blockwork. Blockwork to be tiled should be first rendered with a cement/sand mix. Fairfaced blockwork can be left plain or painted.

External finishes

External boarding or hanging tiles should be fixed to battens, separated from the blockwork with a breather membrane. For external rendering, a spatterdash coat should be applied initially on dense blockwork, followed by two coats of cement/lime/sand render. The first 10 mm coat should be the stronger mix (e.g. 1:1:6) the 5 mm second coat must be weaker (e.g. 1:2:9). Cement/sand mixes are not recommended, as they are more susceptible to cracking and crazing than mixes incorporating lime. The render should termi-

nate at DPC level with a drip or similar weathering detail.

FOUNDATIONS

Foundation blocks laid flat offer an alternative to trench fill or cavity masonry. Portland cement blocks should not be used for foundations where sulfate-resisting cement mortar is specified, unless they are classified as suitable for the particular sulfate conditions. Sulfates present in soil and groundwater are classified on a scale from 1 (lowest) to 5 (highest), according to the BRE Digest 363. Foundation blocks can be of either dense or appropriate lightweight concrete; the latter provides enhanced floor-edge insulation.

Beam and block flooring

Inverted T-beam and concrete block construction (Fig. 2.10) offers an alternative flooring system to traditional solid ground floors within domestic construction. The infill blocks can be standard 100 mm blocks with a minimum transverse crushing strength of 3.5 N/mm^2. For first and subsequent floors, the infill may be full-depth solid blocks or hollow pots and additionally may require a screed to comply with the Building Regulations.

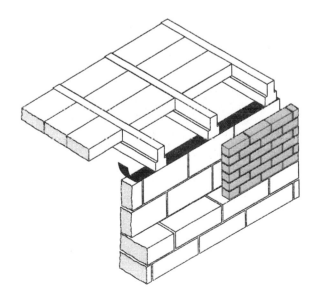

Fig. 2.10 Beam and block flooring

Block paving

Concrete block-paving units are manufactured to a wide range of designs, as illustrated in Fig. 2.11. Blocks may be of standard brick form (200 × 100 mm) to thicknesses of 60, 80 or 100 mm, depending upon the anticipated loading. Alternative designs include tumbled blocks, which emulate granite setts, and various interlocking forms giving designs based on polygonal and curvilinear forms. Colours range from red, brindle, buff, brown, charcoal and grey through to silver and white, with smooth, textured or simulated stone finishes. For most designs, ranges of kerb blocks, drainage channels, edging and other accessory units are available. Concrete paving blocks are usually laid on a compacted sub-base with 50 mm of sharp sand. Blocks are frequently nibbed to create a narrow joint to be filled with kiln-dried sand. For the wider joints that occur between the simulated stone setts a coarser grit can be used to prevent loss by wind erosion.

Fig. 2.11 A selection of concrete block pavings

References

FURTHER READING

Roper, P.A. 1987: *A practical guide to blockwork*. London: International Thomson.

STANDARDS

BS 743: 1970. Materials for damp-proof courses.
BS 1014: 1985. Pigments for Portland cement and Portland cement products.
BS 1243: 1978. Specification for metal ties for cavity wall construction.
BS 5628. Code of practice for use of masonry:
    Part 1: 1992. Structural use of unreinforced masonry.
    Part 2: 1985. Structural use of reinforced and pre-stressed masonry.
    Part 3: 1985. Materials and components, design and workmanship.
BS 5977. Lintels:
    Part 1: 1981. Method for assessment of load.
    Part 2: 1983. Specification for prefabricated lintels.
BS 6073. Precast concrete masonry units:
    Part 1: 1981. Specifications for precast concrete masonry units.
    Part 2: 1981. Method for specifying precast concrete masonry units.
BS 6100. Glossary of building and civil engineering terms:
    Part 5. Masonry.
    Sec. 5.1: 1992. Terms common to masonry.
    Sec. 5.3: 1992. Brick and blocks.
BS 6178. Joist hangers:
    Part 1: 1990. Specification for joist hangers for building into masonry walls of domestic dwellings.
BS 6457: 1984. Specification for reconstructed stone masonry units.
BS 6676. Thermal insulation of cavity walls using man-made mineral fibre batts (slabs):
    Part 1: 1986. Specification for man-made mineral fibre

batts (slabs).

Part 2: 1986. Code of practice for installation of batts (slabs) filling the cavity.

BS 6717. Precast concrete paving blocks:

Part 1: 1993. Specification for paving blocks.

Part 3: 1989. Code of practice for laying.

BS 7533: 1992. Guide for structural design of pavements constructed with clay or concrete block pavers.

BS 8000. Workmanship on building sites:

Part 3: 1989. Code of practice for masonry.

BS 8208. Guide to assessment of suitability of external cavity walls for filling with thermal insulation:

Part 1: 1985. Existing traditional cavity construction.

BS 8215: 1991. Code of practice for design and installation of damp-proof courses in masonry construction.

CP 111: 1970. Structural recommendations for loadbearing walls.

DD 140. Wall ties:

Part 1: 1986. Methods of test for mortar joint and timber frame connections.

Part 2: 1987. Recommendations for design of wall ties.

BUILDING RESEARCH ESTABLISHMENT PUBLICATIONS

BRE Digests

BRE Digest 246: 1981. Strength of brickwork and blockwork walls: design for vertical load.

BRE Digest 359: 1991. Repairing brick and block masonry.

BRE Digest 360: 1991. Testing bond strength of masonry.

BRE Digest 362: 1991. Building mortar.

BRE Digest 363: 1991. Sulphate and acid resistance of concrete in the ground.

BRE Digest 380: 1993. Damp-proof courses.

TRADE ASSOCIATIONS

Aggregate Concrete Block Association, 60 Charles Street, Leicester LE1 1FB (0116 253 6161).

British Concrete Masonry Association, Grove Crescent House, 18 Grove Place, Bedford MK40 3JJ (01234 353745).

Mortar Producers Association Ltd., PO Box 143, Wokingham, Berks. RG40 3YS (01344 761661).

3

LIME, CEMENT AND CONCRETE

Introduction

In the broadest sense, the term *cement* refers to materials which act as adhesives. However, in this context, its use is restricted to that of a binding agent for sand, stone and other aggregates within the manufacture of mortar and concrete. Hydraulic cements and limes set and harden by internal chemical reactions when mixed with water. Non-hydraulic materials will harden only slowly by absorption of carbon dioxide from the air.

Lime was used throughout the world by the ancient civilisations as a binding agent for brick and stone. The concept was brought to Britain in the first century AD by the Romans, who used the material to produce lime mortar. Outside Britain, the Romans frequently mixed lime with volcanic ashes, such as pozzolana from Pozzuoli in Italy, to convert a non-hydraulic lime into a hydraulic cement suitable for use in constructing aqueducts, baths and other buildings. However, in Britain, lime was usually mixed with artificial pozzolanas, for example crushed burnt clay products such as pottery, brick and tile. In the eighteenth century, a so-called *Roman cement* was manufactured by the burning of *cement stone* (argillaceous or clayey limestone), collected from the coast around Sheppey and Essex.

In 1824, Joseph Aspdin was granted his famous patent for the manufacture of *Portland cement*, from limestone and clay. Limestone powder and clay were mixed into a water slurry which was then evaporated by heat in *slip pans*. The dry mixture was broken into small lumps, calcined in a kiln to drive off the carbon dioxide, burnt to clinker and finally ground into

a fine powder for use. The name Portland was used to enhance the prestige of the new concrete material by relating it to Portland stone, which, to some degree, it resembled. Early manufacture of Portland cement was by intermittent processes within bottle, and later chamber, kilns. The introduction of the rotating furnace in 1877 offered a continuous burning process with consequent reductions in fuel and labour costs. The early rotating kilns formed the basis for the development of the various production systems that now exist. In 1989, the peak production year, 18 million tonnes of cement were manufactured within the UK. About half of this was required by the ready-mixed concrete industry; the remainder was divided roughly equally between concrete-product factories and bagged cement for general use.

Lime

MANUFACTURE OF LIME

Lime is manufactured by calcining natural calcium carbonate, typically hard-rock carboniferous limestone. The mineral is quarried, crushed, ground, washed and screened to the required size range. The limestone is burnt at approximately 950°C in either horizontal rotary kilns or vertical shaft kilns which drive off the carbon dioxide to produce quicklime or lump lime (calcium oxide).

$$\underset{\text{calcium carbonate}}{CaCO_3} \xrightarrow{950°C} \underset{\text{lime}}{CaO} + \underset{\text{carbon dioxide}}{CO_2}$$

Slaking of lime

Slaking – that is, the addition of water to quicklime – is a highly exothermic reaction. The controlled addition of water to quicklime produces *high-calcium hydrated lime* (calcium hydroxide) as a dry powder conforming to BS 890: 1995:

$$CaO + H_2O \longrightarrow Ca(OH)_2$$
lime   water   calcium hydroxide

It is suitable for use within mortars or in the manufacture of certain aerated concrete blocks. Generally, the addition of lime to cement mortar, render or plaster increases its water-retention properties, thus retaining workability, particularly when the material is applied to absorbent substrates such as porous brick. Lime also increases the cohesion of mortar mixes, allowing them to spread more easily. Lime-based mortars remain sufficiently flexible to allow movement, but additionally, because of the presence of uncarbonated lime, any minor cracks are subsequently healed by the action of rainwater. Hydrated lime absorbs moisture and carbon dioxide from the air, and should therefore be stored in a cool, draught-free building and used while still fresh.

Lime putty

Lime putty is produced by slaking quicklime with an excess of water for a period of several weeks until a creamy texture is produced. Alternatively, it can be made by stirring hydrated lime into water, followed by conditioning for at least 24 hours. However, the traditional direct slaking of quicklime produces finer particle sizes in the slurry, and the best lime putty is produced by maturing for at least six months. Lime putty may be blended with Portland cement in mortars where its water-retention properties are greater than those afforded by hydrated lime. Additionally, lime putty, often mixed with sand to form *coarse stuff*, is used directly as a pure lime mortar, particularly in restoration and conservation work. It sets, not by reaction with sand and water, but only by carbonation and is therefore described as *non-hydraulic*. Lime wash, as a traditional surface coating, is made by the addition of sufficient water to lime putty to produce a thin creamy consistency.

Carbonation

Lime hardens by the absorption of carbon dioxide from the air, which gradually reconverts the calcium oxide back to calcium carbonate:

$$CaO + CO_2 \xrightarrow{\text{slow}} CaCO_3$$
lime   carbon dioxide   calcium carbonate

The carbonation process is slow, being controlled by the diffusion of carbon dioxide into the bulk of the material. When sand or stone dust aggregate is added to the lime putty to form a mortar or render, the increased porosity allows greater access of carbon dioxide and a speedier carbonation process. The maximum size of aggregate mixed into lime mortars should not exceed half the mortar-joint width. Typical lime mortar mixes are within the range 1:2½ and 1:3, lime putty:aggregate ratio. Because of the slow carbonation process, masonry lifts are limited, and the mortar must be allowed some setting time to prevent its expulsion from the joints.

HYDRAULIC LIMES

Hydraulic limes are manufactured from chalk or limestone containing various proportions of clay impurities. The materials produced have some of the properties of Portland cement, and partially harden through hydration processes, rather than solely through carbonation as happens with non-hydraulic pure calcium oxide lime. Hydraulic limes rich in the clay impurities are more hydraulic and set more rapidly than those with only a low silica and alumina content. Hydraulic limes are categorised as *feebly*, *moderately* or *eminently hydraulic* depending upon their clay content, which is in the ranges 0–8%, 8–18% and 18–25%, respectively. Grey semi-hydraulic lime is still produced within the UK in small quantities from chalk containing a proportion of clay.

Hydraulic lime, manufactured in Somerset or imported from France, is mainly used for the restoration of historic buildings where the use of modern materials would be inappropriate. It is gauged with sand only, giving a mix which develops an initial set within a few hours, but which hardens over an extended period of time. The workable render or mortar mixes adhere well and, because the material is flexible, the risks of cracking and poor adhesion are reduced. The dried mortar is off-white in colour and contains very little alkali, which in Portland cement mortars can cause staining, particularly on limestone. Hydraulic lime may be used for interior lime washes, and also for fixing glass bricks where a flexible binding agent with minimum shrinkage is required. Unlike hydrated lime, hydraulic lime is little affected by exposure to air during storage.

Cement

MANUFACTURE OF PORTLAND CEMENT

Portland cement is manufactured from calcium carbonate in the form of crushed limestone or chalk and an argillaceous material such as clay, marl or shale. Minor constituents such as iron oxide or sand may be added, depending upon the composition of the raw materials and the exact product required. In principle, the process involves the decarbonisation of calcium carbonate (chalk or limestone) by expulsion of the carbon dioxide, and sintering, at the point of incipient fusion, the resulting calcium oxide (lime) with the clay and iron oxide. Depending upon the raw materials used and their water content at extraction, four key variations in the manufacturing process have been developed. These are the *wet*, *semi-wet*, *semi-dry* and the *dry* processes.

Wet process

The wet process (Fig. 3.1), which was the precursor to the other developments, is still used in some areas for processing chalk and marl clay. Clay is mixed with water to form a slurry, when any excess sand is removed by settlement. An equivalent slurry is prepared from

the chalk, which is then blended with the clay slurry, screened to remove any coarse material, and stored in large slurry tanks. After final blending, the slurry is fed into the top of large, slowly rotating kilns. The kilns, which are refractory brick-lined steel cylinders up to 200 m long, are fired to approximately 1450°C, usually with pulverised coal. The slurry is dried, calcined and finally sintered to hard grey/black lumps of cement clinker.

A major development in energy conservation has been the elimination or reduction in the slurry water content required in the manufacturing process, as this consumed large quantities of heat energy during its evaporation.

Semi-wet process

In the semi-wet process, chalk is broken down in water and blended into a marl-clay slurry. The 40% water content within the slurry is reduced to 19% in a filter press; the resulting *filter cake* is nodularised by extrusion onto a travelling preheater grate or reduced in a crusher/dryer to pellets. Heating to between 900°C and 1100°C in tower cyclones precalcines the chalk; the mix is then transferred to a short kiln at 1450°C for the clinkering process.

Semi-dry process

In the semi-dry process, dry shale and limestone powders are blended. About 12% water is added to nodularise the blend, which is then precalcined and clinkered as in the semi-wet process.

Dry process

In the dry process (Fig. 3.2), limestone, shale and sand (typically 80%, 17% and 3%, respectively) are

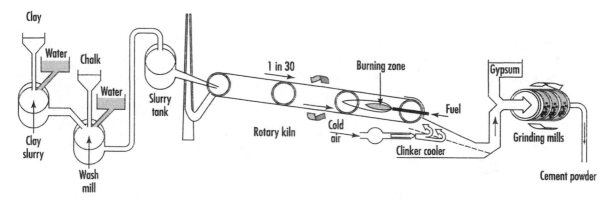

Fig. 3.1 Manufacture of Portland cement – the wet process

milled to fine powders, then blended to produce the *dry meal*, which is stored in silos. The meal is passed through a series of cyclones, initially using recovered kiln gases to preheat it to 750°C, then with added fuel to precalcine at 900°C, prior to passage into a fast-rotating 60 m kiln for clinkering at 1450°C. In all processes an intimately mixed feedstock to the kiln is essential for maintaining quality control of the product. Most plants operate primarily with powdered coal, but additionally other fuels, including petroleum coke, waste tyre chips, smokeless fuel plant residues, or reclaimed spoil-heap coal are used when available. Oil, natural gas and landfill gas have also been used when economically viable. The grey/black clinker manufactured by all processes is cooled with full heat recovery and ground up with 5% added gypsum (calcium sulfate) retarder to prevent excessively rapid *flash* setting of the cement.

The older cement-grinding mills are *open circuit,* allowing one pass of the clinker, which produces a wide range of particle size. This product is typically used for concrete production. The newer cement mills are closed circuit, with air separators to extract fine materials and with recycling of the oversize particles for regrinding. This product is frequently used in the ready-mixed market, since it can be controlled to produce cement with higher later strength. To reduce grinding costs, manufacturers accept load shedding and use off-peak electrical supplies where possible. The Portland cement is stored in silos prior

to transportation in bulk, by road or rail, or in palletised packs. Currently, 50 kg cement bags are being phased out in favour of 25 kg bags for reasons of health and safety.

With dry processing and additional increases in energy efficiency, a tonne of pulverised coal can now produce in excess of six tonnes of cement clinker compared to only three tonnes with the traditional wet process. Because the cement industry is so large, the combined output of carbon dioxide to the atmosphere, from fuel and the necessary decarbonation of the limestone or chalk, represents about 2% of the carbon dioxide emissions in Britain. Emissions of oxides of sulfur from the fuel are low, since these gases are trapped into the cement clinker; however, the escape of oxides of nitrogen and dust, largely trapped by electrostatic precipitators, can only be controlled by constantly improving process technologies. On the basis of the final production of concrete, cement manufacture releases considerably less carbon dioxide per tonne than does primary steel manufacture.

COMPOSITION OF PORTLAND CEMENT

The starting materials for Portland cement are chalk or limestone and clay, which consist mainly of lime, silica, alumina and iron oxide. Table 3.1 illustrates a typical composition.

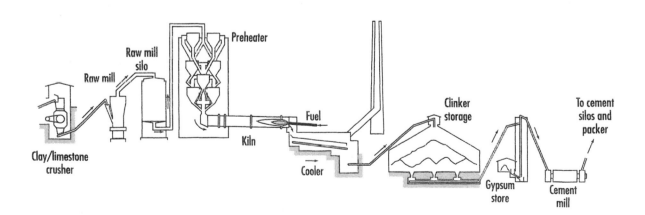

Fig. 3.2 Manufacture of Portland cement – the dry process

Table 3.1 Typical composition of starting materials for Portland cement manufacture

Component	Percentage
Lime	68
Silica	22
Alumina	5
Iron oxide	3
Other oxides	2

Minor constituents, including magnesium oxide, sulfur trioxide, sodium and potassium oxides, amount to approximately 2%. (The presence of the alkali oxides in small proportions can be the cause of the *alkali–silica* reaction, which leads to cracking of concrete when certain silica-containing aggregates are used.) During the clinkering process, the starting materials react together to produce the four key components of Portland cement (Table 3.2).

The relative proportions of these major components significantly affect the ultimate properties of the cements and are therefore adjusted in the manufacturing process to produce the required product range. Typical compositions of Portland cements are shown in Table 3.3.

A small reduction in the lime content within the initial mix will greatly reduce the proportion of tricalcium silicate and produce an equivalent large increase in the dicalcium silicate component of the product. The cement produced will harden more slowly, with a slower evolution of heat. As tricalcium aluminate is vulnerable to attack by soluble sulfates it is the proportion of this component that is reduced in the manufacture of sulfate-resisting cement.

Under the European Standard ENV 197 Part 1: 1995, except with sulfate-resisting cement, up to 5% of minor additional constituents may be added to cement. These fillers must be materials that do not increase the water requirements of the cement, reduce the durability of the mortar or concrete produced, or cause increased corrosion to any steel reinforcement. In the UK, typical fillers include limestone powder and dry meal or partially calcined material from the cement-manufacturing processes.

SETTING AND HARDENING OF PORTLAND CEMENTS

Portland cement is hydraulic: when mixed with water it forms a paste, which sets and hardens as a result of various chemical reactions between the cementitious compounds and water. Setting and hardening are not dependent upon drying out; indeed, Portland cement will harden under water. Only a small proportion of the added water is actually required for the chemical hydration of the

Table 3.2 Major constituents of Portland cement and their specific properties

Compound	Chemical formula	Cement notation	Properties
Tricalcium silicate	$3CaO.SiO_2$	C_3S	Rapid hardening, giving early strength and fast evolution of heat
Dicalcium silicate	$2CaO.SiO_2$	C_2S	Slow hardening, giving slow development of strength and slow evolution of heat
Tricalcium aluminate	$3CaO.Al_2O_3$	C_3A	Quick setting which is retarded by gypsum; Rapid hardening and fast evolution of heat but lower final strength; vulnerable to sulfate attack
Tetracalcium aluminoferrite	$4CaO.Al_2O_3.Fe_2O_3$	C_4AF	Slow hardening; causes grey colour in cement

Table 3.3 Typical compositions of Portland cements

Type	Class	Composition				Fineness (m²/kg)
		$\%C_3S$	$\%C_2S$	$\%C_3A$	$\%C_4AF$	
Portland cement	42.5	55	20	10	8	340
	52.5	55	20	10	8	440
White Portland cement	62.5	65	20	5	2	400
Sulfate-resisting Portland cement	42.5	60	15	2	15	380

cementitious constituents to hydrated calcium silicates. The additional water is needed to ensure the *workability* of the mix when aggregates are added, so that concrete, for example, can be successfully placed within formwork containing steel reinforcement. Water in excess of that required for hydration will ultimately evaporate, leaving capillary pores in the concrete and mortar products. Typically, an increase in void space of 1% reduces crushing strength by 6%. It is therefore necessary to control carefully the water content of the mix by reference to the water/cement ratio. A minimum water/cement ratio of 0.23 is required to hydrate all the cement, although, as the cement powder is hydrated it expands, and thus a ratio of 0.36 represents the point at which cement gel fills all the water space. However, a water/cement ratio of 0.42 more realistically represents the minimum water content to achieve full hydration without the necessity for further water to be absorbed during the curing process.

The setting and hardening processes should be distinguished. Setting is the stiffening of the cement paste which commences immediately the cement is mixed with water. Because the major cementitious constituents set at different rates it is convenient to refer to *initial set* and *final set*. Typically, initial set, or the formation of a plastic gel, occurs after one hour and final set, or the formation of a rigid gel, within 10 hours. The setting process is controlled by the quantity of gypsum added to the cement in the final stages of production. Hardening is the gradual gain in strength of the set cement paste. It is a process which continues, albeit at a decreasing rate, over periods of days, months and years. The rate of hardening is governed partially by the particle-size distribution of the cement powder. Finely ground cement hydrates more rapidly, and therefore begins to set and harden more quickly. Furthermore, the relative proportions of tricalcium silicate and dicalcium silicate have a significant effect upon the rate of hardening, as indicated in Table 3.2. During hydration, any sodium and potassium salts within the Portland cement are released into the pore water of the concrete, giving rise to a highly alkaline matrix. This effectively inhibits corrosion of any reinforcing steel embedded within the concrete, but if active silica is present in any of the aggregates it may react to form an alkali–silica gel, which absorbs water, swells and causes cracking of the concrete. This alkali–silica reaction can, however, be effectively prevented by limiting the total alkali content in the cement to less than 3 kg/m^3. (Cement manufacturers normally specify alkali content in terms of equivalent percentage of sodium oxide.)

TYPES OF CEMENT

Cements are classified primarily on the main constituents, such as Portland cement or Portland fly-ash cement. (In addition there may be minor constituents up to 5% and also additives up to 1% by weight.)

The British Standards describe Portland cement (BS 12: 1996); sulfate-resisting Portland cement (BS 4027: 1996); Portland cement with granulated blast-furnace slag (BS 146: 1996); Portland cement with pulverised fuel ash (BS 6588: 1996 and BS 6610: 1996); and Portland cement with limestone (BS 7583: 1996). The European Standard ENV 197-1: 1995 lists five types of cement (types I to V), which have a wider range of permitted constituents, including additionally blends of Portland cement with silica fume, natural or industrial pozzolanas, calcareous or siliceous fly ash and burnt shale. A comparison between the British and European Standards is given in Table 3.4. Calcium aluminate cement (formerly high-alumina cement) has a totally different formulation from the range of Portland cements based on calcium silicates.

STRENGTH CLASSES OF CEMENT

The standard strength classes of cement are based on the 28 day compressive strength of mortar prisms, made and tested to the requirements of EN 196 Part 1: 1994. The test uses specimens which are 40 × 40 × 160 mm, cast from a mix of 3 parts of CEN (European Committee for Standardisation) standard sand, 1 part of cement and 0.5 part of water. The sample is vibrated and cured for the appropriate time, then broken in halves and compression tested across the 40 mm face. Three specimens are used to determine a mean value from the six pieces.

Each cement strength class (32.5, 42.5, 52.5 and 62.5) has sub-classes associated with the rapid (R), normal (N) or low (L) development of early strength (Table 3.5). (It is anticipated that class 62.5 will be withdrawn in the final version of EN 197-1.) The strength classes and sub-classes give production

Table 3.4 Cements to European Standard ENV 197-1: 1995 and British Standards

Cement	Type	Notation	Portland cement clinker content (%)	Additional main constituent (%)	British Standard
Portland cement	I	CEM I	95–100	0	BS 12: 1996
Portland slag cement	II	CEM II/A-S	80–94	6–20	BS 146: 1996
		CEM II/B-S	65–79	21–35	
Portland silica fume cement	II	CEM II/A-D	90–94	6–10	
Portland pozzolana cement	II	CEM II/A-P	80–94	6–20	
		CEM II/B-P	65–79	21–35	
		CEM II/A-Q	80–94	6–20	
		CEM II/B-Q	65–79	21–35	
Portland fly ash cement	II	CEM II/A-V	80–94	6–20	BS 6588: 1996
		CEM II/B-V	65–79	21–35	BS 6588: 1996
		CEM II/A-W	80–94	6–20	
		CEM II/B-W	65–79	21–35	
Portland burnt shale cement	II	CEM II/A-T	80–94	6–20	
		CEM II/B-T	65–79	21–35	
Portland limestone cement	II	CEM II/A-L	80–94	6–20	BS 7583: 1996
		CEM II/B-L	65–79	21–35	
Portland composite cement	II	CEM II/A-M	80–94	6–20	
		CEM II/B-M	65–79	21–35	
Blastfurnace cement	III	CEM III/A	35–64	36–65	BS 146: 1996 BS 4246: 1996
		CEM III/B	20–34	66–80	BS 4246: 1996
		CEM III/C	5–19	81–95	BS 4246: 1996
Pozzolanic cement	IV	CEM IV/A	65–89	11–35	
		CEM IV/B	45–64	36–55	BS 6610: 1996
Composite	V	CEM V/A	40–64	36–60	
		CEM V/B	20–39	61–80	

The code letters used in the European Standard are:

D silica fume   L limestone   Q industrial pozzolana   V siliceous fly ash
F filler   M mixed   S granulated blastfurnace slag   W calcareous fly ash
K Portland cement clinker   P natural pozzolana   T burnt shale

standards for cements, but do not specify how a particular mix of cement, aggregate and admixtures will perform as a concrete; this needs to be determined by separate testing.

The most commonly used cement within the UK (formerly ordinary Portland cement or OPC) is currently designated to the British Standard BS 12: 1996 as:

PC   42.5   N   PC42.5N

type of cement   strength class   normal strength development

Under the European regulations, EN 197-1, it is defined as:

CEM I   42.5   CEMI 42.5

type of cement   strength class

Similarly, rapid-early-strength Portland slag cement is defined to EN 197-1 as:

CEM II/A   S   42.5   R   CEMII/A-S 42.5R

type of cement /proportion of clinker   sub-type, slag   strength class   rapid early strength

Table 3.5 Strength classes of cements to European Standard ENV 197-1: 1995 and British Standards

Cement	Strength class	Minimum strength (N/mm²)			Maximum strength (N/mm²)	Standard
		2 day	7 day	28 day	28 day	
European Standard						
Portland cement	32.5		16.0	32.5	52.5	ENV 197-1: 1992
	32.5R	10		32.5	52.5	
	42.5	10		42.5	62.5	
	42.5R	20		42.5	62.5	
	52.5	20		52.5		
	52.5R	30		52.5		
British Standards						
Portland cement	62.5	20		62.5		BS 12: 1996
Portland blastfurnace cement	52.5L	10		52.5		BS 146: 1996
	42.5L		20	42.5	62.5	
High slag blastfurnace cement	32.5L		12	32.5		BS 4246: 1996
Pozzolanic pulversied-fuel ash cement	22.5		12	22.5		BS 6610: 1996

The code letters in the standards are: R rapid early strength development   L low-heat cement

Portland cements

Portland cements – strength classes 32.5, 42.5 and 52.5
The Portland cement classes 32.5, 42.5 and 52.5 correspond numerically to their lower characteristic strengths in newtons per square millimetre at 28 days. The 32.5 and 42.5 classes have upper characteristic strengths which are 20 N/mm² greater than the lower characteristic strengths, as designated by the class number. The class 52.5 has no upper strength limit. Statistically, the tested strengths must fall with no more than 5% of the tests below the lower limit or 10% of the tests above the upper limit. Thus class 42.5 Portland cement (formerly ordinary Portland cement) has a strength within the range 42.5 N/mm² to 62.5 N/mm², with a maximum of 5% of test results being below 42.5 N/mm² and a maximum of 10% of the test results being above 62.5 N/mm².

Each class also has lower characteristic strength values at two days, except for class 32.5, which has a lower characteristic strength at seven days. Where high early strength is required, for example to allow the early removal of formwork in the manufacture of precast concrete units, class 52.5 or class 42.5R is used. These Portland cements are more finely ground than class 42.5 to enable a faster hydration of the cement in the early stages. Class 32.5 cements for general-purpose and DIY use frequently contain up to 1% additives to improve workability and frost resistance, together with up to 5% minor additional constituents such as pulverised fuel ash, granulated blastfurnace slag or limestone filler. Portland cement of strength class 42.5 accounts for approximately 90% of total cement production within the UK.

White Portland cements
White Portland cement is manufactured from materials virtually free of iron oxide and other impurities, which impart the grey colour to Portland cement. Generally, china clay and limestone are used and the kiln is fired with natural gas or oil rather than pulverised coal. Iron-free mills are used for the grinding process to prevent colour contamination. Currently, most white Portland cement used within the UK is imported from Denmark and is of the highest strength class (62.5). Because of the specialist manufacturing processes used, it is approximately twice the price of the standard grey product.

Sulfate-resisting Portland cement
Sulfate-resisting Portland cement (BS 4027: 1996) is suitable for concrete and mortar in contact with soils and groundwater containing soluble sulfates up to the maximum levels (measured as sulfur trioxide) of 2% in soil or 0.5% in groundwater. In normal

Portland cements the hydrated tricalcium aluminate component is vulnerable to attack by soluble sulfates, but in sulfate-resisting Portland cement this component is restricted to a maximum of 3.5%. For maximum durability a high-quality, dense, non-permeable concrete is required. Many sulfate-resisting cements are also defined as low-alkali (LA) to BS 4027: 1996, containing less than 0.6% alkali (measured as sodium oxide). Thus durable concrete, without the risk of subsequent alkali–silica reaction, can be manufactured with alkali-reactive aggregates, using up to 500 kg/m³ of cement, provided that no other alkalis are present.

Low-heat Portland cement

Low-heat Portland cement (BS 1370: 1979) is appropriate for use in mass concrete, where the rapid internal evolution of heat could cause cracking. It contains a higher proportion of dicalcium silicate, which hardens and evolves heat more slowly.

Blended Portland cements

Blended Portland cements include not only masonry cement, with its specific end use, but also the wide range of additional materials, now classified within the European Standard ENV 197-1: 1995.

Masonry cements

Portland cement mortar is unnecessarily strong and concentrates any differential movement within brickwork or blockwork into a few large cracks which are unsightly and may increase the risk of rain penetration. Masonry cement produces a weaker mortar, which accommodates some differential movement, and ensures a distribution of hairline cracks within joints, thus preserving the integrity of the bricks and blocks. Masonry cements contain water-retaining mineral fillers, usually ground limestone, and air-entraining agents, to give a higher workability than unblended Portland cement. They should not normally be blended with further admixtures but mixed with building sand in ratios between 1:4 and 1:6½, depending upon the degree of exposure of the brick or blockwork. The air entrained during mixing increases the durability and frost resistance of the hardened mortar. Masonry cement is also appropriate for use in renderings but not for floor screeds or concreting. It is therefore generally used as an alternative to Portland cement with hydrated lime or plasticiser.

Portland slag and blastfurnace cements

Granulated blastfurnace slag, formerly termed ground granulated blastfurnace slag (GGBS), is a cementitious material which, in combination with Portland cement and appropriate aggregates, makes a durable concrete. The material is a by-product of the iron-making process within the steel industry. Iron ore, limestone and coke are fed continuously into blastfurnaces, where, at 1500°C, they melt into two layers. The molten iron sinks, leaving the blastfurnace slag floating on the surface, from where it is tapped off at intervals. The molten blastfurnace slag is rapidly cooled by water quenching in a granulator or pelletiser to produce a glassy product. After drying, the blastfurnace slag granules or pellets are ground to the fine off-white powder, granulated blastfurnace slag. The composition of the material is broadly similar to that of Portland cement, as illustrated in Table 3.6.

Table 3.6 Typical compositions of granulated blastfurnace slag and Portland cement

	Granulated blastfurnace slag (%)	Portland cement (%)
Lime	41	68
Silica	35	22
Alumina	11	5
Iron oxide	1	3
Other	2	2

Granulated blastfurnace slag may be intimately ground with Portland cement clinker in the cement mill, although usually it is mixed with Portland cement on site. The British Standards refer to ranges of blends between granulated blastfurnace slag (BS 6699: 1992) and Portland cement (BS 12: 1996), as shown in Table 3.7. The European Standard ENV 197-1: 1995 refers to Portland slag cement for mixes containing 6–35% slag and to blastfurnace cement for mixes with 36%–95% granulated blastfurnace slag (Table 3.4).

Concrete manufactured from a blend of Portland and granulated blastfurnace slag cements has a lower permeability than Portland cement alone; this enhances resistance to attack from sulfates and weak acids, and to the ingress of chlorides, which can cause rapid corrosion of steel reinforcement, for example in marine environments and near roads

Table 3.7 Granulated blastfurnace slag blends with Portland cement

Granulated blastfurnace slag content (%)	Cement designation to British Standard	British Standard
5–34	Portland slag cement	BS 146: 1996
35–62	Portland blastfurnace cement	BS 146: 1996
50–85	High slag blastfurnace cement	BS 4246: 1996

subjected to de-icing salts. Sulfate attack is also reduced by the decrease in tricalcium aluminate content. Typically, a 70% granulated blastfurnace slag mix would be appropriate for groundwater sulfate levels of up to 6.0 g/l (Class 3 and 4 soils). The more gradual hydration of granulated blastfurnace slag cement evolves less heat and more slowly than Portland cement alone; thus a 70% granulated blastfurnace slag mix can be used for mass concrete, where otherwise a significant temperature rise could cause cracking. The slower evolution of heat is associated with a more gradual development of strength over the first 28 day period. However, the ultimate strength of the mature concrete is comparable to that of the equivalent Portland cement. The initial set with granulated blastfurnace slag blends is slower than for Portland cement alone, and the fresh concrete mixes are more plastic, giving better flow for placing and full compaction. The risk of alkali–silica reaction caused by reactive silica aggregates can be reduced by the use of granulated blastfurnace slag to reduce the active alkali content of the concrete mix to below the critical 3.0 kg/m³ level.

Portland fly ash and pozzolanic cements
Pozzolanic materials are natural or manufactured materials containing silica, which react with the calcium hydroxide produced in the hydration of Portland cement to produce further cementitious products. Within the UK, natural volcanic pozzolanas are little used, but fly ash, formerly termed pulverised fuel ash (PFA), the waste product from coal-fired electricity-generating stations, is used either factory mixed with Portland cement or blended in on site. Portland fly ash cement cures and evolves heat more slowly than Portland cement; it is therefore appropriate for use in mass concrete to reduce the risk of thermal cracking. Additions of up to 25% fly ash in Portland cement are often used; the concrete

produced is darker than that produced with Portland cement alone. Concrete made with blends of 25–40% by weight of fly ash in Portland cement has good sulfate-resisting properties. However, in the presence of groundwater with high magnesium concentrations (greater than 1.0 g/l), sulfate-resisting Portland cement should be used. Fly ash concretes also have enhanced resistance to chloride ingress, which is frequently the cause of corrosion to steel reinforcement.

The fly ash produced in the UK by burning pulverised bituminous coal is siliceous, containing predominantly reactive silica and alumina. In addition to siliceous fly ash, the European Standard ENV 197-1: 1995 does allow for the use of calcareous fly ash, which additionally contains active lime, giving some self-setting properties. Natural pozzolanas of volcanic origin and industrial pozzolanas from other industrial processes in Europe are used with Portland cement and are categorised under ENV 197-1: 1995 as pozzolanic cements.

Portland limestone cement
The addition of up to 5% limestone filler to Portland cement has little effect on its properties. The addition of up to 25% limestone gives a performance similar to that of Portland cement, with a proportionally lower cementitious content; thus, if equivalent durability to Portland cement is required, then cement contents must be increased.

Silica fume
Silica fume or microsilica, a by-product from the manufacture of silicon and ferro-silicon, consists of ultra-fine spheres of silica. The material, because of its high surface area when blended as a minor addition to Portland cement, increases the rate of hydration, giving the concrete a high early strength and also a reduced permeability. This in turn produces greater resistance to chemical attack and abrasion. Silica fume may be added up to 5% as a filler, or in Portland silica fume cement to between 6 and 10%.

Burnt shale
Burnt shale is produced by heating oil shale to 800°C in a kiln. It is similar in nature to blastfurnace slag, and is weakly cementitious. The European Standard ENV 197-1: 1995 allows for the use of burnt shale as a filler to 5%, or between 6 and 35%

in Portland burnt shale cement. There is no corresponding British Standard for this material.

Fillers

Fillers, up to 5% by weight of the cement content, may be added to cements to the Standard ENV 197-1: 1995. They should be materials that do not increase the water requirements of the cement. Fillers may be any of the permitted alternative main constituents (e.g. granulated blastfurnace slag, pozzolanas, fly ash, burnt shale, silica fume or limestone), or other inorganic materials, provided that they are not already present as one of the main constituents. The most common fillers are limestone and either raw meal or partially calcined material from the cement-making process.

CEMENT ADMIXTURES

Admixtures may be defined as materials that are added in small quantities to mortars or concretes during mixing, in order to modify one or more of their physical or visual properties.

Plasticisers

Plasticisers, or water-reducing admixtures, are added to increase the workability of a mix, thus enabling easier placing and compaction. Where increased workability is not required, water reducers may be used to lower the water/cement ratio, giving typically a 15% increase in strength and better durability. The plasticisers, which are usually lignosulfonates or hydroxylated polymers, act by dispersing the cement grains. Some air entrainment may occur with the lignosulfonates, causing a 6% reduction in crushing strength for every 1% of air entrained.

Superplasticisers

Superplasticisers, such as sulfonated naphthalene or sulfonated melamine formaldehyde, when added to a normal 50 mm slump concrete produce a flowing, self-levelling concrete which can be placed, even within congested reinforcement, without vibration. Alternatively, significantly reduced water contents can be used to produce early-, and ultimately higher-, strength concretes. As the effect of superplasticisers lasts for less than an hour, the admixture is usually added to ready-mixed concrete on site prior to discharge and placing. Self-levelling mixes for screeds between 3 and 20 mm thick can be adjusted to take light foot traffic after 3 to 24 hours. Renovation mixes, usually incorporating fibre-mat reinforcement, can be used over existing floor surfaces to thicknesses usually in the range 4–30 mm.

Accelerators

Accelerators increase the rate of reaction between cement and water, thus increasing the rate of set and development of strength. This can be advantageous in precasting, where early removal of the formwork is required, and in cold weather when the heat generated speeds up the hardening processes and reduces the risk of frost damage. Only chloride-free accelerators, such as calcium formate, should be used in concrete, mortar or grout where metal will be embedded, because calcium chloride accelerators can cause extensive metallic corrosion. Accelerators producing a rapid set are not normally used within structural concrete.

Retarders

Retarders, typically phosphates or hydroxycarboxylic acids, decrease the rate of set, thus extending the time between initial mixing and final compaction, but they do not adversely affect 28 day strength. Retarders can be applied to formwork, to retard the surface concrete where an exposed aggregate finish is required, by washing after the formwork is struck. Retarders are also frequently used in ready-mixed mortars to extend their workable life up to 36 hours. The mortars are usually delivered on site in date-marked containers of 0.3 m³ capacity.

Air-entraining admixtures

Air-entraining admixtures, typically wood resins or synthetic surfactants, stabilise the tiny air bubbles which become incorporated into concrete or mortar as it is mixed. The bubbles, which are between 0.05 and 0.5 mm in diameter, do not escape during transportation or vibration, improve the workability of the mix, reduce the risk of segregation and greatly enhance frost resistance. However, the incorporation of void space within concrete decreases its crushing strength by 6% for every 1% of air entrained; thus for a typical 3% addition of entrained air, a reduction of 18% in crushing strength is produced. This is partially offset by the increase in plasticity, which generally produces a higher-quality surface and allows a lower water content to be used. The increased cohesion of air-entrained concrete may trap air against moulded vertical formwork, reducing the quality of the surface.

Water-repellent admixtures

Water penetration through concrete can be reduced by the incorporation of hydrophobic materials, such as stearates and oleates, which coat the surface of pores, and by surface-tension effects discourage the penetration of damp. The use of water-reducing admixtures also reduces water penetration by reducing the water/cement ratio, thus decreasing pore size within the concrete. For mortars and renders a styrene–butadiene latex emulsion admixture may be used to reduce permeability.

Foaming agents

Foamed concrete or mortar contains up to 80% by volume of void space, with densities as low as 400 kg/m^3 and 7 day strengths between 1 and 10 N/mm^2. It is typically produced by blending cement, sand or fly ash and water into a preformed foam or by mechanically foaming the appropriate mix using an air-entraining agent. Foamed concrete is free-flowing, can be pumped and requires no compaction. It is therefore used for trench reinstatement, filling cellars or to provide thermal insulation under floors or in flat roofs.

Pumping agents

Not all concrete mixes are suitable for pumping. Mixes low in cement or with some lightweight aggregates tend to segregate and require thickening with a pumping agent. Conversely, high-cement-content mixes require plasticising to make them pumpable. A range of pumping agents is therefore produced to suit the requirements of various concrete mixes. Lightweight aggregate concrete is often pumped into place for floor slabs.

Pigments

A wide range of coloured pigments is available for incorporation into concrete and mortars. Titanium oxide can be added to enhance the whiteness of white cement. Carbon black is used with grey Portland cement, although the black loses intensity with weathering. The most common colours are the browns, reds and yellows produced with synthetic iron oxides (BS 1014: 1975). The depth and shade of colour depends upon the dose rate (between 1 and 10%), and on the colour of the sand and any other aggregates. To produce pastel shades, pigments can be added to white Portland cement.

CALCIUM ALUMINATE CEMENT

Calcium aluminate cement (formerly known as high-alumina cement) is manufactured from limestone and bauxite (aluminium oxide ore). The ores in roughly equal proportions are charged together into a vertical furnace which is heated to approximately 1600°C (Fig. 3.3). The mixture melts and is continuously run off into trays, where it cools to produce the clinker, which is then milled, producing high-alumina cement to BS 915 Part 2: 1972. The dark grey cement composition differs from that of Portland cement as it is based on calcium aluminates rather than calcium silicates. Although calcium aluminate cement can be produced over a wide range of compositions, the standard product has a 40% alumina content. The European Standard prENV 197-10 proposes an alumina content within the range of 36–55%.

Calcium aluminate cement should not be used for structural purposes; however, it is useful where rapid strength gain is required to allow the fast removal of formwork within 6 to 24 hours. The fast evolution of heat allows concreting to take place at low temperatures. The material also has good heat-resistant properties, so may be used to produce refractory concrete. When mixed with Portland cement it produces a rapid-setting concrete, suitable for non-structural repairs and sealing leaks. Good-quality calcium aluminate cement is generally resistant to chemical attack by dilute acids, chlorides and oils, but not by alkalis.

Some structural failures associated with calcium aluminate cement have been caused by *conversion* of the concrete, in which changes in the crystal structure, accelerated by high temperatures and humidity, have caused serious loss of strength, increased porosity and subsequent chemical attack. Depending upon the degree of conversion, calcium aluminate cement becomes friable and a deeper brown in colour; the exact degree of conversion can be determined only by chemical analysis of a core sample. It is now recognised that such failures can be prevented by using a minimum cement content of 400 kg/m^3, limiting the water/cement ratio to a

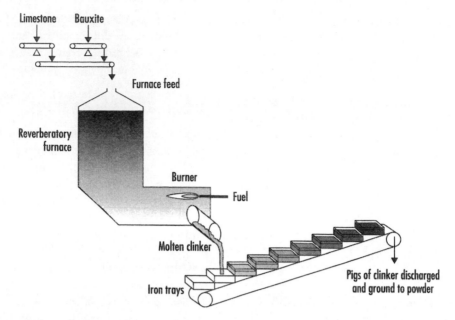

Fig. 3.3 Manufacture of calcium aluminate cement

maximum of 0.4, and by ensuring controlled curing during the 6 to 24 hour initial hardening stage. The concrete should be covered or sprayed to prevent excessive water loss, particularly where substantial increases in temperature may occur. Additionally, to prevent alkaline hydrolysis of the concrete, aggregates containing soluble alkalis should not be used; hard limestone is generally considered to be the best aggregate. Coloured calcium aluminate concrete has the advantage that it is free from calcium hydroxide, which causes efflorescence in Portland cements.

Concrete

Concrete is a mixture of cement, aggregates and water, together with any other admixtures which may be added to modify the placing and curing processes or the ultimate physical properties. Initially, when mixed, concrete is a *plastic* material, which takes the shape of the mould or formwork. When hardened it may be a dense, loadbearing material or a lightweight, thermally insulating material, depending largely on the aggregates used. It may be reinforced or prestressed by the incorporation of steel.

AGGREGATES FOR CONCRETE

Aggregates form a major component of concretes, typically approximately 80% by weight in cured mass concrete. Aggregate properties, including crushing strength, size, grading and shape, have significant effects on the physical properties of the concrete mixes and hardened concrete. Additionally, the appearance of visual concrete can be influenced by aggregate colour and surface treatments.

Aggregates for concrete are normally classified as lightweight, dense or high-density. Standard dense aggregates are classified by size as fine (i.e. sand) or coarse (i.e. gravel). Additionally, steel or polypropylene fibres, or gas bubbles, may be incorporated into the mix for specialist purposes.

Dense aggregates

Source and shape

Dense aggregates are quarried from pits and from the sea bed. In the south-east of England, most land-based sources are gravels, typically flint, whereas further north and west, both gravels and a variety of crushed quarried rocks are available. Marine aggregates are smooth and rounded, and require washing to remove deleterious matter such as salts, silt and organic debris. The shape of aggregates can significantly affect the properties of the mix and cured concrete. Generally, rounded aggregates require a lower water content to achieve a given mix workability, compared to the equivalent mix using angular aggregates. However, cement paste ultimately bonds more strongly to angular aggregates with rough surfaces than to the smoother gravels, so a higher crushing strength can be achieved with crushed rocks as aggregate. Excessive proportions of long and flaky coarse aggregate should be avoided, as they can reduce the durability of concrete.

Aggregate size

For most purposes, the maximum size of aggregate should be as large as possible, consistent with ease of placement within formwork and around any steel reinforcement. Typically, 20 mm aggregate is used for most construction work, although 40 mm aggregate is appropriate for mass concrete, and a maximum of 10 mm for thin sections. The use of the largest possible aggregate reduces the quantity of sand and therefore cement required in the mix, thus controlling shrinkage and minimising cost. Large aggregates have a low surface area/volume ratio, and therefore produce mixes with greater workability for a given water/cement ratio, or allow water/cement ratios to be reduced for the same workability, thus producing a higher-crushing-strength concrete.

Grading

To obtain consistent quality in concrete production, it is necessary to ensure that both coarse and fine aggregates are well graded. A typical *continuously graded* coarse aggregate will contain a good distribution of sizes, such that the voids between the largest stones are filled by successively smaller particles down to the size of the sand. Similarly, a well graded sand will have a range of particle sizes, but with a limit (BS 882: 1992) on the proportion of fine clay or silt, because too high a content of *fines* (of size less than 75 μm) would increase the water and cement requirement for the mix. This overall grading of aggregates ensures that all void spaces are filled with the minimum proportion of fine material and expensive cement powder. In certain circumstances, coarse aggregate may be graded as *single-sized* or *gap graded*. The former is used for controlled blending in *designed mixes* while the latter is used particularly for exposed aggregate finishes on visual concrete. Sands are classified into three categories according to the proportion passing through a 600 μm sieve: coarse

(15–54%), medium (25–80%) and fine (55–100%). Only the coarse and medium categories of sands should be used for heavy-duty concrete floor finishes.

Sampling and sieve analysis

To determine the grading of a sample of coarse or fine aggregate, a representative sample has to be subjected to a sieve analysis. Normally, at least ten samples would be taken from various parts of the stock pile, and these would be reduced down to a representative sample using a *riffle box*, which successively divides the sample by two until the required test volume is obtained (Fig. 3.4).

Fig. 3.4 Riffle box

Aggregate gradings are determined by passing the representative sample through a set of standard sieves (BS 410: 1986). For coarse aggregates these are 50, 37.5, 20, 14, 10 and 5 mm and for fine aggregates 10, 5, 2.36, 1.18 mm, and 600, 300 and 150 μm. Fine aggregates are those that pass through a 5 mm sieve; conversely, coarse aggregates are predominantly retained on a 5 mm sieve. The sieve analysis is determined by assessing the cumulative percentage of material that passes through each sieve size. This is plotted against the sieve size and compared to the BS 882: 1992 gradings (Fig. 3.5).

Aggregates for concreting are normally *batched* from stockpiles of 20 mm coarse aggregate and concreting sand in the required proportions to ensure consistency, although *all-in aggregate*, which contains both fine

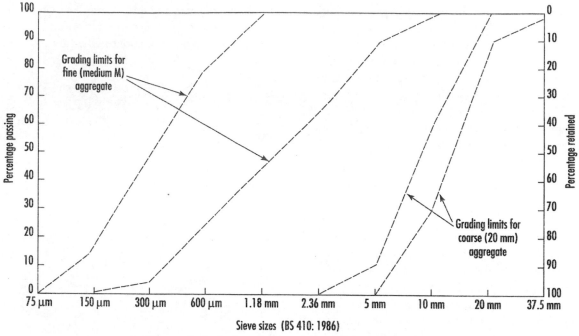

Grading ranges for fine (medium M) and coarse (20 mm) aggregates to BS 882: 1992

Fig. 3.5 Grading of fine (M) and coarse aggregates

and coarse aggregates, is also available as a less well controlled, cheaper alternative, where a lower grade of concrete is acceptable. Where exceptionally high control of the mix is required, single-size aggregates may be batched to the customer's specification. The batching of aggregates should normally be done by weight, as free surface moisture, particularly in sand, can cause *bulking*, which is an increase in volume by up to 40% (Fig. 3.6). Accurate batching must take into account the water content in the aggregates in the calculations of both the required weight of aggregates and the quantity of water to be added to the mix.

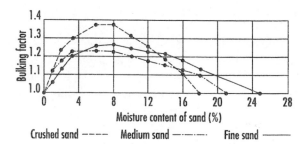

Fig. 3.6 Bulking of sands in relation to moisture content

Impurities within aggregates

Where a high-quality exposed concrete finish is required, the aggregate should be free of iron pyrites, which causes spalling and rust staining of the surface. Alkali–silica reaction (ASR) can occur when active silica, present in certain aggregates, reacts with the alkalis within Portland cement, causing cracking.

High-density aggregates

Where radiation shielding is required, high-density aggregates such as barytes (barium sulfate), magnetite (iron ore), lead or steel shot are used. Hardened concrete densities between 3000 and 5000 kg/m³, double that for normal concrete, can be achieved.

Lightweight aggregates

Natural stone aggregate concretes typically have densities within the range 2200 to 2500 kg/m³, but where densities below 2000 kg/m³ are required, an appropriate lightweight concrete must be used.

Lightweight concretes in construction exhibit the following properties in comparison to dense concrete:

■ they have enhanced thermal insulation but reduced compressive strength;

- they have increased high-frequency sound absorption but reduced sound insulation;
- they have enhanced fire resistance over most dense aggregate concretes (e.g. granite spalls);
- they are easier to cut, chase, nail, plaster and render than dense concrete;
- the reduced self-weight of the structure offers economies of construction;
- the lower formwork pressures enable the casting of higher lifts.

The three general categories of lightweight concrete are lightweight aggregate concrete, aerated concrete and no-fines concrete (Fig. 3.7).

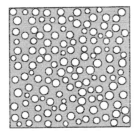
Aerated concrete –
voids in a cement matrix

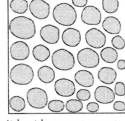
Lightweight aggregate concrete –
voids in the aggregate pellets

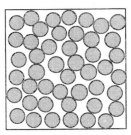
Polystyrene-bead
aggregate cement –
very light aggregate

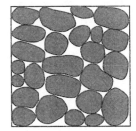
No-fines concrete –
dense aggregate with
voids between

Fig. 3.7 Lightweight concretes

Many of the lightweight aggregate materials are produced from by-products of other industrial processes or directly from naturally occurring minerals. The key exception is expanded polystyrene, which has the highest insulation properties, but is expensive because it is manufactured from petrochemical products.

Pulverised fuel ash

Pulverised fuel ash, or fly ash, is the residue from coal-fired electricity-generating stations. The fine fly ash powder is moistened, pelleted and sintered to produce a uniform lightweight PFA aggregate, which can be used in loadbearing applications.

Foamed blastfurnace slag

Blastfurnace slag is a by-product from the steel industry. Molten slag is subjected to jets of water, steam and compressed air to produce a pumice-like material. The foamed slag is crushed and graded to produce aggregate, which can be used in loadbearing applications. Where rounded pelletised expanded slag is required, the material is further processed within a rotating drum.

Expanded clay and shale

Certain naturally occurring clay materials are pelletised, then heated in a furnace. This causes gases to be evolved which expand and aerate the interior, leaving a hardened surface crust. These lightweight aggregates can be used for loadbearing applications.

Expanded perlite

Perlite is a naturally occurring glassy volcanic rock which, when heated almost to its melting point, evolves steam to produce a cellular material of low density. Concrete made with expanded perlite has good thermal insulation properties but low compressive strength and high drying shrinkage.

Exfoliated vermiculite

Vermiculite is a naturally occurring mineral, composed of thin layers like mica. When heated rapidly the layers separate, expanding the volume of the material by up to 30 times, producing a very lightweight aggregate. Exfoliated vermiculite concrete has excellent thermal insulation properties but low compressive strength and very high drying shrinkage.

Expanded polystyrene

Expanded polystyrene beads offer the highest level of thermal insulation, but with little compressive strength. Polystyrene-bead aggregate cement (PBAC) is frequently used as the core insulating material within precast concrete units.

Aerated concrete

Aerated concrete is manufactured using foaming agents or aluminium powder as previously outlined in the section on foaming agents. Densities in the range 400–1600 kg/m³ give compressive strengths ranging from 1 to 10 N/mm². Drying shrinkages for the lowest-density materials are high (0.3%), but thermal conductivity can be as low as 0.1 W/m K, offering excellent thermal insulation properties. Factory-autoclaved aerated concrete blocks have greatly reduced drying shrinkages and enhanced compressive strength over site-cured concrete. Aerated concrete is generally frost resistant but should be rendered externally to prevent excessive water absorption. The material is easily worked on site, as it can be cut and nailed.

No-fines concrete

No-fines concrete is manufactured from single-sized aggregate (usually between 10 and 20 mm) and cement paste. Either dense or lightweight aggregates can be used, but care has to be taken in placing the mix to ensure that the aggregate remains coated with the cement paste. The material should not be vibrated. Drying shrinkage is low, as essentially the aggregate is stacked up within the formwork, leaving void spaces; these increase the thermal-insulation properties of the material in comparison with the equivalent dense concrete. The rough surface of the cured concrete forms an excellent key for rendering or plastering, which is necessary to prevent rain, air or sound penetration. Dense aggregate no-fines concrete can be used for loadbearing applications.

Fibres

Either steel or polypropylene fibres can be incorporated into concrete, as an alternative to secondary reinforcement, particularly in heavily trafficked floor slabs. The fibres reduce the shrinkage and potential cracking that can occur during initial setting and give good abrasion and spalling resistance to the cured concrete. The low-modulus polypropylene fibres, which do not pose a corrosion risk after carbonation of the concrete, enhance the energy-absorbing characteristics of the concrete, giving better impact resistance. Steel fibres increase flexural strength as well as impact resistance but are more expensive. Typically, polypropylene fibres are added at the rate of 0.2% by weight (0.5% by volume) and steel at the rate of 3–4% by weight. Both polypropylene and steel-fibre concretes can be pumped (glass-fibre reinforced cement is described in Chapter 11).

POLYMER CONCRETE

The incorporation of pre-polymers into concrete mixes, the pre-polymers then polymerising as the concrete sets and hardens, can reduce the penetration of water and carbon dioxide into cured concrete. Typical polymers include styrene-butadiene

rubber. Epoxy resin and acrylic-latex modified mortars are used for repairing damaged and spalled concrete because of their enhanced adhesive properties. Similarly, polymer-modified mortars are used for the cosmetic filling of blowholes and blemishes in visual concrete.

WATER FOR CONCRETE

The general rule is that if water is of a quality suitable for drinking, then it is satisfactory for making concrete (BS 3148: 1980).

CONCRETE MIXES

Concrete mixes are designed to produce concrete with the specified properties at the most economical price. The most important properties are usually strength and durability, although thermal and acoustic insulation, the effect of fire, and appearance in visual concrete may also be critical.

In determining the composition of a concrete mix, consideration is given to the *workability* or ease of placement and compaction of the fluid mix and to the properties required in the hardened concrete. The key factor that affects both these properties is the free-water content of the mix after any water is absorbed into the aggregates. This quantity is defined by the water/cement ratio.

Water/cement ratio

$$\text{Water/cement ratio} = \frac{\text{weight of free water}}{\text{weight of cement}}$$

The free water in a mix is the quantity remaining after the aggregates have absorbed water to the *saturated surface-dry condition*. The free water is used to hydrate the cement and to make the mix workable. With low water/cement ratios below 0.4, some of the cement is not fully hydrated. At a water/cement ratio of 0.4, the hydrated cement just fills the space previously occupied by the water, giving a dense concrete. As the water/cement ratio is increased above 0.4, the mix becomes increasingly workable but the resulting cured concrete is more porous, owing to the evaporation of the excess water leaving void spaces. Figure 3.8 shows the typical relationship between water/cement ratio and concrete crushing strength.

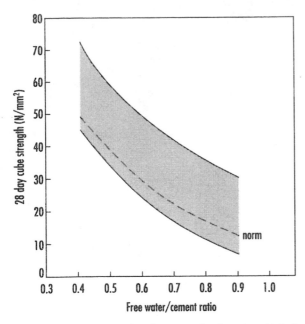

Fig. 3.8 Typical variation of crushing strengths about the published norm for the range of water/cement ratios

Workability

Workability describes the ability of the concrete mix to be placed within the formwork, around any reinforcement, and to be successfully compacted by hand or mechanical means to remove trapped air pockets. Mixes should be cohesive, so that they do not segregate during transportation or placing. Workability is affected by not only the water/cement ratio but also the aggregate content, size, grading and shape, and the addition of admixtures. It is measured on site with the slump test (Fig. 3.9). Table 3.8 shows the relationship between water/cement ratio and workability for crushed and uncrushed aggregates at different cement contents.

Free water
The workability of concrete is highly dependent upon the free water within the mix. An increase in free-water content causes a significant increase in workability, which would result in a greater slump measured in a slump test.

Aggregate shape
Rounded aggregates make a mix more workable than if crushed angular aggregates are used with the same water/cement ratio. However, because the bonding between cured cement and crushed aggregate is stronger than that to rounded aggregates, when other parameters are comparable, crushed aggregates produce a stronger concrete.

Aggregate size
The size of aggregate also affects the workability of the mix. The maximum practical size of coarse aggregate compatible with placement around reinforcement and within the concrete section size should be used to minimise the water content necessary for adequate workability. With fine aggregates, excessive quantities of the fine material (passing through a 600 μm test sieve) would increase considerably the water requirement of a particular mix to maintain workability. This is because the smaller particles have a larger surface

Table 3.8 Typical relationship between water/cement ratio, workability and Portland cement 42.5 content for uncrushed and crushed aggregates

Water/cement ratio	Type of aggregate (20 mm maximum)	Workability		
		Low slump 10–30 mm	Medium slump 25–75 mm	High slump 65–135 mm
		Cement content (kg/m³)	Cement content (kg/m³)	Cement content (kg/m³)
0.7	uncrushed	230	260	285
	crushed	270	300	330
0.6	uncrushed	265	300	330
	crushed	315	350	380
0.5	uncrushed	320	360	400
	crushed	380	420	460
0.4	uncrushed	400	450	500
	crushed	475	525	575

area/volume ratio and therefore require more water to wet their surfaces. As additional water in the mix will decrease the cured concrete strength, for good-quality dense concrete, well graded coarser sands are preferable.

Aggregate/cement ratio

For a particular water/cement ratio, decreasing the aggregate/cement ratio, which therefore increases proportionally both the cement and water content, increases workability. However, as cement is the most expensive component in concrete, cement-rich mixes are more costly than the lean mixes.

Air-entraining

Workability may be increased by air-entraining, although 1% voids in the cured concrete produce a decrease in compressive strength of approximately 6%. Thus in air-entraining there is a balance between the increased workability and resultant improved compaction, versus the void space produced with its associated reduced crushing strength.

Slump test

The slump test is used for determining the workability of a mix on site. It gives a good indication of consistency from one batch to the next, but it is not effective for very dry or very wet mixes. The slump test is carried out as shown in Fig. 3.9. The base plate is placed on level ground and the cone filled with the concrete mix in three equal layers, each layer being tamped down 25 times with a 16 mm diameter tamping rod. The final excess of the third layer is struck off and the cone lifted off from the plate to allow the concrete to slump. The drop in level (mm) is the recorded slump, which may be a *true slump*, a *shear slump* or a *collapse slump*. With a shear slump the material is retested. With a collapse slump the mixture is too wet for most purposes. Typical slump values would be zero to 25 mm for very dry mixes, frequently used in road making; 25–50 mm (low workability) for use in foundations with light reinforcement; 50–100 mm (medium workability) for normal reinforced concrete placed with vibration and over 100 mm for high-workability concrete. Typically, slump values between 10 mm and 175 mm may be measured, although accuracy and repeatability are reduced at both extremes of the workability range. The slump test is not appropriate for aerated, no-fines or gap-graded concretes.

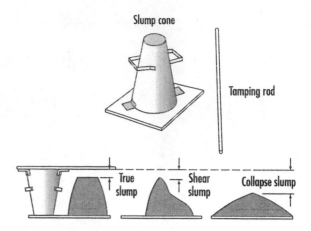

Fig. 3.9 Slump test (after Everett A. 1994: *Mitchell's Materials*, 5th edition. Longman Scientific & Technical)

Compaction

After placing within the formwork, concrete requires compaction to remove air voids trapped in the mix before it begins to stiffen. Air voids weaken the concrete, increase its permeability, and therefore reduce durability. In reinforced concrete, lack of compaction reduces the bond to the steel, and, on exposed visual concrete, blemishes such as blowholes and honeycombing on the surface are aesthetically unacceptable and difficult to make good successfully. Vibration, to assist compaction, can be manual through rodding or tamping for small works; but normally poker vibrators and beam vibrators are used for mass and slab concrete, respectively. Vibrators which clamp onto the formwork are sometimes used when the reinforcement is too congested to allow access for poker vibrators.

The degree of compaction achieved by a standard quantity of work can be measured by the compacting-factor test. In this test a fresh concrete sample is allowed to fall from one hopper into another. The weight of concrete contained in the lower hopper, when struck off flush, compared with a fully compacted sample, gives the compacting factor. The compacting factor for a medium-workability concrete is usually about 0.9.

Concrete cube tests

To maintain quality control of concrete, representative test-cube samples should be taken, cured under controlled conditions and tested for compressive strength after the appropriate 3, 7 or 28 day period.

Steel cube moulds (Fig. 3.10), either 100 or 150 mm, are filled in layers with either hand or mechanical vibration. For hand tamping, a 100 mm cube would be filled in two equal layers, each tamped 25 times with a 25 mm square-end standard compacting bar; mechanical vibration would normally be with a vibrating table or pneumatic vibrator. The mix is then trowelled-off level with the mould. Cubes are cured under controlled moisture and temperature conditions for 24 hours, then stripped and cured under water at 18–20°C until required for testing. Concrete cylinders, 150 mm diameter and 300 mm high, are also used for testing cured concrete, as they tend to give more uniform results for nominally similar concrete specimens.

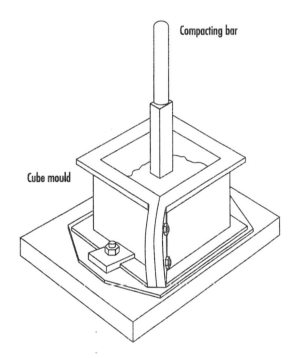

Fig. 3.10 Cube test

DURABILITY OF CONCRETE

While good-quality, well compacted concrete with an adequate cement content and a low water/cement ratio is generally durable, concrete may be subjected to external agencies which cause deterioration, or, in certain circumstances, such as alkali–silica reaction, it may be subject to internal degradation. The durability of concrete is defined in the European Standard DD ENV 206 by prescriptive specification of the minimum grade and the maximum water/cement ratio for a series of environmental conditions.

Sulfate attack

Sulfates are frequently present in soils, but the rate of sulfate attack on concrete is dependent upon the soluble sulfate content of the groundwater. Thus the presence of sodium or magnesium sulfate in solution is more critical than that of calcium sulfate, which is relatively insoluble. Soluble sulfates react with the tricalcium aluminate (C_3A) component of the hardened cement paste, producing calcium sulfoaluminate (ettringite). This material occupies a greater volume than the original tricalcium aluminate, and therefore expansion causes cracking, loss of strength and increased vulnerability to further sulfate attack. The continuing attack by sulfates depends upon the movement of sulfate-bearing groundwater. With magnesium sulfates, deterioration may be more serious, as the calcium silicates within the cured concrete are also attacked. The use of sulfate-resisting Portland cement or combinations of Portland cement and fly ash (pulverised fuel ash (PFA)) or granulated blastfurnace slag (GGBS) reduces the risk of sulfate attack in well-compacted concrete. In the presence of high soluble-sulfate concentrations concrete requires surface protection. The BRE Digest 363: 1991 classifies soil and groundwater conditions from Class 1 to Class 5, according to increasing sulfate and magnesium salt contents.

Frost resistance

Weak, permeable concrete is particularly vulnerable to the absorption of water into capillary pores and cracks. On freezing, the ice formed will expand, causing frost damage. The use of air-entraining agents, which produce discontinuous pores within concrete, reduces the risk of surface frost damage. Concrete is particularly vulnerable to frost damage during the first two days of early hardening. Where new concrete is at risk, frost precautions are necessary to ensure that the mix temperature does not fall below 5°C until a strength of 2 N/mm² is achieved.

Fire resistance

Up to 250°C, concrete shows no significant loss of strength, but by 450°C, depending upon the duration of heating, the strength may be reduced to half and by 600°C little strength remains. However, as concrete is a good insulator, it may take four hours within a building fire for the temperature 50 mm below the surface of the concrete to rise to 650°C (Fig. 3.11).

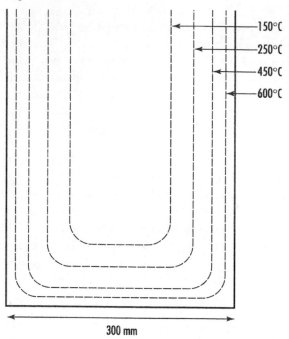

Fig. 3.11 Temperature profile within dense concrete exposed to fire for 60 minutes

The effect of heat on concrete causes colour changes to pink at 300°C, grey at 600°C and to buff by 1000°C. The aggregates used within concrete have a significant effect on fire resistance. For fire protection, limestone aggregates perform better than granites and other crushed rocks, which spall owing to differential expansion. Where the concrete cover over reinforced steel is greater than 40 mm, secondary reinforcement with expanded metal gives added protection to the structural reinforcement. Lightweight-aggregates concretes, owing to their enhanced thermal properties, perform significantly better in fires.

Chemical attack

The resistance of cured concrete to acid attack is largely dependent upon the quality of the concrete, although the addition of granulated blastfurnace slag (GGBS) or fly ash (pulverised-fuel ash (PFA)) increases the resistance to acids. Limestone-aggregate concrete is more vulnerable to acid attack than concretes with other aggregates.

Crystallisation of salts

The crystallisation of salts, particularly from seawater, within the pores of porous concrete can cause sufficient internal pressure to disrupt the concrete.

Alkali–silica reaction

Alkali–silica reaction may occur between cements containing sodium or potassium alkalis and any active silica within the aggregate. In severe cases, expansion of the gel produced by the chemical reaction causes *map* cracking of the concrete, which is characterised by a random network of very fine cracks bounded by a few larger ones. The risk of alkali–silica reaction when using sand containing potentially active silica can, however, be controlled by restricting the alkali content of the Portland cement to a maximum of 0.6% or the soluble alkali content of the concrete to 3 kg/m³.

Carbonation

Carbon dioxide from the atmosphere is slowly absorbed into moist concrete and reacts with the calcium hydroxide content to form calcium carbonate. The process occurs mainly at the surface and penetrates only very slowly into the bulk material. The rate of penetration is dependent on the porosity of the concrete, the temperature and the humidity; it generally becomes problematic only when the concrete surrounding steel reinforcement is affected. Carbonation turns strongly alkaline hydrated cement (pH 12.5) into an almost neutral medium (pH 8.3), in which steel reinforcement will corrode rapidly if subjected to moisture.

$$\underset{\text{hydrated cement}}{Ca(OH)_2} + \underset{\text{carbon dioxide}}{CO_2} \longrightarrow \underset{\text{calcium carbonate}}{CaCO_3}$$

Good-quality dense concrete may show carbonation only to a depth of 5–10 mm after 50 years, whereas a low-strength permeable concrete may carbonate to a depth of 25 mm within 10 years. If reinforcement is not correctly located with sufficient cover it corrodes, causing expansion, spalling and rust staining. The depth of carbonation can be determined by testing a core sample for alkalinity using phenolphthalein chemical indicator, which turns pink in contact with the uncarbonated alkaline concrete. Where steel reinforcement has become exposed owing to carbonation and rusting, it can be coated with a rust-inhibiting cement and the cover restored with polymer-modified mortar which may contain fibre reinforcement. Additional protection against further attack can be achieved by the final application of an acrylic-based anti-carbonation coating.

PHYSICAL PROPERTIES OF CONCRETE

Thermal movement

The coefficient of thermal expansion of concrete varies between 7 and 14×10^{-6} deg C, according to the type of aggregate used, the mix proportions and curing conditions.

Moisture movement

During the curing process, concrete exhibits some irreversible shrinkage which must be accommodated within the construction joints. The extent of the shrinkage is dependent upon the restraining effect of the aggregate and is generally larger when smaller or lightweight aggregates are used. High-aggregate-content mixes with low workability tend to have small drying shrinkages.

The reversible moisture movement for cured concrete is typically 2–6×10^{-4} deg C, depending upon the aggregate.

Creep

Creep is the long-term deformation of concrete under sustained loads (Fig. 3.12). The extent of creep is largely dependent upon the modulus of elasticity of the aggregate. Thus an aggregate with a high modulus of elasticity offers a high restraint to creep. The extent of creep may be several times that of the initial elastic deformation of the concrete under the same applied load. Where rigid cladding is applied to a concrete-frame building, compression joints at each storey must be sufficiently wide to take up any deformation due to creep in addition to normal cyclical movements.

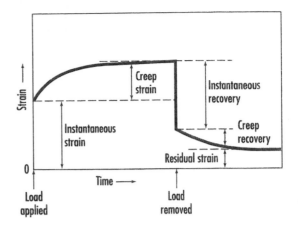

Fig. 3.12 Creep and creep recovery in concrete

CONCRETE STRENGTH CLASSES

Concrete should be specified, placed and cured according to ENV 206: 1992. The preferred strength classes of concrete are shown in Table 3.9, in which the numbers refer to the test sample crushing strengths of a 150×300 mm cylinder and a 150 mm cube, respectively.

SPECIFICATION OF CONCRETE MIXES

There are four methods for specifying concrete mixes described in BS 5328: 1991.

The four methods are:

- designated mixes;
- designed mixes;
- prescribed mixes;
- standard mixes.

If the application can be considered to be routine, then the designated-mix method is usually appropriate. If, however, the purchaser requires specific performance criteria and accepts the higher level of responsibility in the specification, then designed or prescribed mixes may be used. For housing and similar construction, standard mixes should give the

Table 3.9 Concrete strength classes

				Strength classes				
C12/15	C16/20	C20/25	C25/30	C30/37	C35/45	C40/50	C45/55	C50/60

Within each strength class the numbers indicate the 28 day crushing strength in N/mm² as determined by the 150/300 mm cylinder test and 150 mm cube test, respectively, to ENV 206: 1992.

required performance, provided that there is sufficient control over the production and quality of materials used.

Designated mixes

The purchaser is responsible for correctly specifying the proposed use and mix designation. The purchaser must also specify workability, specify whether the concrete is to be reinforced or prestressed, and indicate the nominal aggregate size if it is not 20 mm. The producer must ensure that the mix fulfils all the performance criteria. Thus, for foundations in Class 3 sulfate conditions, the designated mix FND 3 is required. This mix may be supplied with sulfate-resisting Portland cement at 330 kg/m^3 and a maximum water/cement ratio of 0.5; or as a 380 kg/m^3 Portland cement with 25% fly ash or 75% granulated blastfurnace slag at a maximum

water/cement ratio of 0.45. Any of these mixes will perform to the required criteria for the specified purpose. For routine work, designated mixes produced by quality-assured plants offer the specifier the least risk of wrong specification. Table 3.10 illustrates typical housing applications for designated mixes.

Designed mixes

The purchaser specifies the performance criteria required, typically strength, durability and workability of the mix, and also specifies a list of permitted materials. The producer selects the mix proportion and tests the product for compliance.

Prescribed mixes

The purchaser fully specifies the materials and all their proportions. The purchaser is therefore responsible for the performance characteristics of the

Table 3.10 Typical housing applications for designated mixes (BS 5328)

Typical application	Mix designation	Recommended workability (nominal slump (mm))
Foundations		
Blinding and mass concrete fill	GEN 1	75
Strip footings (non-aggressive soils)	GEN 1	75
Mass concrete foundations (non-aggressive soils)	GEN 1	75
Trench-fill foundations (non-aggressive soils)	GEN 1	125
Reinforced foundations (Class 1 sulfate conditions)	RC 35	75
Foundations (Class 2 sulfate conditions)	FND 2	75
Foundations (Class 3 sulfate conditions)	FND 3	75
Foundations (Class 4A sulfate conditions)	FND 4A	75
Foundations (Class 4B sulfate conditions)	FND 4B	75
General applications		
Kerb bedding and backing	GEN 0	10 (very low)
Oversite below suspended slabs (non-aggressive soils)	GEN 1	75
Drainage works – immediate support (non-aggressive soils)	GEN 1	10 (very low)
Drainage works (non-aggressive soils)	GEN 1	50
Fill to wall cavities	GEN 1	125
Solid filling under steps	GEN 1	75
Floors		
Garage floors with no embedded metal	GEN 3	75
House floors with no embedded metal		
— permanent finish to be added (screed or floating floor)	GEN 1	75
— no permanent finish to be added (e.g. carpeted)	GEN 2	75
House floors with embedded metal	RC 30	50
Paving		
House drives, domestic parking and external paving	PAV 1	75
Heavy-duty external paving	PAV 2	50

concrete. Prescribed mixes are particularly used for specialist finishes such as exposed aggregate visual concrete.

Standard mixes

The standard mixes are a set of standard recipes, which can be mixed on site, with a restricted range of materials. They are used where quality control and strength are less critical. Standard mixes can be made to either low, medium or high workabilities.

IN SITU CONCRETE TESTING

The compressive strength of hardened concrete can be estimated *in situ* by mechanical or ultrasonic measurements. The Schmidt hammer or sclerometer measures the surface hardness of concrete by determining the rebound of a steel plunger fired at the surface. In the *pull-out* test, the force required to extract a previously cast-in standard steel cone gives a measure of concrete strength. Ultrasonic devices determine the velocity of ultrasound pulses through concrete. Since pulse velocity increases with concrete density, the technique can be used to determine variations within similar concretes. The test gives a broad classification of the quality of concrete, but not absolute data for concretes of different materials in unknown proportions.

Reinforced concrete

Concrete is strong in compression, with crushing strengths typically in the range 20–40 N/mm², and up to 100 N/mm² for high-strength concretes. However, the tensile strength of concrete is usually only 10% of the compressive strength. Steel is the universally accepted reinforcing material, as it is strong in tension, forms a good bond and has a similar coefficient of thermal expansion to concrete. The location of the steel within reinforced concrete is critical, as shown in Fig. 3.13, to ensure that the tensile and shear forces are transferred to the steel. The longitudinal bars carry the tensile forces, while the links or stirrups combat the shear forces and also locate the steel during the casting of the concrete. Links are therefore more concentrated around locations of high shear, although inclined bars can also be used to resist the shear forces. Fewer or thinner

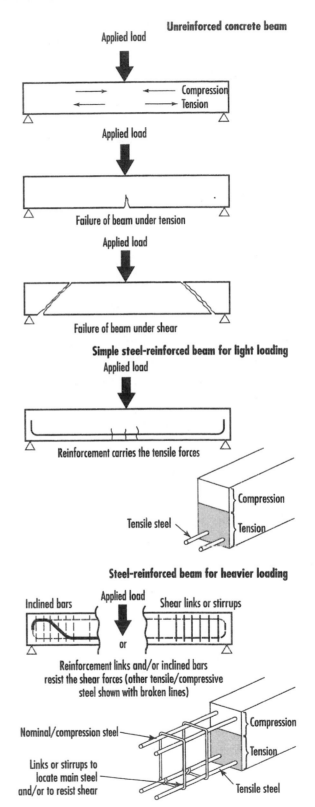

Fig. 3.13 Reinforced concrete

steel bars may be incorporated into reinforced con-crete to take a proportion of the compressive loads in order to minimise the beam dimensions.

Steel reinforcement for concrete is manufactured within the UK from recycled scrap into round, ribbed or ribbed and twisted bars (Fig. 3.14). Mild steel is used for round bars, which are used mainly for the bent links. Hot-rolled high-yield steel is used for ribbed bars, and high-yield steel is cold worked to produced ribbed and twisted bars. High-yield steel has a minimum yield stress of 460 N/mm², roughly double that of mild steel at 250 N/mm². Stainless steel to BS 6744: 1986 can be used for concrete reinforcement where failure due to corrosion is a potential risk. Type 304 (18% chromium, 10% nickel) stainless steel is used for most applications, but the higher-grade type 316 (17% chromium, 12% nickel, 2.5% molybdenum) is used in more corrosive envi-ronments. Welded-steel-mesh reinforcement is used for slabs, roads and within sprayed concrete. The European Standard refers to two ductility classes for reinforcement: High (H) and Normal (N).

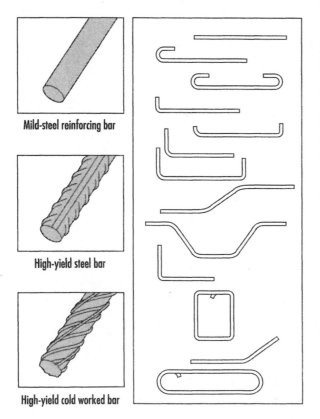

Mild-steel reinforcing bar

High-yield steel bar

High-yield cold worked bar

Fig. 3.14 Types of reinforcement for concrete and standard forms

Bond between steel and concrete

For reinforced concrete to act efficiently as a com-posite material the bond between the concrete and steel must be secure. This ensures that any tensile forces within the concrete are transferred to the steel reinforcement. The shape and surface condition of the steel and the quality of the concrete all affect the bond strength.

To obtain the most efficient mechanical bond with concrete, the surface of the steel should be free of flaky rust, loose scale and grease, but the thin layer of rust, typically produced by short-term stor-age on site, should not be removed before use. The use of hooked ends in round bars reduces the risk of the steel being pulled out under load, but high bond strength is achieved with ribbed bars, which ensure a good bond along the full length of the steel. Steel *rebars* are usually supplied either in stock lengths, or cut and bent ready for making up into cages. Sometimes the reinforcement is supplied as prefabricated cages, which can be welded rather than fixed with iron wire as would be the case on site. Steel reinforcement, although weldable, is rarely welded on site. Rebar joints can easily be made with proprietary fixings, such as steel sleeves fastened by shear bolts. Spacers are used to ensure the correct separation between reinforcement and formwork.

Good-quality dense concrete gives the strongest bond to the steel. Concrete should be well compact-ed around the reinforcement; thus the maximum aggregate size must not bridge the minimum rein-forcement spacing.

Corrosion of steel within reinforced concrete

Steel is protected from corrosion provided that it has an adequate cover of a good-quality, well com-pacted and cured concrete. The strongly alkaline environment of the hydrated cement renders the steel passive. However, insufficient cover caused by incorrect fixing of the steel reinforcement or the formwork can allow the steel to corrode. Rust expansion causes surface spalling, then exposure of the steel allows accelerated corrosion, followed by rust staining of the concrete surface. Calcium chlo-ride accelerators should not normally be used in reinforced concrete, as the residual chlorides cause accelerated corrosion of the steel reinforcement. Additional protection from corrosion can be

Table 3.11 Concrete exposure classes to Eurocode 2

Exposure classes			Typical environmental conditions
1	Dry environment		Interior of dwelling or office
2	Humid environment	a	Interior of building with high humidity exterior components components in non-aggressive soils
		b	Exterior components subject to frost exposure
3	Humid environment with frost and de-icing salts		Components exposed to frost and de-icing salts
4	Seawater environment	a	Components exposed to seawater or saturated salt sea air
		b	Components exposed to seawater or saturated salt sea air and frost
5	Aggressive chemical environment	a	Slightly aggressive chemical environment
		b	Moderately aggressive chemical environment
		c	Highly aggressive chemical environment

Table 3.12 Cover to concrete reinforcement and strength class for durability to Eurocode 2

Exposure class	Nominal cover (mm)				
1	20	20	20	20	20
2a		35	35	30	30
2b			35	30	30
3			40	35	35
4a			40	35	35
4b			40	35	35
5a			35	30	30
5b				30	30
5c					45 (plus physical barrier)
Minimum concrete strength class	C25/30	C30/37	C35/45	C40/50	C45/55 (or better)

achieved by the use of galvanised epoxy-coated or stainless steel reinforcement. The protective alkalinity of the concrete is reduced at the surface by *carbonation*. The depth of carbonation depends upon the permeability of the concrete, the moisture content and any surface cracking. Therefore the nominal cover for concrete reinforcement is calculated from the anticipated degree of exposure (Table 3.11) and the concrete strength class, as in Table 3.12. The cover specified relates to all reinforcement, including any wire ties and secondary reinforcement. Some reduction in carbonation rate can be achieved through the application of protective coatings to the concrete surface.

Where the depth of concrete cover over reinforcement is in doubt it can be measured with a *covermeter*. If the reinforcement is corroding, cathodic protection by the application of a continuous direct current to the steel reinforcement can prevent further deterioration and lead to realkalisation of the carbonated concrete.

Fire resistance of reinforced concrete

The depth of concrete cover required over the steel reinforcement to ensure various periods of fire resistance is shown in Table 3.13. Where cover exceeds 40 mm, additional reinforcement will be needed to prevent surface spalling of the concrete.

Table 3.13 Cover to concrete reinforcement for fire resistance to Eurocode 2

Fire resistance (hours)	Nominal cover to reinforcement (mm)						
	Beams		Floors		Ribs		Columns
	Simply supported	Continuous	Simply supported	Continuous	Simply supported	Continuous	
0.5	20	20	20	20	20	20	20
1.0	20	20	20	20	20	20	20
1.5	20	20	25	20	35	20	20
2.0	40	30	35	25	45	35	25
3.0	60	40	45	35	55	45	25
4.0	70	50	55	45	65	55	25

Where cover exceeds 40 mm additional reinforcement is required to prevent spalling.

PRESTRESSED CONCRETE

Concrete has a high compressive strength, but is weak in tension. Prestressing with steel wires or tendons ensures that the concrete component of the composite material always remains in compression when subjected to flexing up to the maximum working load. The tensile forces within the steel tendons act upon the concrete, putting it into compression, such that only under excessive loads would the concrete go into tension and crack. Two distinct systems are employed: in pre-tensioning, the tendons are tensioned before the concrete is cured and in post-tensioning the tendons are tensioned after the concrete is hardened (Fig. 3.15).

Pre-tensioning

Large numbers of precast concrete units, including flooring systems, are manufactured by the pre-tensioning process. Tendons are fed through a series of beam moulds and the appropriate tension applied. The concrete is placed, vibrated and cured. The tendons are cut at the ends of the beams, putting the concrete into compression. As with precast reinforced concrete it is vital that prestressed beams are installed the correct way up, according to the anticipated loads.

Post-tensioning

In the post-tensioning system the tendons are located in the formwork within sheaths or ducts. The concrete is placed, and when it is sufficiently strong, the tendons are stressed against the concrete and locked off with special anchor grips incorporated into the ends of the concrete. Usually, reinforcement

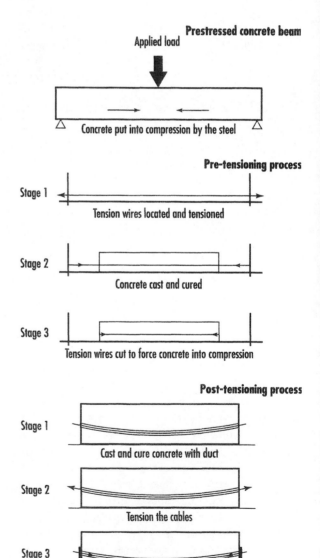

Fig. 3.15 Prestressed concrete

is incorporated into post-tensioned concrete, especially near the anchorages, which are subject to very high localised forces. In the bonded system, after tensioning, the free space within the ducts is grouted up. This then limits reliance on the anchorage fixing; however, in the unbonded system the tendons remain free to move independently of the concrete. Tendon ducts are typically manufactured from galvanised-steel strip or high-density polythene.

Post-tensioning has the advantage over pre-tensioning that the tendons can be curved to follow the most efficient prestress lines. In turn this enables long spans with minimum floor thickness to be constructed. During demolition or structural alteration work, unbonded post-tensioned structures should be de-tensioned, although experience has shown that, if demolished under tension, structures do not fail explosively. In alteration work, remaining severed tendons may subsequently require re-tensioning and re-anchoring to recover structural performance. However the use of post-tensioning does not preclude subsequent structural modifications.

Visual concrete

The production of visual concrete, whether precast or *in situ*, requires not only a high standard of quality control in manufacture, but also careful consideration of the correct specification and detailing of the material to ensure a quality finish which weathers appropriately.

The appearance of visual concrete is affected by three key factors:

- the composition of the concrete mix;
- the formwork used;
- any surface treatment after casting.

DESIGN CONSIDERATIONS

The satisfactory production of large areas of smooth concrete is difficult because of variations in colour and the inevitability of some surface blemishes which can be improved but not eradicated by remedial work. Externally smooth concrete weathers unevenly owing to the build-up of dirt deposits and the flow of rainwater. Therefore, if concrete is to be used externally as a visual material early design considera-

tion must be given to the use of textured or profiled surfaces to control the flow of rainwater. Generally the ranges of finishes and quality control offered by precasting techniques are wider than those available for *in situ* work, but frequently construction may involve the use of both techniques. The use of external renderings offers an alternative range of finishes for concrete and other substrates. Figure 3.16 illustrates the range of processes available in the production of visual concrete.

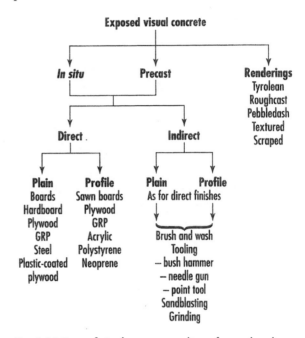

Fig. 3.16 Types of visual concrete according to formwork and surface treatment

PRECAST CONCRETE

Precast-concrete units can be cast vertically or horizontally, although most factory operations use the latter, either face-up or face-down, as better quality control can be achieved through this method. Moulds are usually manufactured from plywood or steel. While steel moulds are more durable for repeated use, plywood moulds are used for the more complex forms; they can also be more readily modified for non-standard units. Moulds are designed to be dismantled for the removal of the cast unit and must be manufactured to tight tolerances to ensure quality control on the finished product. As high costs are involved in the initial production of the moulds, economies of construction can be achieved by limiting the number of variations. This can have significant effects on the overall building aesthetic. Fixing and lifting systems for transportation must be incorporated into precast units, usually in conjunction with the steel reinforcement. In addition to visual concrete panels, units faced with natural stone, brickwork or tiles extend the range of precast architectural claddings.

IN SITU CONCRETE

The quality of *in situ* visual concrete is heavily dependent upon the formwork, as any defects will be mirrored in the concrete surface. The formwork must be strong enough to withstand, without distortion, the pressure of the fresh concrete, and the joints must be tight enough to prevent leakage, which can cause honeycombing of the surface. A wide range of timber products, metals and plastics can be used as formwork, depending upon the surface finish required.

The Independent Television News building in London (Plate 2), built in *in situ* concrete, is characterised by its atrium, which allows daylight to diffuse down the central core, past a series of stepped terraces and cantilevered balconies in ribbed concrete. The illumination of the restrained central space is enhanced by sun and light penetration through the frosted-glass south wall. The front facade is undercut below the second floor, with the exposed concrete columns creating a sense of enclosure to the main entrance.

CONCRETE FINISHES

Smooth finishes

In direct as-cast concrete, the surface texture and water absorbancy of the formwork, or any formwork lining, directly determine the final exposed fairfaced finish. A high level of quality control is therefore required to ensure a visually acceptable finish. Hard, shiny, non-absorbent formwork materials, such as steel, glass-reinforced polyester (GRP) or plastic-coated plywood, can give surfaces which suffer from *map crazing* due to differential shrinkage between the surface and underlying bulk material. Additionally, *blow holes* caused by air bubbles trapped against the form face may spoil the surface if the concrete has not been sufficiently vibrated. Where the absorbency of the formwork varies, because of the mixing of new and reused formwork, or variations within the

softwood timbers, or because of differing application of release agent to the formwork, permanent colour variations may be visible on the concrete surface. Release agents prevent bonding between the concrete and the formwork, which might cause damage to the concrete on striking the formwork. Cream emulsions and oils with surfactant are typically used as release agents for timber and steel, respectively. Formwork linings with controlled porosity can improve the quality of *off-the-form* finishes, by substantially reducing the number of blow holes. The linings allow the escape of air and excess moisture, but not cement, during vibration. A good-quality direct-cast concrete should exhibit only a few small blow holes and modest colour variation.

Textured finishes

A variety of textured finishes can be achieved by the use of rough-sawn boards as formwork. The grain effect can be enhanced by abrasive blasting, and a three-dimensional effect can be achieved by using variations in board thickness. Plastic materials, such as glass-reinforced polyester (GRP), vacuum-formed thermoplastic sheeting, neoprene rubber and polystyrene, can be used as formwork linings to give different pattern effects. Colour variations are reduced by the use of matt finishes, which retain the mould release agent during compaction of the concrete. The number of blow holes is reduced by the use of slightly absorbent materials such as timber and polystyrene. Concrete panels cast face-up can be textured by rolling or tamping the concrete while it is still plastic.

Ribbed and profiled finishes

Ribbed concrete is typically cast *in situ* against vertical timber battens fixed to a plywood backing. So that the formwork can be removed without damage to the cured concrete, the battens must be splayed and smooth. A softer ribbed appearance is achieved by hammering off the projecting concrete to a striated riven finish. Profiled steel formwork and rope on plywood produce alternative finishes. Where deep profiles are required, expanded polystyrene and polyurethane foam can be carved out to produce highly sculptural designs.

Abraded, acid-etched and polished finishes

Light abrasion with sandpaper can be applied to *in situ* or precast concrete. Acid etching is normally used only on precast concrete because of the hazards associated with using acids on site. Both techniques remove the surface laitance (cement-rich surface layer) to create a more stone-like finish, with some exposure of the aggregate. Polishing with carborundum abrasives produces a hard shiny finish, imparting full colour brightness to the aggregate. It is, however, a slow and therefore expensive process.

Exposed aggregate finishes

The exposure of the coarse aggregate in concrete, by removal of the surface smooth layer formed in contact with the formwork, produces a concrete with a more durable finish and better weathering characteristics, which is frequently aesthetically more pleasing. Smooth, profiled and deeply moulded concrete can all be treated, with the visual effects being largely dependent upon the form and colour of the coarse aggregates used. While gap-graded coarse aggregates can be used in both precast and *in situ* exposed aggregate finishes, precasting gives additional opportunities for the uniform placement of the aggregate. In face-down casting, flat stones can be laid on the lower face of the mould, which can be pretreated with retardant to slow the hardening of the surface cement. In face-up casting, individual stones can be pressed into the surface either randomly or to prescribed patterns without the use of retardants. Alternatively, a special facing mix can be used on the fairfaced side of the panel, with the bulk material made up with a cheaper standard mix. The aggregate

has to be exposed by washing and brushing when the concrete has cured sufficiently to be self-supporting. The use of a retarder applied to the formwork face allows the timing of this process to be less critical. The surface should be removed to a depth of no more than one third of the thickness of the aggregate to eliminate the risk of its becoming detached. An alternative method of exposing the aggregate in both precast and *in situ* concrete involves the use of abrasive blasting. Depending upon the size of grit used and the hardness of the concrete, a range of finishes including sculptural designs can be obtained.

Tooled concrete finishes

A range of textures can be obtained by tooling hardened concrete either by hand or mechanically. Generally, a high-quality surface must be tooled, as blemishes can be accentuated rather than eliminated by tooling. Only deep tooling removes minor imperfections, such as blow holes and the effects of slight formwork misalignment. Hand tooling is suitable for a light finish on plain concrete and club hammering can be used on a ribbed finish. Where deep tooling is anticipated, allowance must be made for the loss of cover to the steel reinforcement. The exposed aggregate colour in tooled concrete is less intense than that produced by wash-and-brush exposure because of the effect of the hammering on the aggregate. Standard mechanical tools are the needle gun, the bush hammer and the point tool (Fig. 3.17). A range of visual concrete finishes is illustrated in Fig. 3.18.

Point tool

Bush hammer

Needle gun

Fig. 3.17 Tools for indirect visual concrete finishes

Concrete cast against rough-sawn timber

Ribbed concrete treated by abrasive blasting

Striated textured finish from formwork lined with rope

Ribbed concrete hammered

Fig. 3.18 Visual concrete finishes

Abrasive blast finish to plain concrete

Gap-graded aggregate washed and brushed

Point-tooled finish

Heavy abrasive blast finish to exposed aggregate

Fig. 3.18 Visual concrete finishes (continued)

Weathering of concrete finishes

The weathering of exposed visual concrete is affected by the local microclimate, the concrete finish itself and the detailing used to control the flow of rainwater over the surface. It is almost impossible to ensure that all sides of a building are equally exposed, as inevitably there will be a prevailing wind and rain direction which determines the weathering pattern. It is therefore likely that weathering effects will differ on the various elevations of any building. Some elevations will be washed regularly, whilst others may suffer from an accumulation of dirt which is rarely washed. However, this broad effect is less likely to cause unsightly weathering than pattern streaking on individual facades.

The choice of concrete finish can have a significant effect on weathering characteristics. Good-quality dense uniform concrete is essential if patchy weathering is to be avoided, and generally a rougher finish is likely to perform better than a smooth as-cast finish. Profiling and the use of exposed aggregates have the advantage of dictating the flow of rainwater, rather than letting it run in a random manner, but dirt becomes embedded in the hollows. Dark aggregates and bold modelling minimise the change in appearance on weathering, but, generally, exposed non-absorbent aggregates are likely to give the best weathering performance. Horizontal surfaces can be subject to organic growths and this effect is increased by greater surface permeability.

Careful detailing is necessary to ensure a dispersed and controlled flow of water over the washed areas. The water should then be collected or shed clear by bold details to prevent pattern staining below. Water collected onto horizontal surfaces should not be allowed to run down facades below, so copings, sills and string courses all should be provided with drips to throw the water off the building face; alternatively, water should be removed by gutters. Multistorey facades should be articulated with horizontal features to throw the water off, at least at each storey level. Only on seriously exposed facades where strong winds are likely to cause rain to be driven upwards should small horizontal drip projections be avoided. Where concrete is modelled, due consideration should be given to the direction of flow and the quantity of rainwater anticipated.

EXTERNAL RENDERING

Renders are used to provide a durable and visually acceptable skin to sound but unattractive construction. Renders can reduce rain penetration and maintain the thermal insulation of walls. The finishes illustrated in Fig. 3.19 are all appropriate for external use. In each case it is essential to ensure good adhesion to the background. Where a good mechanical key, such as raked-out brickwork joints, is not present, an initial stipple coat of sand, cement, water and an appropriate bonding agent (e.g. styrene-butadiene rubber) is needed to create a key. Bonding is also affected by the suction or absorbency of the background; where suction is very high, walls may be lightly wetted before the rendering is applied. Metal lathing can be used over timber, steel or friable masonry to give a sound background. Two or three coats of rendering are normally applied; the successive coats are made weaker by a reduction in the thickness or strength of the mix. Smooth renders are not recommended for external work, as they tend to craze, particularly if finished off with a steel rather than wooden float. Generally, permeable renders are more durable than dense impermeable renders, as the latter may suffer cracking and subsequent localised water penetration. Sands for external renderings should be sharp rather than soft and conform to the Type A and Type B gradings in BS 1199: 1976. The design detailing of rendering is important to ensure durability. The top edges of rendering should be protected from the ingress of water by flashings, copings or eaves details. Rendering should stop above DPC level and be formed into a drip with an appropriate edging bead. Rainwater run-off from sills and opening heads should be shed away from the rendering to prevent excessive water absorption at these points, which would lead to deterioration and detachment of the rendering. A range of rendered finishes can be produced, as detailed below.

Roughcast render

Roughcast render consists of a wet mix of cement (1 part), lime (½ part), sand (3 parts) and 5–15 mm shingle or crushed stone (1½ parts) which is applied to walls by throwing from a hand scoop.

Dry-dash render

A 10 mm coat of cement (1 part), lime (1 part) and sand (5 parts) is applied to the wall and while it is

Roughcast

Tyrolean finish

Dry-dash

Travertine finish

Fig. 3.19 Render finishes

Scraped finish

Textured finish

Fig. 3.19 Render finishes (continued)

still wet, calcined flint, spar or shingle are thrown onto the surface and tamped in with a wooden float.

Scraped finish

A final coat of cement (1 part), lime (2 parts) and sand (9 parts) is applied and allowed to set for a few hours, prior to scraping with a rough edge (e.g. saw blade) to remove the surface material. After it has been scraped the surface is lightly brushed over to remove loose material.

Textured finishes

A variety of finishes can be obtained by working the final rendering coat with a float, brush, comb or other tool to produce a range of standard textured patterns. Pargeting, in which more sophisticated patterns are produced, has its cultural roots in Suffolk and Essex.

Tyrolean finish

For a Tyrolean finish, cement mortar is spattered onto the wall surface from a hand-operated machine. Coloured mixes can be used.

Painted rendered finishes

Most renderings do not necessarily need painting, but smooth renderings are frequently painted with masonry paint to reduce moisture absorption and give colour. Once they are painted, walls will need repainting at regular intervals.

Concrete components

In addition to the use of concrete for the production of large *in situ* and precast units, concrete bricks (Chapter 1) and concrete blocks (Chapter 2), the material is widely used in the manufacture of small components, particularly concrete tiles, slates and paving slabs.

CONCRETE ROOFING TILES AND SLATES

Concrete plain and interlocking slates and tiles form a group of very economic pitched roofing materials, with concrete interlocking tiles remaining the cheapest visually acceptable unit pitched-roof product. Plain and feature double-lap and interlocking tiles are manufactured to a range of designs, many of which emulate the traditional clay tile forms (Fig. 3.20).

Concrete plain tiles can be used on pitches down to 35°, while ornamental tiles are appropriate for vertical hanging and pitches down to 70°. The ranges of colours usually include both granular and through colour finishes. Standard ranges of concrete interlocking tiles and slates can be used in certain cases down to roof pitches of 17.5°, and for some shallow-pitched roofs the concrete tiles are laid to broken bond. One interlocking product emulates the appearance of plain tiles, but can be used down to a minimum pitch of 22.5°. Colours include brown, red, rustic and grey, in granular and smooth finish. A limited range of polymer-surfaced concrete interlocking tiles can be used at roof rafter pitches as low as 12.5°, provided that all tiles are clipped to prevent wind lift.

Concrete interlocking slates are manufactured with either a deep flat profile, giving a stone/slate appearance, or with a thin square or chamfered leading edge to copy natural slate. Surfaces can be simulated riven or smooth in a range of colours including grey, blue, brown, buff and red. Matching accessories for either traditional mortar bedding or dry-fixing for ridges, hips and verges are available, together with appropriate ventilation units.

CONCRETE PAVING SLABS AND TILES

Grey concrete paving slabs are manufactured from Portland cement mixes, with pigments added to produce the standard buff, pink and red colours. Standard sizes include 900 × 600 mm, 750 × 600 mm and 600 × 600 × 50 mm, but a wide range of smaller and thinner units is available for the home-improvement market including 600 × 600 mm, 600 × 450 mm, 450 × 450 mm and 400 × 400 mm by 40 to 30 mm. Thicker units (65 mm and 70 mm) are manufactured to withstand light traffic. Plain pressed slabs may have slightly textured surfaces, while cast slabs are available with smooth, simulated riven stone, terrazzo or textured finishes. Tooled textured-finished slabs and associated products are available for use in visually sensitive locations. In addition to the standard square and rectangular units, a wide range of decorative designs including hexagonal, simulated bricks and edging units is generally available.

Tile units for roof terraces, balconies and external pedestrian areas in frost-resistant Portland cement concrete are manufactured to square and hexagonal designs in a range of standard red, brown and buff colours. They are suitable for laying on asphalt, built-up felt, inverted roofs and sand/cement screed. Typical sizes are 305 × 305 mm and 457 × 457 mm with thicknesses ranging from 25 to 50 mm.

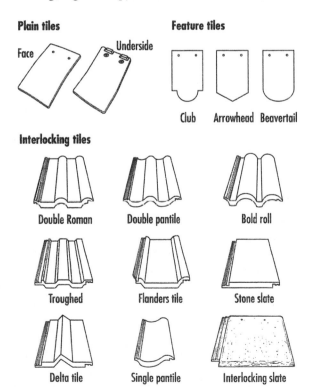

Fig. 3.20 Concrete roofing tiles and slates

References

FURTHER READING

Architectural Cladding Association. 1990: *Handbook – A guide to the design, detailing and economics of precast concrete claddings*. Leicester: Architectural Cladding Association.

Ashurst, J. and Ashurst, N. 1988: *Plasters, mortars and renders*. Practical Building Conservation 3. Aldershot: Gower Technical Press.

Blackledge, G.F. 1990: *Concrete practice.* Crowthorne: British Cement Association.

British Cement Association. 1980–88: *Appearance matters.* Booklets 1–9. Slough: Cement and Concrete Association (now British Cement Association).

British Cement Association. 1991: *Admixtures for concrete.* Crowthorne: British Cement Association.

British Cement Association. 1993: *Concrete on site.* Booklets 1–11. Crowthorne: British Cement Association.

British Cement Association. 1993: *Concrete in the environment.* Crowthorne: British Cement Association.

British Cement Association. 1994: *Post-tensioned concrete foors in multi-storey buildings.* Publication no. 97.347. Crowthorne: British Cement Association.

British Cement Association. 1994: *Worked examples for the design of concrete buildings based on Eurocode 2 – Design of concrete structures, Part 1 General rules and rules for building.* Crowthorne: British Cement Association.

Dhir, R. and Jones, M.R. (ed.) 1994: *Euro-cements – impact of ENV 197 on concrete construction.* London: E. & F.N. Spon.

Francis, A.J. 1977: *The cement industry, 1796–1914: A history.* Newton Abbot: David & Charles.

MacGinley, T.J. and Choo, B.S. 1990: *Reinforced concrete design theory and examples.* 2nd ed. London: E. & F.N. Spon.

Goodchild, C.H. 1993: *Cost study model.* BCA publication 97.333. Crowthorne: British Cement Association.

Goodchild, C.H. 1995: *Hybrid concrete construction.* BCA publication 97.337. Crowthorne: British Cement Association.

Mosley, W.H., Hulse, R. and Bungey, J.H. 1996: *Reinforced concrete design to Eurocode 2.* London: Macmillan.

Narayanan, R.S. (ed.) 1994: *Concrete structures: Eurocode EC2 and BS 8110 compared.* Harlow: Longman Scientific & Technical.

Neville, A.M. 1995: *Properties of concrete,* 4th ed. Harlow: Longman Scientific & Technical.

Ready-mixed Concrete Bureau. 1994: *The essential ingredient.* Crowthorne: The Ready-mixed Concrete Bureau.

Reinforced Concrete Council. 1994: *Concrete in architecture.* Educational Package. Crowthorne: Reinforced Concrete Council.

Spooner, D.C. 1995: *A guide to the properties and selection of cements conforming to British and European Standards.* Interim Technical Report 13. Crowthorne: British Cement Association.

White, G.R. 1991: *Concrete technology,* 3rd ed. New York: Delmar Publishers.

STANDARDS

BS 12: 1996. Specification for Portland cement.

BS 146: 1996. Specification for Portland blastfurnace cements.

BS 410: 1986. Specification for test sieves.

BS 473 and 550: 1990. Concrete roofing tiles and fittings.

BS 812. Testing aggregates:
    Part 2 and Parts 100, 101–103, 105, 106, 109–114, 117–121, 124.

BS 882: 1992. Specification for aggregates from natural sources for concrete.

BS 890: 1995. Specification for building limes.

BS 915. High alumina cement:
    Part 2: 1972. Metric units.

BS 1014: 1975. Pigments for Portland cement and Portland cement products.

BS 1047: 1983. Specification for air-cooled blastfurnace slag aggregate for use in construction.

BS 1197. Concrete flooring tiles and fittings:
    Part 2: 1973. Metric units.

BS 1199: 1976. Sands for external renderings, internal plastering with lime and Portland cement, and floor screeds.

BS 1200: 1976. Sands for mortar for plain and reinforced brickwork, blockwalling and masonry.

BS 1370: 1979. Specification for low heat Portland cement.

BS 1881. Testing concrete:
    Part 5 and Parts 101–122, 124, 125, 127, 129, 201–209.

BS 3148: 1980. Methods of test for water for making concrete (including notes on the suitability of the water).

BS 3797: 1990. Lightweight aggregates for masonry units and structural concrete.

BS 3892. Pulverized-fuel ash:
    Part 1: 1993. Specification for pulverized-fuel ash for use with Portland cement.
    Part 2: 1984. Specification for pulverized-fuel ash for use in grouts and for miscellaneous uses in concrete.

BS 4027: 1996. Specification for sulfate-resisting Portland cement.

BS 4246: 1996. Specification for high slag blastfurnace cement.

BS 4248: 1974. Supersulphated cement.

BS 4449: 1988. Specification for carbon steel bars for the reinforcement of cement.

BS 4466: 1989. Specification for scheduling, dimensioning, bending and cutting of steel reinforcement for concrete.

BS 4483: 1985. Specification for steel fabric for the reinforcement of concrete.

BS 4486: 1980. Specification for hot rolled and hot rolled

and processed high tensile alloy steel bars for the prestressing of concrete.

BS 4550. Methods of testing cement:
Parts 0 and 2–6.

BS 4551: 1980. Methods of testing mortars, screeds and plasters.

BS 4721: 1981. Specification for ready-mixed building mortars.

BS 4887. Mortar admixtures:
Part 1: 1986. Specification for air-entraining (plasticizing) admixtures.
Part 2: 1987. Specification for set-retarding admixtures.

BS 5075. Concrete admixtures:
Part 1: 1982. Specification for accelerating admixtures, retarding admixtures, and water-reducing admixtures.
Part 2: 1982. Specification for air-entraining admixtures.
Part 3: 1985. Specification for superplasticizing admixtures.

BS 5224: 1995. Masonry cement.

BS 5262: 1991. Code of practice for external rendered finishes.

BS 5328. Methods for specifying concrete, including ready-mixed concrete:
Part 1: 1991. Guide to specifying concrete.
Part 2: 1991. Methods for specifying concrete mixes.
Part 3: 1990. Specification for the procedures to be used in producing and transporting concrete.
Part 4: 1990. Specification for the procedures to be used in sampling, testing and assessing compliance of concrete.

BS 5642. Sills and copings:
Part 1: 1978. Specification for window sills of precast concrete, cast stone, clayware, slate and natural stone.
Part 2: 1983. Specification for coping of precast concrete, cast stone, clayware, slate and natural stone.

BS 5838. Specification for dry packaged cementitous mixes:
Part 1: 1980. Prepacked concrete mixes.
Part 2: 1980. Prepacked mortar mixes.

BS 5896: 1980. Specification for high tensile steel wire and strand for the prestressing of concrete.

BS 5977. Lintels:
Part 1: 1981. Method for assessment of load.
Part 2: 1983. Specification for prefabricated lintels.

BS 6073. Precast concrete masonry units:
Part 1: 1981. Specification for precast concrete masonry units.
Part 2: 1981. Method for specifying precast concrete masonry units.

BS 6089: 1981. Guide to assessment of concrete strength in existing structures.

BS 6100. Glossary of building and civil engineering terms:
Part 6: 1984/1990 Concrete and plaster.

BS 6463. Quicklime, hydrated lime and natural calcium carbonate.
Part 1: 1984. Methods of sampling.
Part 2: 1984. Methods of chemical analysis.
Part 3: 1987. Methods of test for physical properties of quicklime.
Part 4: 1987. Methods of test for physical properties of hydrated lime and lime putty.

BS 6588: 1996. Specification for Portland pulverized-fuel ash cements.

BS 6610: 1996. Specification for pozzolanic pulverized-fuel ash cement.

BS 6699: 1992. Specification for ground granulated blast-furnace slag for use with Portland cement.

BS 6744: 1986. Specification for austenitic stainless steel bars for the reinforcement of concrete.

BS 7295. Fusion bonded epoxy coated carbon steel bars for the reinforcement of concrete:
Part 1: 1990. Specification for coated bars.
Part 2: 1990. Specification for coatings.

BS 7542: 1996. Method of test for curing compounds for concrete.

BS 7583: 1996. Specification for Portland limestone cement.

BS 8000. Workmanship on building sites:
Part 2: 1990. Code of practice for concrete work.
Part 9: 1989. Code of practice for cement/sand floor screeds and concrete floor toppings.
Part 10: 1989. Code of practice for plastering and rendering.

BS 8103 Structural design of low-rise buildings:
Part 1: 1995. Code of practice for stability, site investigation, foundations and ground floor slabs for housing.
Part 4: 1995. Code of practice for concrete suspended floors for housing.

BS 8110. Structural use of concrete:
Part 1: 1985. Code of practice for design and construction.
Part 2: 1985. Code of practice for special circumstances.
Part 3: 1985. Design charts for singly reinforced beams, doubly reinforced beams and rectangular columns.

BS 8204. In-situ floorings:
Part 1: 1987. Code of practice for concrete bases and screeds to receive in-situ floorings.
Part 2: 1987. Code of practice for concrete wearing surfaces.
Part 3: 1993. Code of practice for polymer modified cementitious wearing surfaces.
Part 4: 1993. Code of practice for terrazzo wearing surfaces.

BS 8297: 1995. Code of practice for design and installation of non-loadbearing precast concrete cladding.

BS EN 196: 1992. Methods of testing cement:

    Part 1: 1994. Determination of strength.

    Part 3: 1995. Determination of setting time and soundness.

    Part 5: 1995. Pozzolanicity test for pozzolanic cements.

    Part 6: 1992. Determination of fineness.

    Part 7: 1992. Methods of taking and preparing samples of cement.

    Part 21: 1992. Determination of the chloride, carbon dioxide and alkali content of cement.

ENV 197. Cement – composition, specifications and conformity criteria.

    DD ENV 197–1: 1995. Common cements.

    DD ENV 197–2: 1996. Cement – conformity evaluation.

    pr ENV 197–10. Calcium aluminate cement.

DD ENV 206: 1992. Concrete performance, production, placing and compliance criteria.

DD EN 413. Masonry cement:

    Part 1: 1995. Specification.

prEN 413-2: 1992. Masonry cement – test methods.

prEN 447: 1991. Grout for prestressing tendons – specification for common grout.

BS EN 450: 1995. Fly ash for concrete – definitions, requirements and quality control.

BS EN 451. Method of testing fly ash:

    Part 1: 1995. Determination of free calcium oxide content.

    Part 2: 1995. Determination of fineness by wet sieving.

BS EN 490: 1994. Concrete roofing tiles and fittings – product specifications.

BS EN 491: 1994. Concrete roofing tiles and fittings – test methods.

BS EN 678: 1994. Determination of the dry density of autoclaved aerated concrete.

BS EN 679: 1994. Determination of the compressive strength of autoclaved aerated concrete.

BS EN 680: 1994. Determination of the drying shrinkage of autoclaved aerated concrete.

BS EN 989: 1996. Determination of the bond behaviour between reinforcing bars and autoclaved aerated concrete by the 'push-out' test.

BS EN 990: 1996. Test methods for verification of corrosion protection of reinforcement in autoclaved aerated concrete and lightweight aggregate concrete with open structure.

BS EN 991: 1996. Determination of the dimensions of prefabricated reinforced components made of autoclaved aerated concrete or lightweight aggregate with open structure.

BS EN 992: 1996. Determination of the dry density of lightweight aggregate concrete with open structure.

PD 6534: 1993. Guide to the use in the UK of DD ENV 206: 1992 Concrete performance, production, placing and compliance criteria.

DD ENV 1992: Eurocode 2: Design of concrete structures:

    Part 1.1: 1992. General rules and rules for building.

    Part 1.2: 1996 General rules –Structural fire design.

    Part 1.3: 1996. General rules – Precast concrete elements and structures.

    Part 1.4: 1996. General rules – Lightweight aggregate concrete with closed structure.

    Part 1.5: 1996. General rules – Structures with unbonded and external prestressing tendons.

    Part 1.6: 1996 General rules – Plain concrete structures

DD ENV 1994: Eurocode 4: Design of composite steel and concrete structures:

    Part 1: 1994. General rules and rules for building.

CP 114: 1969. The structural use of reinforced concrete in buildings.

CP 204. In-situ floor finishes:

    Part 2: 1970. Metric units.

DD 83: 1983. Assessment of the composition of fresh concrete.

DD 92: 1984. Method for temperature-matched curing of concrete specimens.

DD 216: 1993. Method for determination of chloride content of fresh concrete.

BUILDING RESEARCH ESTABLISHMENT PUBLICATIONS

BRE Digests

BRE Digest 263: 1982. The durability of steel in concrete: Part 1 Mechanism of protection and corrosion.

BRE Digest 264: 1982. The durability of steel in concrete: Part 2 Diagnosis and assessment of corrosion-cracked concrete.

BRE Digest 265: 1982. The durability of steel in concrete: Part 3 The repair of reinforced concrete.

BRE Digest 325: 1987. Concrete Part 1: Materials.

BRE Digest 326: 1987. Concrete Part 2: Specification, design and quality control.

BRE Digest 330: 1991. Alkali aggregate reactions in concrete.

BRE Digest 342: 1989. Autoclaved aerated concrete.

BRE Digest 357: 1991. Shrinkage of natural aggregate in concrete.

BRE Digest 361: 1991. Why do buildings crack?

BRE Digest 362: 1991. Building mortar.

BRE Digest 363: 1991. Sulphate and acid resistance of concrete in the ground.

BRE Digest 389: 1993. Concrete cracking and corrosion of reinforcement.

BRE Digest 392: 1994. Assessment of existing high alumina cement concrete construction in the UK.

BRE Digest 405: 1995. Carbonation of concrete and its effects on durability.

BRE Digest 410: 1995. Cementitious renders for external walls.

BRE Digest 413: 1996. Reinforced autoclaved aerated concrete planks.

BRE Good Building Guides

BRE GBG 18: 1994. Choosing external rendering.

BRE GBG 23: 1995. Assessing external rendering for replacement or repair.

BRE GBG 24: 1995. Repairing external rendering.

BRE Information Papers

BRE IP 8/88. Update on assessment of high alumina cement concrete.

BRE IP 14/88. Corrosion-protected and corrosion-resistant reinforcement in concrete.

BRE IP 7/89. The effectiveness of surface coatings in reducing carbonation of reinforced concrete.

BRE IP 8/89. BREMORTEST: a rapid method of testing fresh mortar for cement content.

BRE IP 16/89. Porous aggregates in concrete: sandstones from North West England.

BRE IP 18/89. Results of exposure tests to evaluate repairs to reinforced concrete in marine conditions.

BRE IP 1/91. Durability of non-asbestos fibre-reinforced cement.

BRE IP 2/91. Magnesian limestone aggregate in concrete.

BRE IP 11/91. Durability studies of pfa concrete structures.

BRE IP 6/92. Durability of blastfurnace slag cement concretes.

BRE IP 15/92. Assessing the risk of sulphate attack on concrete in the ground.

BRE IP 6/93. European concreting practice: a summary.

BRE IP 16/93. Effects of alkali–silica reaction on concrete foundations.

BRE IP 5/94. The use of recycled aggregates in concrete.

BRE IP 7/96 Testing anti-carbonation coatings for concrete.

BRE Reports

BR 106: 1988. Design of normal concrete mixes.

BR 114: 1987. A review of carbonation in reinforced concrete.

BR 164: 1992. Sulphate resistance of buried concrete.

BR 216: 1994. Durability of pfa concrete.

BR 243: 1993. Efficient use of aggregates and bulk construction materials. Volume 1: An overview.

BR 244: 1993. Efficient use of aggregates and bulk construction materials. Volume 2: Technical data and results of surveys.

BR 245: 1993. Performance of limestone-filled cements.

BR 254: 1994. Repair and maintenance of reinforced concrete.

BR 279: 1995. Sulphate and acid attack on concrete in the ground: recommended procedures for soil analysis.

BR 314: 1996. Review of the effect of flyash and slag on alkali-aggregate reaction in concrete.

TRADE ASSOCIATIONS

Architectural Cladding Association, 60 Charles Street, Leicester LE1 1FB (0116 253 6161).

British Aggregate Construction Materials Industries Ltd., 156 Buckingham Palace Road, London SW1W 9TR (0171 730 8194).

British Cement Association, Telford Avenue, Crowthorne, Berks. RG11 6YS (01344 762676).

British Precast Concrete Federation Ltd., 60 Charles Street, Leicester LE1 1FB (0116 253 6161).

British Ready Mixed Concrete Association, The Bury, Church Street, Chesham, Bucks. HP5 1JE (01494 791050).

Cement Admixtures Association, Harcourt, The Common, King's Langley, Herts. WD4 8BL (01923 264314).

Concrete Society, 3 Eatongate, Windsor Road, Slough SL1 2JA (01753 693313).

Concrete Society Advisory Service, 33–35 Cowbridge Road, Pontyclun CF7 9EB (01443 237210).

The Lime Centre, Long Barn, Morestead, Winchester, Hants. SO21 1LZ (01962 713636).

Mortar Producers Association Ltd., PO Box 143, Wokingham, Berks. RG40 3YS (01344 761661).

Prestressed Concrete Association, 60 Charles Street, Leicester LE1 1FB (0116 253 6161).

Ready-mixed Concrete Bureau, Century House, Telford Avenue, Crowthorne, Berks. RG11 6YS (01344 725732).

Sprayed Concrete Association, Association House, 235 Ash Road, Aldershot, Hampshire GU12 4DD (01252 21302).

Structural Precast Association, 60 Charles Street, Leicester LE1 1FB (0116 253 6161).

Reinforced Concrete Council, Century House, Telford Avenue, Crowthorne, Berks. RG45 6YS (01344 725735).

TIMBER AND TIMBER PRODUCTS

Introduction

Timber, arguably the original building material, retains its prime importance within the construction industry because of its versatility, diversity and aesthetic properties. About one third of the earth's land mass is covered by forests, divided roughly two-thirds as hardwoods in temperate and tropical climates and one third as softwoods within temperate and colder regions. Approximately a third of the annual worldwide timber harvest is used in construction, and the rest is consumed for paper-production, as a fuel, or wasted during the logging process.

Environmental issues, raised by the need to meet current and future demands for timber, can be resolved only by sustainable forest developments. In temperate climate forests, clear cutting, in which an area is totally stripped, followed by replanting, is the most economical way of cropping timber, but the shelterwood method, involving a staged harvest over several years, ensures that replacement young trees become established as the mature ones are felled. The deforestation of certain tropical regions has allowed wind and rain to erode the thin topsoil leaving inhospitable or desert conditions; furthermore, the overall reduction in world rainforest areas is contributing significantly to the *greenhouse effect* by reducing the rate of extraction of carbon dioxide from the atmosphere.

Compared to the other major construction materials, timber as a renewable resource is environmentally acceptable. Brick, steel, aluminium and plastics all use more energy in their production, thus contributing considerably to carbon dioxide emissions. Trees require little energy for their conversion into usable timber, and young replacement trees are particularly efficient at absorbing carbon dioxide and releasing oxygen into the atmosphere. Temperate and tropical hardwoods, suitably managed, can be brought to maturity within a human lifespan; softwoods within half that period. Timber products manufactured from reconstituted and waste wood add to the efficient use of forestry.

Timber

The Study Centre at Darwin College, Cambridge (Plate 3), which occupies a narrow site overlooking the River Cam, is designed to accommodate both books and computers. It is a loadbearing masonry and timber building which features the extensive use of English oak, including massive paired columns to the first-floor reading room which is partly cantilevered over the river. The columns in green oak have characteristic shakes and splits, giving an impression of great age, and these contrast with the refined oak and oak veneer of the floors, window frames and furniture. Joints in the green oak are held by stainless steel fixings, which can be tightened as the timber dries and shrinks. The use of oak throughout gives unity to the building, which sits comfortably within its highly sensitive location.

METABOLISM OF THE TREE

The tree, a complex living organism, can be considered in three main sections: the branches with their leaves, the trunk (or bole) and the roots (Fig. 4.1). The

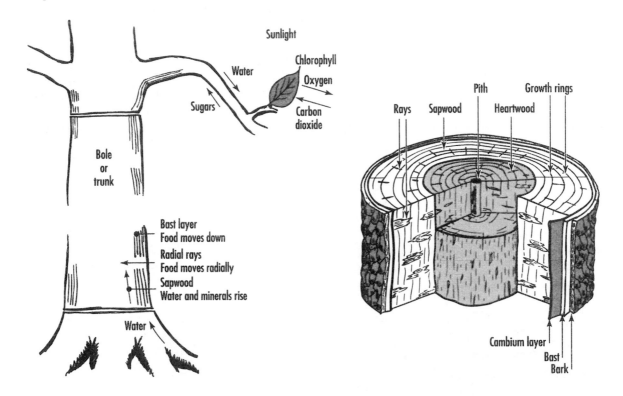

Fig. 4.1 Metabolism of the tree (after Everett A. 1994: *Mitchell's Materials*, 5th edition. Longman Scientific & Technical)

roots anchor the tree to the ground and absorb water with dissolved minerals from the soil. The leaves absorb carbon dioxide from the air and in the presence of sunlight, together with chlorophyll as a catalyst, combine carbon dioxide with water to produce sugars. The oxygen, a byproduct of the process, diffuses out of the leaves. The sugars in aqueous solution are transported down the branches and trunk to be subsequently converted, where required for growth, into the cellulose of the tree. The trunk gives structural strength to the tree, and acts as a store for minerals and food such as starch and also as a two-way transport medium.

The tree is protected from extremes of temperature and mechanical damage by the bark, inside which is the bast layer which transports downwards the sugars synthesised in the leaves. Radial rays then move the food into the sapwood cells for storage. Inside the bast is the thin and delicate cambium, which is the growing layer for the bark and sapwood. Growth takes place only when the cambium layer is active, which in temperate climates is during the spring and summer seasons.

A transverse section through the bole shows the growth rings. These are sometimes referred to as annual rings, but unusual growth patterns can lead to multiple rings within one year, and in tropical climates, where seasonal changes are less pronounced, growth rings may be indistinct and not annual. The growth rings are apparent because the *early wood* produced at the start of the growing season tends to be made from larger cells of thinner walls and is thus softer and more porous than the *late wood* produced towards the end of the growing season. Each year as the tree matures with the production of an additional growth ring, the cells of an inner ring are strengthened by a process of *secondary thickening*. This is followed by lignification, in which the cell dies. These cells are no longer able to act as food stores, but now give increased structural strength to the tree. The physical changes are often associated with a darkening of the timber due to the incorporation into the cell walls of so-called *extractives*, such as resins in softwoods or tannins in oak. These are natural wood preservatives which make heartwood more durable than sapwood.

CONSTITUENTS OF TIMBER

The main constituents of timber are cellulose, hemi-cellulose and lignin, which are natural polymers. Cellulose, the main constituent of the cell walls, is a polymer made from glucose, a direct product from photosynthesis within the leaves of the tree. Glucose molecules join together to form cellulose chains containing typically 10 000 sugar units (Fig. 4.2). Alternate cellulose chains, running in opposite directions to each other, form a predominantly well ordered crystalline material. It is this crystalline chain structure which gives cellulose its fibrous properties, and accounts for approximately 45% of the dry weight of the wood.

Hemicelluloses, which account for approximately 25% of the weight of wood, have more complex partially crystalline structures, being composed of a variety of other sugars. The molecular chains are shorter than those in cellulose, producing a more gelatinous material. Lignin (approximately 25% by weight of the timber) is an insoluble non-crystalline polymeric material. Its main constituents are derivatives of benzene combined to form a complex branched-chain structure.

The three major components are combined to form *microfibrils* which are in turn the building blocks for the cell walls. Crystalline cellulose chains are surrounded by semi-crystalline hemi-cellulose, then a layer of non-crystalline cellulose, and are finally cemented together with lignin (Fig. 4.3). Millions of these microfibrils are built up in layers to form the individual cell walls. It is this composite

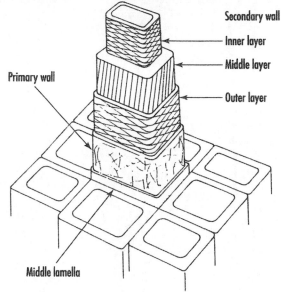

Fig. 4.3 Cell structure of timber (after Desch H.E. 1981: *Timber: Its structure properties and utilisation*, 6th edition. Macmillan Education – Crown Copyright)

Photosynthesis

$$6CO_2 + 6H_2O \xrightarrow{\text{sunlight/chlorophyll}} C_6H_{12}O_6 + 6O_2$$

carbon dioxide　water　　　　　　glucose　oxygen

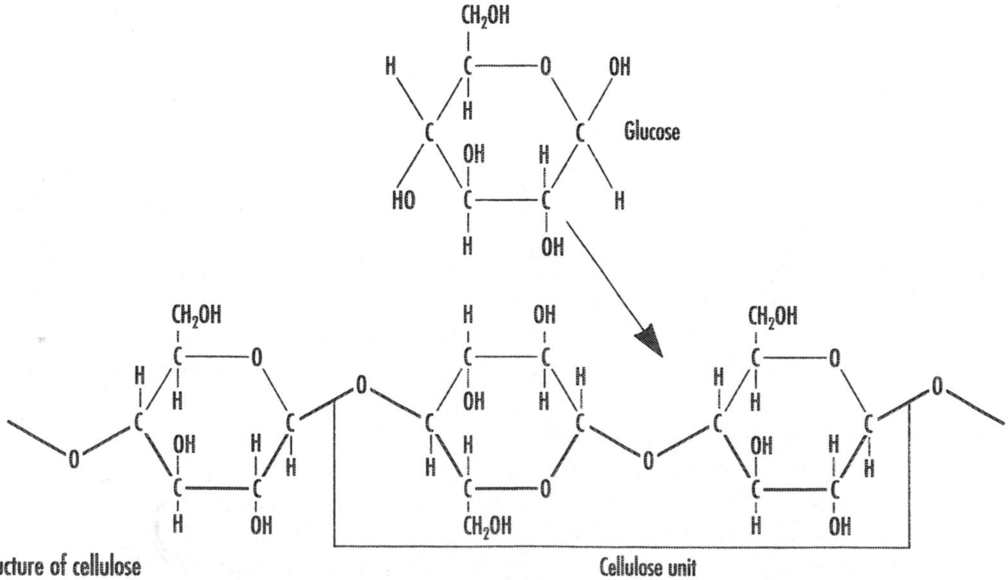

Fig. 4.2 Structure of cellulose

structure that gives timber its physical strength, with the cellulose contributing mainly to the tensile properties and the hemicellulose and lignin to the compressive strength and elasticity.

In addition to the three major constituents and significant quantities of water, timbers contain many minor constituents; some, such as resins, gums and tannins, are associated with the conversion of sapwood to heartwood. Starch present in sapwood is attractive to fungi, and inorganic materials such as silica make working certain tropical hardwoods, such as teak, difficult. The various colours present in different timbers arise from these minor constituents, as the various celluloses and lignin are virtually colourless. Some colours are fixed to the polymeric chains, but others are light-sensitive natural dyes which fade on prolonged exposure to sunlight unless the timber is coated with an ultraviolet-absorbing finish.

HARDWOODS AND SOFTWOODS

Commercial timbers are defined as hardwoods or softwoods according to their botanical classification rather than their physical strength. Hardwoods (angiosperms) are from broad-leafed trees, which in temperate climates are deciduous, losing their leaves in autumn; although in tropical climates, where there is little seasonal variation, old leaves are constantly being replaced by new. Softwoods (gymnosperms) are from conifers, characteristically with needle-shaped leaves, and growing predominantly in the northern temperate zone. Most conifers are evergreen, with the notable exception of the European larch (*Larix decidua*), and they include the Californian redwood (*Sequoia sempervirens*), the world's largest tree, with a height of over 100 metres. Although the terms hardwood and softwood arose from the physical strength of the timbers, paradoxically, balsa (*Ochroma lagopus*), used for model-making, is botanically a hardwood, while yew (*Taxus baccata*), a strong and durable material, is defined botanically as a softwood. Under microscopic investigation, softwoods show only one type of cell which varies in size between the rapid growth of spring and early summer (early wood) and the slow growth of the late summer and autumn (late wood). These cells, or tracheids, perform the food and water conducting functions and give strength to the tree. Hardwoods, however, have a more complex cell structure, with large cells or vessels for the conducting

functions and smaller cells or wood fibres which provide mechanical support. According to the size and distribution of the vessels, hardwoods are divided into two distinct groups. Diffuse-porous hardwoods, which include beech (*Fagus sylvatica*), birch (*Betula pendula*) and most tropical hardwoods, have vessels of a similar diameter distributed approximately evenly throughout the timber. Ring-porous hardwoods, however, including oak (*Quercus robur*), ash (*Fraxinus excelsior*) and elm (*Ulmus procera*), have large vessels concentrated in the early wood, with only small vessels in the late wood (Fig. 4.4).

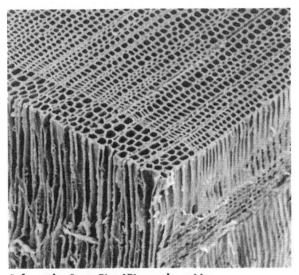

Softwood – Scots Pine (*Pinus sylvestris*)

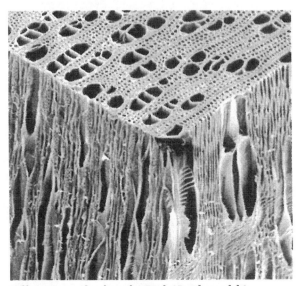

Diffuse-porous hardwood – Birch (*Betula pendula*)

Fig. 4.4 Cell structures of hardwoods and softwoods

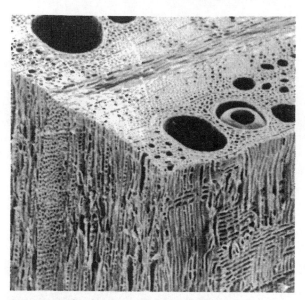

Ring-porous hardwood – Oak (*Quercus robur*)

Fig. 4.4 Cell structures of hardwoods and softwoods (continued)

TIMBER SPECIES

Any specific timber can be defined through the correct use of its classification into family, genus and species. Thus oak and beech are members of the Fagaceae family; beech is one genus (*Fagus*) and oak (*Quercus*) another. The oak genus is subdivided into several species, including the most common, the pedunculate oak (*Quercus robur*), and the similar but less common sessile oak (*Quercus petraea*). Such exact timber nomenclature is, however, considerably confused by the use of lax terminology within the building industry; for example, both Malaysian meranti and Philippine lauan are frequently referred to as Philippine mahogany, and yet they are from a quite different family and genus from that of true mahogany (*Swietenia*) from the West Indies, or Central America. This imprecision can cause the erroneous specification or supply of timber with serious consequences. Where there is a risk of confusion, users should specify the correct family, genus and species.

Softwood accounts for approximately 80% of the timber used in the UK construction industry. Pine (European redwood) and spruce (European whitewood) are imported from Northern and Central Europe, while western hemlock, spruce, pine and fir are imported in quantity from North America. Forest management in these areas ensures that supplies will continue to be available. Smaller quantities of western red cedar, as a durable lightweight cladding material, are imported from North America, together with American redwood from California, pitch pine from Central America and parana pine from Brazil. Increasingly, New Zealand, South Africa and Chile are becoming significant exporters of renewable timber. The UK production of pine and spruce provides only about 10% of national requirements while Ireland plans to be self-sufficient early in the next century.

Over 100 different hardwoods are used in the UK, although together ash, beech, iroko, mahogany (American and Brazalian), meranti, oak (American and European), ramin and teak account for over half of the requirements. Approximately half of the hardwoods used in the UK come from temperate forests in North America and Europe including Britain, but the remainder, including the durable timbers such as iroko, mahogany, sapele and teak, are imported from the tropical rain forests. Since 1965, 6.5% of the Amazon forest has been lost, but much of this deforestation has been for agricultural purposes, with more than three quarters of the trees felled used as a local fuel rather than exported as timber. With the growing understanding of the environmental effects of widespread deforestation, some producer governments are now applying stricter controls to prevent clear felling, and to encourage sustainable harvesting through controlled logging.

CONVERSION

Conversion is the process of cutting boles or logs into sections prior to seasoning. Subsequent further cutting into usable sizes is called manufacture. Finishing operations involving planing and sanding produce a visually smooth surface but reduce the absorption of penetrating wood stains. Timber for solid sections is sawn, whereas thin layers for plywood are peeled and veneers are usually sliced across the face of the log to maximise the visual effect of colour and figure, which is the pattern effect seen on the longitudinal surface of cut wood.

Types of cut

The two main types of cut, *plain sawn* and *quarter sawn*, refer to the angle between the timber face and the growth rings. This is best observed from the end of the timber, as in Fig. 4.5. If the cut is such that the growth rings meet the surface at less than 45° then

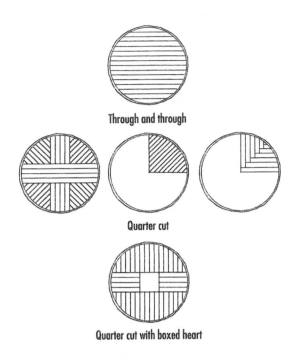

Through and through

Quarter cut

Quarter cut with boxed heart

Fig. 4.5 Conversion of timber

the timber is plain sawn. Timber with this type of cut tends to have a more decorative appearance but a greater tendency to distort by *cupping*. Timber cut with the growth rings meeting the surface at not less than 45° is quarter sawn. Such timber is harder wearing, weather-resistant and less likely to flake. If a log is cut *through and through*, which is most economical, then a mixture of plain and quarter-sawn timber is produced. Quarter sawing is more expensive as the log requires resetting for each cut and more waste is produced; however, the larger sections will be more dimensionally stable. The centre of the tree, the pith, is frequently soft and may be weakened by splits or shakes. In this case the centre is removed as a *boxed heart*.

Sizes

BS 4471 Part 1: 1996 defines the standard sizes of sawn softwood timbers at a 20% moisture content (Table 4.1). Widths over 225 mm and lengths over 5 m are scarce and expensive, but finger jointing (BS 5291: 1989), which can be as strong as continuous timber, does allow longer lengths to be specified. Planing on all faces, or 'processed all round' (PAR), reduces, for example, a 47 × 100 mm section to 44 × 97 mm. Hardwood sizes (BS 5450: 1977) are more variable because of the diversity of hardwood species

Table 4.1 Standard sizes of softwoods and hardwoods

Standard sizes of sawn softwood (20% moisture content) to BS 4471: 1996

Thickness (mm)	Width (mm)								
	75	100	125	150	175	200	225	250	300
16	✓	✓	✓	✓					
19	✓	✓	✓	✓					
22	✓	✓	✓	✓	✓	✓	✓		
25	✓	✓	✓	✓	✓	✓	✓	✓	✓
32	✓	✓	✓	✓	✓	✓	✓	✓	
36	✓	✓	✓	✓					
38	✓	✓	✓	✓	✓	✓	✓	✓	
44	✓	✓	✓	✓	✓	✓	✓	✓	
47	✓	✓	✓	✓	✓	✓	✓	✓	
50	✓	✓	✓	✓	✓	✓	✓	✓	
63	✓	✓	✓	✓	✓	✓	✓		
75		✓	✓	✓	✓	✓	✓	✓	✓
100		✓		✓		✓	✓	✓	✓
150				✓			✓		✓
200						✓			
250								✓	
300									✓

Standard lengths for sawn softwood are:
1.80, 2.10, 2.40, 2.70, 3.00, 3.30, 3.60, 3.90, 4.20, 4.50, 4.80, 5.10, 5.40, 5.70, 6.00, 6.30, 6.60, 6.90 and 7.20 m.
Lengths over 6 m may not be easily obtainable.

Standard sizes of sawn hardwood (15% moisture content) to BS 5450: 1977

Thickness (mm)	Width (mm)										
	50	63	75	100	125	150	175	200	225	250	300
19			✓	✓	✓	✓	✓				
25	✓	✓	✓	✓	✓	✓	✓	✓	✓	✓	✓
32			✓	✓	✓	✓	✓	✓	✓	✓	✓
38			✓	✓	✓	✓	✓	✓	✓	✓	✓
50				✓	✓	✓	✓	✓	✓	✓	✓
63						✓	✓	✓	✓	✓	✓
75						✓	✓	✓	✓	✓	✓
100						✓	✓	✓	✓	✓	✓

(Table 4.2). Hardwoods are usually imported in random widths and lengths; certain structural hardwoods such as iroko (*Chlorophora excelsa*) are available in long lengths (6–8 m) and large sections. Tolerances for acceptable deviations from target sizes are given in BS 4471: 1996. The European Standard EN 336: 1995 defines two tolerance classes; T1 for sawn timber and T2 for planed timber. A specification to BS EN 336 would therefore give target sizes and permitted

Table 4.2 Maximum permitted reduction from basic sizes of softwoods and hardwoods by planing two opposed faces

Maximum reductions from basic softwood sizes by planing two opposed faces

Typical application	Reduction from basic size (mm)			
	15–35	36–100	101–150	over 150
Constructional timber	3	3	5	5
Matching and interlocking boards (not flooring)	4	4	6	6
Wood trim	5	7	7	9
Joinery and cabinet work	7	9	11	13

Maximum reductions from basic hardwood sizes by planing two opposed faces

Typical application	Reduction from basic size (mm)				
	15–25	26–50	51–100	101–150	151–300
Constructional timber	3	3	3	5	6
Flooring, matchings, interlocked boarding and planed all round	5	6	7	7	7
Wood trim	6	7	8	9	10
Joinery and cabinet work	7	9	10	12	14

deviations from the target sizes, e.g. 47 mm (T2) × 100 mm (T2), indicates the actual required finished sizes in planed timber, irrespective of the original sawn size.

MOISTURE CONTENT AND SEASONING

As a tree is a living organism, the weight of water within it is frequently greater than the dry weight of the wood itself. The water content of a tree is equal in winter and in summer, but one advantage of winter felling is that there is a reduced level of insect and fungal activity. After felling, the wood will lose the water held within the cell cavities without shrinkage, until the *fibre saturation point* is reached, when the cells are empty. Subsequently, water will be removed from the cell walls, and it is during this process that the timber becomes harder and shrinkage occurs. As cellulose is a hygroscopic material, the timber will eventually reach equilibrium at a moisture content dependent upon the atmospheric conditions. Subsequent reversible changes in dimension are called movement. The controlled loss of moisture from green timber to the appropriate moisture content for use is called seasoning.

The primary aim of seasoning is to stabilise the timber to a moisture content that is compatible with the equilibrium conditions under which it is to be used, so that subsequent movement will be negligible. BS 5268: Part 2 and Eurocode 5 define three conditions or service classes 1, 2 and 3, which relate to conditions which would give average timber moisture contents not exceeding 12% and 20%, and over 20% respectively. As timber is seasoned, the reduction in water content to below 20% will arrest any incipient fungal decay, which can only commence above this critical level. Drying occurs with evaporation of water from the surface, followed by movement of moisture from the centre of the timber outwards due to the creation of a vapour-pressure gradient. The art of successful seasoning is to control the moisture loss to an appropriate rate. If the moisture loss is too rapid then the outer layers shrink while the centre is still wet and the surface sets in a distended state (case-hardening) or opens up in a series of cracks or checks. In extreme cases as the centre subsequently dries out and shrinks it may honeycomb.

$$\text{Moisture content} = \frac{\text{weight of wet specimen} - \text{dry weight of specimen}}{\text{dry weight of specimen}} \times 100\%$$

Air seasoning

Timber, protected both from the ground and from rain, is stacked in layers separated by strips of wood called stickers which, depending on their thickness, control the passage of air. The air, warmed by the sun and circulated by the wind, removes moisture from the surface of the timbers. The timber ends are protected by waterproof coatings (bituminous paint) to prevent rapid moisture loss, which would cause splitting. Within the UK a moisture content of between 17 and 23% can be achieved within a few months for softwoods or over a period of years for hardwoods.

Kiln drying

Kiln drying or seasoning is effected by heating within a closed chamber, which can be programmed to a precise schedule of temperature and humidity. Thus, drying to any desired moisture content can be achieved without significant degradation of the timber, although some early examples of kiln-dried timber showed serious damage through the use of inappropriate drying schedules. For economic reasons, timber is frequently air-seasoned to fibre saturation point, followed by kiln drying to the required moisture content. This roughly halves the necessary kiln time and fuel costs. A typical softwood load would be dried from fibre saturation point within a few days and hardwood within two to three weeks.

Seasoned timber, if exposed to rain on site, will reabsorb moisture. Good site management is therefore necessary to protect timber from both physical damage and wetting prior to its use. The heating up of new buildings by central heating systems can cause rapid changes in the moisture content of joinery timber and lead to shrinkage, cracking and splitting.

MOISTURE MOVEMENT

Wood is an anisotropic material, with differing moisture movements along the three principal axes: tangential, radial and longitudinal (Fig. 4.6). The highest moisture movement is tangential to the grain, next being radial with the least along the grain. Typical figures are given in Table 4.3. The larger the ratio between tangential and radial movement, the greater the distortion. Moisture movements are conventionally quoted for a change in relative humidity from 90% to 60% at 25°C. The BRE classifies

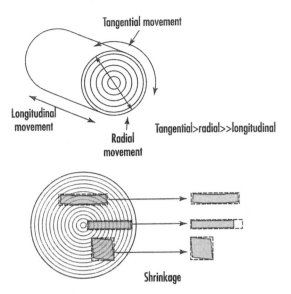

Fig. 4.6 Moisture movement and initial drying shrinkage

Table 4.3 Moisture movement of some hardwoods and softwoods normally available in the UK

Hardwoods

Small moisture movement (less than 3%)	Medium moisture movement (3.0–4.5%)	Large moisture movement (over 4.5%)
Afrormosia	Ash	Beech, European
Iroko	Elm, English	Ramin
Jelutong	Keruing	
Mahogany, African	Oak, American	
Mahogany, American	Oak, European	
Meranti	Sapele	
Teak	Utile	

Softwoods

Small moisture movement (less than 3%)	Medium moisture movement (3.0–4.5%)
Douglas fir	European redwood
Sitka spruce	European whitewood
Western hemlock	Parana pine
Western red cedar	

Moisture movement is assessed on the sum of the radial and tangential movements for a change in environmental conditions from 60 to 90% relative humidity.

woods into three categories according to the sum of radial and tangential movement effected by this standard change in relative humidity. Small movement is defined as less than 3%, medium between 3% and 4.5% and large over 4.5%.

TIMBER DEFECTS

Timber, as a natural product, is rarely free from blemishes or defects, although in some instances, such as knotty pine, waney-edge fencing timber or burr veneers, the presence of the imperfections enhances the visual quality of the material. Timber imperfections can be divided into the three main categories: natural, conversion and seasoning defects, according to whether they were present in the living tree, or arose during subsequent processing. Additionally, timber may be subject to deterioration by weathering, fungal and insect attack, and fire. These latter effects are discussed later in the chapter.

Natural defects

Knots

Knots are formed where branches of the tree join the trunk (Fig. 4.7). Where the wood fibres of the branch are continuous with the trunk, then a live knot is produced. If, however, the branch is dead, or bark becomes incorporated into the trunk, a dead knot is produced. This is liable to be loose, lead to incipient decay and cause structural weakness.

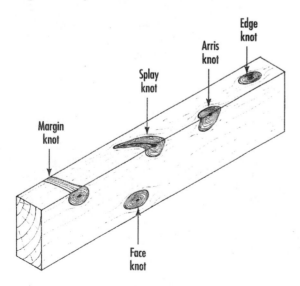

Fig. 4.7 Knots (after Porter, B. and Rose, R. 1996: *Carpentry and joinery: Bench and site skills.* Arnold)

Knots are described as face, edge, splay, margin or arris, dependent upon how they appear on the faces of converted timber. Additionally, knots may appear as clusters, and range in size from insignificant to many millimetres across. Frequently they are hard to work, and in softwoods contain quantities of resin, which will continue to seep out unless the wood is sealed before painting.

Natural inclusions

Many minor defects occur to varying degrees in different varieties of timber. Bark pockets occur where pieces of bark have been enclosed within the timber as a result of earlier damage to the cambium or growth layer. Pitch pockets and resin streaks, containing fluid resin, are frequently seen along the grain of softwoods.

Compression and tension wood

Trees leaning owing to sloping ground, or subject to strong prevailing winds, produce reaction wood to counteract these forces. In softwoods, compression wood is produced which is darker in colour owing to an increased lignin content. In hardwoods, tension wood is produced, which is lighter in colour owing to the presence of an extra cellulose layer in the cell walls. Both types of reaction wood have an abnormally high longitudinal shrinkage, causing distortion on seasoning; furthermore, tension wood tends to produce a rough surface when it is machined.

Abnormal growth rings

The width of the growth rings is an indicator of the growth rate and timber strength, with the optimum ranged around five rings per centimetre for softwoods and three rings per centimetre for hardwoods, depending on the species. Excessively fast or slow growth rates give rise to weaker timber owing to a reduction in the proportion of the stronger late wood or its production with thinner-walled fibres.

Conversion defects

Sloping grain

For maximum strength, timber should be approximately straight-grained. This is because as the slope of the grain increases (Fig. 4.8), there is a proportionate reduction in bending strength, ranging typically from 4% at 1 in 25 to 19% at 1 in 10. The British Standard (BS 5756: 1996) limits the slope of grain in tropical hardwoods for structural use to 1 in 11, and BS 4978: 1996 refers to the slope of grain in

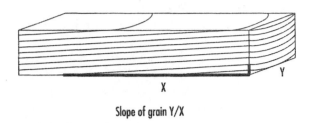

Slope of grain Y/X

Fig. 4.8 Sloping grain

visually graded softwoods including those for the manufacture of laminated timber.

Wane

Wane is the loss of the square edge of the cut timber owing to the incorporation of the bark or the curved surface of the trunk. A degree of wane is acceptable in structural and floor timbers (BS 4978: 1996 and BS 1297: 1987), and is a special feature in waney-edge fencing.

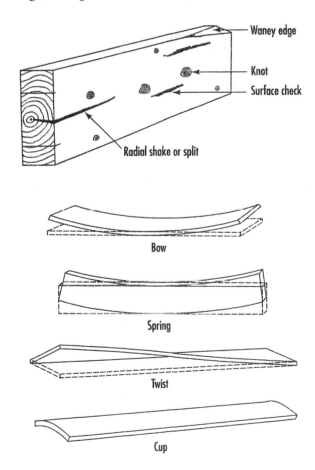

Fig. 4.9 Warping, splits and checks

Seasoning defects

Some of the commonest defects in timber are associated with the effects of seasoning. During the seasoning process, the contraction of the timber is different in the three major directions; furthermore, as described under 'Moisture movement', the outside of the timber tends to dry out more rapidly than the interior. These combined effects cause distortion of the timber, including warping and the risk of rupture of the timber to produce surface checks and splits (Fig. 4.9).

Shakes

Major splits within timber are termed shakes, and these can result from the release of internal stresses within the living tree on felling and seasoning; however, some fissures may be present within the growing timber. Commonly, shakes are radial from the exterior of the trunk, but star shakes which originate at the centre or pith may be associated with incipient decay. Ring shakes follow round a particular growth ring and are frequently caused by the freezing of the sap in severe winters.

SPECIFICATION OF TIMBER

The building industry uses timber for a wide range of purposes from rough-sawn structural members to claddings, trim and highly machined joinery. The specification of timber for each use may involve defining the particular hardwood or softwood, where particular visual properties are required. However, for the majority of general purposes, where strength and durability are the key factors, timber is specified by a strength class, which combines timber species and strength grades.

In addition to strength class, the specification of structural timber should include: lengths and cross-section target sizes, surface finish, moisture content and any preservative or special treatments (BRE Digest 416: 1996 gives guidance).

Strength grading

Strength grading, formerly known as stress grading, is the measurement or estimation of the strength of individual timbers, which allows each piece to be used to its maximum efficiency. It may be done visually, a slow and skilled process, or within a grading machine, which tests stiffness.

Visual strength grading

Each piece of timber is inspected for distortions, growth-ring size and slope of grain, then checked against the allowed standards for the number and severity of the natural defects such as knots, waney-edge, and fissures. The timber is then assigned to a grade and stamped accordingly. Softwood grades are special structural grade (SS) and general structural grade (GS). Temperate hardwood grades are THA and THB for sizes over 100 mm and TH1 and TH2 for smaller sizes. The tropical hardwood grade is HS.

Machine strength grading

Each piece of timber is rapidly inspected for any distortions which may cause it to be rejected manually, or serious defects within 500 mm of either end, at which points the machine testing is ineffective. The timber is then moved through a series of rollers which press it firmly against a curved metal plate (Fig. 4.10). The force required to bend the timber to this standard curvature is determined by a series of transducers and from these data the timber strength is computed. As the sample leaves the machine it may be sprayed at close intervals with colour-coded dye to continuously record its strength. Finally, each piece will be stamped with details of its overall grade, dependent on its weakest part, together with information on its species group, wet/dry state, the testing agency and individual machine (Fig 4.10). The machine gradings and dye colour codes are given in Table 4.4.

Table 4.4 Strength classes, former machine strength grading categories and their associated colour codings

Strength class	Former strength grading	Colour code
C27	M75	red
C24	MSS (machine-graded special structural)	purple
C22	M50	blue
C16	MGS (machine-graded general structural)	green

Strength classes

The BS EN Eurocode 5, *Design of timber structures*, will ultimately become the key British Standard, but as an interim measure the pre-standard BS ENV 1995-1-1: 1994 Eurocode 5 has been published and this will run concurrently with BS 5268 Part 2: 1996. Strength classes to BS EN 338: 1995 (Table 4.5), are defined as C14 to C40 and D30 to D70, where the prefix C refers to softwoods (coniferous) and D to hardwoods (deciduous). The number refers to the characteristic bending strength in newtons per square metre. The full specification of the strength classes to BS EN 338: 1995 gives characteristic values for density and a wide range of strength and stiffness properties, all based on sample test values. The data do not take into account any safety factors to be included in the design process.

The previous classification (BS 5268 Part 2: 1991) defined strength classes as SC1 to SC5 for softwoods and SC5 to SC9 for hardwoods. Generally, BS 5268: 1991 strength classes SC3, SC4 and SC5 are covered by the BS EN 338: 1995 classes C16, C24 and C27.

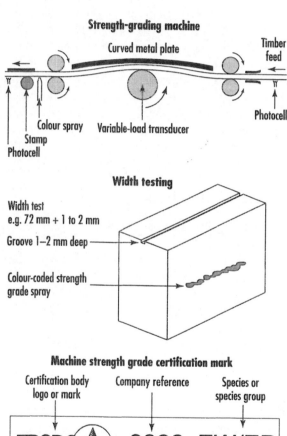

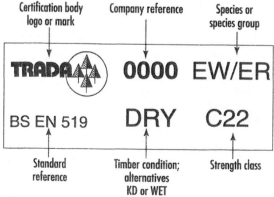

Fig. 4.10 Strength-grading machine and certification mark

Table 4.5 Strength classes and characteristic values to BS EN 338: 1995 and BS 5268 Part 2: 1996

Strength classes to BS EN 338: 1995

	C14	C16	C18	C22	C24	C27	C30 / D30	C35 / D35	C40 / D40	D50	D60	D70
Strength properties (N/mm²)												
Bending	14	16	18	22	24	27	30	35	40	50	60	70
Stiffness properties (kN/mm²)												
Modulus of elasticity parallel to the grain	7	8	9	10	11	12	12 / 10	13 / 10	14 / 11	14	17	20

Strength classes to BS 5268 Part 2: 1996

	C14	C16	C18	C22	C24	C27	C30	C35	C40	D30	D35	D40	D50	D60	D70
Strength properties (N/mm²)															
Bending	4.1	5.3	5.8	6.8	7.5	10.0	11.0	12.0	13.0	9.0	11.0	12.5	16.0	18.0	23.0
Stiffness properties (kN/mm²)															
Modulus of elasticity parallel to the grain	6.8	8.8	9.1	9.7	10.8	12.3	12.3	13.4	14.5	9.5	10.0	10.8	15.0	18.5	21.0

C refers to coniferous softwoods and D refers to deciduous hardwoods

Guidance to the Building Regulations refers in the Approved Document A to strength classes SC3 and SC4 for structural floor, ceiling and roof members, in relation to housing up to three storeys. Table 4.6 shows the strength classes to BS EN 338: 1995 for commonly used timber species. BS 4978: 1988 has now been revised as BS 4978: 1996 to refer only to visually strength-graded timber of grades GS (general structural) and SS (special structural).

Limit state design

Eurocode 5 represents a significant change for designers in timber as it is based on *limit state design*, rather than permissible stress as in the BS 5268: 1996. This brings timber into line with steel and concrete, for which this approach has already been taken. There are generally two limit states to be considered: first, the *ultimate limit state* beyond which parts of the structure may collapse; and secondly the *serviceability limit state* beyond which excessive deflection or vibration would render the structure unfit for its purpose. The ultimate limit states are determined from the *characteristic values of the loads* or actions and the material properties, to which partial safety factors are applied. Generally, the characteristic values of the material properties in BS EN 338: 1995 are higher than those in the BS 5268: 1996 grades, as they are derived from laboratory tests without reductions for long-term loading or safety factors, which become the responsibility of the designer.

JOINERY TIMBER

The term joinery applies to the assembly of worked timber and timber panel products, using timber which has been planed to a smooth finish. By contrast, carpentry refers to the assembly of the structural carcase of a building, usually with rough-sawn timbers. Joinery work, including the production of windows, doors, staircases, fitted furniture, panelling and mouldings, requires timber that is dimensionally stable, appropriately durable, with acceptable gluing properties, and which can be machined well to a good finish. Joinery-grade timber is categorised into four quality classes (Table 4.7) according to number and size of natural defects, particularly knots. These classes are subdivided into two surface categories, exposed and concealed, according to whether the timber is to be visible in use. (BRE Digest 407 lists the softwoods and hardwoods most frequently used for joinery in the UK.) Softwood flooring, cladding and profiled boards should not be specified as joinery.

DETERIORATION OF TIMBER

The major agencies causing the deterioration of timber in construction are weathering, fungi, insects and fire.

Table 4.6 Softwood species/grade combinations which satisfy the requirements of the BS EN 338: 1995 strength classes C14–C30 (grading to EN 519, BS 4978 or North American)

Species	Origin	Grading rules	European Standard BS EN 338: 1995 Strength classes						
			C14	C16	C18	C22	C24	C27	C30
Redwood	Europe	EN 519	✓	✓	✓	✓	✓	✓	✓
		BS 4978		GS			SS		
Whitewood	Europe	EN 519	✓	✓	✓	✓	✓	✓	✓
		BS 4978		GS			SS		
Douglas fir	UK	BS 4978	GS		SS				
Scots pine	UK	EN 519	✓	✓	✓	✓	✓	✓	
		BS 4978	GS			SS			
European spruce	UK	EN 519	✓	✓	✓	✓	✓		
		BS 4978	GS		SS				
Larch	UK	BS 4978		GS			SS		
Sitka spruce	Canada	Canada	1,2		Sel				
		BS 4978	GS		SS				
Douglas fir—larch	Canada USA	BS 4978		GS			SS		
		Can/USA		1,2			Sel		
Hem—fir	Canada USA	EN 519	✓	✓	✓	✓	✓	✓	✓
		Can/USA		1,2			Sel		
		BS 4978		GS			SS		
Spruce—pine—fir	Canada	EN 519	✓	✓	✓	✓	✓	✓	✓
		Canada		1,2			Sel		
		BS 4978		GS			SS		
Western whitewood	USA	USA	1,2		Sel				
		BS 4978	GS		SS				
Southern pine	USA	BS 4978			GS		SS		
		USA		3		1,2			
Pine	Chile	EN 519	✓	✓	✓	✓	✓	✓	
Pine	Zimbabwe	EN 519	✓	✓	✓	✓	✓	✓	
Pitch pine	Caribbean	BS 4978				GS		SS	
Parana pine	Imported	BS 4978		GS			SS		
Western red cedar	Imported	BS 4978	GS		SS				

Grading: EN 519 refers to machine grading; BS 4978 refers to visual grading, GS and SS are General Structural and Special Structural grades, respectively. The Canadian and US visual grading standards are NLGA and NGRDL, respectively. In the Canadian and US gradings 1, 2, 3 and Sel refer to No.1, No. 2, No. 3 and Select, respectively, ✓ indicates available to the grade indicated.

Weathering

On prolonged exposure to sunlight, wind and rain, external timbers gradually lose their natural colours and turn grey. Sunlight and oxygen break down some of the cellulose and lignin into water-soluble materials which are then leached out of the surface, leaving it grey and denatured. Moisture movements, associated with repeated wetting and drying cycles, raise the surface grain, open up surface checks and cracks and increase the risk of subsequent fungal decay. Provided that the weathering is superficial, the original appearance of the timber can be recovered by removing the denatured surface.

Table 4.7 Classes of timber for joinery use

Joinery class	Joinery use
Class CSH	'Clear' grades of softwood and hardwood
Class 1	High-quality or specialised joinery
Class 2	General-purpose joinery
Class 3	General-purpose joinery

Fungal attack

Fungi are simple plants, which, unlike green plants, cannot synthesise chlorophyll, and therefore must obtain their nutrients by metabolising organic material, breaking it down into soluble forms for absorption into their own system. For growth they need oxygen and a supply of food and water, a minimum moisture content of 20% being necessary for their growth in timber. The optimum temperature for growth is different for the various species of fungi, but usually within the range 20–30°C. Little growth takes place below 5°C and fungi will be killed by prolonged heating to 40°C. Some timbers, particularly the heartwoods of certain hardwoods, are resistant to attack because their minor constituents or *extractives* are poisonous to fungi.

All fungi have a similar life cycle (Fig. 4.11), commencing with the microscopic spores which are always present in quantity in the air. Under favourable conditions, spores within the surface cracks of timber will germinate and produce fine filaments or hyphae, which feed on the cellulose of the timber. The hyphae branch and grow through the timber cells, feeding on both the walls and their contents. With increasing colonisation of the timber, the fine hyphae combine to produce a white matrix or mycelium, which is then visible to the eye. After a period of growth, the mycelium at the surface produces fruiting bodies which generate many thousands of spores to continue the life cycle. The spores, which are less than 10 microns in size, are readily distributed by air movement.

Moulds and stains

Moulds and stains are fungi that metabolise only the starch and sugar food reserves stored within the timber cells; therefore sapwoods are generally more vulnerable than heartwood, since during the conversion of sapwood to heartwood the stored food is removed. Generally, there is little loss of strength

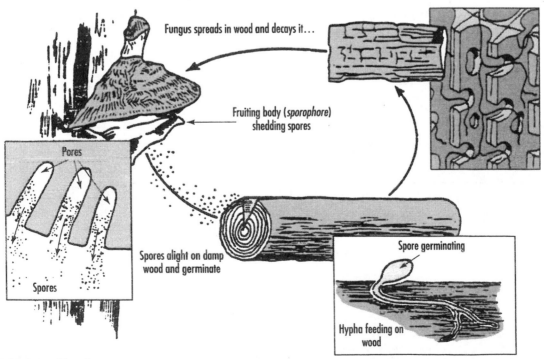

Fig. 4.11 Fungus life cycle

associated with such an attack, although one variety, *blue stain*, aesthetically degrades large quantities of timber and its presence may indicate conditions for incipient wood-rotting fungal attack. It is best prevented by kiln drying to reduce quickly the surface moisture content, unless infection has already occurred within the forest. Generally softwoods are more susceptible to attack than hardwoods.

Wet and dry rots

The name dry rot, attributed to one variety of fungus, is a misnomer, as all fungal growths require damp conditions before they become active. Destructive fungi can be categorised as soft, brown or white rots.

Soft rots, which belong to a group of microfungi, are restricted to very wet conditions such as timbers buried in the ground and are therefore not experienced with normal construction. They are usually found only within the timber surface, which becomes softened when wet and powdery when dry.

The brown rots preferentially consume the cellulose within timber, leaving more of the lignin, tannin and other coloured extractives; thus the timber becomes progressively darker. In contrast, the white rots consume all the constituents of the cells, so the timber becomes lighter in colour as the attack proceeds.

A major cause of deterioration of timber within buildings is *Serpula lacrymans*, the so-called *dry rot*. Under damp conditions, above 20% moisture content, the mycelium forms cotton-wool-like masses over the surface of the timber, which becomes wet and slimy. The mycelium strands, up to 20 mm in diameter, can grow through brickwork and past inert materials to infect otherwise dry timber. Under drier conditions the mycelium forms a grey-white layer over the timber, with patches of bright yellow and occasionally lilac. The fruiting bodies, or fructifications, are plate-like forms which disperse the rust-red spores. In some circumstances the fruiting bodies may be the first signs of attack by dry rot. After an attack by dry rot the timber breaks up both along and across the grain into cube-shaped pieces, becoming dry and friable: hence the name dry rot.

Wet rot or cellar fungus (*Coniophora puteana*) is the most common cause of timber decay within buildings in the UK. It requires a higher moisture content than dry rot (40–50%) and is therefore frequently associated with water ingress owing to leaks or condensation. The decayed timber is darkened and tends to crack mainly along the grain. The thin individual strands or hyphae are brown or black, and the fruiting bodies, rarely seen, are olive green in colour. Frequently the decay is internal without significantly affecting the exposed faces of the timber.

Phellinus contiguus (*Poria contigua*) causes decay to external softwood joinery, particularly window frames, causing the timber to decompose into fibrous lengths. Another variety, *Phellinus megaloporus*, is known to attack oak timbers, ultimately leaving a white mass.

Insect attack

Insect attack on timber within the UK is limited to a small number of species, and tends to be less serious than fungal attack. This is the reverse of the situation in hotter climates, where termites and other insects can cause catastrophic damage. The main damage by insects within the UK comes from beetles, which during their larval stage bore through the timber, mainly within the sapwood, causing loss of mechanical strength. For other species, such as the pinhole borers (*Platypus cylindricus*), the adult beetle bores into the timber to introduce a fungus on which the larvae live. The elm bark beetle (*Scolytus scolytus*) was responsible for the spread of *Dutch elm disease* in the 1970s. The larvae tunnelled under the bark, within the bast and cambium layers, preventing growth and spreading the destructive fungus which eventually killed large numbers of the trees across the UK.

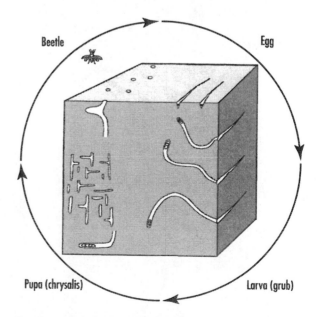

Fig. 4.12 Life cycle of wood-boring beetles

Common furniture beetle (*Anobium punctatum*)

Actual size approx. 3 to 5 mm long

Flight holes

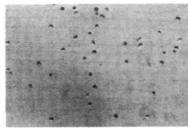

Bore dust

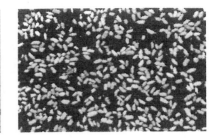

Death watch beetle (*Xestobium rufovillosum*)

Actual size approx. 6 mm long

Typical damage

Bore dust

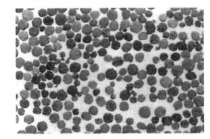

House longhorn beetle (*Hylotrupes bajulus*)

Actual size approx. 25 mm long

Typical damage to rafters

Bore dust

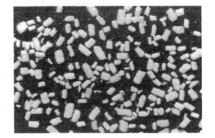

Powder post beetle (*Lyctus brunneus*)

Actual size approx. 5 to 6 mm long

Severe internal damage and apparently superficial external damage

Bore dust

Fig. 4.13 Wood-boring beetles common within the UK

Wood-boring weevil (*Pentarthrum huttoni*)

Actual size approx. 3 to 5 mm long

Typical internal damage

Bore dust

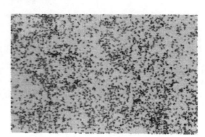

Fig. 4.13 Wood-boring beetles common within the UK (continued)

The typical life cycle (Fig. 4.12) commences with eggs laid by the adult beetle in cracks or crevices of timber. The eggs develop into the larvae, which tunnel through the timber, leaving behind their powdery waste or frass. Dependent on the species, the tunnelling process can continue for up to several years before the development of a pupa close to the surface of the timber, prior to the emergence of the fully developed adult beetle, which eats its way out, leaving the characteristic flight hole. The insects which attack well-seasoned timber within the UK are the common furniture beetle, the death watch beetle, the house longhorn beetle and the powder post beetle. Wood-boring weevils attack only timber that has been previously affected by fungal decay (Fig. 4.13).

Common furniture beetle

The common furniture beetle (*Anobium punctatum*) attacks mainly the sapwood of both hardwoods and softwoods; it can be responsible for structural damage in cases of severe attack, and is thought to be present in up to 20% of all buildings within the UK. The brown beetle is 3–5 mm long and leaves flight holes of approximately 2 mm in diameter. Both waterborne and organic-solvent insecticides offer effective treatments.

Death watch beetle

The death watch beetle (*Xestobium rufovillosum*) characteristically attacks old hardwoods, particularly oak, and is therefore responsible for considerable damage to historic buildings. Attack is normally on the sapwood, but heartwood softened by moisture and fungal decay will attract infestation; adjacent softwood may also be affected. The brown beetle is approximately 8 mm long and leaves a flight hole of 3 mm diameter. Remedial measures should include the eradication of damp and the application of organic-solvent insecticides.

House longhorn beetle

The house longhorn beetle (*Hylotrupes bajulus*) is a serious pest in some parts of southern England, particularly in Surrey. The Building Regulations 1991 – Approved Document to Support Regulation 7: 1992 edition lists the specific areas of southern England where roof timbers must be treated against this pest. House longhorn beetle can infest and cause serious structural damage to the sapwood of seasoned softwood roof timbers. With an average life cycle of six years and a larva that is up to 35 mm long, this beetle can cause serious damage before evidence of the infestation is observed. The affected timbers bulge where tunnelling occurs just below the surface. The eventual flight holes of the black beetle are oval and up to 10 mm across. Where sufficient serviceable timber remains, remedial treatment with organic-solvent or paste formulations is appropriate.

Powder post beetle

The powder post beetle (*Lyctus brunneus*) attacks the sapwood of certain hardwoods, particularly oak and ash. Only timbers with sufficient starch content within the sapwood are vulnerable to attack as the larvae feed on starch rather than the cell walls. The eggs are laid by the adult female beetle into the vessels, which are the characteristically large cells within hardwoods. Timbers with low starch content or fine vessels are immune, and the extended soaking of vulnerable timbers in water can reduce the risk of attack, but, owing to the long time scale involved, this is not commercially viable. The 4 mm reddish-brown beetle leaves a flight hole of approximately 1.5 mm diameter. Timbers are attacked only until all the sapwood is consumed, so in older buildings damage is usually extinct. In new buildings, coatings of paint or varnish make treatment impractical so replacement is the usual option.

Wood-boring weevils

Wood-boring weevils attack only timber previously softened by fungal decay. The most common weevil (*Pentarthrum huttoni*) produces damage similar in appearance to the common furniture beetle, but removal of decayed timber will eliminate the secondary infestation.

Preservation of timber

Wood preservatives contain pesticides in the form of insecticides and fungicides. Their use is therefore strictly controlled to limit unnecessary or accidental environmental damage. Preservative treatments should involve only materials currently approved by the Control of Pesticides Regulations (1986) and they should be used in accordance with the COSHH (Control of Substances Hazardous to Health 1988) regulations, the manufacturers' instructions and by operatives wearing appropriate protective clothing. Timber treatments may be divided into the application of preservatives to new timber, and remedial treatments used to eradicate or reduce an existing problem.

Preservative treatments for new timber

For the preservation of new timber within industrial plants, the risks to the environment and users are strictly controlled, and therefore more hazardous chemicals may be used with safety. The two industrial processes involve the use of vacuum and pressure impregnation.

The double-vacuum process, using organic-solvent-borne preservatives, is suitable for low- and medium-risk timber, such as external joinery. The timber, at less than 28% moisture content, is loaded into a low-pressure vessel which is evacuated to extract the air from within the timber. The vessel is flooded with preservative and a low positive pressure applied for between several minutes and one hour, depending upon the permeability of the timber. The vessel is then drained and evacuated to remove excess preservative from the timber surface. Formulations consist of either fungicides or

insecticides, or both, dissolved in volatile organic solvents. The solvents penetrate well into the timber but have a strong odour and are highly flammable. Pentachlorophenol (PCP) and tri-butyl tin oxide (TBTO) are the standard fungicides, with lindane (gamma hexachlorocyclohexane) used as the insecticide. A water repellent may also be incorporated in the preservative formulation.

The pressure/vacuum process is similar to the double-vacuum process, but uses waterborne preservatives and the application of high pressure within a pressure vessel to ensure deep penetration. The standard waterborne wood preservative is a copper/chromium/arsenate (CCA) mixture. The copper salt acts as the fungicide, the arsenate component as the insecticide and the sodium dichromate fixes the active ingredients within the timber, preventing their loss through leaching. Timber treated with proprietary products such as *Tanalith* is coloured slightly green but can be directly painted. Other formulations for wood preservation include: copper/chromium/boron (CCB), which is good for hardwoods; fluor/chrome/arsenate/phenol (FCAP), which is effective against attack by termites and house longhorn beetle; and sodium pentachlorophenate for preventing attack by *Serpula lacrymans*. Timbers to be built into high-risk situations, such as industrial roofs, frames and floors, timbers embedded in masonry, sole plates, sarking boards, tile battens, etc., should be treated by this process.

The use of pentachlorophenol (PCP) and tri-butyl tin oxide (TBTO) is normally restricted to controlled industrial use, where environmental hazards are minimised.

Remedial treatment for timber

Remedial treatments to existing buildings should be limited to those strictly necessary to deal with fungal or insect attack. The use of combined fungicides and insecticides is not advised when the attack is by one agent only. Within the UK, much timber decay is caused by building failures. As fungal decay can occur only in damp conditions, the first remedial measure must be to restore dry conditions. This should remove the need for frequent chemical applications.

The orthodox approach to the eradication of fungal and wood-boring beetle attack involves the removal of severely decayed or affected timber, followed by appropriate preservative treatment to the remaining timber. For fungal attack, at least 300 mm of apparently sound timber should be removed beyond the last visible sign of decay, and the adjoining timbers treated with fungicide. For wood-boring beetle, unless the infestation is widespread, preservative treatment should be applied only up to 300 mm beyond the visible holes. Organic-solvent fungicides and insecticides applied by brush or spray offer some protection from further attack, but applications of pastes which deliver higher quantities of the active ingredients are usually more effective. Insecticidal smoke treatments need to be repeated annually, as they are only effective against emerging beetles, but they may be useful in situations where brushing or spraying is impracticable.

The environmental approach to the eradication of fungal decay relies heavily on the removal of the causes of damp. On the basis that fungal attack will cease when timber is at less than 20% moisture content, increased ventilation and the rectification of building defects should prevent further attack. Only seriously affected timbers need to be replaced, and affected masonry sterilised; however, continual monitoring is required, as dormant fungal decay will become active if the timber moisture content rises again above 20%. *Rothounds* (specially trained sniffer dogs) and fibre-optics systems offer non-destructive methods for locating active dry rot before it becomes visible.

Pesticides used professionally for remedial treatment include permethrin and cypermethrin as insecticides, with boron esters, copper naphthenate and acypetacs zinc as fungicides. In remedial work, copper-based products should not be used near aluminium, and, during permethrin treatment, sarking felt, electrical wiring and roof insulation should be protected. These pesticides are currently considered acceptable for treatment in areas inhabited by bats, which are a protected species under the Wildlife and Countryside Act 1981.

Under the European Standards EN 351-1: 1996 and BS EN 335-1: 1992, timber preservative treatments against wood-destroying organisms are categorised by performance standards and not to the individual chemical preservative treatments. The standards define wood preservatives according to their effectiveness in a range of environmental conditions.

Hazard Class 1   Above ground, covered and permanently dry – moisture content less than 20%.

Hazard Class 2   Above ground, covered but with risk of high humidity and occasional wetting – moisture content occasionally over 20%.

Hazard Class 3   Above ground, not covered and frequently wet – moisture content frequently over 20%.

Hazard Class 4   Ground or fresh water contact, permanently wet – moisture content permanently over 20%.

Hazard Class 5   In salt water, permanently wet – moisture content permanently over 20%.

The level of treatment required to give the necessary performance is classified according to penetration into the wood and by retention or loading within the appropriate part of the wood.

Fire

Timber is an organic material and therefore combustible. As timber is heated it initially evolves any absorbed water as vapour. By the time it reaches a temperature of about 230–250°C, decomposition takes place with the production of charcoal, and combustible gases such as carbon monoxide and methane are evolved, which cause the flaming. Finally the charcoal smoulders to carbon dioxide and ash.

However, despite its combustibility, timber, particularly in larger sections, performs better in a fire than the equivalent sections of exposed steel or aluminium. Timber has a low thermal conductivity, which, combined with the protection afforded by the charred surface material, insulates the interior from rapid rises in temperature and loss of strength. The rate of charring of timber under the standard Fire Resistance Test ranges between 30 mm and 50 mm per hour per surface exposed, according to the timber density (Table 4.8). It is therefore possible to predict the fire resistance of any timber component using the British Standard (BS 5268 Part 4: 1978). Additionally, as all timbers have a low coefficient of expansion, timber beams will not push over masonry walls, as sometimes occurs with steel beams and trusses during fires.

Table 4.8 Rate of burning for timber from each exposed face

Rate of burning	Timber	Typical density (kg/m³)
30 mm per hour	Hardwoods (e.g. keruing, teak)	over 650
40 mm per hour	Structural softwoods e.g. European redwood/ European whitewood	450–550
50 mm per hour	Western red cedar	380

Flame retardants

Within a fire, volatile combustible components are evolved from the surface of the timber and these cause the flaming. To reduce this effect, timber can be impregnated by vacuum and pressure with inorganic chemicals which on heating evolve non-combustible gases. Timbers should be machined to their final dimensions before treatment. For interior use, typical compositions include waterborne inorganic salts, such as ammonium sulfate or phosphate with sodium borate or zinc chloride. As these materials are hygroscopic, the timber should not be used in areas of high humidity. For exterior use, a leach-resistant flame-retardant material based on an organo-phosphate is used, as this is heat fixed by polymerisation within the timber. Surface treatments, including antimony trioxide flame-retardant paints, are suitable for both interior and exterior use. Intumescent coatings are suitable for most environments if overcoating is applied. However, the protection afforded by surface treatments may be negated by unsuitable covering or removal by redecoration. Untreated timber, which is normally Class 3 spread of flame to BS 476 Part 7, can be improved to Class 1 by surface treatments.

TIMBER CONNECTORS

A range of steel timber connectors is commercially available. Trussed rafters, which account for a large market, are usually constructed with galvanised-steel nail plates (Fig. 4.14). Plates are hydraulically pressed into both sides of the timbers to be connected at the butt joints. Other types of connector include single- and double-sided circular toothed plates fixed with a central bolt. Laminated timber beams are usually fixed with purpose-made bolted shoes or plates.

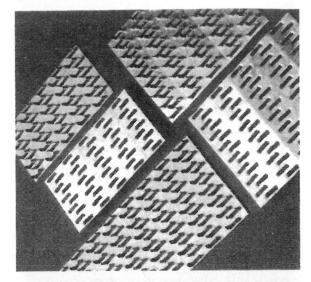

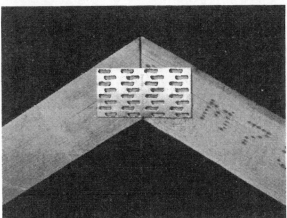

Fig. 4.14 Nail plates

Timber products

A wide range of products is manufactured from wood material, ranging in size from small timber sections and thin laminates through chips and shavings down to wood fibres. The physical properties of the materials produced reflect a combination of the subdivision of the wood, the addition of any bonding material and the manufacturing process. The physical properties then determine products' appropriate uses within the building industry. Many products are manufactured from small timber sections or timber by-products from the conversion of solid timber which otherwise would be wasted. Compressed straw slabs, thatch and shingles are additionally included in this section.

The product range includes:

- laminated timber;
- engineered timber;
- plywood;
- blockboard and laminboard;
- particleboard;
- fibreboard;
- wood wool slabs;
- compressed straw slabs;
- thatch;
- shingles.

LAMINATED TIMBER

Manufacture

Large solid-timber sections are limited by the availability of appropriate lumber; in addition, their calculated strength must be based on the weakest part of the variable material. Laminated-timber sections overcome both of these difficulties and offer additional opportunities to the designer. Laminated timber is manufactured by curing, within a jig, layers of accurately cut smaller timber sections which are continuously glued together with a resin adhesive. The use of strength-graded timber and the staggering of individual scarf or finger joints ensures uniformity of strength within the product; although, under BS 5268 Part 2: 1996 and prEN 387, large finger joints through the whole section of a *glulam* member are permissible. The manufacturing process ensures greater dimensional stability and fewer visual defects than in comparable solid timber sections. Laminated timber may be homogeneous, with all laminates of the same strength class of timber, or combined, in which lower-strength-class laminates are used for the centre of the units. Table 4.9 gives the European strength classes to prEN 1194: 1995 for the two alternatives.

Forms

Sections can be manufactured up to any transportable size, typically 30 m, although spans over 50 m are pos-

sible. Standard-size straight sections (315 × 65 and 90 mm; 405 × 90 and 115 mm; and 495 × 115 mm) are stock items, but common sizes range from 180 × 65 mm to 1035 × 215 mm. Sections can be manufactured to order, to any uniform or non-uniform linear or curved form. Figure 4.15 illustrates typical laminated timber arches, columns and portal frames as generators of structural forms. The aesthetic properties of laminated timber can be enhanced by the application of suitable interior or exterior timber finishes. The majority of laminated timber structures are manufactured from softwoods such as European redwood or whitewood, although the rib members within the roof structure of the Thames Flood Barrier were manufactured from the West African hardwood, iroko. Steel fixing devices and joints may be visually expressed or almost unseen by the use of concealed bolted steel plates. Laminated timber performs predictably under fire conditions with a charring rate of

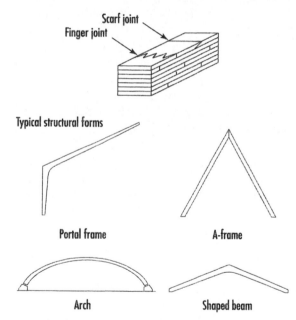

Fig. 4.15 Glued laminated timber beams (glulam)

Table 4.9 Strength classes to prEN 1194: 1995 for homogeneous and combined glulam

Glulam strength class	GL18	GL20	GL22	GL24	GL26	GL28	GL30	GL32	GL34	GL36	GL38
Homogeneous glulam:											
Strength class of laminates	C14	C16	C18	C22	C24	C27	C30		C35		C40
Combined glulam:											
Strength class of outer laminates		C16	C22	C22	C27		C30	C35	C40	C40	
Strength class of inner laminates		C14	C16	C18	C22		C24	C27	C30	C35	

40 mm per hour, as defined within BS 5268: Part 4 section 4, 1978. Preservative treatments are necessary when the material is to be used under conditions in which the moisture content is likely to exceed 20%. The three service classes of glulam structures relate to the environmental conditions.

Service Class 1 Internal conditions with heating and protection from damp.
Service Class 2 Protected, but unheated conditions.
Service Class 3 Exposed to the weather.

ENGINEERED TIMBER

Engineered timber (Fig. 4.16), a relatively new product, is more economical than laminated timber as there is little waste in the production process. It is manufactured to three grades by laminating timber strands with polyurethane resin under heat and pressure. In one process, logs are cut into flat timber strands 300 mm long; these are then treated with resin, aligned and hot pressed into billets of reconstituted wood. In the other processes, 3 mm thick timber strands or sheets of veneer are coated with waterproof adhesive and bundled together with the grain parallel. The strands or veneers are pressed together and microwave cured to produce structural timber billets or sheets up to 20 m long. The uniform material is suitable for use in columns, beams, purlins and trusses and can be machined as solid timber. I-section joists up to 20 m in length, with engineered timber flanges and web, are suitable for flat and pitched roofs and for floor construction.

Fig. 4.16 Engineered timber

PLYWOOD

Manufacture

Plywood is manufactured by laminating a series of thin timber layers, or plies, to the required thickness. The timber log is softened by water or steam treatment and rotated against a full-length knife to peel off a veneer or ply of constant thickness (Fig. 4.17). The ply is then cut to size, dried and coated with adhesive prior to laying up to the required number of layers. Not all the plies are of the same thickness; often, thicker plies of lower-grade material are used in the core. However, the sheets, must be balanced about the centre to prevent distortions caused by differential movement. Plies are normally built up with adjacent grain directions at right angles to each other to give uniform strength and reduce overall moisture movement, although with even plywoods, the central pair of plies have parallel grains. The laminate of plies and glue is cured in a hot press, sanded and trimmed to standard dimensions for packaging. Decorative veneers of

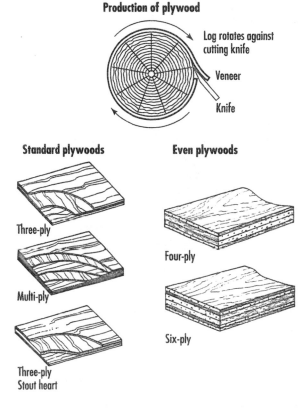

Production of plywood

Log rotates against cutting knife

Veneer

Knife

Standard plywoods

Three-ply

Multi-ply

Three-ply
Stout heart

Even plywoods

Four-ply

Six-ply

Fig. 4.17 Manufacture and standard types of plywood

hardwood or plastic laminate may be applied to one or both faces. Plywood imported from North America is typically manufactured from softwood; from northern Europe it comes mainly from birch and from the Far East predominantly from tropical hardwoods.

The standard sheet size is 2440 × 1220 mm, with some manufacturers producing sheet sizes of up to 3100 × 1530 mm or slightly larger. Sheet thicknesses range from 4 mm to 25 mm for normal construction use, although thinner sheets are available for specialist purposes.

Grades

The grade of plywood is determined partly by the adhesive used. The predominant and most durable grade, WBP (weather and boil proof, BS 6566: 1985), can be used externally without delamination, provided that the timber itself is durable or suitably protected against deterioration. Phenol formaldehyde resins are the most frequently used adhesives for WBP-grade plywood. Marine plywood (BS 1088/4079: 1966) is a combination of a moderately durable timber with phenol formaldehyde resin. The common lower grades of plywood, in order of decreasing durability, are CBR (cyclic boil resistant), MR (moisture resistant) and INT (interior), respectively. These are bonded with melamine–urea formaldehyde or urea formaldehyde resins. In addition to the grade of adhesive and the durability of the timber itself, the quality of plywood is affected by the number of plies for a particular thickness and the surface condition of the outer plies, which ranges from near perfect, through showing repaired blemishes to imperfect. Factory-applied treatments to improve timber durability and fire resistance are normally available.

The European Standard prEN 635 Parts 2 and 3: describes five classes of allowable defects (E, and I to IV), according to decreasing quality of surface appearance; Class E has almost no surface defects.

The European Standard prEN 636: 1996 gives performance specifications for plywood to be used in dry, humid or exterior conditions against criteria of bonding strength and durability with respect to biological decay.

Class 1 Interior applications under dry conditions (Hazard Class 1).

Class 2 Humid conditions – protected exterior applications (Hazard Class 2).

Class 3 Exterior applications – unprotected exterior use (Hazard Class 3).

Uses

Considerable quantities of plywood are used by the construction industry because of its strength, versatility and visual properties. The strength of plywood in shear is used in the manufacture of plywood box and I-section beams in which the plywood forms the web. Increased stiffness can be generated by forming the plywood into a sinusoidal web. Plywood box beams can be manufactured to create pitched and arched roof forms, as illustrated in Fig. 4.18. Stiffened and stressed skin panels, in which plywood and softwood timbers are continuously bonded to act as T or I-beams, will span greater distances as floor structures than the same depths of traditional softwood joists with nailed boarding. Such structural units can also be used to form pitched roofs, or to form folded-plate roof structures or barrel vaulting (Fig. 4.18). Plywood of 8–10 mm thickness is frequently used as the sheeting material in timber-frame construction and for complex roof forms such as domes. The lower-grade material is extensively used as formwork for *in situ* concrete.

CORE PLYWOOD

The standard core-plywood products are blockboard and laminboard. Both are manufactured with a core of, usually, softwood strips sandwiched between one or two plies (Fig. 4.19). In blockboard the core strips are between 7 mm and 30 mm wide, but in laminboard, the more expensive product, they are below 7 mm in width and continuously glued throughout. As with plywood, the grain directions are perpendicular from layer to layer. Most core plywoods are bonded with urea formaldehyde adhesives appropriate to interior applications only. The standard sheet size is 2440 × 1220 mm, with a thickness range of 12–25 mm, although larger sheets up to 45 mm thick are available. Blockboard can be finished with a wide range of decorative wood, paper or plastic veneers for use in fitted furniture. Variants on the standard products include plywood with phenolic foam, polystyrene or a particleboard core. Battenboard,

Plywood beams

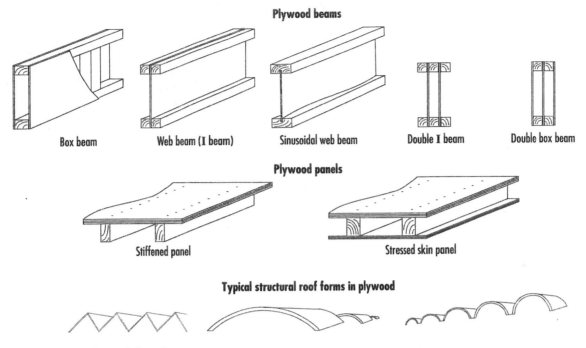

Box beam   Web beam (I beam)   Sinusoidal web beam   Double I beam   Double box beam

Plywood panels

Stiffened panel   Stressed skin panel

Typical structural roof forms in plywood

Fig. 4.18 Structural uses of plywood

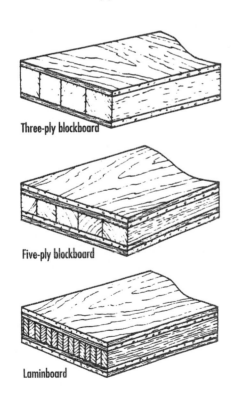

Three-ply blockboard

Five-ply blockboard

Laminboard

Fig. 4.19 Core plywoods

which has core blocks wider than 30 mm, is available, but no longer in common use.

PARTICLEBOARD

Manufacture

Particleboard or chipboard is manufactured from wood waste or forest thinnings which are converted into wood chips, dried and graded according to size. The chips are coated with adhesive to approximately 8% by weight and then formed into boards (Fig. 4.20). The woods chips are either formed randomly into boards, giving a uniform cross-section, or distributed with the coarse material in the centre and the finer chips at the surface to produce a smoother product. The boards are then compressed and cured between the plates of a platen press at 200°C. Boards are finally trimmed, sanded and packed. In an alternative manufacturing process, the mixture of wood chip and resin is extruded through a die into a continuous board; however, in this method, the wood chips are predominantly orientated at right angles to the board face, thus giving a weaker material. In the *Mende* process a continuous ribbon of 3 to 6 mm chipboard is produced by calendering the mix around heated rollers.

The standard sizes of particleboard are 2440 × 1220 mm, 3050 × 1220 mm and 3600 × 1220 mm, with the most common thicknesses ranging from 12 mm to 40 mm, although much larger sheet sizes and a wider range of thicknesses are available.

Types

The durability of particleboards is dependent upon the resin adhesive. Much UK production uses urea formaldehyde resin, although the moisture-resistant grades are manufactured with melamine–urea formaldehyde or phenol formaldehyde resins.

Particleboards are classified into six types to BS 5669 Part 2: 1989.

Type C1   General-purpose packaging and hoarding boards.

Type C1A Slightly improved strength and surface finish (furniture).

Type C2   Enhanced mechanical properties (domestic flooring).

Type C3   Improved moisture resistance over Type 1 (kitchen worktops).

Type C4   Moisture resistance of Type 3 but with specified impact resistance (flooring subject to occasional wetting).

Type C5   Highest moisture resistance and mechanical performance (structural purposes subject to occasional wetting in service).

BS 5669: Part 2 1989 refers to specifications and

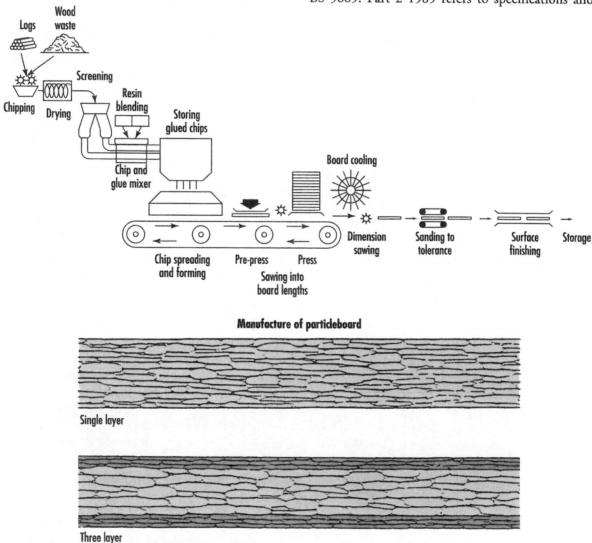

Manufacture of particleboard

Single layer

Three layer

Fig. 4.20 Manufacture and standard types of particleboard

applications for particleboards. Sheets should be colour-coded for identification along two opposite edges.

The European Standard BS EN 312: 1996 covers six grades of particleboard according to their anticipated loading and environmental conditions.

Part 2 General-purpose boards for use in dry conditions (Hazard Class 1).
Part 3 Boards for interior fitments and furniture for use in dry conditions (Hazard Class 1).
Part 4 Loadbearing boards for use in dry conditions (Hazard Class 1).
Part 5 Loadbearing boards for use in humid conditions (Hazard Class 2).
Part 6 Heavy-duty loadbearing boards for use in dry conditions (Hazard Class 1).
Part 7 Heavy-duty loadbearing boards for use in humid conditions (Hazard Class 2).

Standard particleboards are hygroscopic and respond to changes in humidity. A 10% change in humidity will typically increase the sheet length and breadth by 0.13% and the thickness by 3.5%. Types C1, C1A and C2 should not be exposed to moisture, even during construction. Types C3, C4 and C5 are tolerant to occasional wetting and relative humidities over 85%. However, no chipboards should be exposed to prolonged wetting, as they are all susceptible to wet-rot fungal attack.

All untreated particleboards have Class 3 spread of flame. However, they can be treated to the requirements of Class 1 by chemical addition in manufacture, by impregnation, or with intumescent paints. Class 0 can also be reached.

A wide range of wood veneer, primed/painted, paper and plastic (PVC, phenolic film or frequently melamine) finishes is available as standard. Pre-cut sizes are available edged to match. Domestic-flooring-grade particleboard, usually 18 mm or 22 mm, may be square-edged or tongued and grooved. The industrial flooring grades are typically from 38 mm upwards in thickness.

Uses

Large quantities of Types C1 and C1A particleboard are used in the furniture industry. Most flat-pack DIY furniture is now manufactured from painted or veneered chipboard. Particleboard can be effectively jointed by using double-threaded particleboard wood screws and various specialist fittings. Where high humidity is anticipated, the moisture-resistant grade, Type C3, should be used. The domestic flooring market uses large quantities of flooring-grade particleboard, Type C4, as it is competitively priced compared with traditional tongued and grooved softwood. BS 5669 specifies that 18/19 mm and 22 mm chipboard require maximum joist centres of 450 mm and 610 mm, respectively. Edges should be tongued and grooved or fully supported. For heavy-duty flooring and structural work to BS 5268 Part 2: 1996, Type C5 must be used. The moisture-resistant grades of particleboard are suitable for flat-roof decking; Type C3 may be used where access is limited, but Type C4 should be specified where normal access is required. Phenolic-film-coated particleboard offers a suitable alternative to plywood as formwork to concrete.

ORIENTED STRAND BOARD

Manufacture

Oriented strand board (OSB) is manufactured from softwood timber flakes, usually pine, tangentially cut and measuring approximately 75×35 mm. These are dried and coated with wax and 2.5% of either phenol formaldehyde or melamine–urea formaldehyde resin. The mix is laid up in three (or occasionally five) layers, with the grains running parallel to the sheet on the outer faces and across or randomly within the middle layer. The boards are then cured under heat and pressure, sanded and packaged (Fig. 4.21).

Grades and uses

There are two grades of flakeboard to BS 5669 Part 3: 1992; both are moisture resistant. Grade F1 is suitable for formwork, while grade F2, which has enhanced properties in terms of strength, moisture resistance and fungal attack, is suitable for roof sarking, flooring and flat-roof decking. Oriented strand board is manufactured to a thickness range of 6–25 mm, although 10–18 mm sheets predominate. In Europe it is manufactured from pine, and in North America from aspen.

The European Standard BS EN 300: 1996 specifies four grades of oriented strand board according to loadbearing requirements and environmental conditions.

Oriented strand board

Wood wool slab

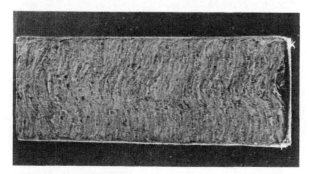

Compressed straw slab

Fig. 4.21 Oriented strand board, wood wool and compressed straw slabs

OSB1 General-purpose boards and boards for interior fitments for use in dry conditions (Hazard Class 1).
OSB2 Loadbearing boards for use in dry conditions (Hazard Class 1).
OSB3 Loadbearing boards for use in humid conditions (Hazard Class 2).
OSB4 Heavy-duty loadbearing boards for use in humid conditions (Hazard Class 2).

CEMENT-BONDED PARTICLEBOARD

Manufacture

Cement-bonded particleboard is manufactured from a mixture of wood particles or filaments (usually softwood), and Portland or accelerated magnesite cement. The boards, which are light grey in colour, have a uniform cementitious surface. The material is approximately 65% wood by volume, with cement filling all the void spaces, producing a material typically with a density of 1000–1250 kg/m^3 (compared with 650–690 kg/m^3 for standard-grade chipboard).

Types and uses

The British Standard BS 5669 Part 4: 1989 refers to two types of cement-bonded particleboard.

Type T1 Based on magnesite cement, the material is unsuitable for damp conditions, is not frost-resistant but is suitable as a lining board.
Type T2 Based on Portland cement, the material has good resistance to fire, water, fungal attack and frost and may therefore be used internally or externally.

While the European Standard BS EN 633: 1994 defines both magnesite- and Portland-cement-based products, BS EN 634: 1996 specifies only one grade of Portland-cement-bonded particleboard, suitable for non-structural purposes both internally and externally.

Boards frequently have a core of coarse wood chips, sandwiched between finer material, producing a good finish, which may be further treated by sanding and priming. Because of its density, cement-bonded particleboard has good sound-insulation properties. Typically, 18 mm board will give sound reduction up to 33 dB. The material is frequently used for soffits, external sheathing and roofing on both modular and timber-frame buildings. The heavier grades, generally tongued and grooved, are suitable for flooring, owing to the high impact resistance of the material.

The material has a Class 0 surface spread of flame to Building Regulations (Class 1 to BS 476 Part 7: 1987). Board sizes are typically 1220 × 2440, 2600 or 3100 mm, with standard thicknesses of 12 and 18 mm, although sheets up to 40 mm in thickness are made.

Gypsum-bonded particleboard

Gypsum-bonded particleboard, available in sheets of 6 mm thickness upwards, is an alternative multipurpose building board.

FIBREBOARDS

Fibreboards are manufactured from wood or other plant fibres by the application of heat and/or pressure. They are bonded by the inherent adhesive properties and felting of the fibres, or by the addition of a synthetic binder. In the *wet* process used for the manufacture of hardboard, mediumboard and softboard, no adhesive is added to the wood fibres. With medium-density fibreboard (MDF), a resin bonding agent is incorporated during the production process.

Manufacture

Wet process
Forest thinnings and wood waste are chipped and then softened by steam heating. The chips are ground down into wood fibres and made into a slurry with water. The slurry is fed onto a moving wire-mesh conveyor, where the excess water is removed by suction and light rolling which causes the fibres to felt together. The *wet lap* is then cut to lengths and transferred to a wire mesh for further pressing and heat treatment to remove the remaining water and complete the bonding process. Boards are then conditioned to the correct moisture content and packaged. The range of products primarily arises from the differing degrees of compression applied during the manufacturing process (Fig. 4.22).

Dry process
The manufacture of medium-density fibreboard (MDF) involves the addition of adhesive, usually urea formaldehyde, to the dry wood fibres, which are laid up to an appropriate thickness, slightly compressed to a density of at least 450 kg/m³ and cut to board lengths. The boards are cured under heat and pressure in a press, trimmed to size and sanded. A moisture-resistant grade (MDFMR) is available. MDF has the advantage of a high-quality machinable finish, and is now used for the production of various mouldings as well as boards. Decorative profiled sheets can be manufactured by laser cutting of MDF panels to individual client designs. Because of fibreboard's uniformity, solid sections can be routed to any form. Mouldings can be supplied primed and undercoated, ready to receive a finishing coat on site.

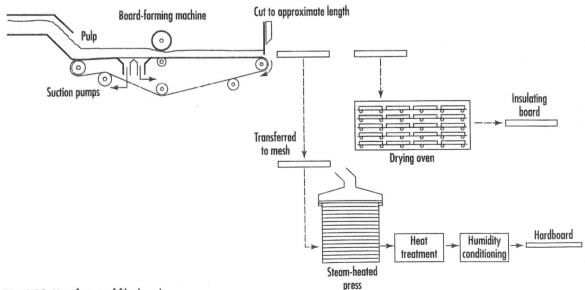

Fig. 4.22 Manufacture of fibreboards

Hardboard

Hardboards are the densest fibreboards, with a minimum density of 900 kg/m³. The boards range in colour from light to dark brown, usually with one smooth surface and a mesh-textured surface on the underside, although *duo-faced* hardboard – smooth on two faces – is available. Standard sheet sizes are 1220 × 2440 mm to 3600 mm, and 1700 × 4880 mm; there are also door sizes. Standard thicknesses range from 3.2 to 6.4 mm, although a wider range is available.

The European Standard BS EN 622 Part 2: 1996 specifies six grades of hardboard according to load-bearing requirements and environmental conditions.

HB   General-purpose boards for use in dry conditions (Hazard Class 1).

HB.LA   Loadbearing boards for use in dry conditions (Hazard Class 1).

HB.H   General-purpose boards for use in humid conditions (Hazard Class 2).

HB.HLA1 Loadbearing boards for use in humid conditions (Hazard Class 2).

HB.HLA2 Loadbearing boards for use in humid conditions (Hazard Class 2).

HB.E   General-purpose boards for exterior use (Hazard Class 3).

Standard hardboard is suitable for internal use, typically panelling, wall and ceiling linings, floor underlays and furniture. A range of perforated, embossed and textured surfaces is available. Applied coatings include primed or painted and various printed woodgrain, PVC or melamine foils.

Tempered hardboard

Tempered hardboards, impregnated with oils during manufacture, are denser and stronger than the standard hardboards, with enhanced water- and abrasion resistance. Tempered hardboards are dark brown to black in colour and have a density usually exceeding 960 kg/m³. Of the two types THN and THE (normal and extra), THE has the better performance.

Tempered hardboards are suitable for structural and exterior applications. The material's high shear strength is used within hardboard-web structural box beams and I-beams. Typical exterior applications include claddings, fasciae and soffits, where weather resistance is important. The moisture resistance of tempered hardboard makes it suitable for lining concrete formwork.

Mediumboard and softboard

Mediumboard and softboard are manufactured by the *wet* process. Mediumboard (high-density and low-density) and softboard exhibit a range of physical properties which reflects the degree of compression applied during the manufacturing process. High-density mediumboard (density 560–900 kg/m³) has a dark-brown shiny surface like hardboard. Low-density mediumboard (density 400–560 kg/m³) has a light-brown soft finish. Softboard (density 210–400 kg/m³) is light in colour, with a fibrous, slightly textured finish. Softboard impregnated with bitumen offers an increased moisture resistance over the untreated material.

High-density mediumboard extra grade (HME) can be used for exterior cladding Both the normal (HMN) and the extra grade (HME) are used for wall linings, sheathing, partitioning, ceilings and floor underlays. Low-density mediumboard (LME – extra and LMN – normal) is used for wall linings, panelling, ceilings and notice boards. It is unsuitable for exterior use. Softboard (SBN) is used for its acoustic and thermal insulating properties. Bitumen-impregnated softboard (SBI and SBS) has enhanced water-resistant properties and is suitable for use as a floor underlay to chipboard on concrete.

The European Standard BS EN 622 Part 3: 1996 specifies ten grades of low- (L) and high- (H) density mediumboard according to loadbearing requirements and environmental conditions.

MBL and MBH   General-purpose boards for use in dry conditions (Hazard Class 1).

MBH.LA1 and MBH.LA2   Loadbearing boards for use in dry conditions (Hazard Class 1).

MBL.H and MBH.H   General-purpose boards for use in humid conditions (Hazard Class 2).

MBH.HLS1 and MBH.HLS2   Loadbearing boards for use in humid conditions (short-term load duration class only) (Hazard Class 2).

MBL.E and MBH.E   General-purpose boards for exterior use (Hazard Class 3).

The European Standard BS EN 622 Part 4: 1996 specifies five grades of softboard according to loadbearing requirements and environmental conditions.

SB   General-purpose boards for use in dry conditions (Hazard Class 1).

SB.LS Loadbearing boards for use in dry conditions (instantaneous load duration class only) (Hazard Class 1).

SB.H General-purpose boards for use in humid conditions (Hazard Class 2).

SB.HLS Loadbearing boards for use in humid conditions (instantaneous load duration class only) (Hazard Class 2).

SB.E General-purpose boards for exterior use (Hazard Class 3).

WOOD WOOL SLABS

Manufacture

Wood wool slabs are manufactured by compressing long strands of chemically stabilised wood fibres coated in Portland cement (Fig. 4.21). The grey product has an open texture which may be left exposed, spray-painted or used as an effective substrate for plastering. It is also a suitable material for permanent shuttering for concrete. Slabs are available in a range of thicknesses, from 25 to 125 mm, typically 600 mm wide and up to 4000 mm in length.

Types and uses

Wood wool slabs are available either plain-edged or with interlocking galvanised-steel channels to the longitudinal edges. Three grades (Type A, B and SB) are specified in British Standard BS 1105: 1981.

Type A are non-loadbearing slabs manufactured to 25, 38 and 50 mm thicknesses and they are suitable for ceilings, partitions, wall linings and permanent concrete shuttering.

Type B are loadbearing slabs manufactured to 50, 75, 100 and 125 mm thicknesses; they are suitable for roof decking.

Type SB are loadbearing slabs with a greater impact resistance than Type B owing to the incorporation into the centre of the slabs of a high-strength nylon mesh. Their primary use is for roof decking.

The steel-channel reinforced slabs are normally manufactured to the Type SB standard. For typical loadings, 4000 mm spans can be achieved in roof decking applications. Where greater spans (up to 6000 mm) are required, reinforced-edge trough sections are available. The material is rated as Class 0 with respect

to Building Regulations and Class I (BS 476 Part 7: 1971) in terms of surface spread of flame. The material is resistant to fungal attack and is unaffected by wetting. Wood wool slabs offer good sound-absorption properties because of their open-textured surface. This is largely unaffected by the application of sprayed emulsion paint. The material is therefore appropriate for partitions, internal walls and ceilings where sound absorption is critical. Acoustic insulation for a pre-screeded 50 mm slab is typically 30 dB. The relatively high proportion of void space affords the material good thermal insulating properties, with a typical thermal conductivity of 0.077 W/m K at 8% moisture content.

The material is workable, being easily cut and nailed. Where a gypsum plaster or cement/lime/sand external rendering is to be applied, all joints should be reinforced with scrim. Wood wool slabs form a suitable substrate for flat roofs finished with built-up bitumen felt, asphalt or metals.

COMPRESSED STRAW SLABS

Compressed straw slabs are manufactured by forming straw under heat and pressure, followed by encapsulation in a fibreglass mesh and plastering-grade paper (Fig. 4.21). Typically used for internal partitioning, the panels are mounted onto a timber sole plate and butt-jointed with adhesive or dry-jointed with proprietary sheradised clip fixings. All joints are jute scrimmed and the whole partitioning finished with a 3 mm skim of board plaster. The slabs are 58 mm thick by 1200 mm wide, in a range of standard lengths from 2270 mm to 2400 mm. Service holes are incorporated into the panels at 300 mm centres for vertical electrical wiring. While normal domestic fixtures can be fitted directly to the panels, heavier loads require coach-bolt fixings through the panels. The product should not be used where it will be subjected to moisture. Compressed straw slabs, when skim plastered, have a 30 minute fire resistance rating, a Class 0 spread of flame, and a sound reduction of typically 35 dB over the range 100–3200 Hz.

THATCH

Thatch was the roof covering used for most buildings until the end of the Middle Ages, and remained the norm in rural areas until the mid-nineteenth century. For most of this century thatch has been used only in conservation work; however, with the new resurgence of interest in the material, partially associated with the reconstruction of the thatched Globe Theatre in London, thatch has once again become a current construction material.

Materials

The three standard materials for thatching within the UK are water reed (*Phragmites australis*), long straw (usually wheat) and combed wheat reed. Water reed is associated with the Norfolk broads, the Fens, south Hampshire and the Tay estuary; long straw, with the Midlands and Home Counties; while combed wheat reed is more common in Devon and Cornwall. Water reed is the most durable, lasting typically 50 years, but long straw and combed wheat reed last approximately 20 and 30 years, respectively, depending upon location and roof pitch. All thatched roofs will need reridging at 10 to 15 year intervals; with water reed this is often done with saw sedge (*Cladium mariscus*), which is more flexible than the reed itself. Both long straw and combed wheat reed are often grown and harvested specifically as thatching materials, to ensure long, undamaged stems. Long straw is threshed wheat, whereas combed wheat straw is wheat with any leaves and the grain head removed.

Appearance

Long-straw roofs show the lengths of the individual straws down the roof surface and are also characterised by the use of split hazel rodding around the eaves and gables to secure the thatch. To prevent attack by birds they are frequently covered in netting. Combed wheat reed and water reed both have a closely packed finish, with the straw ends forming the roof surface. A pitch of 50–60° is usual for thatch with a minimum of 45°, the steeper pitches being more durable. The ridge, which may be a decorative feature, is produced by either wrapping wheat straw over the apex or butting-up reeds from both sides of the roof. Traditionally hazel twigs are used for fixings, although these can be replaced with stainless steel wires.

Properties

Fire
The fire hazards associated with thatched roofs are evident; however, fire retardants can be used,

although these may denature the material. At the Globe Theatre in London, a sparge water-spray system has been installed. Electrical wiring and open-fire chimneys are the most common causes of thatch fires, although maintenance work on thatched roofs is also a risk if it is not carefully managed.

Insulation
Thatch offers good insulation, keeping buildings cool in summer and warm in winter; a typical 300 mm of water reed achieves a U-value of 0.35 W/m² K. Felt underlay is not used with long straw or combed wheat reed, which are applied wet. With water reed, which is applied dry, an underlay is not usually advised unless it is required to seal the building while waiting for the thatch.

SHINGLES

Western red cedar (*Thuja plicata*), as a naturally durable material, is frequently used as shingles or shakes for roofing or cladding. Shingles are cut to shape, whereas shakes are split to the required thickness, usually between 10 and 13 mm. Both shakes and shingles may be tapered or straight. Shingles, typically 400, 450 or 600 mm long and between 75 and 355 mm wide, may be treated with copper/chrome/arsenate (CCA) wood preservative to improve their durability. Additionally they may be treated with flame retardant to satisfy the AA fire rating of BS 476. Shingles should be fixed with corrosion-resistant nails, leaving a spacing of 5–6 mm between adjacent shingles. A minimum pitch of 14° is necessary and three layers are normally required. While the standard laying pattern is straight coursing, staggered patterns and the use of profiled shingles on steeper pitches can create decorative effects.

The Queens Building, De Montfort University, Leicester (cover illustration), incorporates fireproofed western red cedar shingles as a lightweight cladding material. The natural colour of the cedar wood complements the red brickwork, giving an overall warmth to the exterior envelope of the building. In exposed locations the red-brown cedar wood surface gradually weathers to a silver-grey, while in very sheltered locations the shingles become green with lichen.

References

FURTHER READING

BRE. 1972: *Handbook of hardwoods.* London: HMSO.

BRE. 1977: *Handbook of softwoods.* London: HMSO.

Brockett, P. and Wright, A. 1986: *The care and repair of thatched roofs.* SPAB Technical Leaflet 10. London: Society for the Protection of Ancient Buildings.

Desch, H.E. 1981: *Timber: Its structure, properties and utilisation,* 6th ed., revised by J.M. Dinwoodie. London: Macmillan Education.

Graystone, J. 1985: *The care and protection of wood.* Slough: ICI Paints Division.

Keyworth, B. and Woodbridge, D. 1992: *Environmental aspects of timber in use in the UK.* Oxford: Timber Tectonics Ltd.

Mettem, C.J. and Richens, A.D. 1991: *Hardwoods in construction.* High Wycombe: TRADA.

Sunley, J. and Bedding, B. (eds.) 1985: *Timber in construction.* London: Batsford/TRADA.

Thatching Advisory Services Ltd. 1994: *The complete thatch guide.* Wokingham.

TRADA. 1992: *Introduction to wood based panel products.* High Wycombe: TRADA.

TRADA. 1993: *Panel products directory.* High Wycombe: TRADA.

TRADA. 1994: *Eurocode 5 – Design guidance.* High Wycombe: TRADA.

TRADA. 1996: *Wood information sheets.* High Wycombe: TRADA.

Wilkinson, J.G. 1979: *Industrial timber preservation.* London: Associated Business Press.

Wood Panel Products Federation. 1994: *Technical information.*

STANDARDS

BS 144. Wood preservation using coal tar creosotes:
    Part 1: 1990. Specification for preservation.
    Part 2: 1990. Methods for timber treatment.

BS 373: 1957. Methods for testing small clear specimens of timber.

BS 476. Fire tests on building materials and structures.
    Part 7: 1987. Method for classification of the surface spread of flame of products.

BS 585. Wood stairs:
    Part 1: 1989. Specification for straight stairs with closed risers for domestic use, including straight and winder flights and quarter or half landings.
    Part 2: 1985. Specification for performance requirements for domestic stairs constructed of wood-based materials.

BS 644. Wood windows:
    Part 1: 1989. Specification for factory assembled windows of various types.
    Part 2: 1958. Wood double-hung sash windows.
    Part 3: 1951. Wood double-hung sash and case windows (Scottish type).

BS 1088: 1966. Marine plywood manufactured from selected untreated tropical hardwoods.

BS 1105: 1981. Specification for wood wool cement slabs up to 125 mm thick.

BS 1142: 1989. Fibre building boards.

BS 1187: 1959. Wood blocks for floors.

BS 1203: 1979. Specification for synthetic resin adhesives (phenolic and aminoplastic) for plywood.

BS 1282: 1975. Guide to the choice, use and application of wood preservatives.

BS 1297: 1987. Specification for tongued and grooved softwood flooring.

BS 1336: 1971. Knotting.

BS 1567: 1953. Wood door frames and linings.

BS 1579: 1960. Connectors for timber.

BS 3444: 1972. Blockboard and laminboard.

BS 3809: 1993. Wood wool permanent formwork and infill units for reinforced concrete floors and roofs.

BS 4046: 1991. Compressed straw building slabs.

BS 4050. Specification for mosaic parquet panels:
    Part 1: 1977. General characteristics.
    Part 2: 1966. Classification and quality requirements.

BS 4072: 1974. Wood preservation by means of copper/chrome/arsenic compositions:
    Part 1: 1987. Specification for preservatives.
    Part 2: 1987. Method for timber treatment.

BS 4079: 1966. Plywood made for marine use and treated against attack by fungi, insects and marine borers.

BS 4169: 1988. Specification for manufacture of glued-laminated timber structural members.

BS 4261: 1985. Glossary of terms relating to timber preservation.

BS 4471: 1996. Specification for sizes of sawn and processed softwood.

BS 4512: 1969. Methods of test for clear plywood.

BS 4787. Internal and external wood doorsets, door leaves and frames:
    Part 1: 1980. Specification for dimensional requirements.

BS 4965: 1991. Specification for decorative laminated plastics sheet veneered boards and panels.

BS 4978: 1996. Specification for visual strength grading of softwood.

BS 5268. Structural use of timber:
    Part 2: 1996. Code of practice for permissible stress design, materials and workmanship.
    Part 3: 1985. Code of practice for trussed rafter roofs.

Part 4: 1978. Fire resistance of timber structures.

Part 5: 1989. Code of practice for the preservative treatment of structural timber.

Part 6: 1996. Code of practice for timber frame walls.

Part 7: 1989/90. Recommendations for the calculation basis for span tables.

BS 5277: 1966. Doors. Measurement of defects of general flatness of door leaves.

BS 5278: 1976. Doors. Measurement of dimensions and of defects of squareness of door leaves.

BS 5291: 1989. Specification for manufacture of finger joints in structural softwood.

BS 5368. Methods of testing windows:

Part 1: 1976. Air permeability test.

Part 2: 1980. Watertightness test under static pressure.

Part 3: 1978. Wind resistance test.

Part 4: 1978. Form of test report.

BS 5369: 1987. Methods of testing doors; behaviour under humidity variations of door leaves placed in successive uniform climates.

BS 5395. Stairs, ladders and walkways:

Part 1: 1977. Code of practice for straight stairs.

Part 2: 1984. Code of practice for the design of helical and spiral stairs.

Part 3: 1985. Code of practice for the design of industrial type stairs, permanent ladders and walkways.

BS 5450: 1977. Specification for sizes of hardwoods and methods of measurement.

BS 5589: 1989. Code of practice for preservation of timber.

BS 5666. Methods of analysis of wood preservatives and treated timber:

Parts 1–7.

BS 5669. Particleboard:

Part 1: 1989. Method of sampling, conditioning and test.

Part 2: 1989. Specification for wood chipboard.

Part 3: 1992. Specification for oriented strand board (OSB).

Part 4: 1989. Specification for cement bonded particleboard.

Part 5: 1993. Code of practice for the selection and application of particleboards for specific purposes.

BS 5707. Solutions of wood preservatives in organic solvents:

Part 1: 1979. Specification for solutions for general purpose applications, including timber that is to be painted.

Part 2: 1979. Specification for pentachlorophenol wood preservative solution for use on timber that is not required to be painted.

Part 3: 1980. Methods of treatment.

BS 5756: 1996. Visual strength grading of hardwood.

BS 5837: 1991. Guide for trees in relation to construction.

BS 6100. Glossary of building and civil engineering terms:

Part 4. Forest products.

BS 6178. Joist hangers:

Part 1: 1990. Specification for joist hangers for building into masonry walls of domestic dwellings.

BS 6446: 1989. Specification for manufacture of glued structural components of timber and wood based panel products.

BS 6559: 1985. General introductory document on European (or CEN) methods of test for wood preservatives.

BS 6566: 1985. Plywood.

BS 7331: 1990. Direct surfaced wood chipboard based on thermosetting resins.

BS 7359: 1991. Commercial timbers including sources of supply.

BS 8103: Structural design of low-rise buildings:

Part 3: 1996 Code of practice for timber floors and roofs for housing.

BS 8201: 1987. Code of practice for flooring of timber, timber products and wood based panel products.

BS EN 20. Wood preservatives – determination of the effectiveness against *Lyctus brunneus:*

Part 2: 1993. Application by impregnation (laboratory method).

BS EN 49. Wood preservatives – determination of the effectiveness against *Anobium punctatum* by egg-laying and larval survival:

Part 1: 1992. Application by surface treatment (laboratory method).

Part 2: 1992. Application by impregnation (laboratory method).

BS EN 300: 1996. Oriented strand board (OSB).

BS EN 309: 1992. Wood particleboards – definition and classification.

BS EN 310: 1993. Wood-based panels – determination of modulus of elasticity in bending and of bending strength.

BS EN 311: 1992. Particleboards – surface soundness of particleboards, test method.

BS EN 312: 1996. Particleboards – specifications.

BS EN 313. Plywood – classification and terminology:

Part 1: 1996. Classification.

Part 2: 1995. Terminology.

BS EN 314. Plywood – bonding quality.

Part 1: 1993. Test methods.

Part 2: 1993. Requirements.

BS EN 315: 1993. Plywood – tolerances for dimensions.

BS EN 316: 1993. Wood fibreboards – definition, classification and symbols.

BS EN 317: 1993. Particleboards and fibreboards – determination of swelling in thickness after immersion in water.

BS EN 318: 1993. Fibreboards – determination of dimensional changes associated with changes in relative humidity.

BS EN 319: 1993. Particleboards and fibreboards – determination of tensile strength perpendicular to the plane of the board.

BS EN 320: 1993. Fibreboards – determination of resistance to axial withdrawal of screws.

BS EN 321: 1993. Fibreboards – cyclic tests in humid conditions.

BS EN 322: 1993. Wood-based panels – determination of moisture content.

BS EN 323: 1993. Wood-based panels – determination of density.

BS EN 324. Wood-based panels – determination of dimensions of boards:
Part 1: 1993. Determination of thickness, width and length.
Part 2: 1993. Determination of squareness and edge straightness.

BS EN 325: 1993. Wood-based panels – determination of test pieces.

BS EN 326. Wood-based panels – sampling, cutting and inspection:
Part 1: 1994. Sampling and cutting of test pieces and expression of test results.

BS EN 330: 1993. Wood preservatives – field test method for determining the relative protective effectiveness of a wood preservative for use under a coating and exposed out-of-ground contact: L-joint method.

BS EN 335. Hazard classes of wood and wood-based products against biological attack:
Part 1: 1992. Classification of hazard classes.
Part 2: 1992. Guide to the application of hazard classes to solid wood.
Part 3: 1996 Application to wood-based panels.

BS EN 336: 1995. Structural timber. Coniferous and poplar – timber sizes – permissible deviations.

BS EN 338: 1995. Structural timber. Strength classes.

BS EN 350. Durability of wood and wood-based products – natural durability of solid wood:
Part 1: 1994. Guide to the principles of testing and classification of the natural durability of wood.
Part 2: 1994. Guide to the natural durability and treatability of selected wood species of importance in Europe.

BS EN 351. Preservative-treated solid wood:
Part 1: 1996. Classification of preservative penetration and retention.
Part 2: 1996. Guidance on sampling for the analysis of preservative-treated wood.

BS EN 380: 1993. Timber structures – test methods – general principles for static load testing.

BS EN 382. Fibreboards – determination of surface absorption:
Part 1: 1993. Test method for dry process fibreboard.
Part 2: 1994. Test method for hardboards.

BS EN 383: 1993. Timber structures – test methods – determination of embedded strength and foundation values for dowel type fasteners.

BS EN 385: 1995. Finger jointed structural timber – performance requirements and minimum production requirements.

BS EN 386: 1995. Glued laminated timber – performance requirements and minimum production requirements.

prEN 387. Glued laminated timber – production requirements for large finger joints. Performance requirements and minimum production requirements.

BS EN 390: 1995. Glued laminated timber – sizes – permissible deviations.

BS EN 408: 1995. Timber structures – structural timber and glued laminated timber.

BS EN 409: 1993. Timber structures – test methods – determination of the yield moment of dowel type fasteners – nails.

BS EN 460: 1994. Durability of wood and wood-based products – natural durability of solid wood – guide to the durability requirements for wood to be used in hazard classes.

BS EN 518: 1995. Structural timber – grading – requirements for visual strength grading standards.

BS EN 519: 1995. Structural timber – grading – requirements for machine strength grading timber and grading machines.

BS EN 594: 1996 Timber structures – test methods – racking strength and stiffness of timber frame wall panels.

BS EN 595: 1995. Timber structures – test methods – test of trusses for the determination of strength and deformation behaviour.

BS EN 596: 1995. Timber structures – test methods – soft body impact test of timber framed walls.

BS EN 599. Performance of wood preservatives as determined by biological tests:
Part 1. Specification according to hazard class.
Part 2. Classification and labelling.

BS EN 622: 1996. Fibreboards – specifications.

BS EN 633: 1994. Cement-bonded particle boards – definition and classification.

BS EN 634. Cement-bonded particle boards – specifications:
Part 1: 1995. General requirement.

BS EN 635. Plywood – classification by surface appearance:
Part 1: 1995. General rules.
Part 2: 1995. Hardwood.
Part 3: 1995. Softwood.

prEN 636: 1996. Plywood – specifications.

BS EN 789: 1996 Timber structures – Test methods –

determination of mechanical properties of wood-based panels.

BS EN 942: 1996 Timber in joinery – general classification of timber quality.

BS EN 975. Sawn timber – appearance grading of hardwoods.

    Part 1: 1996 Oak and Beech.

BS EN 1014: 1996 Wood preservatives – creosote and creosoted timber – methods of sampling and analysis.

BS EN 1072: 1995. Plywood – description of bending properties for structural plywood.

BS EN 1087. Particleboards – determination of moisture resistance:

    Part 1: 1995. Boil test.

BS EN 1128: 1996 Cement-bonded particle boards – determination of hard body impact resistance.

BS EN 1193. Timber structures – test methods – structural and glued laminated timber. Determination of additional physical and mechanical properties.

prEN 1194: 1995. Timber structures – glued laminated timber – strength classes and determination of characteristic values.

BS EN 26891: 1991. Timber structures – joints made with mechanical fasteners – general principles for the determination of strength and deformation characteristics.

BS EN 28970: 1991. Timber structures – testing of joints made with mechanical fasteners – requirements for wood density.

DD 839: 1994. Wood preservatives – determination of the preventative efficacy against wood-destroying basidiomycete fungi.

DD ENV 1250: 1995. Wood preservatives. Method of measuring losses of active ingredients and other preservative ingredients from treated timber.

DD ENV 1390: 1995. Wood preservatives – determination of the eradication action against *Hylotrupes bajulus (Linnaeus)* larvae – laboratory method.

BS ENV 1995: Eurocode 5: Design of timber structures:

    Part 1.1: 1994. General rules and rules for buildings.

REGULATIONS

Control of Pesticides Regulations 1986.
Control of Substances Hazardous to Health 1988.
Wildlife and Countryside Act 1981.

BUILDING RESEARCH ESTABLISHMENT PUBLICATIONS

BRE Digests

BRE Digest 194: 1976. The use of elm timber.
BRE Digest 208: 1988. Increasing the fire resistance of existing timber floors.

BRE Digest 296: 1985. Timbers: their natural durability and resistance to preservative treatment.

BRE Digest 299: 1993. Dry rot: its recognition and control.

BRE Digest 301: 1985. Corrosion of metals by wood.

BRE Digest 304: 1985. Prevention of decay in external joinery.

BRE Digest 307: 1996. Identifying damage by wood-boring insects.

BRE Digest 314: 1986. Gluing wood successfully.

BRE Digest 323: 1992. Selecting wood-based panel products.

BRE Digest 327: 1993. Insecticidal treatments against wood boring insects.

BRE Digest 340: 1989. Choosing wood adhesives.

BRE Digest 345: 1989. Wet rots: recognition and control.

BRE Digest 351: 1990. Re-covering old timber roofs.

BRE Digest 354: 1990. Painting exterior wood.

BRE Digest 364: 1991. Design of timber floors to prevent decay.

BRE Digest 371: 1992. Remedial wood preservatives: use them safely.

BRE Digest 373: 1992. Wood chipboard.

BRE Digest 375: 1992. Wood-based panel products: their contribution to the conservation of forest resources.

BRE Digest 378: 1993. Wood preservation: application methods.

BRE Digest 387: 1993. Natural finishes for exterior wood.

BRE Digest 393: 1994. Specifying preservative treatments: the new European approach.

BRE Digest 394: 1994. Plywood.

BRE Digest 400: 1994. Oriented strand board.

BRE Digest 407: 1995. Timber for joinery.

BRE Digest 416: 1996 Specifying structural timber.

BRE Digest 417: 1996 Hardwoods for construction and joinery, current and future sources of supply.

BRE Defects Action Sheets

BRE DAS 13: 1983. Wood windows: arresting decay.
BRE DAS 14: 1983. Wood windows: preventing decay.
BRE DAS 74: 1986. Suspended timber ground floors: repairing rotted joists.
BRE DAS 103: 1987. Wood floors: reducing risk of recurrent dry rot.

BRE Good Building Guide

BRE GBG 21: 1995. Joist hangers.

BRE Information Papers

BRE IP 7/88. The design and manufacture of ply-web beams.
BRE IP 5/90. Preservation of hem-fir timber.
BRE IP 7/91. Serviceability design of ply-web roof beams.

BRE IP 9/91. Blue staining of timber in service: its cause, prevention and treatment.

BRE IP 10/91. The selection of timber for exterior joinery from the genus *Shorea*.

BRE IP 12/91. Fibre building board: types and uses.

BRE IP 14/91. In situ treatment of exterior joinery using boron-based implants.

BRE IP 11/92. Schedules for the preservation of hem-fir timber.

BRE IP 14/92. Cement-bonded particleboard.

BRE IP 19/92. Wood-based panel products: moisture effects and assessing the risk of decay.

BRE IP 9/93. Perspectives on European Standards for wood-based panels.

BRE IP 8/94. House longhorn beetle: geographical distribution and pest status in the UK.

BRE IP 2/96. An assessment of exterior medium density fibreboard (MDF).

BRE Reports

BR 76: 1986. Timber drying manual. Second edition.

BR 226: 1992. A review of tropical hardwood consumption.

BR 229: 1992. Wood preservation in Europe: development of standards for preservatives and treated wood.

BR 232: 1992. Recognising wood rot and insect damage in buildings.

BR 241: 1992. The strength properties of timber.

BR 249: 1990. Long-term field trials on preserved timber out of ground contact.

BR 256: 1994. Remedial treatment of wood rot and insect attack in buildings.

BR 276: 1995. Long-term field trials on preserved timber in ground contact.

TRADA PUBLICATIONS

Wood Information Sheets

WIS 1–6: 1995 Glued laminated timber – an introduction.

WIS 1–25: 1996 Introduction and supply of timber to BS 5268 Part 2: 1996.

WIS 1–37: 1995 Eurocode 5 – an introduction.

WIS 1–38: 1995 Glued laminated timber – European standards.

WIS 2/3–29: 1996 British structural softwood and span tables under BS 5268.

WIS 2/3–37: 1995 Softwood sizes – European standards.

WIS 2/3–38: 1995 Durability and preservative treatments of wood – European standards.

WIS 2/3–41: 1995 Particleboards – key British and European standards.

WIS 2/3–42: 1995 Particleboards – European standards.

WIS 2/3–45: 1995 Fibreboard – key British and European standards.

WIS 2/3–46: 1995 Fibreboards – European standards.

WIS 2/3–48: 1995 Plywood – key British and European standards.

WIS 2/3–49: 1995 Plywood – European standards.

WIS 4–20: 1995 Structural softwoods – key British and European standards.

WIS 4–21: 1995 European strength classes and strength grading.

WIS 4–26: 1996 Strength graded British-grown softwood.

TRADE ASSOCIATIONS

Association of British Plywood and Veneer Manufacturers Ltd., Riverside Industrial Estate, Morson Road, Ponders End, Enfield EN3 4TS (0181 804 2424).

British Timber Merchants' Association, Stocking Lane, Hughenden Valley, High Wycombe, Bucks. HP14 4JZ (01494 563602).

British Wood Preserving and Damp Proofing Association, 6 Office Village, 4 Romford Road, Stratford, London E15 4EA (0181 519 2588).

British Woodworking Federation, Broadway House, Tothill Street, London SW1H 9NQ (0171 222 1511).

Council of Forest Industries, Tileman House, 131–133 Upper Richmond Road, Putney, London SW15 2TR (0181 788 4446).

Council for Small Industries in Rural Areas, 141 Castle Street, Salisbury, Wiltshire SP1 3TP (01722 336255).

English Nature, Northminster House, Peterborough, Cambs. PE1 1UA (01733 340345).

Finnish Plywood International, PO Box 99, Welwyn Garden City, Herts. AL6 0HS (01438 798305).

Glued Laminated Timber Association, Chiltern House, Stocking Lane, Hughenden Valley, High Wycombe, Bucks. HP14 4ND (01494 565180).

International Truss Plate Association, 41 Bowes Hill, Rowlands Castle, Hants. PO9 6BP (01705 412689).

Nordic Timber Council, 17 Exchange Street, Retford, Notts. DN22 6BL (01777 706616).

Thatching Advisory Services Ltd., Faircross Offices, Stratfield Sate, Reading, Berks. RG7 2BT (01256 880828).

Timber and Brick Information Council, Gable House, 40 High Street, Rickmansworth, Herts. WD3 1ES (01923 778136).

Timber Research and Development Association, Stocking Lane, Hughenden Valley, High Wycombe, Bucks. HP14 4ND (01494 563091).

Wood Panel Products Federation, 1 Hanworth Road, Feltham, Middx. TW13 5AF (0181 751 6107).

Wood Wool Slab Manufacturers Association, 26 Store Street, London WC1E 7BT (0171 323 3770).

5

FERROUS AND NON-FERROUS METALS

—

Introduction

A wide range of ferrous and non-ferrous metals and their alloys are used within construction, but iron, steel, aluminium, copper, lead and zinc predominate. Recent trends have been towards the development of more durable alloys and the use of coatings both to protect and to give visual diversity to the product ranges. Generally the metals require a large energy input for their production from raw materials; however, this high embodied energy is partially offset by the long life and recycling of most metals. Approximately 50% of current steel production is from scrap.

Ferrous metals

Ferrous metals are defined as those in which the element iron predominates. The earliest use of the metal was for the manufacture of implements and weapons in the Iron Age commencing in Europe *circa* 1200 BC. Significant developments were the use by Wren in 1675 of a wrought iron chain in tension to restrain the outward thrust from the dome of St Paul's Cathedral, the use of cast iron in compression for the iron bridge at Coalbrookdale in 1779, and the use of cast iron by Paxton in the prefabricated sections of the Crystal Palace in 1851. Steel is a relatively recent material, only being available in quantity after the development of the Bessemer converter in the late nineteenth century. The first steel-frame high-rise building of 10 storeys was built

in 1885 in Chicago by William le Baron Jenney.

The platform level of the Waterloo International Terminal in London (Plate 4) is covered by curved and tapered 3-pin steel arches, which are designed to accommodate the flexing inevitably caused by the movement of trains at this level. The steel arches, each consisting of two prismatic bow-string trusses connected by a knuckle joint, are asymmetrical to allow for the tight curvature of the site. The tops of the longer trusses are covered with toughened glass providing views towards old London, with profiled stainless steel spanning between. The area spanned by the shorter trusses is fully glazed. The structure is designed for a minimum lifetime of 100 years.

MANUFACTURE OF STEEL

The production of steel involves a sequence of operations which are closely interrelated in order to ensure maximum efficiency of a highly energy-intensive process. The key stages in the production process are the making of pig iron, its conversion into steel, the casting of the molten steel and its formation into sections or strip. Finally coils of steel strip are cold-rolled into thin sections and profiled sheet.

Manufacture of pig iron

The raw materials for the production of iron are iron ore, coke and limestone. Most iron ore is imported from America, Australia and Scandinavia, where the iron content of the ore is high. Coke is produced from coking coal, mainly imported from Europe, in batteries of coking ovens. Some of this coke is then sintered with iron ore prior to the iron-making process.

Iron ore, coke, sinter and limestone are charged into the top of the blastfurnace (Fig. 5.1). A hot air blast, sometimes enriched with oxygen, is fed through the tuyères into the base of the furnace. This heats the furnace to white heat, converting the coke into carbon monoxide which then reduces the iron oxide to iron. The molten metal collects at the bottom of the furnace. The limestone forms a liquid slag, floating on the surface of the molten iron. Purification occurs as impurities within the molten iron are preferentially absorbed into the slag layer.

$$2C + O_2 \longrightarrow 2CO$$
carbon (coke)   oxygen   carbon monoxide

$$Fe_2O_3 + 3CO \longrightarrow 2Fe + 3CO_2$$
iron ore   carbon monoxide   iron   carbon dioxide
(haematite)

The whole process is continuous, since relining the blastfurnace with the special refractory bricks is expensive and time consuming. From time to time as the molten slag level rises, excess is tapped off for subsequent disposal as a by-product of the steel-making

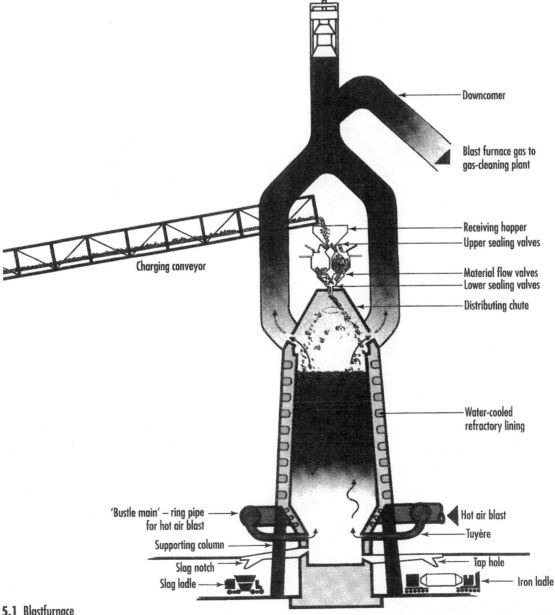

Fig. 5.1 Blastfurnace

industry. When *hot metal* is required for the subsequent steel-making process it is tapped off into huge ladles for transportation direct to the steel converter. At this stage the iron is only 90–95% pure with sulfur, phosphorus, manganese and silicon as impurities and a carbon content of 4–5%. Waste gases from the blastfurnace are cleaned and recycled as fuel within the plant. A blastfurnace will typically operate nonstop for ten years producing 40 000 tonnes per week.

Steelmaking

There are two standard processes used within the UK for making steel. The basic oxygen process is used for the manufacture of bulk quantities of standard-grade steels. The electric arc furnace process is used for the production of high-quality special steels and particularly stainless steel.

Basic oxygen process

Bulk quantities of steel are produced by the basic oxygen process in a refractory lined steel furnace which can be tilted for charging and tapping. A typical furnace (Fig. 5.2) will take a charge of 350 tonnes and convert it into steel within 30 minutes. Initially scrap metal, accounting for one quarter of the charge, is loaded into the tilted furnace, followed by the remainder of the charge as hot metal direct from

the blastfurnace. A water-cooled lance is then lowered to blow high-pressure oxygen into the converter. This burns off impurities and reduces the excess carbon content while raising the temperature. Argon and a small quantity of nitrogen are introduced at the bottom of the furnace. Lime is added to form a floating slag to remove further impurities and alloying components are added to adjust the steel composition, prior to tapping. Finally the furnace is inverted to run out any remaining slag, prior to the next cycle.

Electric arc process

The electric arc furnace (Fig. 5.3) consists of a refractory lined hearth, covered by a removable roof, through which graphite electrodes can be raised and lowered. With the roof swung open, scrap metal is charged into the furnace, the roof is closed and the electrodes lowered to near the surface of the metal. A powerful electric arc is struck between the electrodes and the metal, which heats the metal up to melting point. Lime and fluorspar are added to form a slag, and oxygen is blown into the furnace to complete the purification process. When the temperature and chemical analysis are correct, the furnace is tilted to tap off the metal, to which appropriate alloying components may then be added. A typical furnace will produce 150 tonnes of high-grade or stainless steel within 90 minutes.

Casting

Traditionally the molten steel was cast into ingots, prior to hot rolling into slabs and then sheet. However, most steel is now directly poured, or teemed, and cast into continuous billets or slabs, which are then cut to appropriate lengths for subsequent processing. Continuous casting (Fig. 5.4), which saves on reheating, is not only more energy efficient than processing through the ingot stage but also produces a better surface finish to the steel. However, components such as the nodes for rectangular and circular hollow-section constructions and large pin-joint units are manufactured directly as individual castings. They can then be welded to the standard milled steel sections to give continuity of structure.

Hot-rolled steel

Sheet steel is produced by passing 25 tonne hot slabs at approximately 1250°C through a series of

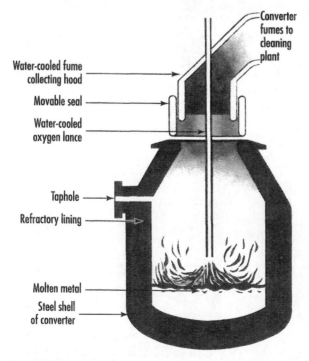

Fig. 5.2 Basic oxygen furnace

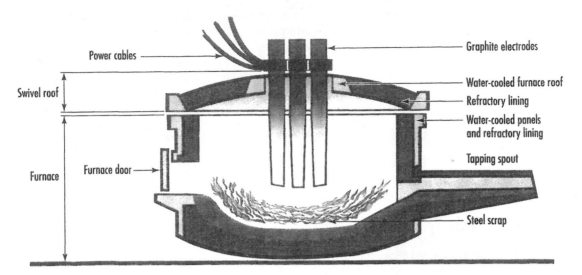

Fig. 5.3 Electric-arc furnace

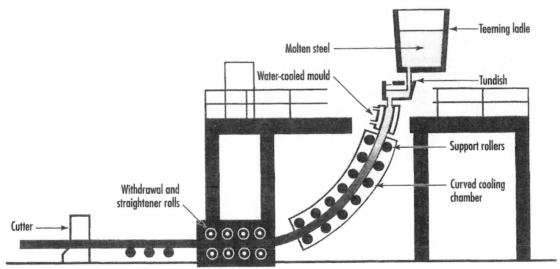

Fig. 5.4 Continuous casting

computer-controlled rollers which reduce the thickness to typically between 1.5 and 20 mm prior to water cooling and coiling. A 25 tonne slab would produce a 1 km coil of 2 mm sheet. Steel sections such as universal beams and columns, channels and angles (Fig. 5.5) are rolled from hot billets through a series of *stands* to the appropriate section.

Cold-rolled steel

Sheet steel may be further reduced by cold rolling, which gives a good surface finish and increases its tensile strength. Light round sections may be processed into steel for concrete reinforcement,

while coiled sheet may be converted into profiled sheet or light steel sections (Fig. 5.5). Cold-reduced steel for construction is frequently factory finished with zinc, alloys including terne (lead and tin) or plastic coating.

CARBON CONTENT OF FERROUS METALS

The quantity of carbon alloyed with iron has a profound influence on the physical properties of the metal owing to its significant effect on the microscopic crystal structure (Fig. 5.6). At ambient temperature a series of crystal forms (ferrite, pearlite and cementite) associated with different proportions

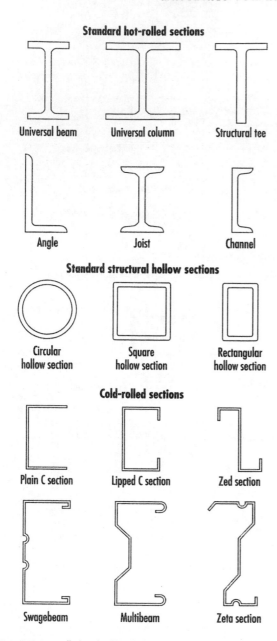

Fig. 5.5 Hot-rolled and cold-rolled sections (first published in Trebilcock, P.J. 1994: *Building design using cold formed steel sections: an architect's guide*. Steel Construction Institute)

otherwise would occur on slow cooling. These effects are exploited within the various heat treatments that are applied to steels in order to widen the available range of physical properties.

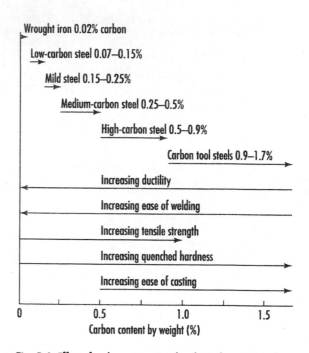

Fig. 5.6 Effect of carbon content on the physical properties of wrought iron and steels

Wrought iron

Wrought iron contains only about 0.02% of carbon. It was traditionally made by remelting and oxidising pig iron in a reverberatory furnace. The process was continued until virtually all the high carbon content of the pig iron had been burnt off to produce a pasty wrought iron which was withdrawn from the furnace and then hammered out. Wrought iron is fibrous in character owing to the incidental incorporation within the metal of slag residues and impurities such as magnesium sulfide, which are formed into long veins by the hammering process. Wrought iron has a high melting point, approaching 1540°C, depending upon its purity. It was traditionally used for components in tension owing to its tensile strength of about 350 N/mm². It is ductile and easily worked or forged when red hot, thus eminently suitable for crafting into ornamental ironwork, an appropriate use because of its greater resistance to corrosion than steel. Because of

of iron and carbon are stable. However, on increasing the temperature, crystal forms that were stable under ambient conditions become unstable and are recrystallised into the high-temperature form (austenite). This latter crystal structure can be trapped at room temperature by the rapid quenching of red-hot steel, thus partially or completely preventing the natural recrystallisation processes which

its high melting point, wrought iron cannot be welded or cast. Production ceased in the UK in 1973 and modern wrought iron is either recycled old material or, more frequently, low-carbon steel, with its attendant corrosion problems.

Cast iron

Cast iron contains in excess of 2% carbon in iron. It is manufactured by the carbonising of pig iron and scrap with coke in a furnace. The low melting point of around 1130°C, and its high fluidity when molten, give rise to its excellent casting properties but, unlike wrought iron, it cannot be hot worked and is generally a brittle material. The corrosion resistance of cast iron has been exploited in its use for boiler castings, street furniture and traditional rain-water goods. Modern foundries manufacture castings to new designs and as reproduction Victorian and Edwardian components for restoration work.

Differing grades of cast iron are associated with different microscopic crystal structures. The common grey cast iron contains flakes of graphite, which cause the characteristic brittleness and impart the grey colour to fractured surfaces. White cast iron contains the carbon as crystals of cementite (iron carbide, Fe_3C) formed by rapid cooling of the melt. This material may be annealed to reduce its brittle character. A more ductile cast iron (spheroidal cast iron) is produced by the addition of magnesium and ferrosilicon and annealing which causes the carbon to crystallise into graphite nodules. This material has an increased tensile strength and significantly greater impact resistance. All cast irons are strong in compression.

Road iron goods, such as manhole covers, made from largely recycled grey cast iron are heavy but brittle. Where increased impact resistance is required for public roads, lighter and stronger ductile iron components are used. Traditional sand-cast rain-water goods are usually manufactured from grey cast iron, while cast iron drainage systems are manufactured from both grey and ductile iron. Unlike steel, cast iron does not soften prematurely in a fire, but may crack if cooled too quickly with water from a fire hose.

Steels

A wide range of steels is commercially available reflecting the differing properties associated with carbon content, the various heat treatments and the addition of alloying components.

Carbon contents of steels range typically between 0.07% and 1.7% and this alone is reflected in a wide spectrum of physical properties. The low-carbon (0.07–0.15%) and mild steels (0.15–0.25%) are relatively soft and can be subjected to extensive cold working. Medium-carbon steels (0.25–0.5%), which are often heat treated, are hard wearing. High-carbon steels (0.5–0.9%) and carbon tool steels (0.9–1.7%) exhibit increasing strength and wear resistance with increasing carbon content.

HEAT TREATMENT OF STEELS

The physical properties of steels can be modified by various heat treatments which involve heating to a particular temperature followed by cooling under controlled conditions.

Hardening

Rapidly quenched steel, cooled quickly from a high temperature in oil or water, thus retaining the high-temperature crystalline form, is hard and brittle. This effect becomes more pronounced for the higher carbon content steels, which are mostly unsuitable for engineering purposes in this state.

Annealing and normalising

These processes involve the softening of the hard steel, by recrystallisation, which relieves internal stresses within the material and produces a more uniform grain structure. For annealing, the steel is reheated and soaked at a temperature of over 700°C, then cooled slowly at a controlled rate within a furnace or cooling pit. This produces the softest steel for a given composition. With normalising, the steel is reheated to a similar temperature for a shorter period and then allowed to cool more rapidly in air. This facilitates subsequent cold working and machining processes.

Tempering

Reheating the steel to a moderate temperature (400–600°C) followed by cooling in air reduces the brittleness, by allowing some recrystallisation of the metal. The magnitude of the effect is directly related to the tempering temperature, with ductility increasing and tensile strength reducing for the higher process temperatures.

Carburising

Components may be case hardened to produce a higher carbon content on the outer surface, while leaving the core relatively soft; thus giving a hard-wearing surface without embrittlement and loss of impact resistance to the centre. Usually this process involves heating the components surrounded by charcoal or other carbon-based material to approximately 900°C for several hours. The components are then heat treated to develop fully the surface hardness.

SPECIFICATION OF STEELS

With the advent of European Standards for steels, the designations of steel grades have been changed from the British Standards, formerly BS 4360: 1986, through an intermediate stage BS EN 10025: 1990

specific to the UK, and finally to the common European Standard BS EN 10025: 1993 (Hot-rolled products of non-alloy structural steels). Specifications for grades of steel initially not covered by BS EN 10025: 1990, were published unchanged within a revised version of BS 4360: 1990, now withdrawn.

In 1993, BS EN 10113: 1993 (Hot-rolled products in weldable fine grain structural steels) and BS EN 10155: 1993 (Structural steels with improved atmospheric corrosion resistance) were published, superseding the specifications for certain higher grades and weather-resistant steels within the revised BS 4360: 1990. Now BS EN 10210 Part 1: 1994 supersedes BS 4360: 1990 with respect to hot-finished hot-rolled structural sections and prEN 10219: 1996 supersedes BS 6363: 1983 for cold-formed structural hollow sections.

Table 5.1 Steel designations for standard grades to BS 4360: 1986 and BS EN 10025: 1990 and 1993

BS EN 10025: 1993 grade	BS EN 10025: 1990 grade	BS 4360: 1986 grade	BS EN 10025: 1993 limits	
			Ultimate tensile strength (N/mm^2)	Minimum yield strength (N/mm^2)
S185	Fe 310-0		290–510	185
S235	Fe 360A	40A	340–470	235
S235JR	Fe 360B		340–470	235
S235JRG1	Fe 360B(FU)		340–470	235
S235JRG2	Fe 360B(FN)	40B	340–470	235
S235J0	Fe 360C	40C	340–470	235
S235J2G3	Fe 360D1	40D	340–470	235
S235J2G4	Fe 360D2	40D	340–470	235
S275	Fe 430A	43A	410–560	275
S275JR	Fe 430B	43B	410–560	275
S275J0	Fe 430C	43C	410–560	275
S275J2G3	Fe 430D1	43D	410–560	275
S275J2G4	Fe 430D2	43D	410–560	275
S355	Fe 510A	50A	490–630	355
S355JR	Fe 510B	50B	490–630	355
S355J0	Fe 510C	50C	490–630	355
S355J2G3	Fe 510D1	50D	490–630	355
S355J2G4	Fe 510D2	50D	490–630	355
S355K2G3	Fe 510DD1	50DD	490–630	355
S355K2G4	Fe 510DD2	50DD	490–630	355

Notes: Fe refers to ferrous metal and S to structural steel.

Sub-grades A to DD in the 1986 designation system indicate increasing impact resistance as measured by the Charpy V-notch test. They are replaced by JR, J0, J2 and K2, respectively, in the 1993 designation. K has a higher impact energy than J; the symbols R, 0 and 2 refer to the impact test at room temperature, 0°C and −20°C respectively.

G1 or FU is rimming steel, G2 or FN is not rimming steel, G3 is normalised, and G4 gives discretion on supply condition to the manufacturer.

Table 5.2 Steel designations for higher grades to BS 4360: 1986 and BS EN 10113: 1993

BS EN 10113: 1993 grade	BS 4360: 1990 grade	BS EN 10113: 1993 limits	
		Ultimate tensile strength (N/mm²)	Minimum yield strength (N/mm²)
S275N	43DD	370–510	275
S275NL	43EE		
S355N	50DD	470–630	355
	50E		
S355NL	50EE		
S420N		520–680	420
S420NL			
S460N	55C	550–720	460
S460NL	55EE		
S275M		360–510	275
S275ML			
S355M		450–610	355
S355ML			
S420M		500–660	420
S420ML			
S460M		530–720	460
S460ML			

Notes: S refers to structural steel.
Sub-grades DD to EE in the 1990 designation system indicate increasing impact resistance as measured by the Charpy V-notch test.
Sub-grades M (thermomechanical rolled) and N (normalised or normalised rolled) relate to the physical state of the steel, and L (low-temperature impact) to high impact resistance.

Table 5.3 Steel designations for weather-resistant grades to BS 4360: 1990 and BS EN 10155: 1993

BS EN 10155: 1993 grade	BS 4360: 1990 grade	BS EN 10155: 1993 limits	
		Ultimate tensile strength (N/mm²)	Minimum yield strength (N/mm²)
S235J0W		340–470	≥235
S235J2W			
S355J0WP	WR50A	490–630	≥355
S355J2WP			
S355J0W	WR50B		
S355J2G1W	WR50C		
S355J2G2W	WR50C		
S355K2G1W			
S355K2G2W			

Notes: S refers to structural steel. Sub-grades A to C in the 1990 designation system indicate increasing impact resistance as measured by the Charpy V-notch test.
Sub-grades J0, J2 and K2 (1993 designation) similarly indicate increasing impact resistance.
Sub-grade WR (1990 designation) or W (1993 designation) refers to weather-resistant steel.
G1 and G2 refer to the supplied condition of the steel and P indicates a high-phosphorus grade.

The correspondences between the standards are illustrated in Tables 5.1, 5.2, 5.3 and 5.4. In the UK 1986 and 1990 gradings, the first grade number referred to the ultimate tensile strength, while the sub-grade letters (e.g. A or C) give an indication of the physical properties of the steel. The higher sub-grade steels have greater impact resistance and improved weldability and fatigue resistance, usually associated with lower carbon content of the steel. The sub-grade letters correlate directly to the impact resistance measured by the standard Charpy V-notch test.

In the 1993 designations, Fe for iron is replaced by S for structural steel, the numbers relate to the yield strength rather than the ultimate tensile strength and the sub-grade letters are replaced by letter codes which take into account not only impact resistance but also other production conditions and compositions, such as W for weather-resistant steel.

The following example illustrates the changes for one particular grade of steel:

1986 designation	1990 designation	1993 designation
43A	Fe430A	S275

(where Fe is the chemical symbol for iron, S refers to structural steel, A is the lowest impact resistant sub-grade, the ultimate tensile strength is 430 N/mm² and the yield strength is 275 N/mm²).

STRUCTURAL STEELS

Weldable structural steels have a carbon content within the range 0.16–0.25%. Structural steels are usually normalised by natural cooling in air after hot rolling. The considerable size effect which causes the larger sections to cool more slowly than the thinner sections gives rise to significant differences in physical properties; thus an 80 mm section can typically have a 10% lower yield strength compared to a 16 mm section of the same steel.

Hollow sections

Circular, square and rectangular hollow sections are usually made from flat sections which are progressively bent until almost round. They are then passed through a high-frequency induction coil to raise the edges to fusion temperature, when they are forced together to complete the tube. Excess metal is removed from the surface. The whole tube may then be reheated to normalising temperature (850–950°C), and hot rolled into circular, rectangular or square sections. For smaller sizes, the tube

Table 5.4 Steel designations for hot-finished structural hollow sections BS 4360: 1990 and BS EN 10210: 1994

BS EN 10210: 1994 grade	BS 4360: 1990 grade	BS EN 10210: 1994 limits Minimum yield strength (N/mm²)
S275J0H	43C	≥275
S275J2H	43D	
S355J0H	50C	≥355
S355J2H	50D	
S275NH		≥275
S275NLH	43EE	
S355NH		≥355
S355NLH	50EE	
S460NH		≥460
S460NLH	55EE	

Notes: S refers to structural steel, and H to hollow sections.
Sub-grades C to EE in the 1990 designation system indicate increasing impact resistance as measured by the Charpy V-notch test.
Sub-grades J0 and J2 (1994 designation) indicate impact resistance at 0°C and −20°C, respectively.
Sub-grades N (normalised or normalised rolled) and L (low-temperature impact) relate to the physical state of the steel.
The standard UK production grades are the S275J2H and S355J2H designations.

is heated to 950–1050°C and stretch reduced to BS EN 10210: 1994 dimensions. The standard steel grades are S275J2H and S355J2H, corresponding to the former 43D and 50D grades respectively (Table 5.4). Cold-formed hollow sections differ in material characteristics from the hot-finished sections and conform to prEN 10219: 1996. The former grades 43 (St44) and 50 (St52) with minimum yield strengths of 360 and 450 N/mm² respectively are standard, although the lower grade (St37) with a minimum yield strength of 235 N/mm² is imported.

Bending of structural sections

Castellated beams, rolled, hollow and other sections can be bent into curved forms by specialist metal bending companies. The minimum radius achievable depends upon the metallurgical properties, thickness and the cross-section. Generally, smaller sections can be curved to smaller radii than the larger sections, although for a given cross-section size the heavier-gauge sections can be bent to smaller

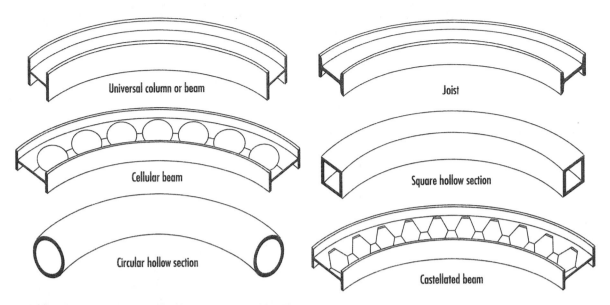

Universal column or beam

Joist

Cellular beam

Square hollow section

Circular hollow section

Castellated beam

Fig. 5.7 Curved steel sections. The photograph shows curved steel sections at Clayton Square, Liverpool.

FIRE PROTECTION OF STRUCTURAL STEEL

The fire protection of structural steel may be approached either by the traditional method involving the application of insulation materials with standard fire resistance periods (Fig. 5.8), or by a structural fire engineering method, which predicts the potential rate of rise of temperature of exposed steel members in each situation, based on the calculated fire load and particular exposure of the steel.

Applied protection to structural steel

Intumescent coatings
Thin film intumescent coatings, which do not seriously affect the aesthetic of exposed structural steelwork, offer up to 120 minutes' fire protection. A full colour range for application by spray, brush or roller can be used on steel and also for remedial work on old cast iron or wrought iron structures.

Sprayed coatings
Sprayed coatings based on either vermiculite cement or mineral-fibre cement may be applied directly to steel to give up to 4 hours' fire protection. The process is particularly appropriate for structural steel in ceiling voids, where the over-spray onto other materials is less critical. The finish, which can be adjusted to the required thickness, is heavily textured, and the products are relatively cheap.

radii than the thinner-gauge sections. Normally, universal sections can be bent to tighter radii than hollow sections of the same dimensions. Elegant structures (Fig. 5.7) can be produced with curved standard sections and also curved tapered beams. The cold bending process work hardens the steel, but without significant loss of performance within the elastic range appropriate to structural steelwork.

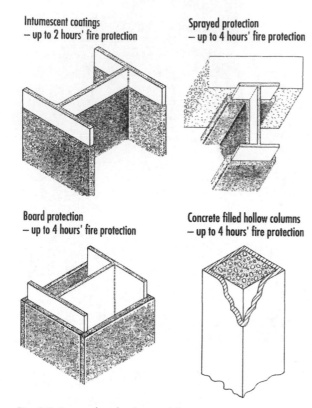

Intumescent coatings
– up to 2 hours' fire protection

Sprayed protection
– up to 4 hours' fire protection

Board protection
– up to 4 hours' fire protection

Concrete filled hollow columns
– up to 4 hours' fire protection

Fig. 5.8 Structural steelwork, typical fire-protection systems

Boarded systems

Lightweight boards boxed around steel sections offer between 30 minutes' and 4 hours' fire protection depending on their thicknesses. Products are generally based on vermiculite or mineral fibres within cement, calcium silicate or gypsum binders. Boarded systems are screwed either directly to the structural steel, to light-gauge steel fixings or to a box configuration. Precoated products are available, or the standard systems may be subsequently decorated.

Preformed casings

Preformed sheet-steel casings which encase lightweight vermiculite plaster give a high-quality appearance and up to 4 hours' fire resistance. The calculated fire resistance is based solely on the thickness of insulation and does not take into account any additional protection afforded by the sheet steel.

Masonry and concrete

Structural steel may be fully encased with masonry or suitably reinforced lightweight concrete in which non-spalling aggregates should be used. Hollow steel columns may be filled with plain, fibre-reinforced or bar-reinforced concrete to give up to 120 minutes' fire resistance. For plain or fibre-reinforced concrete a minimum section of 140 mm × 140 mm or 100 mm × 200 mm is required and 200 mm × 200 mm or 150 mm × 250 mm for bar-reinforced concrete filling.

Water-filled systems

Interconnecting rectangular or circular hollow steel sections can be given fire protection by filling with water as part of a gravity feed or pumped system. Water loss is automatically replaced from a tank, where corrosion inhibitor and anti-freeze agents are added to the system as appropriate.

Fire engineering

The heating rate of a structural steel section within a fire depends upon the severity of the fire and the degree of exposure of the steel. Where a steel section has a low surface/cross-sectional area (Hp/A) ratio (Fig. 5.9), its temperature will rise at a slower rate than a section with a high Hp/A ratio. Fire-engineered solutions calculate the severity of a potential fire based on the enclosure fire loads, ventilation rates and thermal characteristics, and then predict temperature rises within the structural steel based on exposure. The stability of the structural member can therefore be predicted, taking into consideration its steel grade, loading and any structural restraint. From these calculations it can be determined whether additional fire protection is required and at what level to give the required fire resistance period. Depending upon the particular circumstances, a fully loaded unprotected column with a section factor (Hp/A) of less than 50 m^{-1} may offer 30 minutes'

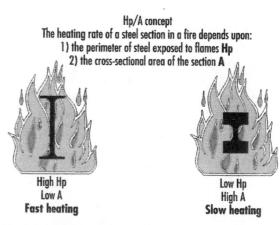

Hp/A concept
The heating rate of a steel section in a fire depends upon:
1) the perimeter of steel exposed to flames **Hp**
2) the cross-sectional area of the section **A**

High Hp
Low A
Fast heating

Low Hp
High A
Slow heating

Fig. 5.9 Hp/A ratios and rates of heating in fire

Shelf angle floor
Up to 60 minutes' fire resistance

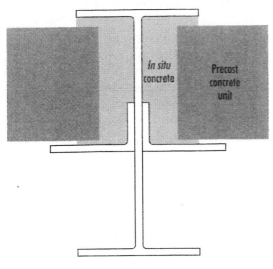

'Slimflor' beam
Up to 60 minutes' fire resistance

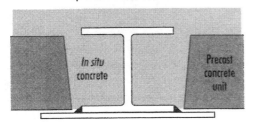

Column with blocked in web
Up to 30 minutes' fire resistance

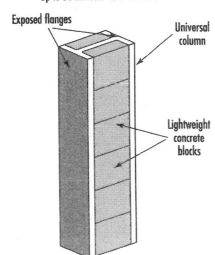

Fig. 5.10 Fire resistance of structural-steel systems

structural fire resistance; similarly, lighter columns with lightweight concrete blocks in the web can achieve 30 minutes' fire resistance. Shelf angle floors of suitable section, and in which a high proportion of the steel is encased by the concrete floor construction, can achieve 60 minutes' fire resistance (Fig. 5.10).

PROFILED STEEL SHEETING

The majority of profiled sheet steel is produced by shaping the precoated strip through a set of rolls which gradually produce the desired section without damage to the applied coating. The continuous profiled sheet is then cut and packaged to customer requirements. The standard sections have a regular trapezoidal profile, with the depth of the section dependent on the loading and required span (Fig. 5.11). In cases where there is the risk of buckling, stiffeners are incorporated into the profile. Curved profiled sheets for eaves and soffits are manufactured

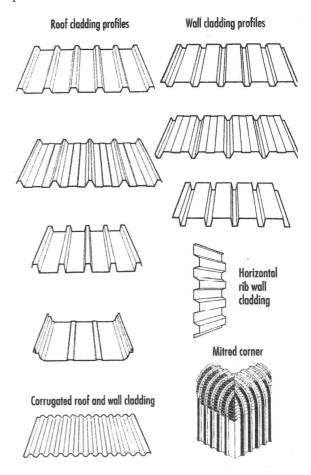

Fig. 5.11 Typical profiles for sheet-steel roofing and cladding

by brake-pressing from the same coated strip. Trapezoidal profiles may be crimped in this process, although sinusoidal sheets and shallow trapezoidal sections can be curved without this effect. The rigidity of curved sections reduces their flexibility and thus the tolerances of these components. Proprietary spring-clip fixings may be used when concealed fixings are required for certain profiled sheet sections.

STEEL CABLES

Steel cables are manufactured by drawing annealed thin steel rods through a series of lubricated and tapered tungsten carbide dies, producing up to a ten-fold elongation. The drawing process increases the strength and reduces the ductility of the steel, thus the higher carbon steels, required for the production of high-tensile wires, need special heat treatment before they are sufficiently ductile for the sequence of drawing processes.

In order to manufacture steel cables for suspended structures or prestressed concrete, a set of individual wires are twisted into a strand, then a series of strands are woven around a central core of steel or fibre strand to produce a rope. A series of ropes are then woven to produce cable to the required specifications. For prestressed concrete all-steel ropes must be used.

Ferrous alloys

WEATHERING STEEL

Weathering steels are structural steels which have been alloyed with small proportions of copper, usually between 0.25 and 0.55%, together with silicon, manganese, chromium and either vanadium or phosphorus as minor constituents. The alloying has the effect of making the naturally formed brown rust coating adhere tenaciously to the surface, thus preventing further loss by spalling. The use of weathering steels is not appropriate within marine environments, and all-weathering steel must be carefully detailed to ensure that the rainwater run-off does not impinge on other materials, particularly concrete and glass, where it will cause severe staining during the first few years of exposure to the elements. *Cor-Ten* is the UK commercial name for weathering steels.

STAINLESS STEELS

Stainless steels are a range of alloys containing at least 12% chromium. The corrosion resistance of the material is due to the natural passive film of chromium oxide which immediately forms over the material in the presence of oxygen; thus, if the surface is subsequently scratched or damaged, the protective film naturally re-forms. The corrosion resistance is increased by the inclusion of nickel and molybdenum as further alloying components. The standard (austenitic) grades used within construction are type 304 (18% chromium, 10% nickel) and type 316 (17% chromium, 12% nickel and 2.5% molybdenum). Type 304 is suitable for use in rural and lightly polluted urban sites, while type 316 is more appropriate for use within normal urban, marine and industrial environments. For certain aggressive environments, the high-alloy type 2205 (duplex) stainless steel should be used. Type 430 (ferritic) stainless steel containing only chromium (17% chromium), with a reduced corrosion resistance, is appropriate for internal building use where corrosion is a less critical factor. European grades to BS EN 10088: 1995 for stainless steels are given in Table 5.5.

Stainless steel is manufactured by a three-stage process. Scrap is melted in an electric arc furnace, then refined in an argon–oxygen decarburiser and alloyed to the required composition in a ladle furnace by the addition of the minor constituents. Most molten metal is continuously cast into billets or slabs

Table 5.5 Stainless steel compositions and grades to BS EN 10088: 1995 for different environmental conditions

UK type	European Grade		Suitable environments
	Number	Name (indicating composition of alloying components)	
Austenitic			
304	1.4301	X5 Cr Ni 18-10	rural and clean urban
316	1.4401	X5 Cr Ni Mo 17-12-2	urban, industrial and marine
Ferritic			
430	1.4016	X6 Cr 17	interior
Duplex			
2205	1.4462	X2 Cr Ni Mo N 22-5-3	severe industrial and marine

(Cr, Ni, Mo and N refer to chromium, nickel, molybdenum and nitrogen respectively, and X2, X5 or X6 refer to the carbon content as 0.02, 0.05 or 0.06% respectively)

for subsequent forming. Stainless steel is hot rolled into plate, bar and sheet, while thin sections may be cold rolled. Heavy universal sections are made up from plates. Stainless steel may be cast or welded and is readily formed into small components such as fixings and architectural ironmongery. Polished, brushed, matt, patterned and profiled finishes are available; additionally, the natural oxide film may be permanently coloured by chemical and cathodic treatment to bronze, blue, gold, red, purple or green according to its final thickness.

Stainless steel is available in square, rectangular and circular hollow sections as well as the standard sections for structural work. It has become a popular material for roofing, cladding, interior and exterior trim owing to its strength and low maintenance. The corrosion resistance of stainless steel makes it eminently suitable for masonry fixings such as corbels, anchor bolts and cavity wall ties. Stainless steel wire ropes and end fittings may be used in tensile structures. Austenitic stainless steels are used for the manufacture of pipework, catering and drainage products where durability and corrosion resistance are critical. Exposed exterior stainless steel should be washed regularly to retain its surface characteristics. Pitting corrosion causing surface pin-point attack, crevice corrosion under tight-fitting washers and stress corrosion cracking, where the material is under high-tensile load, may occur where inappropriate grades are used in aggressive environments.

HEAT-TREATED STEELS

The size effect, which causes a reduced yield strength in large sections due to their slower cooling rates as compared to the equivalent thin sections, can be ameliorated by the addition of small quantities of alloying elements such as chromium, manganese, molybdenum and nickel.

Coated steels

ZINC-COATED STEEL

The zinc coating of steel has, for many years, been a standard method for its protection against corrosion. The zinc coating may be applied by hot-dipping or spraying with the molten metal, sheradising in heated zinc powder or electrodeposition. In hot-dip galvanising the steel is cleaned by pickling in acid followed by immersion in molten zinc or iron–zinc alloy. The zinc coating protects the steel by acting as a physical barrier between the steel and its environment, and also by sacrificially protecting the steel where it is exposed by cutting or surface damage. The iron–zinc alloy coating gives a better surface for painting or welding. The durability of the coated steel is dependent upon the thickness of the coating (standard 275 g/m^2, i.e. 137.5 g/m^2 per face) and the environment. Coastal situations and industrial environments with high concentrations of salt and sulfur dioxide respectively may cause rapid deterioration. The alkalis in wet cement, mortar and plaster etch zinc coatings, but once dry, corrosion is slow; however, calcium chloride used as an accelerator in plaster is aggressive and should only be used sparingly. Fixings for zinc-coated sheet should be carefully chosen to avoid the formation of bimetallic couples, which can cause accelerated corrosion. In particular, no copper or brass should make contact with either zinc or iron–zinc alloy coated steel. Other metals, such as lead, aluminium and stainless steel, have less serious effects in clean atmospheres, but generally all fixings should be sealed and insulated by rubber-faced washers. Where zinc-coated steel is to be fixed to unseasoned timber or timber impregnated with copper-based preservatives, the wood should be coated with bitumen paint. Where damaged in cutting, fixing or welding, the zinc coating should be repaired with the application of zinc-rich paint.

Zinc-coated steel may be painted for decoration or improved corrosion resistance. However, the *normal spangle* zinc finish will show through paint, and the *minimised spangle* or iron–zinc alloy finish are more appropriate for subsequent painting.

ALUMINIUM–ZINC ALLOY COATED STEEL

Steel coated with an alloy of aluminium (55%), zinc (43.5%) and silicon (1.5%) is more durable than that coated with an equivalent thickness of pure zinc, and may be used without further protection in non-aggressive environments. It is also used as the substrate for certain organic coatings.

TERNE-COATED AND LEAD-CLAD STEEL

Lead and terne, an alloy of lead (80–90%) and tin (20–10%), are used as finishes to steel and stainless steel for cladding and roofing units. Terne can be applied to sheet stainless steel as a 20 micron layer by immersion in the molten alloy. Terne-coated stainless steel does not suffer from bimetallic corrosion and can normally be used in contact with lead, copper, aluminium or zinc. Thermal movement is similar to that for stainless steel, allowing for units up to 9 m in length to be used for roofing and cladding. The composite material, lead-clad steel, is produced by cold-roll bonding 0.75 mm lead to 1.0 mm terne-plated steel or to 0.8 mm terne-plated stainless steel. Lead-clad steel is suitable for cladding and roofing systems and has the appearance and corrosion resistance of milled lead. Because of the support afforded by the steel substrate, lead-clad steel or stainless steel can be used for self-supported fasciae, soffits, gutters and curved sections. Joints can be lead-burned and soldered as traditional lead. Cut ends should be protected by soldering in the case of lead-clad steel, although the stainless steel version requires no protective treatment. Unlike traditional lead, the material is virtually theft-proof and does not suffer significantly from creep. Patination oil should be applied to the lead surface after installation to prevent staining effects.

ORGANIC COATED STEEL

Since the 1960s, a range of heat-bonded organic coatings for steel have been developed including: PVC plastisol (*Colorcoat*), polyvinylidene fluoride (PVF$_2$), polyesters and PVC film (*Stelvetite*). Within this product range the PVC plastisol currently has the largest market share for cladding and roofing within the UK.

PVC plastisol coating

PVC plastisol is applied to zinc- or aluminium/zinc-coated steel to a thickness of 0.2 mm. It has a tough leather grain finish and is available in a wide range of colours, although the pastel shades are recommended for roofing applications. The reverse side is usually coated with a grey corrosion-resistant primer and polyester finish, although PVC plastisol may be specified for unusually aggressive internal environments. Careful site storage and handling are required to prevent physical damage to the surface. For non-marine environments the most durable colours will give a period to first maintenance of greater than 20 years. Very deep colours, and the non-pastel shades in coastal locations, will have reduced periods to first repainting.

PVF$_2$ coating

PVF$_2$, an inert fluorocarbon, when applied as a 0.027 mm coating to zinc-coated steel, has good colour stability at temperatures of up to 120°C, making it suitable for world-wide use and for buildings which are likely to be extended at a later date. The finish is smooth and self-cleaning, although considerable care is required on site to prevent handling damage. A period to first maintenance of 15 years is typical within the UK for non-coastal locations. The wide colour range includes metallic silver.

Polyester coating

Polyester and silicone polyester-coated galvanised steels are economic products, but offer only medium-term life in non-aggressive environments. Externally the period to first maintenance will be typically 10 years in unpolluted inland locations, but they are suitable for internal use. Silicone polyester should not be used in marine or hot, humid environments. Polyester and silicone polyester coatings are smooth and typically 0.025 mm in thickness.

Enamel coating

Organic enamel-coated steels offering good light reflectance are suitable for internal use as wall and roof linings. Coatings, usually 0.022 mm thick, are typically applied to hot-dip zinc/aluminium alloy-coated steel and are easily cleaned. The standard colour is brilliant white, but a range of light colours is also available.

PVC film coating

PVC film (0.02 mm) in a range of colours, decorative patterns and textured finishes is calendered to zinc-coated steel strip. The product is suitable only for internal applications.

Steel tiles and slates

Lightweight steel tile and slate units, manufactured from galvanised steel coated with acrylic resin and a granular finish, give the appearance of traditional slate or pantile roofs. The products have the advantage, particularly for refurbishment work, of lightness in comparison to the traditional materials. Units can typically be used for roof pitches between 12° and 90°. A span of 1200 mm allows for wider spacing of roof trusses. Units in a range of traditional material colours are available with appropriate edge and ventilation accessories.

Aluminium

Aluminium has only been available as a construction material for about a hundred years. Possibly the most well known early use of the metal was for the cast statue of Eros which has stood in Piccadilly Circus, London, since 1893.

MANUFACTURE

Aluminium, the most common metallic element in the earth's crust, is extracted from the ore bauxite, an impure form of aluminium oxide or alumina. The bauxite is dissolved in caustic soda, filtered, reprecipitated to remove impurities and dried. The pure alumina is then dissolved in fused cryolite (sodium aluminium fluoride) within a carbon-lined electrolytic cell. Electrolysis of the aluminium oxide produces oxygen and the pure aluminium, which is tapped off periodically and cast. The process is highly energy intensive and frequently reliant on cheap hydroelectric power. Typically the production of 1 tonne of aluminium requires 14 000 kWh of electrical energy, although recycling waste aluminium requires only one twentieth of this energy. Cast ingots or slabs are hot-rolled at 500°C into 5 mm coiled sheets which subsequently can be cold rolled into thinner sheets or foil. Owing to the ductility of aluminium, the metal can be extruded into complex shapes or drawn into wire. Forming and machining processes are generally easier than with steel. Aluminium components may also be formed by casting.

PROPERTIES

Aluminium is one of the lightest metals with a density of 2700 kg/m^3, compared to steel 7900 kg/m^3. Standard-grade aluminium (99% pure) has a tensile strength between 70 and 140 N/mm^2, depending on temper; however, certain structural aluminium alloys (e.g. alloy 5083) achieve 345 N/mm^2, comparable to the 410–560 N/mm^2 for S275 (Fe 430A) steel. This compares favourably on a strength to weight basis, but the modulus of elasticity for aluminium is only one-third that of steel, so deflections will be greater unless deeper sections are used. For an aluminium section to have the same stiffness as an equivalent steel member, the aluminium section must be enlarged to approximately half the weight of the steel section.

DURABILITY

The durability of aluminium as a construction material is due to the protection afforded by the natural oxide film, which is always present on the metal surface. The aluminium oxide film, which is immediately produced when the surface of the metal is cut or scratched, is naturally only 0.01 micron thick, but may be thickened by the process of anodisation.

FIRE

The strength of aluminium is halved from its ambient value at a temperature of 200°C, and for many of the alloys is minimal by 300°C.

CONTACT WITH OTHER BUILDING MATERIALS

While dry cement-based materials do not attack aluminium, the alkalinity of wet cement, concrete and mortar causes rapid corrosion. Thus, where these materials make contact during the construction process, the metal should be protected by a coating of bitumen paint. Furthermore, anodised and, in particular coloured sections, such as glazing units, can be permanently damaged by droplets of wet cement products, and should be protected on site by a removable lacquer or plastic film. Under dry conditions aluminium is unaffected by contact with timber; however, certain timber preservatives, particularly those containing copper compounds, may cause corrosion under conditions of high humidity. Where this risk is present the metal should be protected with a coating of bitumen.

Although aluminium is highly resistant to corrosion in isolation, it can be seriously affected by corrosion when in contact with other metals. The most serious effects occur with copper and copper-based alloys, and rainwater must not flow from a copper roof or copper pipes into contact with aluminium. Except in marine and industrial environments it is safe to use stainless steel fixings or lead with aluminium, although zinc and zinc-coated steel fixings are more durable. Unprotected mild steel should not be in electrical contact with aluminium.

ALUMINIUM ALLOYS

Aluminium alloys fall into two major categories, either cast or wrought. Additionally, the wrought alloys may be subjected to heat treatment. The majority of aluminium used in the construction industry is wrought, the content and degree of alloying components being directly related to the physical properties required, with the pure metal being the most malleable. BS EN 485: 1994 designates aluminium alloys into categories according to their major alloying components (Table 5.6).

Table 5.6 Broad classification of aluminium alloys

Alloy series	Major alloying components
1000	greater than 99% aluminium
3000	manganese alloys (maximum 1.8% manganese)
4000	silicon alloys (maximum 2% silicon)
5000	magnesium alloys
6000	magnesium and silicon alloys
7000	zinc alloys
8000	tin alloys

(In many cases minor alloying components are also present.)

For flashings where on site work is necessary, 99.8% pure aluminium (alloy 1080A) or 99.5% (alloy 1050A) offer the greatest malleability, although the standard commercial-grade 99% pure aluminium (alloy 1200) is suitable for insulating foils and for continuously supported sheet roofing.

Profiled aluminium for roofing and cladding, requiring additional strength and durability, is alloyed with 1.25% manganese (alloy 3103). It is produced from the sheet by roll-forming, and can be manufactured into curved sections to increase design flexibility. Preformed rigid flashings to match the profile sheet are manufactured from the same alloy and finish. The alloy with 2% magnesium (alloy 5251) is more resistant to marine environments. Aluminium rainscreen cladding panels up to 2.8 × 1.5 m in size may also be shaped using the superplastic forming (SPF) process, which relies on the high extensibility of the alloy 5083SPF. Sheet alloy, typically 2 mm in thickness, is heated to 380–500°C, and forced by air pressure into the three-dimensional form of the mould. Horizontal or vertical ribs are frequently manufactured to give enhanced rigidity, but cladding panels may be formed to individual designs including curvature in two directions. Coloured finishes are usually polyester powder or PVF_2 coatings.

Extruded sections for curtain walling, doors and windows require the additional strength imparted by alloying the aluminium with magnesium and silicon (alloy 6063). Thermal insulation within such extruded sections is achieved by a hidden thermal break or by an internal plastic or timber insulating cladding.

Structural aluminium for loadbearing sections and space frames typically contains magnesium, silicon and manganese (alloy 6082). Tempering increases the tensile strength to the range 270–310 N/mm², which is more comparable to the standard grade of structural steel S275 (minimum tensile strength 410 N/mm²).

FINISHES FOR ALUMINIUM

Anodising

The process of anodising thickens the natural aluminium oxide film to typically 10–25 microns. The component is immersed in sulfuric acid and electrolytically made anodic, which converts the surface metal into a porous aluminium oxide film, which is then sealed by boiling in water. The anodising process increases durability and can be used for trapping dyes within the surface to produce a wide range of coloured products. Some dyes fade with exposure to sunlight, the most durable colours being gold, blue, red and black. Exact colour matching for replacement or extensions to existing buildings may be difficult, and manufacturers will normally produce components within an agreed band of colour variation. If inorganic salts of tin are incorporated into the surface during the anodising process then colour-fast bronzes are produced. Depending upon the period of exposure to the electrolytic anodisation process, a range of colours from pale bronze to black may be produced. Different aluminium alloys respond differently to the anodising treatment. Pure aluminium will produce a silver mirror finish, whereas the aluminium–silicon alloys (e.g. alloy 6063) produce a grey finish.

Surface textures

A range of surface textures is achieved by mechanical and chemical processing. Finishes include bright-polished, matt, etched and pattern-rolled according to the pretreatments applied, usually before anodising, and also the particular alloy used.

Plastic coatings

Polyester coatings, predominantly white, but with a wide range of colour options, are used for double-glazing systems, cladding panels and rainwater goods. The polyester is applied electrostatically as a powder and heat cured to a smooth self-cleaning finish. PVC simulated wood-grain and other pattern finishes may also be applied to aluminium extrusions and curtain-wall systems.

Paint

Where aluminium is painted for decorative purposes it is important that the appropriate primer is used. The aluminium should be abraded or etched to give a good key to the paint system, although cast aluminium normally has a sufficiently rough surface. Oxide primers are appropriate but red lead should be avoided.

Maintenance of finished aluminium

For long-term durability all external aluminium finishes should be washed regularly with a mild detergent solution, at intervals not normally exceeding three months. Damaged paint coatings may be touched-up on site, but remedial work does not have the durability of the factory-applied finishes.

ALUMINIUM IN BUILDING

Typical applications for aluminium and its alloys in building include roofing and cladding, curtain wall and structural glazing systems, flashings, rainwater goods, vapour barriers and, internally, ceilings, panelling, luminaires, ducting, architectural hardware and walkways.

Thermal breaks in aluminium

In order to overcome thermal bridging effects where aluminium extrusions are used for double-glazing systems, thermal breaks are inserted between the aluminium in contact with the interior and exterior spaces. These may be manufactured from preformed polyamide strips or alternatively the appropriate extrusions are filled with uncured polymer, then the bridging aluminium is milled out after the plastic has set.

Jointing methods

Aluminium components may be joined mechanically with aluminium bolts or rivets; non-magnetic stainless steel bolts are also appropriate. If aluminium is to be electric-arc welded, the use of an inert-gas shield, usually argon, is necessary to prevent oxidation of the metal surface. A filler rod, compatible with the alloy to be welded, supplies the additional material to make up the joint. Strong adhesive bonding of aluminium components is possible, providing that the surfaces are suitably prepared.

Copper

Copper was probably one of the first metals used by man, and evidence of early workings suggests that the metal was smelted as early as 7000 BC. Later it was discovered that the addition of tin to copper improved the strength of the material and by 3000 BC the Bronze Age had arrived. The Romans made extensive use of copper and bronze for weapons, utensils and ornaments. Brass from the alloying of copper and zinc emerged from Egypt during the first century BC. By the mid-eighteenth century South Wales was producing 90% of the world's output of copper, with the ore from Cornwall, but now the main sources are the Americas, Russia and Africa.

MANUFACTURE

The principal copper ores are the sulfides (e.g. chalcocite), and sulfides in association with iron (e.g. chalcopyrite). Ores typically contain no more than 1% copper and therefore require concentrating by flotation techniques before the copper is extracted through a series of furnace processes. The ores are roasted then smelted to reduce the sulfur content and produce *matte,* which contains the copper and a controlled proportion of iron sulfide. The molten matte is refined in a converter by a stream of oxygen. This initially oxidises the iron, which concentrates into the slag and is discarded; sulfur is then burnt off to sulfur dioxide, leaving 99% pure metal which, on casting, evolves the remaining dissolved gases and solidifies to *blister* copper. The blister copper is further refined in a furnace to remove the remaining sulfur with air and then oxygen with methane or propane. Finally, electrolytic purification produces 99.9% pure metal. Approximately 40% of copper and the majority of brass and bronze used within the UK is recycled from scrap.

GRADES OF COPPER

Only four of the numerous grades of copper are commonly used within the construction industry.

Electrolytic tough pitch high-conductivity copper (C101)

Electrolytic tough pitch high-conductivity copper is used mainly for electrical purposes; however, the sheet material is also used for fully supported traditional and long-strip copper roofing. It contains approximately 0.05% dissolved oxygen, which is evolved as steam if the copper is heated to 400°C in a reducing flame, thus rendering the metal unsuitable for welding or brazing.

Fire refined tough pitch copper (C102)

Fire refined tough pitch copper has a similar specification to C101, but with marginally more impurities.

Tough pitch non-arsenical copper (C104)

Tough pitch non-arsenical copper is used for general building applications. It is suitable for sheet roofing.

Phosphorus deoxidised non-arsenical copper (C106)

Phosphorus deoxidised non-arsenical copper is the standard grade for most building applications including roofing but not for electrical installations. The addition of 0.05% phosphorus to refined tough pitch copper isolates the oxygen, rendering the metal suitable for welding and brazing. It is therefore used for plumbing applications where soldering is inappropriate.

COPPER FORMS AND SIZES

Copper is available as wire, rod, tube, foil, sheet and plate. Typical roofing grades are 0.45, 0.6 and 0.7 mm. The metal is supplied dead soft (fully annealed), one quarter or one eighth hard, half-hard or full-hard. It rapidly work hardens on bending, but softness can be recovered by annealing at red heat. Copper can be worked at any temperatures, since, unlike zinc, it is not brittle when cold. The standard grade of copper used for roofs, pipes and domestic water-storage cylinders is phosphorus deoxidised non-arsenical copper C106, although the other tough-pitch grades C101, C102 and C104 may also be used for roofs. Copper for pipework is supplied in annealed coils for mini/microbore systems, in 6 m lengths half-hard and hard for general plumbing work. The hard-temper pipes cannot be bent. Plastic-coated tubes, colour coded to identify the service (e.g. yellow – gas), are available.

PATINA

The green patina of basic copper sulfate or carbonate on exposed copper gradually develops according to the environmental conditions. On roofs within a marine or industrial environment the green patina develops within five years; under heavy pollution it may eventually turn dark brown or black. Within a town environment, the patina on roofs will typically develop over a period of ten years. However, vertical copper cladding will normally remain a deep brown, owing to the fast rainwater run-off, except in marine environments, when the green colour will develop. On site treatment to accelerate the patinisation process is unreliable, but pre-patinised copper sheet is available if the effect is required immediately. Green pre-patinised copper sheet should not be welded, brazed or soldered as heat treatment causes discolouration of the patina. The factory-generated green patina will weather according to the local environmental conditions, often turning quickly to a blue-green. Tinned copper, which is grey in colour, quickly weathers to a matt surface with the appearance of zinc or lead, but has the durability and workability of copper.

CORROSION

Generally copper itself is resistant to corrosion; however, rainwater run-off may cause staining on adjacent materials and severe corrosion to other metals. Zinc, galvanised steel and non-anodised aluminium should not be used under copper, although in this respect lead, stainless steel and brass are unaffected. Copper may cause corrosion to steel or anodised aluminium in direct contact, if moisture is present. Specifically, copper should not be installed below exposed bitumen, bitumen paint, or cedarwood shingles where leaching action producing acid solutions can cause localised attack on the metal. Additionally, some corrosion may arise from the acid produced by algae on tiled roofs. The accidental splashing of lime or cement mortar onto copper causes a blue-green discolouration; however, this can readily be removed with a soft brass brush. Some corrosion of copper pipework may be caused by soft water, particularly if high levels of dissolved carbon dioxide are present; hard waters generally produce a protective film of calcium compounds which inhibits corrosion. Pitting corrosion has been reported in rare cases associated with either hard, deep-well waters or hot, soft waters with a significant manganese content. Additionally, excessive acidic flux residues not removed by flushing the system may cause corrosion. Within heating systems in which oxygen in the primary circulating water is constantly being replenished through malfunction or poor design, bimetallic corrosion will occur between steel radiators and copper pipework. This will result in the build-up of iron oxide residues at the bottom of the radiators. The use of appropriate inhibitors will reduce this effect.

COPPER ROOFING SYSTEMS

Traditional and long-strip systems

Copper roofing systems may be categorised as traditional or long-strip. The latter have the advantage that bays as long as 8.5 m may be constructed without the necessary cross welts on sloping roofs or drips on flat roofs appropriate to the traditional system. This has significant cost benefits in terms of installation costs.

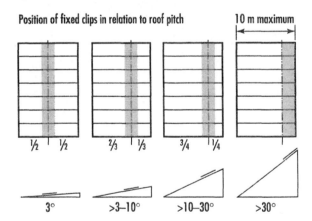

Position of fixed clips in relation to roof pitch — 10 m maximum

½ | ½   ⅔ | ⅓   ¾ | ¼

3°   >3–10°   >10–30°   >30°

Recommended widths and standing seam centres for long-strip copper roofing

Width of strip (mm)	450	600	670
Standing seam centres (mm)	375	525	595

(using 0.6/0.7 mm copper strip at ¼ or ½ hard temper with a fixed zone of 1 metre)

Fig. 5.12 Long-strip copper roofing

The long-strip copper roof system (Fig. 5.12) with bays up to 600 mm wide may be laid on roofs with pitches between 5° and 45° and uses one quarter or one eighth hard temper 0.6 mm copper strip. The system requires specified areas of the roof to be fixed with conventional welted joint clips, and the remain-

der with expansion clips which allow for the longitudinal expansion of the bays, but ensure a secure fixing to the substructure. Lateral thermal movement is accommodated by a space at the base of the standing seams. Long-strip copper is laid on a felt underlay which allows free movement between the metal and the structure, while isolating the copper from any ferrous fixings in the structure and providing some sound reduction from the effects of wind and rain. All fixings should be made from the same copper as the roof. Nails should be copper or brass.

Within the traditional copper roofs (Fig. 5.13), standing seams or batten roll jointing systems are used depending on the pitch and appearance required. For pitches of 5° or less, batten rolls are appropriate, as standing seams are vulnerable to accidental flattening and subsequent failure by capillary action. Cross welts may be continuous across roofs where batten rolls are used, but should be staggered where standing seams are used. Either soft or one quarter hard temper copper is normally used. The substructure, felt and fixed clips are as used in long-strip roofing. These differences in articulation within the traditional roofing systems and particularly by contrast to the smooth line of long-strip system offer alternative visual effects to the designer of copper roofs. Copper rainwater systems are available with a range of standard components.

Bonded copper systems

Proprietary systems offer similar visual effects to traditional copper, aluminium, stainless and ternecoated stainless steel roofing systems, by using the metal bonded to either particleboard or roofing felt. (The latter is referred to in Chapter 6 on Flat Roofing Materials.) Copper bonded to 18 mm high-density moisture-resistant particleboard offers a smoother finish than that achieved by traditional roofing and cladding methods, while still showing the articulation of standing or flat seams.

COPPER ALLOYS

Copper may be alloyed with zinc, tin, aluminium, nickel or silicon to produce a range of brasses and bronzes.

Brass

Brass is an alloy of copper and zinc, most commonly with a zinc content between 10% and 45%. It is

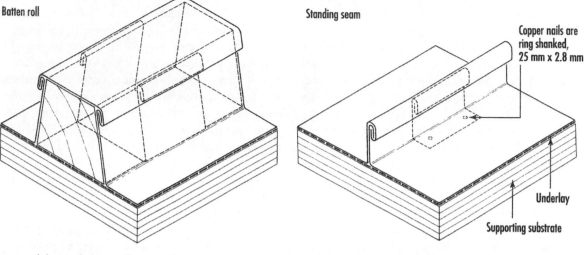

Batten roll

Standing seam

Copper nails are ring shanked, 25 mm x 2.8 mm

Underlay

Supporting substrate

Recommended centres for batten roll copper roofing

Width of sheet (mm)   600
Batten roll centres (mm)   500
(using 0.6 mm copper strip to a maximum 1.8 m length in soft or ¼ hard temper)

Recommended centres for standing seam copper roofing

Width of sheet (mm)   600
Standing seam centres (mm) 525
(using 0.6 mm copper strip to a maximum 1.8 m length in soft or ¼ hard temper)

Copper shingles

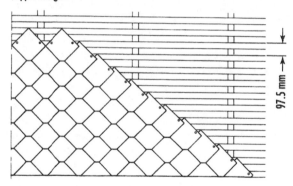

97.5 mm

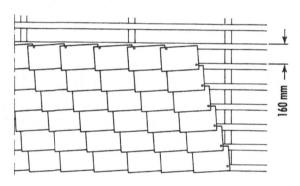

160 mm

Fig. 5.13 Traditional copper roofing and copper shingles

used for small components such as architectural ironmongery, door and window furniture, handrails and balustrades. It may be lacquered to prevent deterioration of the polished finish, although externally and in humid environments the lacquer fails, requiring the brass to be cleaned with metal polish to remove the tarnish. Brass plumbing fittings manufactured from 60/40 (copper/zinc) brass may corrode in soft, high-chloride content waters by dezincification. The process produces insoluble zinc corrosion products and ultimately porous metal fittings which may cause failure of the system. In situations where this problem is likely, dezincification-resistant (DZR) fittings made from alloy CZ132 containing 2% lead should be used. Such components are marked with the '℟' dezincification-resistant symbol.

Bronze

Bronze is an alloy of copper and tin, used for high-quality door furniture and engraved nameplates. Bronzes are usually harder and more durable than the equivalent brasses and exhibit a greater resistance to corrosion. Phosphor bronze contains up to 0.5% phosphorus in an 8% tin bronze. Because of its load-bearing properties and durability, it is frequently used as corbel plates and fixings for stone and precast concrete cladding panels. Aluminium-Bronze (copper and aluminium), silicon–bronze (copper and silicon) and gunmetals (copper–tin–zinc alloys) are also used for masonry fixings and cast components by virtue of their strength and durability. Nickel–bronze alloys (copper, nickel and zinc) can be manufactured to highly polished *silver* finishes, particularly appropriate for interior fittings.

Lead

The Egyptians used lead in the glazing of their pottery and for making solder by 5000 BC. It was mined in Spain by the Phoenicians around 2000 BC.

MANUFACTURE

Lead occurs naturally as the sulfide ore, galena. The manufacturing process involves the concentration of the ore by grinding and flotation. The sulfide is converted to the oxide by roasting, then reduced to the metal in a blastfurnace charged with limestone and coke. Further refining removes impurities which otherwise would reduce the softness of the metal.

LEAD SHEET

The majority of lead sheet for roofing, cladding, flashings and gutter linings is produced by milling thick sheet down to the required thickness. Continuous machine-cast lead, which accounts for approximately 10% of the UK market, is manufactured by immersing a rotating water-cooled metal drum in a bath of molten lead at constant temperature. The lead solidifies on the surface of the drum and is peeled off as it emerges from the melt. The thickness can be adjusted by altering the speed of rotation of the drum. The sheet produced is without the anisotropic directional grain structure associated with the standard rolling process. Unlike most other building materials, sheet lead thicknesses are defined by the old code numbers as shown in Table 5.7. Sand-cast lead sheet is still manufactured by the traditional method, which involves pouring molten lead onto a prepared bed of sand. The sheet thickness is controlled by drawing a piece of timber across the molten metal surface to remove the excess material. Sand-cast lead is normally only used for conservation work on key historic buildings, when much of the old lead may be recycled in the process.

CORROSION

Freshly cut lead has a bright finish, but it rapidly tarnishes in the air with the formation of a blue-grey film of lead carbonate and lead sulfate. In damp conditions a white deposit of lead carbonate is produced, and in cladding this can both be aesthetically unacceptable and cause some staining of the adjacent materials. The effect can be prevented by the application of patination oil after the lead has been fixed. Lead is generally resistant to corrosion owing to the protection afforded by the insoluble film; however, it is corroded by

Table 5.7 Lead sheet codes and typical applications

Code	3	4	5	6	7	8
Colour code	green	blue	red	black	white	orange
Nominal thickness (mm)	1.32	1.80	2.24	2.65	3.15	3.55
Nominal weight (kg/m²)	15.0	20.4	25.4	30.1	35.7	40.3
Typical application:						
Flat roofing			✓	✓	✓	✓
Pitched roofing			✓	✓	✓	✓
Vertical cladding		✓	✓			
Soakers	✓	✓				
Hip and ridge flashings		✓	✓			
Parapets, box and tapered valley gutters			✓	✓	✓	✓
Pitched valley gutters		✓	✓			
Weatherings to parapets		✓	✓	✓		
Apron and cover flashings		✓	✓			
Chimney flashings		✓	✓			

organic acids. Acidic rainwater run-off from mosses and lichens may cause corrosion, and contact with damp timbers, particularly oak, teak and western red cedar, should be avoided by the use of building paper or bitumen paint. Trapped condensation under sheet lead may cause significant corrosion, so consideration must be given to the provision of adequate ventilation underneath the decking which supports the lead. Dew points must be checked to ensure that condensation will not occur and be trapped under the lead sheet in either new work or renovation. Generally lead is stable in most soils; however, it is attacked by the acids within peat and ash residues. Electrolytic corrosion rarely occurs when lead is in contact with other metals, although within marine environments aluminium should not be used in association with lead. Corrosion does occur between wet Portland cement or lime products and lead during the curing process, thus in circumstances where the drying out will be slow, the lead should be isolated from the concrete with a coat of bitumen paint.

FATIGUE AND CREEP

In order to prevent fatigue failure due to thermal cycling or creep, that is, the extension of the metal under its own weight over extended periods of time, it is necessary to ensure that sheet sizes, thicknesses and fixings are in accordance with the advice given by the Lead Sheet Association in their technical manuals. The metal must be relatively free to move with temperature changes, so that alternating stresses are not focused in small areas leading to eventual fatigue fracture. A geotextile separating underlay of non-woven polyester or crimped filament polypropylene may be used. The addition of 0.06% copper to 99.9% pure lead refines the crystal structure giving increased fatigue resistance without significant loss of malleability. The composition of lead sheet is strictly controlled by BS 1178: 1982.

LEAD ROOFING

Lead roofing requires a smooth, continuous substrate. Generally the bay sizes depend upon the roof geometry and the thickness of lead to be used (Fig. 5.14). For flat roofs (from 1 in 80 to 10°), joints are generally wood-cored rolls down the fall and drips across. For pitched roofs (10° to 80°), joints in the direction of the fall may be wood-cored or hollow rolls, with laps across the fall, unless for aesthetic reasons the bays are to be divided by drips. For steep pitches welts are used, and over 80°, standing seams are appropriate (Fig. 5.14). Fixings are copper or stainless steel nails and clips within the rolls, welts or standing seams. Lead as a highly malleable material can be formed or *bossed* into shape with the specialist tools including the bossing stick and bossing mallet. Welding or leadburning involves the joining of lead to lead using additional material to make the joint thicker by one third than the adjacent material.

The David Mellor Cutlery Factory, Hathersage, Derbyshire (Plate 6), illustrates a traditionally detailed lead roof. The wood-cored roll-jointed lead is supported on a stepped deck manufactured from prefabricated stressed-skin insulated plywood boxes, tapered to fit the radial design. These units are supported on a series of lightweight steel trusses, tied at the perimeter by a steel tension ring and at the centre lantern by a ring-truss. Around the perimeter, the lead is burnt to ensure a vertical seal.

LEAD SHEET CLADDING

For cladding the thickness of lead to be used dictates the maximum spacing between vertical joints and distance between laps. Vertical joints may be wood-cored rolls or welts and occasionally standing seams or hollow rolls, where the risk of physical damage from ladders is negligible. The lead is hung by nailing at the head, with allowance for up to 6 mm thermal movement to occur within the lap joints.

An alternative form of lead cladding is the use of preformed lead-clad panels, which are then clipped onto the building facade. Typically; 25 mm exterior-grade plywood covered with Code 4 or Code 5 lead is used. The panels are set against a lead-faced timber structural support leaving 25 mm joints for thermal movement.

FLASHINGS

Lead, because of its malleability and durability, is an ideal material from which to form gutters and gutter linings, ridge and hip rolls, and the full range of standard and specialist flashings, including ornamental work to enhance design features. For most flashing applications, lead sheets of Codes 3, 4 and 5 are used, fixed with copper or stainless steel and occasionally lead itself.

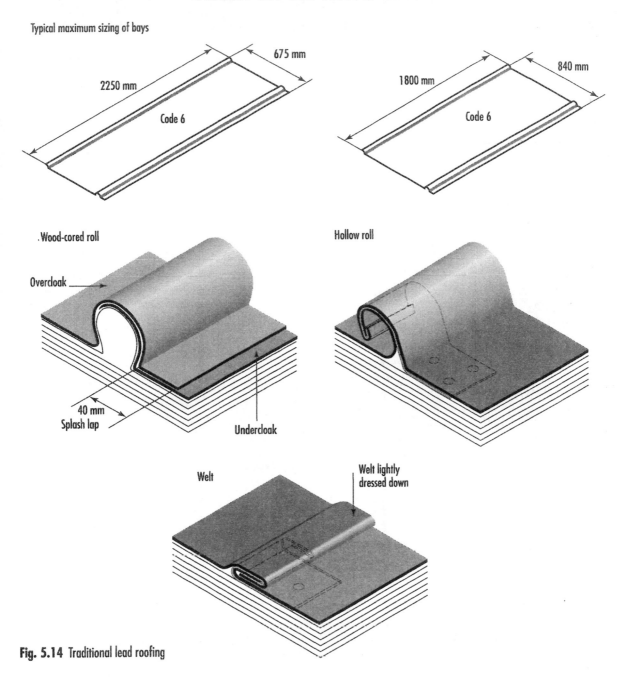

Typical maximum sizing of bays

675 mm
2250 mm
Code 6

840 mm
1800 mm
Code 6

.Wood-cored roll

Overcloak

40 mm
Splash lap

Undercloak

Hollow roll

Welt

Welt lightly
dressed down

Fig. 5.14 Traditional lead roofing

ACRYLIC-COATED LEAD SHEET

Acrylic-coated lead sheet is produced to order and in the standard colours, white, slate grey, terracotta and dark brown for use in colour-coordinated flashings. The colour-coated Code 4 (1.80 mm) milled lead is produced in widths of 250, 300, 450 and 600 mm. The material is moulded by bossing as for standard lead sheet and where welded, the exposed grey metal may be touched-up if necessary.

Zinc

Zinc was known to the Romans as the alloy, brass, but it was not produced industrially until the mid-eighteenth century, and was not in common use on buildings until the nineteenth century. The cut surface tarnishes quickly to a light grey owing to the formation of a patina of basic zinc carbonate. The metal is hard at ambient temperatures and brittle when cold. It should therefore not be worked at metal temperatures below 10°C without prior warming, and heavy impacts should not be used within the forming processes of bending and folding.

MANUFACTURE

Zinc occurs naturally as the sulfide ore, zinc blende. The ore is first concentrated and then roasted to produce zinc oxide. The addition of coal reduces zinc oxide to the metal, which is evolved as the vapour and then condensed. High-grade zinc is produced by the electrolysis of a purified zinc sulfate solution.

ZINC SHEET

Zinc sheet is manufactured by continuous casting and rolling in a range of thicknesses (Table 5.8), to a standard sheet size of 914 mm × 2438 mm, and up to 1000 mm wide in coil. The two standard products are the pure metal (99.995% pure) and the alloy with small additions of titanium and copper (e.g. 0.07% and 0.08% minima respectively). The rolling process modifies the grain structure, particularly in the pure metal; however, this does not affect the working of the sheets. The alloy has improved performance with respect to strength and creep resistance but also a reduced coefficient of thermal expansion which enables the construction of bays up to 9 or 12 m in length depending upon design considerations including bay width. Titanium/copper alloy (BS 6561: 1985) may be folded or curved to produce interlocking cladding panels for vertical, horizontal or diagonal installation. Both the pure metal and the titanium alloy can be worked by hand at room temperature and do not work harden.

PATINA

Bright zinc tarnishes in the air with the production of a thin oxide film, which is rapidly converted into basic zinc carbonate by the action of water and carbon dioxide. The patina then prevents further degradation of the surface. Ordinary zinc has a lighter blue-grey patina than the alloyed sheet, so the two materials should not be mixed within the same construction. Pre-weathered alloys are available if light or slate grey patinated surfaces are required immediately. The lifetime of zinc depends directly upon the thickness. A 0.8 mm roof should last for 40 years in urban conditions, whereas the same sheet as cladding, washed clean by rain, could last for 60 years. The titanium alloy with considerably improved durability has a predicted life of up to 100 years in a rural environment, depending upon the pitch of the application.

LACQUERED ZINC SHEET

A factory-applied 25 micron heat-treated polyester lacquer finish to zinc gives a range of colour options through white, brown, terracotta, green/grey and blue.

CORROSION

Zinc should not be used in contact with copper or where rainwater draining from copper or copper alloys would discharge onto zinc. It may, however, be used in association with aluminium or lead. In contact with steel or stainless steel, the zinc must be the major component to prevent significant corrosion effects. Unprotected cut edges of galvanised steel located above zinc can cause unsightly rust stains and should be avoided. If the underside of zinc sheet remains damp owing to condensation for extended periods of time then pitting corrosion will occur, causing eventual failure. It is therefore necessary to ensure that the substructure is designed appropriately with vapour barrier, insulation and ventilation to prevent interstitial condensation. Sulfur dioxide within polluted atmospheres prevents the formation of the protective carbonate film and causes corrosion.

Zinc is not affected by Portland cement mortars or concrete, although it should be coated with a hard-drying bitumen paint where it will be in contact with soluble salts from masonry or cement additives. Zinc

Table 5.8 Zinc sheet thicknesses and weights

Nominal thickness (mm)	0.65	0.7	0.8	0.9	1.0
Nominal weight (kg/m²)	4.7	5.0	5.8	6.5	7.2
Weight of standard sheet (kg) 914 x 2438 mm	10.4	11.2	12.8	14.5	16.1

Titanium zinc is also available in sheet thicknesses of 0.5, 0.6 and 1.10 mm.

may be laid directly onto seasoned softwoods, unless impregnated with copper-salt preservatives; however, it should be isolated with an underlay from acidic timbers such as oak and western red cedar. Furthermore, zinc should not be used in association with western red cedar shingles, which generate an acidic discharge. The acidic products from the effect of ultraviolet radiation on bitumen can cause corrosion in zinc. If the bitumen is not protected from direct sunlight by reflective chippings, then any zinc subjected to the rainwater discharge should itself be protected with a dense bitumen coating.

FIXINGS

Fixings for zinc should be of galvanised or stainless steel. Clips are made of zinc, cut along the rolled direction of the sheet and folded across the grain. Watertight joints may be made by soldering using tin/lead solder in conjunction with zinc chloride flux.

ROOFING AND CLADDING

Both the roll-cap and standing seam systems are appropriate for fully supported zinc roofing (Fig. 5.15). Welted joints are standard practice across the bays at pitches steeper than 15°; below 15° drips are necessary. A minimum fall of 3° is recommended, although a pitch in excess of 7° will ensure self-cleaning, preventing the accumulation of dirt which reduces service life. Where the bay length is greater than 3 m, a section 1 m in length is fixed rigidly, while the remaining area is secured to the substructure with sliding clips which accommodate the thermal movement. Titanium zinc sheets are available in lengths of up to 6 m. Timber roof boarding or plywood forms the ideal substructure for zinc, but particleboard is inappropriate except for cladding, and concrete must be sealed against trapped moisture. For cladding, the vertical joints may be welted, standing seam or roll cap with the horizontal joints welted. Self-supporting cladding and roofing systems may also be constructed in titanium zinc with bays set at 300 mm centres and a profile depth of 38 mm. Titanium zinc rainwater systems are available with an appropriate range of standard components.

Titanium zinc alloy pre-weathered interlocking square or parallelogram tiles are appropriate for vertical hanging and roof pitches down to 25°. They are fixed with soldered and sliding clips to timber battens.

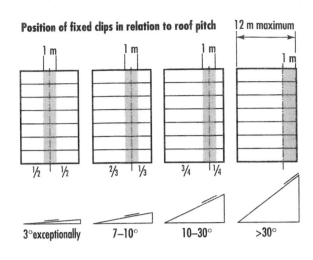

Position of fixed clips in relation to roof pitch

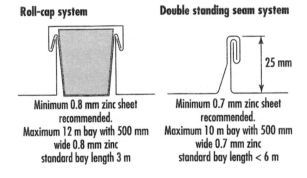

Roll-cap system

Minimum 0.8 mm zinc sheet recommended. Maximum 12 m bay with 500 mm wide 0.8 mm zinc standard bay length 3 m

Double standing seam system

Minimum 0.7 mm zinc sheet recommended. Maximum 10 m bay with 500 mm wide 0.7 mm zinc standard bay length < 6 m

Interlocking tiles

Standard sizes (a)   square 450, 280, and 200 mm
rhombus 280, 250, and 200 mm

Fig. 5.15 Zinc roofing and interlocking tiles

Process of metallic corrosion

Corrosion is an electro-chemical process, which can only occur in the presence of an electrolyte, that is, moisture containing some dissolved salts. The process may be understood by considering the action of a simple Daniell cell as shown in Fig. 5.16.

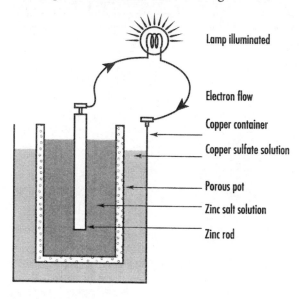

Fig. 5.16 Daniell cell

When the cell operates, two key processes occur. At the anode, the zinc gradually dissolves, generating zinc ions in solution and electrons which flow along the wire and light up the lamp as they move through its filament. At the copper cathode, the electrons are received at the surface of the metal and combine with copper ions in solution to plate out new shiny metal on the inside of the copper container.

Anode

$$Zn \longrightarrow Zn^{++} + 2e^-$$
zinc   zinc ions   electrons

Cathode

$$Cu^{++} + 2e^- \longrightarrow Cu$$
copper ions   electrons   copper

An equivalent process takes place in the dry Leclanché cell – the standard torch battery (Fig. 5.17). However, in this case the central carbon rod replaces the copper and the liquid is replaced by an aqueous paste. The anode process is the same as in the Daniell cell with the gradual dissolution of the zinc container.

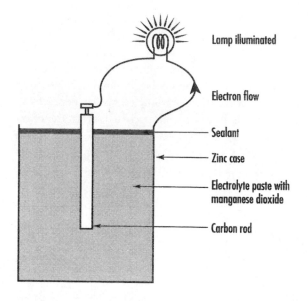

Fig. 5.17 Dry Leclanché cell

Anode

$$Zn \longrightarrow Zn^{++} + 2e^-$$
zinc   zinc ions   electrons

At the cathode the carbon rod is surrounded by manganese dioxide, which oxidises the hydrogen gas that would otherwise have been produced there by the reaction between water and the electrons.

Cathode

$$H_2O + O + 2e^- \longrightarrow 2OH^-$$
water   oxygen   electrons   hydroxyl ions
(from manganese dioxide)

This sequence is similar to that seen in the corrosion of iron (Fig. 5.18). In this case the presence of both an electrolyte and oxygen are necessary for corrosion to occur.

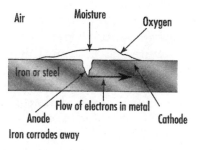

Fig. 5.18 Corrosion of iron

Anode

$$Fe \longrightarrow Fe^{++} + 2e^-$$

iron   iron ions   electrons

Cathode

$$2H_2O + O_2 + 4e^- \longrightarrow 4OH^-$$

water oxygen electrons hydroxyl ions
(from the air)

Rust formation

$$Fe^{++} + 2OH^- \longrightarrow Fe(OH)_2 \longrightarrow Fe_2O_3.H_2O$$

iron ions hydroxyl ions iron hydroxide rust

Overall summary

$$4Fe + 3O_2 + 2H_2O \longrightarrow 2Fe_2O_3.H_2O$$

iron   oxygen   water   rust

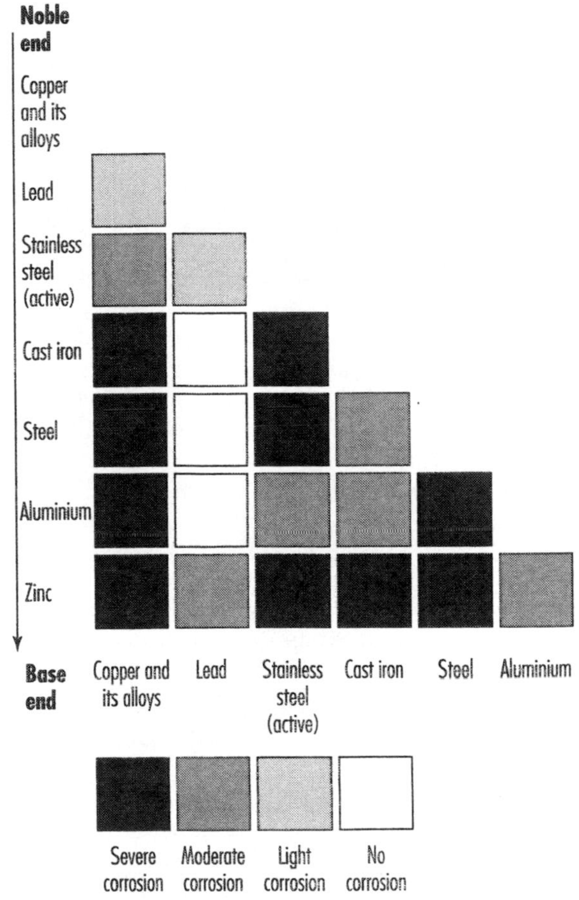

Indication of typical corrosion rates between pairs of metals in contact in the presence of moisture. The metal lower down the series copper (noble end) to zinc (base end) corrodes. The rate of corrosion will be generally increased within more aggressive environments.

Fig. 5.19 Bimetallic corrosion between pairs of metals in building applications

FACTORS AFFECTING THE RATE OF CORROSION

The key factors which accelerate the rate of corrosion are the presence of two dissimilar metals in mutual contact and the degree of pollution within any moisture surrounding the metals. If the more base metal is small in quantity compared to the more noble metal, then rapid corrosion of the more base metal will occur. Figure 5.19 shows which pairs of metals commonly used in construction should not generally be allowed into contact. Within a single metal minor surface variations, such as crystal grain boundaries, the effects of cold working or welding, the presence of impurities or alloying components within the metal, variable cleanliness or access to aerial oxygen, may all cause accelerated corrosion.

References

FURTHER READING

Aluminium Federation. 1993: *The properties of aluminium and its alloys,* 9th ed. Birmingham: Aluminium Federation.

ASFPCM 1992: *Fire protection for structural steel in buildings,* 2nd ed. Aldershot: Association of Specialist Fire Protection Contractors and Manufacturers Ltd.

Blanc, A., McEvoy, M. and Plank, R. (ed.) 1993: *Architecture and construction in steel.* London: E. & F.N. Spon.

British Iron and Steel Producers Association 1994: *Iron and steel specifications,* 8th ed. London: BISPA.

British Steel Corporation 1992: *Roof and cladding in steel.* London: British Steel plc.

British Steel. 1995: *Steel or concrete – The economics of commercial buildings.* Publication No. SPC39 3 2/95. London: British Steel plc.

Copper Development Association. 1986: *Copper and copper alloys: Composition and properties.* TN10. Potters Bar: CDA.

Copper Development Association. 1985: *Copper in roofing: Design and installation.* TN32. Potters Bar: CDA.

Eggen, A.P. and Sandaker, B.N. 1995: *Steel, structure and architecture: A survey of the material and its applications.* New York: Whitney Library of Design.

Lane, J. 1992: *Aluminium in building.* Aldershot: Ashgate.

Lead Sheet Association. 1990: *The lead sheet manual: A guide to good practice* vol. 1: *Lead sheet flashings.* London: Lead Sheet Association.

Lead Sheet Association. 1992: *The lead sheet manual: A guide to good practice* vol. 2: *Lead sheet roofing and cladding.* Tunbridge Wells: Lead Sheet Association.

Llewellyn, D.T. 1994: *Steels, metallurgy and applications.* Oxford: Butterworth-Heinemann.

Polmear, I.J. 1989: *Light alloys: Metallurgy of the light metals,* 2nd ed. Metallurgy and Materials Science Series. London: Edward Arnold.

National Federation of Roofing Contractors. 1991: *Profiled sheet metal and cladding – A guide to good practice,* 2nd ed. London: National Federation of Roofing Contractors Ltd.

Rheinzink. 1988: *Architecture with Rheinzink: Roofing and wall cladding.* Datteln: Rheinzink.

Steel Construction Institute. 1993: *Concise Eurocode 3 for the design of steel buildings in the United Kingdom.* Ascot: The Steel Construction Institute.

Steel Construction Institute. 1993: *Steelwork design guide to Eurocode 3,* Part 1.1: *Introducing Eurocode 3.* Ascot: The Steel Construction Institute.

Zinc Development Association. *Zinc in building design.* London: Zinc Development Association.

STANDARDS

BS 4. Structural steel sections:
  Part 1: 1993. Specification for hot-rolled sections.
BS 405: 1987. Specification for uncoated expanded metal carbon steel sheets for general purposes.
BS 416. Discharge and ventilating pipes and fittings sand-cast or spun in cast-iron:
  Part 1: 1990. Specification for spigot and socket systems.
  Part 2: 1990. Specification for socketless systems.
BS 417. Galvanised mild steel cisterns and covers, tanks and cylinders:
  Part 2: 1987. Metric units.
BS 437: 1978. Specification for cast iron spigot and socket drain pipes and fittings.
BS 449. Specification for the use of structural steel in building:
  Part 2: 1969. Metric units.
BS 460: 1964. Cast-iron rainwater goods.
BS 493: 1970. Airbricks and gratings for wall ventilation.
BS 699: 1984. Specification for copper direct cylinders for domestic purposes.
BS 729: 1971. Hot dip galvanized coatings on iron and steel articles.
BS 779: 1976. Cast iron boilers for central heating and indirect water supply (rated output 44 kW and above).
BS 864. Capillary and compression tube fittings of copper and copper alloy:
  Part 2: 1983. Specification for capillary and compression fittings for copper tubes.
BS 1091: 1963. Pressed steel gutters, rainwater pipes, fittings and accessories.
BS 1161: 1977. Specification for aluminium alloy sections for structural purposes.

BS 1178: 1982. Specification for milled lead sheet for building purposes.
BS 1189: 1986. Specification for baths made from porcelain enamelled cast iron.
BS 1202. Nails:
  Part 1: 1974. Steel nails.
  Part 2: 1974. Copper nails.
  Part 3: 1974. Aluminium nails.
BS 1210: 1963. Wood screws.
BS 1211: 1958. Centrifugally cast (spun) iron pressure pipes for water, gas and sewage.
BS 1243: 1978. Specification for metal ties for cavity wall construction.
BS 1245: 1975. Metal door frames (steel).
BS 1329: 1974. Metal hand rinse basins.
BS 1390: 1990. Baths made from vitreous enamelled sheet steel.
BS 1431: 1960. Wrought copper and wrought zinc rainwater goods.
BS 1449. Steel plate, sheet and strip:
  Part 1: 1991. Specification for carbon manganese plate, sheet and strip.
  Part 2: 1983. Specification for stainless and heat-resisting steel plate, sheet and strip.
BS 1452: 1990. Specification for flake graphite cast iron.
BS 1470: 1987. Specification for wrought aluminium and aluminium alloys for general engineering purposes: plate sheet and strip.
BS 1554: 1990. Stainless and heat-resisting steel round wire.
BS 1566. Copper indirect cylinders for domestic purposes:
  Part 1: 1984. Specification for double feed indirect cylinders.
  Part 2: 1984. Specification for single feed indirect cylinders.
BS 1615: 1987. Method for specifying anodic oxidation coatings on aluminium and its alloys.
BS 1706: 1990 . Method for specifying electroplated coatings of zinc and cadmium on iron and steel.
BS 2870: 1980. Rolled copper and copper alloys. Sheet, strip and foil.
BS 2874: 1986. Specification for copper and copper alloy rods and sections.
BS 2875: 1969. Copper and copper alloys. Plate.
BS 2994: 1976. Cold rolled steel sections.
BS 2997: 1958. Aluminium rainwater goods.
BS 3083: 1988. Specification for hot-dip zinc coated and hot-dip aluminium/zinc coated corrugated steel sheets for general purposes.
BS 3198: 1981. Specification for copper hot water storage combination units for domestic purposes.
BS 3830: 1973. Vitreous enamelled steel building components.

BS 3987: 1991. Anodic oxide coatings on wrought aluminium for external architectural applications.

BS 4127: 1994. Light gauge stainless steel tubes, primarily for water applications.

BS 4447: 1973. The performance of prestressing anchorages for post-tensioned construction.

BS 4449: 1988. Specification for carbon steel bars for the reinforcement of concrete.

BS 4513: 1969. Lead bricks for radiation shielding.

BS 4604. The use of high strength friction grip bolts in structural steelwork. Metric series:
> Part 1: 1970. General grade.
> Part 2: 1970. Higher grade (parallel shank).

BS 4622: 1970. Grey iron pipes and fittings.

BS 4842: 1984. Specification for liquid organic coatings for application to aluminium alloy extrusions, sheet and preformed sections for external architectural purposes.

BS 4848. Hot-rolled structural steel sections:
> Part 2: 1991. Specification for hot-finished hollow sections.
> Part 4: 1972. Equal and unequal angles.

BS 4868: 1972. Profiled aluminium sheet for building.

BS 4873: 1986. Specification for aluminium alloy windows.

BS 4921: 1988. Specification for sheradised coatings on iron and steel.

BS 5286: 1978. Specification for aluminium framed sliding glass doors.

BS 5427: 1976. Code of practice for performance and loading criteria for profiled sheeting in building.

BS 5493: 1977. Code of practice for protective coating of iron and steel structures against corrosion.

BS 5950. Structural use of steelwork in building:
> Part 1: 1990. Code of practice for design in simple and continuous construction: hot rolled sections.
> Part 2: 1992. Specification for materials, fabrication and erection: hot rolled sections.
> Part 3: 1990. Design in composite construction.
> Part 4: 1994. Code of practice for design of composite slabs with profiled steel sheeting.
> Part 5: 1987. Code of practice for design of cold formed sections.
> Part 7: 1992. Specification for materials and workmanship: cold formed sections.
> Part 8: 1990. Code of practice for fire resistant design.
> Part 9: 1994. Code of practice for stressed skin design.

BS 5977. Lintels:
> Part 1: 1981. Method for assessment of load.
> Part 2: 1983. Specification for prefabricated lintels.

BS 6362: 1990. Stainless steel tubes suitable for screwing in accordance with BS 21.

BS 6363: 1983. Specification for welded cold formed steel structural hollow sections.

BS 6496: 1984. Specification for powder organic coatings for application and stoving to aluminium alloy extrusions, sheet and preformed sections for external architectural purposes.

BS 6497: 1984. Specification for powder organic coatings for application and stoving to hot-dip galvanised hot-rolled steel sections and preformed steel sheet.

BS 6510: 1984. Specification for steel windows, sills, window boards and doors.

BS 6536: 1985. Specification for continuously hot-dip aluminium/silicon coated cold reduced carbon steel sheet and strip.

BS 6561: 1985. Specification for zinc alloy sheet and strip for building.

BS 6582: 1985. Specification for continuously hot-dip lead alloy (terne) coated cold reduced carbon steel flat rolled products.

BS 6681: 1986. Specification for malleable cast iron.

BS 6744: 1986. Specification for austenitic stainless steel bars for the reinforcement of concrete.

BS 6781: 1986. Specification for continuously organic coated steel flat products.

BS 6830: 1987. Specification for continuously hot-dip aluminium/zinc alloy coated cold rolled carbon steel flat products.

BS 7613: 1994. Hot rolled quenched and tempered weldable structural steel plates.

BS 7364: 1990. Galvanised steel studs and channels for stud and sheet partitions and linings using screw fixed gypsum wallboards.

BS 7668: 1994. Specification for weldable structural steels. Hot finished structural hollow sections in weather resistant steels.

BS 8118. Structural use of aluminium:
> Part 1: 1991. Code of practice for design.
> Part 2: 1991. Specification for materials, workmanship and protection.

BS 8202. Coatings for fire protection of building elements:
> Part 1: 1987. Code of practice for the selection and installation of sprayed mineral coatings.
> Part 2: 1992. Code of practice for the use of intumescent coating systems to metallic substrates for providing fire resistance.

BS EN 124: 1994. Gully tops and manholes – design requirements, type, testing, marking, quality control.

BS EN 485. Aluminium and aluminium alloys – sheet, strip and plate:
> Part 1: 1994. Technical conditions for inspection and delivery.
> Part 3: 1994. Tolerances on shape and dimensions for hot-rolled products.
> Part 4: 1994. Tolerances on shape and dimensions for

cold-rolled products.

BS EN 486: 1994. Aluminium and aluminium alloys – extrusion ingots – specifications.

BS EN 487: 1994. Aluminium and aluminium alloys – rolling ingots – specifications.

BS EN 545: 1995. Ductile iron pipes, fittings, accessories and their joints for water pipelines – requirements and test methods.

BS EN 573: 1995. Aluminium and aluminium alloys – chemical composition and form of wrought products.

BS EN 586. Aluminium and aluminium alloys – forgings:
Part 2: 1994. Mechanical properties and additional property requirements.

BS EN 598: 1995. Ductile iron pipes, fittings, accessories and their joints for sewerage applications – requirements and test methods.

BS EN 754: 1996. Aluminium and aluminium alloys – cold drawn rod/bar and tube.

BS EN 755: 1996. Aluminium and aluminium alloys – extruded rod/bar, tube and profile.

prEN 877: 1996. Cast iron pipes, fittings, accessories and their joints.

BS EN 969: 1996. Specification for ductile iron pipes, fittings, accessories and their joints for gas applications – requirements and test methods.

BS EN 1057: 1996. Copper and copper alloys. Seamless, round copper tubes for water and gas in sanitary and heating applications.

BS EN 1173: 1996. Copper and copper alloys – material condition or temper designation.

BS EN 1412: 1996. Copper and copper alloys. European numbering system.

BS EN 10025: 1993. Hot rolled products of non-alloy structural steels and their technical delivery conditions.

BS EN 10034: 1993. Structural steel I and H sections – tolerances on shape and dimensions.

BS EN 10051: 1993. Specification for continuously hot-rolled uncoated plate, sheet and strip of non-alloy and alloy steels – tolerances on dimensions and shape.

BS EN 10056. Specification for structural steel equal and unequal leg angles:
Part 2: 1993. Tolerances, shape and dimensions.

BS EN 10088. Stainless steels:
Part 1: 1995. List of stainless steels.
Part 2: 1995. Technical delivery conditions for sheet, plate and strip for general purposes.
Part 3: 1995. Technical delivery conditions for semi-finished products, bars, rods and sections for general purposes.

prEN 10095. Heat resisting steels and alloys.

BS EN 10113. Hot-rolled products in weldable fine grain structural steels:
Part 1: 1993. General delivery conditions.

Part 2: 1993. Delivery conditions for normalized/normalized rolled steels.
Part 3: 1993. Delivery conditions for thermo-mechanical rolled steels.

BS EN 10130: 1991. Specification for cold rolled low carbon steel flat products for cold forming: Technical delivery conditions.

BS EN 10131: 1991. Cold milled uncoated low carbon and high yield strength steel flat products for cold forming – Tolerances on dimensions and shape.

BS EN 10142: 1991. Specification for continuously hot-dip zinc coated low carbon steel sheet and strip for cold forming – Technical delivery conditions.

BS EN 10147: 1992. Continuously hot-dip zinc coated structural steel sheet and strip– Technical delivery conditions.

BS EN 10149. Specification for hot-rolled flat products made of high yield strength steels for cold forming:
Part 1: 1996. General delivery conditions.

BS EN 10152: 1994. Specification for electrolytically zinc coated cold rolled steel flat products: Technical delivery conditions.

BS EN 10155: 1993. Structural steels with improved atmospheric corrosion resistance: Technical delivery conditions.

BS EN 10210: Hot finished structural hollow sections of non-alloy and fine grain structural steels:
Part 1: 1994. Technical delivery conditions.
Part 2: 1996. Tolerances, dimensions and sectional properties.

prEN 10219: Cold formed structural hollow sections of non-alloy and fine grained structural steels:
Part 1: 1996. Technical delivery requirements.
Part 2: 1996. Tolerances, dimensions and sectional properties.

BS EN 10242: 1995. Threaded pipe fittings in malleable cast iron.

prEN 10250. Open die forgings for general purposes:
Part 5. Stainless steels.

BS EN 22263: 1994. Metallic and other inorganic coatings – thermal spraying – zinc, aluminium and their alloys.

BS EN ISO 7441: 1995. Corrosion of metals and alloys – determination of bimetallic corrosion in outdoor exposure corrosion tests.

CP 118: 1969. The structural use of aluminium.

CP 143. Sheet roof and wall coverings:
Part 1: 1958. Aluminium, corrugated and troughed.
Part 5: 1964. Zinc.
Part 10: 1973. Galvanised corrugated steel. Metric units.
Part 11: 1970. Lead. Metric units.
Part 12: 1970. Copper. Metric units.

Part 15: 1973. Aluminium. Metric units.

CP 1021: 1973. Cathodic protection.

CP 3012: 1972. Cleaning and preparation of metal surfaces.

DD ENV: 1993. Eurocode 3: Design of steel structures:

Part 1.1: 1992. General rules and rules for building.

Part 1.2: 1995. General rules – Structural fire design.

DD ENV: 1994. Eurocode 4: Design of composite steel and concrete structures:

Part 1.1: 1994. General rules and rules for building.

BUILDING RESEARCH ESTABLISHMENT PUBLICATIONS

BRE Digests

BRE Digest 83: 1980. Plumbing with stainless steel.

BRE Digest 301: 1985. Corrosion of metals by wood.

BRE Digest 305: 1986. Zinc-coated steel.

BRE Digest 317: 1990. Fire resistant steel structures: free-standing blockwork-filled columns and stanchions.

BRE Digest 349:1990. Stainless steel as a building material.

BRE Report

BR 142: 1989. The use of light-gauge cold-formed steelwork in construction: developments in research and design.

TRADE ASSOCIATIONS

Aluminium Federation Ltd., Broadway House, Calthorpe Road, Five Ways, Birmingham, W. Midlands B15 1TN (0121 456 1103).

Aluminium Finishing Association, Broadway House, Calthorpe Road, Five Ways, Birmingham, W. Midlands B15 1TN (0121 456 1103).

Aluminium Rolled Products Manufacturers Association, Broadway House, Calthorpe Road, Five Ways, Birmingham, W. Midlands B15 1TN (0121 456 1103).

Association of Specialist Fire Protection Contractors and Manufacturers, Association House, 235 Ash Road, Aldershot, Hants. GU12 4DD (01252 21322).

British Constructional Steelwork Association Ltd., 4 Whitehall Court, Westminster, London SW1A 2ES, (0171 839 8566).

British Iron and Steel Producers Association, 5 Cromwell Road, London SW7 2HX (0171 581 0231).

British Non-Ferrous Metals Federation, 10 Greenfield Crescent, Edgbaston, Birmingham, W. Midlands B15 3AU (0121 456 3322).

British Stainless Steel Association, 8th Floor, Bridge House, Smallbrook, Queensway, Birmingham, W. Midlands B5 4JP (0121 643 3377).

British Steel Structural Advisory Service, Steel House, Redcar, Cleveland TS10 5QW (01642 474242).

Cast Iron Drainage Association, Custard Factory, 1–103 Gibb Street, Birmingham, W. Midlands B9 4BR (0121 693 9909).

Cold Rolled Sections Association, Centre City Tower, 7 Hill Street, Birmingham, W. Midlands B5 4UU (0121 643 5494).

Copper Development Association, Orchard House, Mutton Lane, Potters Bar, Herts. EN6 3AP (01707 650711).

Council for Aluminium in Building, 11 Cleeve Cloud Lane, Prestbury, Cheltenham, Glos. GL52 5SE (01242 677459).

Lead Sheet Association, St. John's Road, Tunbridge Wells, Kent TN4 9XA (01892 513351).

Metal Cladding and Roofing Manufacturers Association, 18 Mere Farm Road, Noctorum, Birkenhead, Merseyside L43 9TT (0151 652 3846).

Metal Finishing Association, Federation House, 10 Vyse Street, Birmingham, W. Midlands B18 6LT (0121 236 2657).

Metal Roof Deck Association, Fields House, Gower Road, Haywards Heath, West Sussex RH16 4PL (01444 440027).

Stainless Steel Advisory Centre, PO Box 161, Shepcote Lane, Sheffield, S. Yorks. S9 1TR (0114 244 0060).

Steel Construction Institute, Silwood Park, Ascot, Berks. SL5 7QN (01344 23345).

Zinc Development Association, 42 Weymouth Street, London W1N 3LQ (0171 499 6636).

6

BITUMEN AND FLAT ROOFING MATERIALS

Introduction

The flat roofing materials, which form an impermeable water barrier, include built-up bitumen felt systems, mastic asphalt, single-ply plastic membranes and liquid coatings. All require continuous support on an appropriate roof decking system. Green roofs are considered as an extension of the standard roofing systems. Metal roofing systems are described in Chapter 5.

Cold, warm and inverted roofs

COLD ROOFS

In cold roof construction, the weatherproof layer is applied directly onto the roof decking, usually particleboard or plywood, and this is directly supported by the roof structure, frequently timber joists (Fig. 6.1). Thermal insulation is laid over the gypsum plasterboard ceiling, leaving cold void spaces between the structural timbers or steel. In this form of roof construction, there is a significant risk of condensation forming on the underside of the decking and this may cause deterioration of the structure. Precautions must be taken to ensure adequate ventilation of the cold voids, and the underside of the deck must not cool below the dew point when the external temperature is −5°C. Any vapour check under the insulation layer is vulnerable to leakage around electrical service cables. In remedial work on cold roofs, if adequate ventilation cannot be

achieved, then conversion to a warm or inverted roof system may be advantageous.

WARM ROOFS

In warm roof construction the thermal insulation is laid between the roof deck and the weatherproof covering (Fig. 6.1). This ensures that the roof deck and its supporting structure are insulated from extremes of temperature, thus limiting excessive thermal movement which may cause damage. As the insulating material is directly under the waterproof layer, it must be sufficiently strong to support any foot traffic associated with maintenance of the roof. The waterproof and insulation layers will require mechanical fixing or ballasting to prevent detachment in strong winds. Surface condensation on the underside of a roof deck within warm roof construction would normally indicate insufficient thermal insulation.

INVERTED ROOFS

In inverted roof construction, both the structural deck and the weatherproof membrane are protected by externally applied insulation (Fig. 6.1). This ensures that the complete roof system is insulated from extremes of hot and cold, and also from damage by solar radiation and maintenance traffic. The insulation layer is usually either ballasted with gravel or fully protected with paving slabs. Disadvantages of inverted roof construction are the greater deadweight, and the difficulty in locating leaks under the insulation layer.

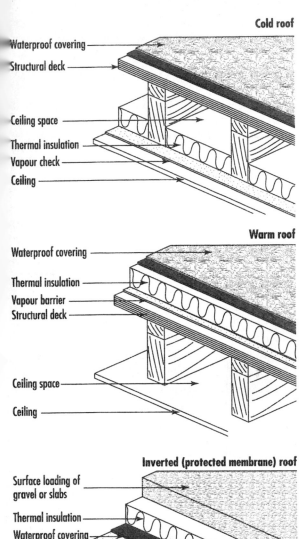

Cold roof

Waterproof covering

Structural deck

Ceiling space

Thermal insulation

Vapour check

Ceiling

Warm roof

Waterproof covering

Thermal insulation

Vapour barrier

Structural deck

Ceiling space

Ceiling

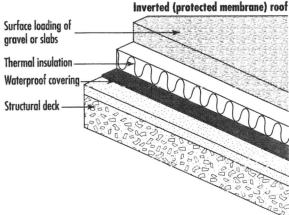

Inverted (protected membrane) roof

Surface loading of gravel or slabs

Thermal insulation

Waterproof covering

Structural deck

Fig. 6.1 Cold, warm and inverted roofs

Built-up roofing

Built-up roofing consists of two or more layers of bitumen felt bonded together with hot bitumen. Bitumen is the residual material produced after the removal by distillation of all volatile products from crude oil. The properties of bitumen are modified by controlled oxidation, which produces a more rubbery material suitable for roofing work. In the manufacture of bitumen felts, a continuous base layer of glass fibre or bitumen-saturated polyester is passed through molten oxidised bitumen containing inert filler; the material is then rolled to the required thickness. The bitumen felt is coated with sand to prevent adhesion within the roll or with mineral chippings to produce the required finish. A range of thicknesses is available and for ease of recognition the classes relating to the base fibre layer are colour-coded along one edge of the rolls.

TYPES OF ROOFING FELT

Roofing felts are classified by BS 747: 1994 according to their base fibre and primary function. Classes are subdivided into types according to their intended layer within a built-up roofing system and any applied surface finish. Only Class 3 and Class 5 felts are considered appropriate for built-up roofing systems (Table 6.1). Class 4 felts are used as underlay for mastic asphalt roofing and Class 1F felts based on natural organic fibres are used as underslating felts, although these are being superseded by reinforced materials such as polyester, which are tear-resistant and more durable. Where the risk of condensation is high, sarking felts which are waterproof but vapour permeable may be appropriate.

Table 6.1 Roofing felts to BS 474: 1994

Class	Base	Type	Use
Class 1	fibre base	Type 1F	underslating felt
Class 3	glass-fibre base	Type 3B	fine granule surface
		Type 3E	mineral surface
		Type 3G	venting base layer
Class 4	sheathing felt	Type 4A	underlay to mastic asphalt
Class 5	polyester base	Type 5B	fine granule surface
		Type 5E	mineral surface
		Type 5U	fine granule underlayer felt

(Class 1 felts with organic fibre bases are being phased out of use in built-up felt roofing systems. Class 2 felts with asbestos-fibre bases are no longer manufactured.)

Built-up roofing systems using the Class 3 glass-fibre based products are standard, but the Class 5 polyester-based products have greater strength and durability at a higher initial cost. A typical three-layer system is illustrated in Fig. 6.2. All oxidised bitumen felts, when exposed to ultraviolet light and ozone, gradually age harden and become less resistant to fatigue failure.

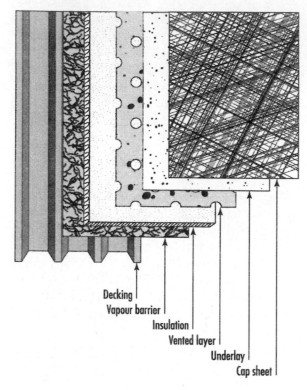

Decking
Vapour barrier
Insulation
Vented layer
Underlay
Cap sheet

Fig. 6.2 Typical three-layer built-up roofing system

ROOFING SYSTEMS

Built-up roofing felt may be applied to roofs constructed from precast or *in situ* concrete, cement screeds, plywood (exterior WBP grade), timber (19 mm tongued and grooved, with preservative treatment and conditioning), particleboard (except in conditions of high humidity where only the cement-bonded product is appropriate), wood wool slabs and profile metal decking (galvanised steel or aluminium). In warm roof applications a vapour check is applied over the decking. Insulation materials include cork, mineral wool, perlite, foamed glass, rigid polyurethane foam (PUR) and high-density extruded polystyrene. Most manufacturers are now able to supply CFC-free insulation products. The heat-sensitive expanded plastics are frequently supplied pre-bonded to a cork, perlite or fibreboard layer to receive the *pour and roll* hot bitumen or

torch-on felt systems. Where suitable falls are not incorporated into the roof structure, the insulation can be supplied ready cut-to-falls. A minimum in-service fall of 1 in 80 is required to prevent *ponding*; this may need to be designed at 1 in 40 to allow for settlement. On sloping roofs the first layer is applied down the slope, but on flat roofs (less than 10°) the direction of the first layer need not relate to the falls. The first layer is either partly or fully bonded depending upon the substrate. Perforated felt is frequently laid loose as the first layer, and becomes spot bonded as the hot bitumen for the second layer is applied. On timber the first layer is nailed. Partial bonding permits some thermal movement between the felt system and the decking, and also allows for the escape of any water vapour trapped in the decking material. The use of proprietary breather vents on large roofs allows the escape of this entrapped air from the roof structure by migration under the partially bonded layer. Side laps of 50 mm and end laps of typically 100 mm should all be staggered between layers. On sloping roofs the first layer should be nailed at the top of each sheet at 50 mm centres and higher melting point 115/15 bitumen should be used for bonding the subsequent layers to prevent slippage. Protection from the effects of ultraviolet light is afforded either by the factory applied mineral surface finish to the *cap* sheet, the application of reflective paint, or on flat roofs typically by a 12 mm layer of reflective white spar stone chippings.

POLYMER-MODIFIED BITUMEN FELTS

High-performance bitumen felts based on polyester bases for toughness and polymer-modified bitumen coatings for increased flexibility, strength and fatigue resistance offer considerably enhanced durability over the standard oxidised bitumen felts. The two types are based on styrene butadiene styrene (SBS) and atactic polypropylene (APP) modified bitumen.

SBS high-performance felts

SBS polymer-modified bitumen felts have greater elasticity than standard oxidised bitumen felts. They are laid either by the traditional pour and roll technique which is used for standard bitumen felts or by torching-on (Fig. 6.3). In the pour and roll process, bonding bitumen is heated to a temperature of between 200 and 250°C and poured in front of the felt as it is unrolled, giving continuous adhesion between the layers. In the torching-on process, as the felt is unrolled the backing is heated to the molten state with propane burners.

APP high-performance felts

APP polymer-modified bitumen contains typically 25% atactic polypropylene in bitumen with some inert filler. The product is more durable than oxidised bitumen and has enhanced high-temperature resistance and low-temperature flexibility. Felts are manufactured with a polyester core, some additionally with a glass-fibre reinforced weathering surface. The APP polymer-modified bitumen felts are bonded by torching the heat-sensitive backing, as the temperature of hot-poured bitumen is too low to form a satisfactory bond.

Hot bitumen bonding roofing felt

Torching-on high-performance felts

Fig. 6.3 Laying built-up roofing felts with poured hot bitumen and by torching-on

METAL-FACED ROOFING FELTS

Metal-faced high-performance SBS felts give visual quality and enhanced durability compared with standard mineral surfaced built-up felt roofing systems. They are available in copper, aluminium and stainless steel, each with a small squared pattern of indentations (Fig. 6.4), which allows for thermal movement between the bonded felt and metal finish. The various metals weather similarly to the traditional sheet metal roofing systems; thus copper, subject to the local environment, will produce a green patina. The metal foil thickness is typically 0.08 mm for aluminium and copper or 0.05 mm for stainless steel.

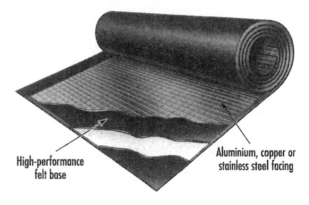

High-performance felt base

Aluminium, copper or stainless steel facing

Fig. 6.4 Metal-faced roofing felts

INVERTED ROOFS

In an inverted roof the built-up felt waterproofing membrane is laid directly onto the roof deck. Non-absorbent insulation, such as extruded polystyrene, is laid onto the membrane, which is then covered with a filter sheet to prevent the ingress of excessive organic material. River washed ballast or pavings on supports protect the system from mechanical and wind damage. Inverted roofs have the advantage that the waterproof membrane is protected from thermal stress by the insulating layer. This in turn is protected from damage by the paving or ballast finish. High-performance built-up felt systems are suitable for inverted roofs.

Mastic asphalt

TYPES OF MASTIC ASPHALT

Mastic asphalt is a blended bitumen-based product. It is manufactured either from the bitumen produced by the distillation of crude oil, or from lake asphalt, a naturally occurring blend of asphalt containing 36% by weight of finely divided clay, mainly imported from Trinidad. The bitumen is blended with limestone powder and fine limestone aggregate to produce the standard roofing types specified in BS 6925: 1988 (Table 6.2).

Table 6.2 Mastic asphalt grades to BS 6925: 1988

Type	Composition
BS 988B	100% bitumen
BS 988T25	75% bitumen, 25% lake asphalt
BS 988T50	50% bitumen, 50% lake asphalt
Specified by manufacturers	polymer-modified grades

The effect of the finely divided clay particles within lake asphalt type BS 988T confers better laying characteristics and enhanced thermal properties; these are advantageous when the material is to be exposed to wide temperature changes, particularly in warm roof construction systems.

Mastic asphalt is usually delivered as blocks, for melting on site prior to laying, although hot molten asphalt is occasionally supplied for larger contracts. Laid mastic asphalt is brittle when cold but softens in hot, sunny weather. The hardness is increased by the re-melting process, and also by the addition of further limestone aggregate. Polymer-modified mastic asphalts, usually containing styrene butadiene styrene block copolymers, are more durable and have enhanced flexibility and extensibility at low temperatures, allowing for greater building movements and better resistance to thermal shock. Where mastic asphalt roofs are subjected to foot or vehicle access, then paving-grade mastic asphalt (BS 1447: 1988) should be applied as a wearing layer over the standard roofing-grade material.

ROOFING SYSTEMS

Mastic asphalt may be laid over a wide variety of flat or pitched roof decking systems, either as warm or cold roof constructions although the latter is generally not recommended owing to condensation risks. As mastic asphalt is a brittle material it requires continuous firm support. Appropriate decks are concrete (*in situ* or precast), plywood (exterior WPB grade), particleboard, wood wool slabs and profiled metal sheeting. A typical concrete warm roof system is illustrated in Fig. 6.5.

In dense concrete construction, a sand and cement screed is laid to falls over the *in situ* slab. The falls should be designed such that, even with inevitable variations on site, they are never less than 1 in 80, as this is essential to ensure the immediate removal of the surface water and to prevent ponding. Plywood, profiled metal and other decking systems would be similarly laid to falls. A layer of bitumen-bonded Type 3B glass-fibre felt is applied over the structure to act as a vapour check.

Insulation

Thermal insulation, to provide the necessary roof U-value, is bonded with hot bitumen. A wide variety of insulation boards or blocks including cork, glass fibre, mineral wool, fibreboard, perlite, foamed glass, high-density extruded polystyrene and polyisocyanurate are suitable, although where insufficient rigidity is afforded by the insulation material, or if it would be affected by heat during application of the hot asphalt, it must be overlaid with firm heat-resistant boards to prevent damage during maintenance or construction. Where falls are not provided by the structure, the insulation may be set appropriately, provided that the thinnest section gives the required thermal properties. A separating layer of loose-laid geotextile material or Type 4A sheathing felt (BS 747: 1994) is then applied to allow differential thermal movement between the decking system and the mastic asphalt waterproof finish.

Mastic asphalt application

Mastic asphalt is laid to 20 mm in two layers on roofs up to 30° and to 20 mm in three layers on slopes greater than 30°. Upstands of 150 mm are required to masonry, rooflights, pipes, etc. where they penetrate the roof membrane. Where adhesion

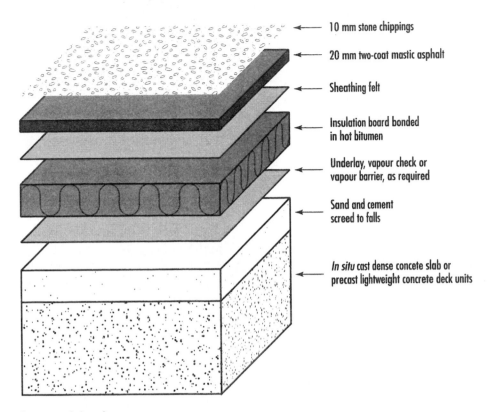

10 mm stone chippings

20 mm two-coat mastic asphalt

Sheathing felt

Insulation board bonded in hot bitumen

Underlay, vapour check or vapour barrier, as required

Sand and cement screed to falls

In situ cast dense concete slab or precast lightweight concrete deck units

Fig. 6.5 Typical mastic asphalt roofing system

on vertical surfaces is insufficient, expanded metal lathing should be used to support the mastic asphalt. An apron flashing should protect the top of the upstand. A layer of sand is rubbed into the top of the final layer while it is hot to break up the skin of bitumen-rich material which forms at the worked surface.

Surface protection

Mastic asphalt gradually hardens over a period of a few years and should be protected from softening under bright sunlight by the application of surface protection. Reflective paint coatings – for example, titanium oxide in polyurethane resin or aluminium pigmented bitumen – are effective until they become dirty, but for vertical surfaces they are the only appropriate measure. Reflective coatings are available in a range of colours giving differing levels of solar reflectivity. For horizontal surfaces and pitches up to 10°, a layer of 10 mm–14 mm white stone chippings will give better protection not only from sunlight but also from ultraviolet light, which gradually degrades bitumen products. Additionally, a layer of stone will

act to reduce the risk of thermal shock during very cold periods. Where traffic is anticipated, the mastic asphalt should be protected with glass-fibre reinforced cement (GRC) tiles or concrete pavings.

INVERTED ROOFS

Mastic asphalt forms a suitable waterproof membrane for externally insulated or inverted roofs. The application of the insulating layer over the mastic asphalt has the advantage that it protects the waterproof layer from thermal shock, impact damage and degradation by ultraviolet light. The insulation, usually extruded polystyrene boards, is held down either by gravel or precast concrete paving slabs.

Single-ply roofing systems

Single-ply roofing systems consist of a continuous membrane usually between 1 and 3 mm thick, covering any form of flat or pitched roof (Fig. 6.6). As waterproofing is reliant on the single membrane, a high quality of workmanship is required and this is normally provided by a specialist installer. In refurbishment work where the substrate may be rough, a polyester fleece may be used to prevent mechanical damage to the membrane from below. Life expectancies are typically quoted as 25 years. The wide range of membrane materials used may generally be categorised into thermoplastic, elastomeric and modified bitumen products. In many cases the single-layer membrane is itself a laminate, incorporating either glass fibre or polyester to improve strength and fatigue resistance or dimensional stability respectively. Both thermoplastic and elastomeric products are resistant to ageing under the severe conditions of exposure on roofs. Fixings offered by the proprietary systems include fully bonded, partially bonded, mechanically fixed and loose laid with either ballast or concrete slabs. Joints are lapped and either heat or solvent welded, usually with THF (tetrahydrofuran). A final seal of the plastic in solvent may be applied to the joint edge after the lap joint has been checked

for leaks. Most manufacturers provide a range of purpose-made accessories such as preformed corners, rainwater outlet sleeves and fixings for lightning protection.

THERMOPLASTIC SYSTEMS

Thermoplastic systems, made from non-cross-linked plastics, can be joined by solvent or heat welding. They generally exhibit good weathering properties and chemical resistance. The dominant thermoplastic systems are based on plasticised PVC (polyvinyl chloride), which is normally available in a range of colours. Certain PVC products contain up to 35% by weight of plasticisers, which can migrate to adjacent materials, leaving the membrane less flexible and causing incompatibility with extruded polystyrene insulation or bitumen products. Products manufactured from VET (vinyl ethylene terpolymer, a blend of 35% ethyl vinyl acetate and 65% PVC with only 4% plasticiser added as lubricant) are more

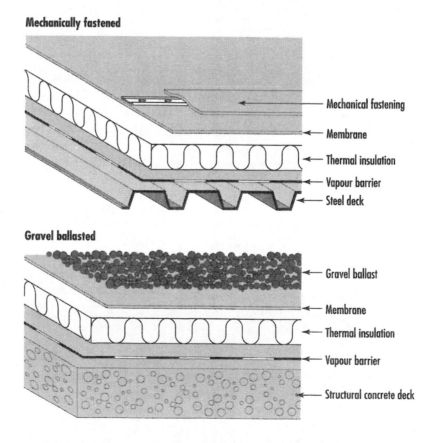

Fig. 6.6 Typical single-ply roofing systems, mechanically fastened and gravel ballasted

compatible with bitumen and polystyrene-based insulation products. Other products include CPE (chlorinated polyethylene), which has enhanced chemical resistant properties, CSPE (chlorosulfonated polyethylene), which is highly weather-resistant, and PIB (polyisobutylene), a relatively soft material which is easily joined. FPA (flexible polypropylene alloy) membranes, based on an alloy of EPR (ethylene propylene rubber) and polypropylene, combine the temperature, chemical resistance and weldability of PVC and the flexibility of the elastomeric single-ply systems.

ELASTOMERIC SYSTEMS

Elastomeric systems are dominated by EPDM (ethylene propylene diene monomer), which is a cross-linked or cured polymer. It is characterised by high elongation and good weathering resistance to ultraviolet light and ozone. The standard material is black or grey in colour but white is also available. Most products are seamed with adhesives or applied tapes as EPDM cannot be softened by solvents or heat; however, EPDM laminated with thermoplastic faces can be heat welded on site.

MODIFIED-BITUMEN SYSTEMS

Most modified-bitumen systems are based on SBS (styrene butadiene styrene), APP (atactic polypropylene) or rubber-modified bitumen. Some products are now combining the durability of APP-modified bitumens with the enhanced flexibility of SBS-modified bitumen. Systems usually incorporate polyester and/or glass-fibre reinforcement for increased dimensional stability.

Liquid coatings

A range of bitumen-based and polymer-based materials are used in the production of liquid roof waterproofing membranes. While some products are installed in new work, most products are used for remedial action on failed existing flat roofs as an economic alternative to re-roofing (Fig. 6.7). They may be appropriate when the exact location of water ingress cannot be located or when re-roofing is not practicable owing to the disruption that it would

cause. It is essential that the nature of the existing roof is correctly determined so that an appropriate material can be applied; also, failures in the substrate must be identified and rectified. The surface of the existing material must be free of loose material and dust to ensure good adhesion with the liquid coating, which can be applied by brush, roller or airless spray. While achieving a uniform thickness is difficult, the systems have the advantage of being seamless. Without further protection, roofs should only be subjected to light maintenance pedestrian traffic. Installation should normally be carried out by specialist roofing contractors.

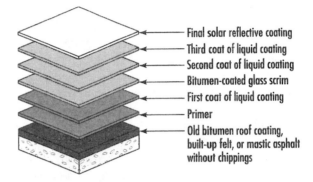

Final solar reflective coating
Third coat of liquid coating
Second coat of liquid coating
Bitumen-coated glass scrim
First coat of liquid coating
Primer
Old bitumen roof coating, built-up felt, or mastic asphalt without chippings

Fig. 6.7 Typical refurbishment of a built-up felt or asphalt roof with a liquid coating system

BITUMEN-BASED SYSTEMS

Most bitumen systems require a primer to seal the existing roof membrane and provide a base for the liquid coating. Two or three coats of bitumen solution or emulsion will normally be required for the waterproofing layer, and a solar reflective finish should be applied after the membrane has fully dried. A layer of glass-fibre reinforcement is usually incorporated during application of the waterproofing membrane to give dimensional stability. Two component systems mixed during the spraying process cure more rapidly, allowing a seamless 4 mm elastomeric coat to be built up in one layer on either flat or pitched roofs. Where the material is ultraviolet light resistant, a solar reflective layer may not be necessary.

POLYMER-BASED SYSTEMS

The range of polymers used for liquid roof finishes is extensive, including acrylic resins, polyurethanes, polyesters, silicones, rubber copolymers and modified bitumens. Some manufacturers offer a range of colours incorporating the necessary solar reflecting properties. Glass-fibre or polyester mat is used as reinforcement within the membrane layer, which is applied in a minimum of two coats. Additives to improve fire resistance such as antimony trioxide and bromine compounds may be incorporated into the formulations. Fire ratings of AA in respect of flame penetration and surface spread of flame (A highest, D lowest – Building Regulations Approved Document B4) can be achieved with some products.

Green roofs

Green roofs are flat or low pitched roofs which are landscaped over the waterproofing layer. The landscaping may include some hard surfaces and have access for leisure and recreational functions as well as the necessary routine maintenance. Green roofs offer not only increased life expectancy for the waterproofing layer by protecting it from physical damage, ultraviolet light and temperature extremes, but also increased usable space and considerable environmental noise, air quality and wildlife habitat benefits. Green roofs (Fig. 6.8) may be waterproofed using modified-bitumen high-performance built-up felts,

single-ply membrane systems or mastic asphalt. Under planting, T-grade mastic asphalt should be laid to 30 mm in three layers rather than the usual two layers to 20 mm thickness.

Green roofs are divided between the *intensive* and the *extensive* systems. Extensive green roofs are designed to be lighter in weight, relatively cheap, usually not open to general access and requiring the minimum of maintenance. Planting should be of drought-tolerant, wind- and frost-resistant species such as mosses and sedums. The complete system, with planting, soil, filter sheet, drainage, moisture retention layer and root barrier, will add between 60 and 200 kg/m² loading to the roof structure, which must be capable of this additional imposed load. Intensive green roofs are generally designed to accept recreational activity and to include the widest range of vegetation from grass to shrubs and semi-mature trees. Depths of soil are typically between 400 and 600 mm, which, together with the necessary 100 mm of lightweight drainage material or a thin proprietary drainage system, generate an additional imposed load of approximately 500 kg/m².

When considering the installation of a green roof the following design factors should be considered:

■ additional dead weight on the existing or proposed structural system;

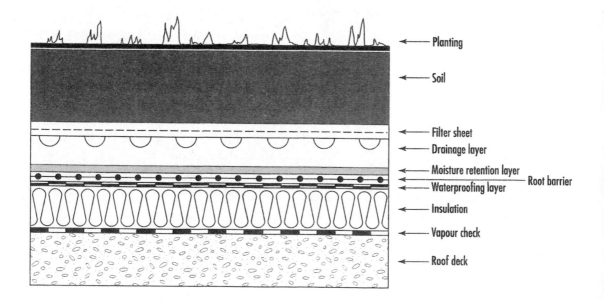

Fig. 6.8 Typical green roof system

- insulation and waterproofing system;
- root barrier (typically polythene or PVC);
- water-retaining layer to reduce quantity of watering required by irrigation or sprinkling;
- water drainage layer (typically gravel, lightweight aggregate or profiled plastic sheeting);
- filter sheet to prevent soil and organic material blocking the drainage system (typically polyester or polypropylene);
- vegetation layer of soil upgraded with organic and mineral additives;
- planting – the anticipated planting dictates the depth of the soil substrate.

Vegetation-free zones will be required for access and maintenance. Care must be taken to ensure that the roof membrane is not damaged by gardening implements.

References

FURTHER READING

British Flat Roofing Council. *Technical Information Sheets*. Nottingham: BFRC.

British Flat Roofing Council. 1993: *Flat roofing: Design and good practice.* London: CIRIA/BFRC.

British Flat Roofing Council. 1994: *The assessment of life-span characteristics and as-built performance of flat roofing systems.* Nottingham: BFRC.

Coates, D.T. 1993: *Roofs and roofing: Design and specification handbook.* Caithness: Whittles.

Mastic Asphalt Council and Employers Federation. 1980: *Roofing handbook.* Haywards Heath: MACEF.

Metal Cladding and Roofing Manufacturers Association. 1991–94: *Design guides – Technical papers 1–8.* Birkenhead: MCRMA.

National Federation of Roofing Contractors. 1989: *Liquid roof coatings*, 2nd ed. London: National Federation of Roofing Contractors.

Property Services Agency. 1987: *PSA technical guide to flat roofing.* 2nd ed. DOE PSA.

Ruberoid. 1995: *Flat roofing – A guide to good practice,* 3rd ed. London: Ruberoid.

STANDARDS

BS 476. Fire tests on building materials and structures.
  Part 3: 1975. External fire exposure roof test.
BS 594. Hot rolled asphalt for roads and other paved areas:

Part 1: 1992. Specification for constituent materials and asphalt mixtures.
BS 743: 1970. Materials for damp-proof courses.
BS 747: 1994. Specification for roofing felts.
BS 1446: 1973. Mastic asphalt (natural rock asphalt fine aggregate) for roads and footways.
BS 1447: 1988. Specification for mastic asphalt (limestone fine aggregate) for roads, footways and pavings in building.
BS 1521: 1972. Waterproof building papers.
BS 4016: 1972. Building papers (breather type).
BS 4841. Rigid polyurethane (PUR) and polyisocyanurate (PIR) foam for building applications:
  Part 3: 1994. Specification for two types of laminated board (roof boards) with auto-adhesively bonded reinforcing facings for use as roofboard thermal insulation for built-up roofs.
BS 6229: 1982. Code of practice for flat roofs with continuously supported coverings.
BS 6367: 1983. Code of practice for drainage of roofs and paved areas.
BS 6398: 1983. Specification for bitumen damp-proof courses for masonry.
BS 6925: 1988. Specification for mastic asphalt for building and engineering (limestone aggregate).
BS 8000. Workmanship on building sites:
  Part 4: 1989. Code of practice for water proofing.
BS 8204. Screeds, bases and in situ floorings:
  Part 5: 1994. Code of practice for mastic asphalt underlays and wearing surfaces.
BS 8217: 1994. Code of practice for built-up felt roofing.
CP 144. Roof coverings:
  Part 4: 1970. Mastic asphalt. Metric units.
CP 153. Windows and rooflights.
  Part 2: 1970. Durability and maintenance.

BUILDING RESEARCH ESTABLISHMENT PUBLICATIONS

BRE Digests

BRE Digest 144: 1972. Asphalt and built-up felt roofings: durability.
BRE Digest 180: 1986. Condensation in roofs.
BRE Digest 190: 1976. Heat losses from dwellings.
BRE Digest 311: 1986. Wind scour of gravel ballast on roofs.
BRE Digest 312: 1986. Flat roof design: the technical options.
BRE Digest 324: 1987. Flat roof design: thermal insulation.
BRE Digest 372: 1992. Flat roof design: waterproof membranes.
BRE Digest 419: 1996. Flat roof design: bituminous waterproof membranes.

BRE Information Papers

BRE IP 15/82. Inspection and maintenance of flat and low pitched timber roofs.

BRE IP 19/82. Considerations in the design of timber flat roofs.

BRE IP 2/89. Thermal performance of lightweight inverted warm deck flat roofs.

BRE IP 8/91. Mastic asphalt for flat roofs: testing for quality assurance.

BRE IP 7/95. Bituminous roofing membranes: performance in use.

BRE Report

BR 302: 1996 Roofs and roofing.

TRADE ASSOCIATIONS

Association of British Roofing Felt Manufacturers Ltd., 38 Bridlesmith Gate, Nottingham NG1 2GQ (0115 958 9209).

British Flat Roofing Council, 38 Bridlesmith Gate, Nottingham NG1 2GQ (0115 950 7733).

European Liquid Roofing Association, Fields House, Gower Road, Haywards Heath, West Sussex RH16 4PL (01444 417458).

Institute of Asphalt Technology, Unit 18, Central Trading Estate, Staines, Middx. TW18 4XE (01784 465387).

International Waterproofing Association, 38 Bridlesmith Gate, Nottingham NG1 2GQ (0115 950 4225).

Mastic Asphalt Council and Employers Federation, Lesley House, 6-8 Broadway, Bexleyheath, Kent DA6 7LE (0181 298 0414).

Metal Cladding and Roofing Manufacturers Association, 18 Mere Farm Road, Noctorum, Birkenhead, Merseyside L43 9TT (0151 652 3846).

National Federation of Roofing Contractors Ltd., 24 Weymouth Street, London W1N 3FA (0171 436 0387).

Single Ply Roofing Association, 38 Bridlesmith Gate, Nottingham NG1 2GQ (0115 950 7733).

Flat Roofing Contractors Advisory Board, Fields House, Gower Road, Haywards Heath, West Sussex RH16 4PL (01444 440027).

7

GLASS

Introduction

The term glass refers to materials, usually blends of metallic oxides, predominantly silica, which do not crystallise when cooled from the liquid to the solid state. It is the non-crystalline or amorphous structure of glass (Fig. 7.1) that gives rise to its transparency.

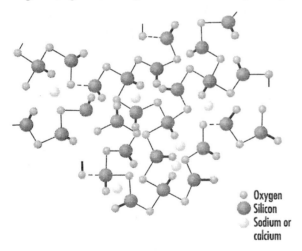

Oxygen
Silicon
Sodium or calcium

Fig. 7.1 Structure of glass (after Button D. and Pye B. (ed.) 1993. *Glass in building*. Butterworth Architecture)

Glass made from sand, lime and soda ash has been known in Egypt for 7000 years, although it probably originated in Assyria and Phoenicia. The earliest man-made glass was used to glaze stone beads and later to make glass beads (*circa* 2500 BC), but it was not until about 1500 BC that it was used to make hollow vessels.

For many centuries glass was worked by drawing the molten material from a furnace. The glass was then rolled out or pressed into appropriate moulds, and finally fashioned by cutting and grinding. Around 100 BC the technique of glass blowing evolved in Assyria, and the Romans developed this further by blowing glass into moulds. Medieval glass produced in the Rhineland contained potash from the burning of wood rather than soda ash. Together with an increase in lime content this gave rise to a less durable product, which has caused the subsequent deterioration of some church glass from that period.

The various colours within glass derived from the addition of metallic compounds to the melt. Blue was obtained by the addition of cobalt, while copper produced blue or red, and iron or chromium produced green. In the fifteenth century white opaque glass was produced by the addition of tin or arsenic, and by the seventeenth century ruby-red glass was made by the addition of gold chloride. Clear glass could only be obtained by using antimony or manganese as a decolouriser to remove the green colouration caused by iron impurities within the sand.

Manufacture

COMPOSITION

Modern glass is manufactured from sand (silica), soda ash (sodium carbonate) and limestone (calcium carbonate), with small additions of salt-cake (calcium sulfate) and dolomite (magnesian limestone). This gives a final composition of typically 70–74% silica, 12–16% sodium oxide, 5–12% calcium oxide, 2–5% magnesium oxide with small quantities of aluminium, iron and potassium oxides. The addition of 25% broken glass or *cullet* to the furnace mix accelerates the melting process and recycles the production waste. Most raw materials are available within the UK, although some dolomite is imported. The production process is relatively energy intensive at 15 000 kWh/m³ (cf. concrete – 625 kWh/m³), but the environmental pay-back arises from its appropriate use in energy-conscious design.

FORMING PROCESSES

Early methods

Early crown glass was formed by spinning a 4 kg cylindrical gob of molten glass on the end of a blow pipe. The solid glass was blown, flattened out and then transferred to a solid iron rod or *punty*. After reheating it was spun until it opened out into a 1.5 m diameter disc. The process involved considerable wastage including the bullion in the centre, which nowadays is the prized piece. An alternative process involved the blowing of a glass cylinder which was then split open and flattened out in a kiln. This process was used for the manufacture of the glass for the Crystal Palace in 1851.

Subsequently, in a major development, a circular metal bait was lowered into a pot of molten glass and withdrawn slowly, dragging up a cylindrical ribbon of glass 13 m high, the diameter of the cylinder being maintained with compressed air. The completed cylinder was then detached, opened up and flattened out to produce flat window glass.

It was only by the early twentieth century with the development of the Fourcault process in Belgium and the Colburn process in America that it became possible to produce flat glass directly. A straight bait was drawn vertically out of the molten glass to produce a ribbon of glass which was then drawn directly up a tower. In the Colburn process the ribbon of glass was turned horizontally through a series of rollers; finally, appropriate lengths were cut off. However, such drawn sheet glass suffered from manufacturing distortions. This problem was overcome by the production of plate glass, which involved horizontal casting and rolling, followed by grinding to remove distortions, and polishing to give a clear, transparent but expensive product. The process was ultimately fully automated into a production line in which the glass was simultaneously ground down on both faces. The plate glass manufacturing process is now obsolete, having been totally replaced by the *float process*, developed by Pilkington in 1959.

Float glass

A furnace produces a continuous supply of molten glass at a temperature of approximately 1100°C, which flows across the surface of a large shallow bath of molten tin contained within an atmosphere of hydrogen and nitrogen (this prevents oxidation of the surface of the molten metal) (Fig. 7.2). The glass ribbon moves across the molten metal, initially at a sufficiently high temperature for the irregularities on both surfaces to become evened out leaving a flat and parallel ribbon of glass. The temperature of the glass is gradually reduced as it moves forward until, at the end of the molten tin, it is sufficiently solid at 600°C not to be distorted when supported on rollers. Thickness is controlled by the speed at which the glass is drawn from the bath. Any residual stresses are removed as the glass passes through the 200 m annealing lehr or furnace, leaving a fire-polished material. The glass is washed and substandard material discarded. The computer controlled cutting, firstly across the ribbon, then the removal of the

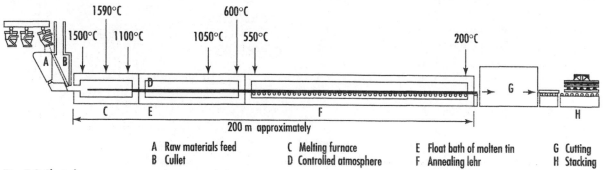

Fig. 7.2 Float glass process

edges, is followed by stacking, warehousing and dispatch. A typical float glass plant will manufacture 5000 tonnes of glass per week, operating continuously for several years.

Float glass for the construction industry is made within the thickness range 2–25 mm, although 0.5 mm is available for the electronics industry. The standard thicknesses are 3, 4, 5, 6, 8, 10 and 12 mm. Surface modified glasses, such as certain solar control glasses, are also produced within the float process, typically by the incorporation of metal ions into the glass through the application of electric fields across the molten tin bath. The recent development of an all-electric melting process offers better quality control and less environmental pollution than previously obtained from conventional oil or gas fired furnaces.

Non-sheet products

GLASS FIBRES

Continuous filament

Continuous glass fibres are manufactured by constantly feeding molten glass from a furnace into a forehearth fitted with 1600 accurately manufactured holes through which the glass is drawn at several thousand metres per second. The fibres (as small as 9 microns in diameter) pass over a size applicator and are gathered together as a bundle prior to being wound up on a collet. The material may then be used as rovings, chopped strand or woven strand mats for the production of glass-fibre reinforced materials such as GRP (glass-fibre reinforced polyester), GRC (glass-fibre reinforced cement), or GRG (glass-fibre reinforced gypsum) – see Chapter 11.

Glass wool

Glass wool is made by the Crown process, which is described in Chapter 13.

CAST GLASS

Glass may be cast and pressed into shape for glass blocks and extruded sections.

Profiled sections

Profiled trough sections in clear or coloured 6 or 7 mm cast glass are manufactured in sizes ranging

from 232 to 498 mm wide, 41 and 60 mm deep and up to 7 m long, with or without stainless steel longitudinal wires (Fig. 7.3). The system can be used horizontally or vertically, as single or double glazing, and as a roofing system spanning up to 3 m. A large radius curve is possible as well as the normal straight butt jointed system and the joints are sealed with one-part translucent silicone. The standard double-glazed system has a U-value of 2.8 W/m² K, but this can be enhanced to 1.8 W/m² K by the use of low-emissivity coated glass. Amber tinted glass is available for solar control. The double-glazed system produces a sound reduction within the 100–3200 Hz range of typically 40 dB.

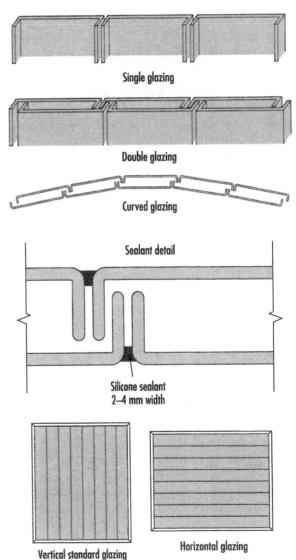

Fig. 7.3 Profiled glass sections

Feature glazed walls in glass blocks

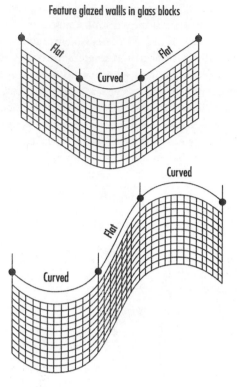

Fig. 7.4 Glass blocks

Glass blocks

Glass blocks for non-loadbearing walls and partitions are manufactured by joining together two hollow halves, and partially evacuating the space, giving a U-value of 2.5 W/m² K. The standard blocks (Fig. 7.4) are 115, 190, 240 and 300 mm square with thicknesses of 80 and 100 mm; rectangular blocks are also available. A variety of patterns including reeded, floral or crystal designs offer a range of light transmission and privacy. Blocks with solar reflective glass or incorporating white glass fibres offer additional solar control; colour may be added to the edge coating or the glass itself. Special blocks are also available to form corners and ends.

For exterior and fire-retarding applications natural or coloured mortar (2 parts Portland cement, 1 part lime, 8 parts sand) is used for the jointing. Walls may be straight or curved; in the latter case, the minimum radius is according to block size and manufacturer's specification. Vandal- and bullet-proof blocks are available for situations requiring higher security. For interior use, blocks may be laid with sealant rather than mortar.

Glass blocks jointed with mortar give a fire resistance of 30 or 60 minutes with respect to stability and integrity but not insulation, according to BS 476 Part 22: 1987. Sound reduction over the 100–3150 Hz range is typically 40 dB. Visible light transmission ranges from 75% downwards according to the desired level of solar control.

FOAMED GLASS

The manufacture of foamed glass as an insulation material is described in Chapter 13.

Sheet products

STANDARD GLASS SIZES

Float glass up to 12 mm in thickness is available to a maximum sheet size of 3180 × 6080 mm; thicker grades (15, 19 and 25 mm) are available to smaller sheet sizes. BS 952 Part 2: 1980 refers to standard glass curvatures while non-standard units can be manufactured by heating annealed glass until it softens and sag-bends over appropriate formers. Bending may be in one or two planes, and the bent glass can subsequently be toughened or laminated.

EMBOSSED PATTERN GLASS

A wide range of 3, 4 and 6 mm patterned glasses is commercially available, offering obscuration factors between 1 (lowest) and 5 (highest) depending upon the depth and design of the pattern, as illustrated in Fig. 7.5. The degree of privacy afforded by the various glasses is dependent not only upon the pattern but also upon the relative lighting levels on either side and the proximity of any object to the glass. The maximum stock sheet size is 2140 × 1320 mm.

Patterned glass is manufactured from a ribbon of molten cast glass which is passed through a pair of rollers, one of which is embossed. Certain strong patterns, such as *Cotswold* or *reeded*, require client choice

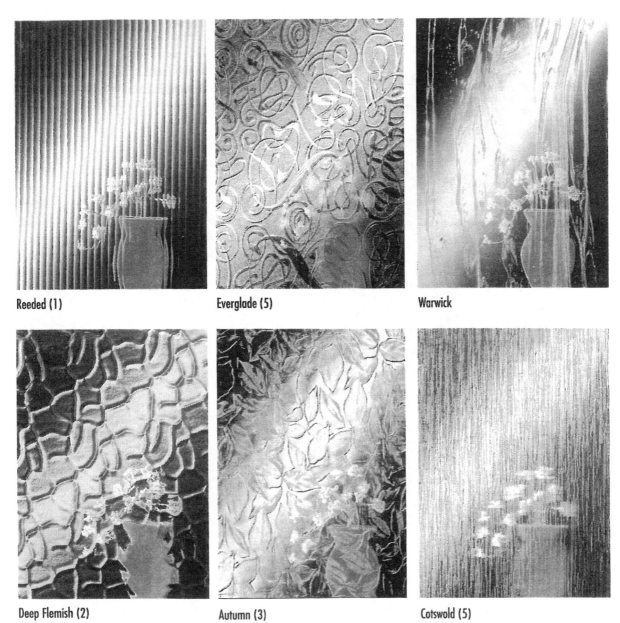

Reeded (1)   Everglade (5)   Warwick

Deep Flemish (2)   Autumn (3)   Cotswold (5)

Fig. 7.5 Typical embossed patterned glasses and relevant obscuration factors

of orientation, whereas the more flowing designs may need appropriate matching. Patterned glasses may be toughened, laminated or incorporated into double-glazing units for thermal or acoustic considerations; a limited range is available in bronze tinted glass.

SCREEN PRINTED GLASS

White or coloured ceramic frit is screen printed onto clear or tinted float glass, which is then toughened and heat soaked, causing the ceramic enamel to fuse permanently into the glass surface. Standard

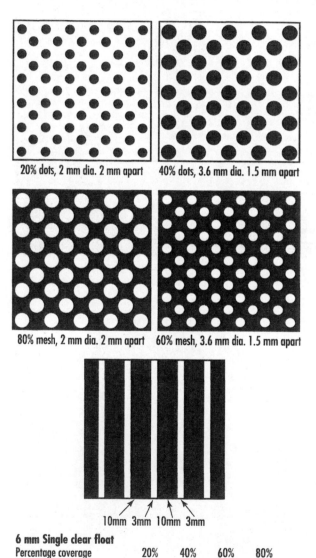

20% dots, 2 mm dia. 2 mm apart   40% dots, 3.6 mm dia. 1.5 mm apart

80% mesh, 2 mm dia. 2 mm apart   60% mesh, 3.6 mm dia. 1.5 mm apart

10mm 3mm 10mm 3mm

6 mm Single clear float

Percentage coverage	20%	40%	60%	80%
Percentage light transmission	75	62	49	37
Shading co-efficient	0.86	0.76	0.66	0.56

Fig. 7.6 Screen printed glass

patterns (Fig. 7.6) or individual designs may be created, giving the required level of solar transmission and privacy. Screen printed glass, which is colourfast and abrasion-resistant, is usually installed with the printed side as the inner face of conventional glazing.

DECORATIVE ETCHED AND SANDBLASTED GLASS

Acid etched glass, 4 mm and 6 mm in thickness, is available to a maximum sheet size of 2140 × 1320 mm with a small range of patterns (Fig. 7.7). These glasses have a low obscuration factor and should not be used in areas of high humidity, as condensation or water causes temporary loss of the pattern. Etched glasses need to be handled carefully on site, as oil, grease and finger marks are difficult to remove completely. Etched glasses may be toughened or laminated. When laminated, the etched side should be outermost to retain the pattern effect; when incorporated into double glazing, the etched glass forms the inner leaf with the etched face towards the air gap. As with embossed glass, pattern matching and orientation is important. Similar visual effects can be achieved by sandblasting techniques, although the surface finish is less smooth. Patterns may be clear on a frosted background or the reverse, depending upon the aesthetic effect and level of privacy required.

DECORATIVE COLOURED GLASS

Traditional coloured glass windows constructed with lead cames, soldered at the intersections and wired to saddle bars, are manufactured from uniform pot, surface flashed or painted glasses. For new work, additional support is afforded by the use of lead cames with a steel core, and non-corroding saddle bars of bronze or stainless steel should be used. A three-dimensional effect is achieved by fixing, with ultraviolet sensitive adhesive, coloured bevelled glass to clear or coloured sheet glass, the thin edges (1.5–2.5 mm) being covered with adhesive lead strip. Such effects can also be simulated by the use of coloured polyester or vinyl film and lead strip acrylic bonded to a single sheet of clear glass. The base glass may be toughened or laminated as appropriate, and the decorative coloured glass laminate can be incorporated into standard double-glazing units.

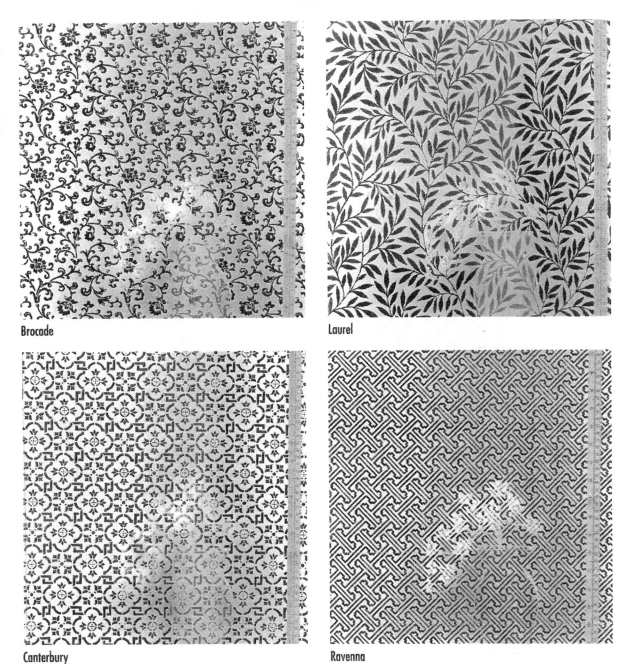

Brocade

Laurel

Canterbury

Ravenna

Fig. 7.7 Etched glass

GEORGIAN WIRED GLASS

Georgian wired glass (Fig. 7.8) is produced by rolling a sandwich of a 13 mm electrically welded steel wire mesh between two ribbons of molten glass. This produces the standard cast 7 mm sheet, suitable when obscuration is required. For visual clarity the cast product is subsequently ground with sand and water then polished with jeweller's rouge to a 6 mm sheet. Both the cast and polished grades have a light transmission of 80%. Wired glass is not stronger than the equivalent thickness of annealed glass; however, when cracked, the pieces remain held together.

On exposure to fire the wire mesh dissipates some heat, but ultimately Georgian glass will crack, particularly if sprayed with water when hot. However, the wire mesh holds the glass in position, thus retaining its integrity and preventing the passage of smoke and flame. Accidental damage may cause the breakage of the glass, but again it is held in position by the mesh, at least until the wires are affected by corrosion.

Georgian wired glass is available in sheet sizes up to 1980 × 3700 mm (cast) and 1980 × 3300 mm (polished). It is easily cut and can be laminated to other glasses but cannot be toughened. Standard Georgian glass is not considered to be a *safety glass* to BS 6206: 1981, which defines three classes with decreasing impact resistance down from Class A to Class C. However, certain laminates or products with increased wire thickness do achieve the impact resistance standards for safety glass to BS 6206: 1981 and should be marked accordingly. They may therefore be used in locations requiring safety glass according to Part N of the Building Regulations.

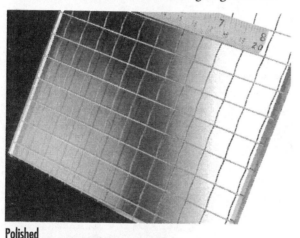

Polished

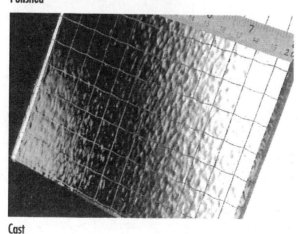

Cast

Fig. 7.8 Georgian wired glass

TOUGHENED GLASS

Toughened glass (Fig. 7.9) is up to four or five times stronger than standard annealed glass of the same thickness. It is produced by subjecting preheated annealed glass at 650°C to rapid surface cooling by the application of jets of air. This causes the outer faces to be set in compression with balancing tension forces within the centre of the glass. As cracking within glass commences with tensile failure at the surface, much greater force can be withstood before this critical point is reached.

Toughened glass cannot be cut or worked, and therefore all necessary cutting, drilling of holes and grinding or polishing of edges must be completed in advance of the toughening process. In the *roller hearth* horizontal toughening process, some bow, roller wave distortions and end edge sag may develop but these will be within narrow tolerances; however, they may be observed in the more reflective glasses when viewed from the outside of a building. In the vertical toughening process the sheet is held by tongs which leave slight distortions where they have gripped the glass.

Toughened glass will withstand considerable extremes of temperature and sudden temperature shocks. If broken, it shatters into small granules which are not likely to cause the serious injuries associated with the accidental breakage of annealed glass. To be classified as a *safety glass* toughened glass must be tested and marked according to required standard BS 6206: 1981. When toughened glass is specified for roof glazing, balustrades and spandrel panels, it is subjected to a heat-soaking process which is destructive to any substandard units. This removes the low risk of spontaneous breakage of toughened glass on site, caused by the presence of nickel sulfide crystals within the material. All standard float, coated, rough cast and some patterned glasses can be toughened.

HEAT-STRENGTHENED GLASS

Heat-strengthened glass is manufactured by a similar process to toughening, but with a slower rate of cooling which produces only half the strength of toughened glass. On severe impact, heat-strengthened glass breaks into large pieces like annealed glass; but it does not require heat-soaking to prevent the spontaneous breakage which occurs occasionally with toughened glass. Heat-strengthened glass is not a safety glass.

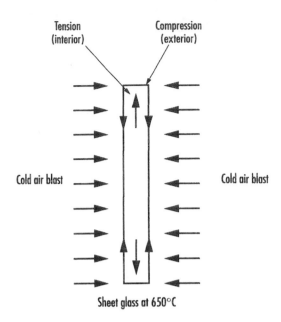

Fig. 7.9 Process for manufacturing toughened glass

LAMINATED GLASS

Laminated glass (Fig. 7.10) is produced by bonding two or more layers of glass together with a plastic interlayer of polyvinyl butyral sheet or a polymethyl methacrylate low-viscosity resin. The low-viscosity resin is more versatile as it allows for the manufacture of curved laminates or the incorporation of patterned glasses. The lamination process greatly increases the impact resistance over annealed glass of the same thickness. Furthermore, on impact the glass laminations crack without splintering or disintegration, being held together by the interlayer. Therefore, laminated glass can be defined as a *safety glass* provided it achieves the appropriate class standard to BS 6206: 1981. Increased impact resistance may be obtained by the use of thicker interlayers, by increasing the numbers of laminates or by the inclusion of polycarbonate sheet. Typically, anti-bandit glass has two or three glass laminates while, depending on the anticipated calibre and muzzle velocity, bullet-resistant glass has four or more glass laminates. To prevent spalling, the rear face of bullet-resistant glass may be sealed with a scratch-resistant polyester film and for fire protection Georgian wired glass may be incorporated. Laminated glasses made from annealed glass can be cut and worked after manufacture.

Specialist properties for X-ray or ultraviolet light control can be incorporated into laminated glasses by appropriate modifications to the standard product. The latter reduces transmissions in the 280–380 nm wavelength ranges, which cause fading to paintings, fabrics and displayed goods.

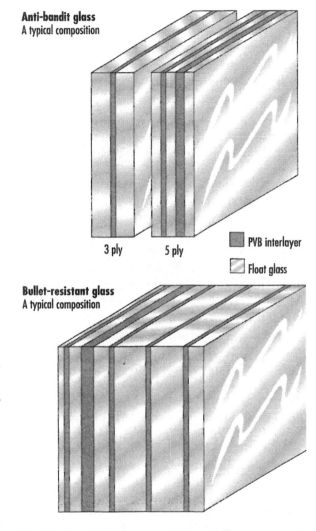

Fig. 7.10 Laminated glass – anti-bandit and bullet-resistant

FIRE-RESISTANT GLASS

The ability of a particular glass to conform to the criteria of integrity and insulation within a fire is a measure of its fire resistance (Table 7.1). However, to achieve a specified performance in fire it is necessary to ensure that the appropriate framing, fixings and glass have all been used, since fire resistance is ultimately dependent upon the whole glazing system and not the glass alone. The European classifications for fire resistance are based on the ability of the material to meet certain test criteria in relation to integrity (E), insulation (I) radiation (W), and also (not normally relevant to glass) loadbearing capacity (R).

Non-insulating glass

Non-insulating glass products will prevent the passage of flame, hot gases and smoke, but will allow heat transmission by radiation and conduction. Therefore, further fire spread may occur through the ignition of secondary fires. Intense radiation through glass areas may render adjacent escape routes impassable.

Georgian wired glass offers a fire resistance rating of up to 120 minutes with respect to integrity, depending upon the panel size and fixings. If the glass cracks within a fire its integrity is retained, as the wire mesh prevents loss of the fractured pieces. Georgian wired glass is cheaper than insulated fire-resistant glasses and may be cut to size on site.

Toughened calcium-silica based glasses can achieve 90 minutes', fire resistance with respect to integrity. The glazing remains intact and transparent, but will break up into harmless granules on strong impact if necessary for escape. Toughened glass cannot be cut or worked after manufacture.

Boro-silicate glass, with a low coefficient of expansion, is more resistant to thermal shock than standard annealed glass and does not crack on exposure to fire. It can be thermally strengthened to increase its impact resistance. Certain ultra-heat-resistant ceramic glasses, with negligible coefficients of thermal expansion, can resist temperatures up to 1000°C, and even the thermal shock of a cold water spray when heated by fire.

Insulating glass

Insulating glasses are manufactured from float glass laminated with either intumescent or gel materials. Intumescent laminated glass has clear interlayers, which, on exposure to fire, expand to a white opaque material, inhibiting the passage of conductive and radiant heat (Fig. 7.11). The glass layers adjacent to the fire crack but retain integrity owing to their adhesion with the interlayers. The fire resistance, ranging between 30 and 120 minutes for insulation and integrity, depends on the number of laminations, usually between 3 and 5. To avoid the green tint associated with thick laminated glass, a reduced-iron-content glass may be used to maintain optimum light transmission. For exterior use the external grade has an additional glass laminate with a protective ultraviolet filter interlayer. Laminates may be manufactured with tinted glass or combined with other patterned or solar control glasses. Insulating glass is supplied cut to size and should not be worked on site. Double-glazed units with two leaves of intumescent laminated glass give insulation and integrity ratings of 120 minutes; alternatively, units may be formed with one intumescent laminate in conjunction with specialist solar control glasses. The fire-resistant laminated glasses conform to the requirements of BS 6206: 1981, in respect of Class A impact resistance.

Table 7.1 Typical fire resistance properties of glass

Fire resistance of non-insulating glass – integrity only

Type	Thickness (mm)	Integrity (min)
Georgian wired glass – cast	7	30–60
Georgian wired glass – polished	6	30–120
Toughened glass	6	30–90
Glass blocks	80	30–60

Fire resistance of insulating glass – integrity and insulation

Type	Thickness (mm)	Integrity (min)	Insulation (min)
Laminated intumescent glass	10	30	–
	12	30	30
	15	60	30
	21	60	60
	50 (double glazing)	120	120

Fire resistance data are significantly dependent upon glazing size, aspect ratio and glazing system.

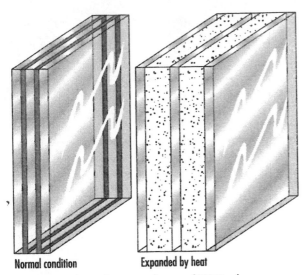

Normal condition   Expanded by heat

The interlayers expand at around 120°C and
transform into a rigid and opaque shield

Fig. 7.11 Fire-resistant glass with intumescent material laminates

Gel insulated glasses are manufactured from laminated toughened glass with the gel layer sandwiched between two or more glass layers. In the event of fire, the gel interlayer, which is composed of a polymer-containing aqueous inorganic salt solution, absorbs heat by the evaporation of water and produces an insulating crust. The process is repeated layer by layer. Depending upon the thickness of the gel layer, fire resistance times of 30, 60, 90 or 120 minutes may be achieved.

Partially-insulating glass

Partially-insulating glass consisting of a 10 mm triple laminate of float glass with one intumescent interlayer and one polyvinyl butyral layer offers a modest increase in fire resistance over non-insulating glass. Surface treatments can also increase the heat reflectance of both glass faces.

GLAZING AND ENERGY CONSERVATION

Current Building Regulations (Approved Document Part L1 (1995)) require that there should be reasonable provision for the conservation of fuel and power in buildings. With respect to glazing, the regulations assume double glazing to be the standard and take into account the combined effect of the frame material and glazing, together with the energy conservation associated with the use of low-emissivity glass. The benefits of useful solar radiation gains may also be taken into account in assessing the overall energy performance of buildings.

Double and triple glazing

Whenever the internal surface of exterior glazing is at a lower temperature than the mean room surface temperature and the internal air temperature, heat is lost by a combination of radiation exchange at the glass surfaces, air conduction and air convection currents inside and out, and by conduction through the glass itself. This heat loss can be reduced considerably by the use of multiple glazing with air, partial vacuum or inert gas fill (Fig. 7.12).

Double glazing reduces the direct conduction of heat by the imposition of an insulating layer of air between the two panes of poorly insulating glass. The optimum air gap is approximately 15 mm, since above this value convection currents between the glass panes reduce the insulating effect of the air. Partial evacuation, or the use (as a filling agent) of argon, which has a lower thermal conductivity than air, further reduces heat transfer by conduction. The use of krypton, or even xenon, within a 16 mm double glazing space in conjunction with low-emissivity glass can achieve a U-value of 1.0 W/m² K. Similar reductions in conducted heat can be achieved by the incorporation of an additional air space within triple

Table 7.2 Typical U-values for single- and multiple-glazing systems

Glass system	U-value (W/m² K)
Single clear glass	5.4
Double clear glass	2.8
Triple clear glass	1.9
Double clear glass with hard low-emissivity coating (e.g. *K Glass*)	1.9
Double clear glass with soft low-emissivity coating (e.g. *Kappafloat*)	1.8
Double clear glass with low-emissivity coating and argon fill	1.5
Double solar glass with low-emissivity coating and argon fill	1.2
Triple clear glass with two low-emissivity coatings and two argon fills	0.8
Double clear glass with hard low-emissivity coating mounted in timber or PVC-U frame (dependent on size of glazing unit)	2.4

The data relate to 6 mm glass and 12 mm spacing.

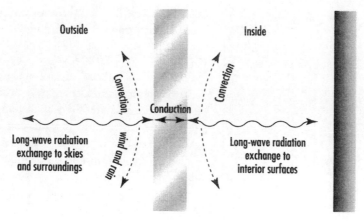

Mechanism for heat loss, through single glass

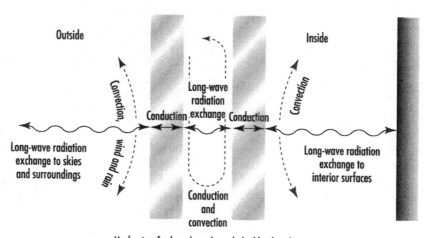

Mechanism for heat loss, through double glazed units

Fig. 7.12 Mechanism of heat loss through single and double glazing (after Button D. and Pye B. (ed.) 1993. *Glass in building.* Butterworth Architecture)

glazing. Thin mylar films incorporating blends of metals and metal oxides tuned to the local climatic conditions can further reduce the U-values of double-glazing units. Typical U-values are shown in Table 7.2.

Low-emissivity glass

Low-emissivity glasses are manufactured from float glass by the application of a transparent low-emissivity coating on one surface. The coating may be applied either on-line, within the annealing lehr at 650°C, as a pyrolytic hard-coat as in *K-Glass* or *Eko-plus*, or off-line after glass manufacture by magnetic sputtering under vacuum, which produces a softer coat as in *Kappafloat* or *Cool-lite*. Only on-line manufactured low-emissivity glasses may normally be toughened after coating, but off-line low-emissivity

coatings may be applied to previously toughened glass. The on-line surface coating is more durable and is not normally damaged by careful handling.

Low-emissivity glass functions by reflecting back into the building the longer wavelength heat energy associated with the building's occupants, heating systems and internal wall surfaces, while allowing in the transmission of the shorter wavelength solar energy (Fig. 7.13). The incoming solar energy is absorbed by the internal walls and re-radiated as longer wavelength energy, which is then trapped by the low-emissivity coating on the glass.

Low-emissivity coatings can reduce by three quarters the radiant component of the thermal transfer between the adjacent surfaces within double glazing. The reduction in emissivity of standard

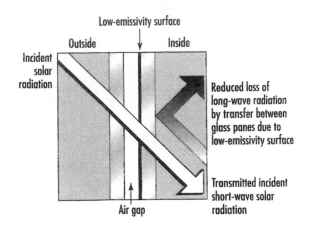

Fig. 7.13 Mechanism of heat loss control with low-emissivity glass

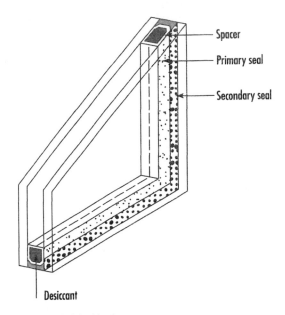

Fig. 7.14 Typical double glazing unit

uncoated glass from 0.84 to below 0.2 gives a decrease in U-value from 2.8 W/m² K for standard double glazing to 1.8 W/m² K with low-emissivity glass. Frequently, low-emissivity glass is protected in use within sealed double-glazed units. The outer leaf in the double-glazing system may be clear or any other specialist glass for security or solar control. Pyrolytic low-emissivity coatings are suitable for incorporation into secondary glazing for existing windows.

Double-glazing units

Hermetically sealed double-glazing units are usually manufactured with aluminium spacers which incorporate moisture adsorbing molecular sieve or silica gel and are sealed typically with two-component

Table 7.3 Typical overall U-values (W/m² K) for windows, doors and roof windows

	Type of frame							
	Wood		Metal		Thermal break		PVC-U	
Glass separation (mm)	6	12	6	12	6	12	6	12
Windows								
Double glazed	3.3	3.0	4.2	3.8	3.6	3.3	3.3	3.0
Double glazed, low E glass	2.9	2.4	3.7	3.2	3.1	2.6	2.9	2.4
Double glazed, argon fill	3.1	2.9	4.0	3.7	3.4	3.2	3.1	2.9
Double glazed, low E, argon fill	2.6	2.2	3.4	2.9	2.8	2.4	2.6	2.2
Triple glazed	2.6	2.4	3.4	3.2	2.9	2.6	2.6	2.4
Double glazed doors								
Half glazed	3.1	3.0	3.6	3.4	3.3	3.2	3.1	3.0
Fully glazed	3.3	3.0	4.2	3.8	3.6	3.3	3.3	3.0
Roof windows less than 70° from horizontal								
Double glazed	3.6	3.4	4.6	4.4	4.0	3.8	3.6	3.4

Other windows/doors	Wood	Metal	Thermal break	PVC-U
Single glazed windows/doors	4.7	5.8	4.3	4.7
Solid timber panel door	3.0			
Half glazed/half timber panel door	3.7			

polyisobutylene, polyurethane, polysulfide or epoxy-sulfide or hot-melt butyl rubber and a protective cap (Fig. 7.14). Frequently a second seal of two-part silicone is used to prevent leakage. To reduce cold bridging and condensation, thin stainless steel spacers offer greater thermal efficiency. Further, particularly with small glazing units, the overall energy efficiency of the unit can be considerably affected by the thermal conductivity of the frame. Current UK Building Regulations require that the overall U-values for the whole window including frames and glazing be taken into consideration. Timber frames offer good insulation, plastics less so owing to their higher conductivity and the incorporation of steel reinforcement, while aluminium frames require the inclusion of a thermal break to reduce the risk of surface condensation and significant heat loss (Table 7.3).

SOLAR CONTROL GLASSES

Solar glasses offer a modified passage of light and heat energy compared to clear glass of the same thickness. A descriptive code indicates the relative quantities of light and heat transmitted for a particular glass (e.g. 50/62 for 6 mm bronze body tinted glass), and this can be related to the equivalent data for clear float glass (87/83 for 6 mm clear). Additionally, as a guide to solar heat radiation control, the shading coefficient relates the solar radiant heat transmitted by a particular glass to that for 3–4 mm clear glass (Table 7.4). The two key methods of control are increased solar absorption as in body tinted glasses or increased solar reflection, although certain solar glasses combine both methods of control. Additionally, double-glazed units may incorporate adjustable blinds or louvres.

Body tinted glass

Body tinted glasses have a uniform through colour of grey, bronze, green, blue, pink or amber. They reduce both the transmitted light and heat compared to equivalent clear float glass, as illustrated in Fig. 7.15. They function by absorbing some of the incident solar radiation, causing the glass to warm. The glass then dissipates this absorbed heat towards both the inside and outside of the building, but owing to the greater movement of air externally, a greater proportion is expelled. Thus in double-glazed units, the body tinted glass must form the outer pane. Additional environmental control can be achieved by

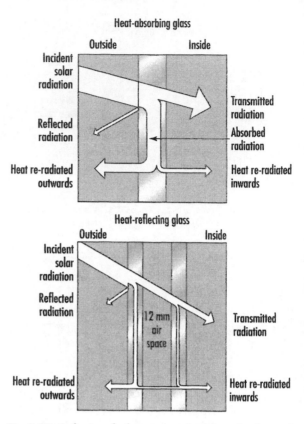

Fig. 7.15 Mechanism of solar gain control with heat-absorbing and heat-reflecting glasses

the use of low-emissivity glass for the inner pane, when a proportion of the heat re-radiated inwards from the body tinted glass is reflected back out again by the low-emissivity coating.

Body tinted glasses may be toughened or laminated for use in hazardous areas. The degree of solar control offered by body tinted glass is categorised as low to medium, being dependent upon both the thickness and colour of the product.

Reflective coated glass

Reflective coated glasses offer medium to high solar gain control by the action of a range of reflective coatings. Coatings may be applied on-line during the float process or subsequently as sputtered surface treatments to clear or body tinted glass. Available colours in reflection are blue, green, grey, silver, gold and bronze, although colours by transmission may be different (e.g. *Reflectafloat* is silver in reflection but bronze in transmission). By combining the range of coatings with different body tinted glasses a wide range of solar control properties are achieved.

Table 7.4 Characteristics of typical heat-absorbing and heat-reflecting solar glasses

Heat-absorbing glass (6 mm — body tinted)

Colour	Code	Light transmittance	Light reflectance	Heat transmittance	Shading coefficient
Green	72/62	0.72	0.06	0.62	0.72
Blue	54/62	0.54	0.05	0.62	0.72
Bronze	50/62	0.50	0.05	0.62	0.72
Grey	42/60	0.42	0.05	0.60	0.69

Heat-reflecting glass (6 mm — pyrolytic coating)

Colour	Coating face	Code	External colour in reflectance	Light transmittance	Light reflectance	Heat transmittance	Shading coefficient
Clear	out	43/55	bright silver	0.43	0.45	0.55	0.63
Clear	in	43/58	silver	0.43	0.40	0.58	0.66
Blue/green	out	33/40	bright silver	0.33	0.45	0.40	0.46
Blue/green	in	33/46	blue/green	0.33	0.30	0.46	0.53
Grey	out	20/41	bright silver	0.20	0.45	0.41	0.47
Grey	in	20/49	grey	0.20	0.13	0.49	0.56
Bronze	out	25/41	bright silver	0.25	0.45	0.41	0.48
Bronze	in	25/49	bronze	0.25	0.18	0.49	0.56
Silver		33/53	silver (bronze in transmission)	0.33	0.43	0.53	0.61

Heat-reflecting glass (6 mm — sputter coating)

Colour	Code	Light transmittance	Light reflectance	Heat transmittance	Shading coefficient
Silver	10/23	0.10	0.38	0.23	0.26
Silver	20/34	0.20	0.23	0.34	0.39
Silver	30/42	0.30	0.16	0.42	0.48
Bronze	12/32	0.12	0.11	0.32	0.37
Bronze	10/24	0.10	0.19	0.24	0.27
Bronze	26/40	0.26	0.17	0.40	0.46
Blue	13/32	0.13	0.12	0.32	0.37
Blue	20/33	0.20	0.20	0.33	0.38
Blue	30/39	0.30	0.16	0.39	0.45
Blue	40/50	0.40	0.10	0.50	0.57
Green	8/25	0.08	0.27	0.25	0.29
Green	17/32	0.17	0.17	0.32	0.37
Grey	10/32	0.10	0.09	0.32	0.37

Standard clear float glass (6 mm)

Colour	Light transmittance	Light reflectance	Heat transmittance	Shading coefficient
Clear float glass	0.87	0.08	0.83	0.95

Where reflective coatings are to be applied after the float manufacturing process, all other working, such as toughening and bending, must be completed prior to the surface treatment. While many mineral coatings are durable in normal use as single glazing, they are damaged by abrasives and may also exhibit minor imperfections, although these are considered acceptable if not observed at a distance less than 3 metres and the imperfections are less than 2 mm in diameter.

ACOUSTIC CONTROL

The level of sound reduction by glazing is influenced by the mass of the glass and the extent of air leakage around the opening lights. Sound insulation for single glazing follows the mass law – doubling the glass thickness reduces sound transmission by approximately 4 dB. Toughened, patterned and wired glass of the same thickness responds as for plain glass, but laminated glass based on polymethyl methacrylate (PMMA) bonding agent has enhanced sound insulation properties. The polymethyl methacrylate, because it is a soft material, changes the frequency response of the composite sheet in comparison with the same weight of ordinary glass.

Double glazing for sound insulation should be constructed with the component glasses differing in thickness by at least 30% to reduce sympathetic resonances; typically 6 mm and 10 mm would be effective. Where the passage of speech noise (630–2000 Hz) is to be reduced, filling the double-glazing units with sulfur hexafluoride is advantageous, but this is detrimental to attenuation of traffic and other low-frequency noises within the range 200–250 Hz. A typical high-performance double-glazing unit giving a U-value of 1.3 $W/m^2 K$ and a sound reduction of 35 dB would be constructed from 6.4 mm laminated glass with a 15.5 mm argon filled cavity and a 4 mm inner pane of low-emissivity glass. For enhanced sound insulation an air gap of at least 100 mm is required, with the economical optimum being 200 mm. The reveals should be lined with sound absorbing material such as fibreboard, to reduce reverberation within the air space. All air gaps must be fully sealed with opening lights closed by multipoint locking systems and compressible seals. An air gap corresponding to only 1% of the window area can reduce the efficiency of sound insulation by 10 dB.

SPANDREL PANELS FOR CURTAIN WALLING

Opaque panels for curtain walling can be manufactured to match or contrast with the range of vision area solar control glasses. Manufactured from toughened heat-soaked glass for impact and thermal shock resistance, they may be single or double glazed, with integral glass fibre or polyurethane foam insulation and an internal finish. Panels are colourfast and scratch-resistant, and may be manufactured from plain or decorative glass.

SPECIALIST GLASSES

One-way observation glass

Where unobserved surveillance is required, one-way observation mirror glass can be installed. In order to maintain privacy, the observer must be at an illumination level no greater than one seventh that of the observed area and wear dark clothing. From the observed area the one-way observation glass has the appearance of a normal mirror.

Alarm glass

Glass containing either a ceramic loop or a series of straight wires can be incorporated into a burglar alarm system, which is activated when the glass is broken. Usually straight wired alarm glass is incorporated into a laminated system, while a ceramic loop circuit would be fixed to the air space face of the toughened outer pane within a double-glazing system.

Electromagnetic radiation shielding glass

Building zones requiring protection to magnetically stored data from accidental or deliberate corruption by external electric fields can be protected by laminated glass incorporating electromagnetic shielding layers. For maximum security, the conducting laminates within the composite glass should be in full peripheral electrical contact with the metal window frames and the surrounding wall surface screening.

Variable transmission glasses

Variable transmission or *smart* glasses change their optical and thermal characteristics under the influence of light (photochromic), heat (thermochromic) or electric potential (electrochromic). These glasses, currently under development for the building industry, offer the potential of highly responsive dynamic climate control to building facades, which currently can only be achieved by the use of sophisticated mechanical shading devices. Photochromic glasses have the disadvantage that they would continually respond to changes in solar radiation rather than to the interior condition of the building; however, electrochromic devices, which can be switched in response to the building's interior requirements, are likely to become the basis of smart windows.

Electrochromic multilayer thin-film systems become coloured in response to an applied low voltage, and are then cleared by reversal of the electric potential. The depth of colouration is dependent upon the magnitude of the applied voltage. Optically stable materials which exhibit electrochromism are the oxides of tungsten, nickel and vanadium. Electrochromic thin-film systems may be laminated to any flat sheet glass.

A laminated glass system (*Priva-lite*) containing a polymer dispersed liquid-crystal layer contained between polyvinyl butyral layers can be electrically switched from transparent to white/translucent for privacy.

Manifestation of glass

Where there is a risk that glazing might be unseen, and thus cause a hazard to the users of a building, particularly at entrances and in circulation spaces, it should be made clear with a solid or broken line, or company logo, at a height of approximately 1500 mm above floor level.

Mirror glass

Standard mirror glass is manufactured by the chemical deposition onto float glass of a thin film of silver, from aqueous silver and copper salt solutions. The film is then protected with two coats of paint or a plastic layer. A recent development is the production of mirror glass by chemical vapour deposition within the float glass process. Mirror glass is produced by the on-line application of a multi-layer coating of silicon–silica–silicon, which acts by optical interference to give the mirror effect. Mirror glass manufactured by this process is less prone to deterioration and may be more easily toughened, laminated or bent than traditional mirror glass.

Glass supporting systems

The fixing of glazing and particularly solar control glasses, should be sufficiently flexible to allow for tolerances and thermal movements. A minimum edge clearance of at least 3 mm is required for single glazing and 5 mm for double-glazing units. Edge cover should be sufficient to cope with the design wind loading, with a minimum normally equal to the glass or unit thickness to ensure a neat sight line. Glass thickness should be checked for suitability against predicted wind speeds, modified appropriately by consideration of the effects of topography, local roughness of the terrain, building height and size of the glazing component.

The Pilkington *Planar System* (Fig. 7.16) offers the designer a flush and uninterrupted facade of glass. The only fixings to be seen on the external facade are the countersunk bolt heads. The system, which can be used for single or double glazing, vertically or sloping, is designed such that each glazing unit is separately supported by the mullion system, so there is no restriction on the height of the building. Thermal and wind movement is taken up by the fixing plate, which is sufficiently flexible to allow some rotation of the glass. In the double-glazed system the units are principally supported by the outer pane. Glass to glass butt joints are sealed with silicone.

The *Financial Times* building in Docklands, London (Plate 5), is designed with a long, clear facade sandwiched between two aluminium-clad solid ends. The glazed section, 96×16 m, consists of a single-glazed suspended toughened glass wall, bolted by circular plate assemblies to external aerofoil

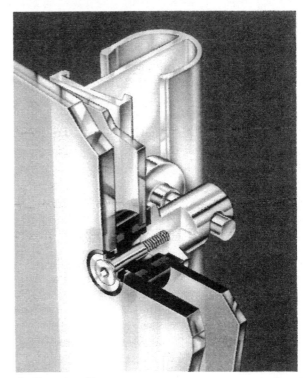

The Planar Assembly

Fig. 7.16 Typical facade glazing system

forms and intermediate cantilevered arms. This creates a wall of uninterrupted glass which is striking by day and transparent at night, when the illuminated printing presses can be clearly seen from the road.

STRUCTURAL GLASS

Glass columns are frequently used as fins to restrain excessive deflection caused by wind loading to all glass walls. Fixings between adjacent units are usually stainless steel clamps bolted through preformed holes in the toughened or laminated glass. However, the use of glass alone as the structural system is innovative. For single-storey structures, laminated or toughened glass columns and beams may be fixed with clear silicone adhesive. Instead of using aluminium spacers to produce the structural double-glazing units, glass spacers sealed with clear silicone offer a totally clear system, although the edges may require etching to conceal the necessary desiccant. Such structural glass systems are reliant on the adhesive properties of high-modulus sealants and require careful design consideration in relation to excessive solar gain.

Glazing check list

Perhaps more than any other building component glazing is expected to perform many functions. It is therefore necessary to ensure that all factors are taken into consideration in the specification of glasses. It is evident that many of the environmental control factors are closely inter-related and the specifier must check the consequences of a design decision against all the parameters:

- view in and out by day and night;
- visual appearance by day and by night – colour and reflectivity;
- energy conscious balance between daylight and artificial lighting;
- sky and reflected glare;
- overheating and solar control;
- passive solar gain and energy efficiency;
- thermal comfort, U-values and condensation;
- ventilation and sound control;
- security – impact damage, vandalism and fire spread.

References

FURTHER READING

Button, D. and Pye, B. (ed.) 1993: *Glass in building: A guide to modern architectural glass performance.* Oxford: Butterworth Architecture.
Pilkington. 1990: *Glass and wind loading.* St. Helens: Pilkington.
Pilkington. 1991: *Glass and transmission properties of windows.* St. Helens: Pilkington.
Pilkington. 1993: *Glass and noise control.* St. Helens: Pilkington.
Pilkington. 1993: *Environmental control glasses.* St. Helens: Pilkington.
Saint Gobain. 1995: *Glass in building – Clearly the best solution.* London: Saint Gobain.
Grundy, T. 1990: *The global miracle of float glass.* St. Helens: T. Grundy.
Burgoyne, I. and Scoble, R. 1983: *Two thousand years of flat glass making.* St. Helens: Chalon Press.

STANDARDS

BS 952. Glass for glazing:
    Part 1: 1995. Classification.
    Part 2: 1980. Terminology for work on glass.
BS 2750. Methods of measurement of sound insulation in buildings and of building elements.
    Part 5: 1980. Field measurements of airborne sound insulation of facade elements and facades.
BS 3447: 1962. Glossary of terms used in the glass industry.
BS 4031: 1966. X-ray protective lead glasses.
BS 4255. Rubber used in preformed gaskets for weather exclusion from buildings:
    Part 1: 1986. Specification for non-cellular gaskets.
BS 4904: 1978. Specification for external cladding for building purposes.
BS 5051. Bullet-resisting glazing:
    Part 1: 1988. Bullet-resistant glazing for interior use.
BS 5252: 1976. Framework for colour co-ordination for building purposes.
BS 5357: 1995. Code of practice for installation of security glazing.
BS 5368. Method of testing windows:
    Part 1: 1976. Air permeability test.
    Part 2: 1980. Water tightness test under static pressure.
    Part 3: 1978. Wind resistance tests.
    Part 4: 1978. Form of test report.
BS 5516: 1991. Code of practice for design and installation of sloping and vertical patent glazing.
BS 5544: 1978. Specification for anti-bandit glazing

(glazing resistant to manual attack).

BS 5713: 1979. Specification for hermetically sealed flat double glazing units.

BS 5821. Methods for rating the sound insulation in buildings and of building elements:

Part 1: 1984. Method for rating the airborne sound insulation in buildings and of interior building elements.

Part 2: 1984. Method for rating the impact sound insulation.

Part 3: 1984. Method for rating the airborne sound insulation of façade elements and façades.

BS 6100. Glossary of building and civil engineering terms:

Part 1 Subsec. 1.4.1: 1990. Glazing.

BS 6180: 1995. Code of practice for protective barriers in and about buildings.

BS 6206: 1981. Specification for impact performance requirements for flat safety glass and safety plastics for use in buildings.

BS 6262: 1982. Code of practice for glazing of buildings:

Part 3: 1996. Fire, security and wind loading.

Part 4: 1994. Safety related to human impact.

BS 6375. Performance of windows:

Part 1: 1989. Classification of weathertightness.

BS 8000. Workmanship on building sites:

Part 7: 1990. Code of practice for glazing.

BS EN 572: 1995. Glass in building:

Part 1. Definition.

Part 2. Float glass.

Part 3. Polished wired glass.

Part 4. Wired patterned glass.

Part 5. Patterned glass.

Part 7. Wired or unwired channel shaped glass.

CP3. Code of basic data for the design of buildings:

Ch. V Part 2: 1972. Wind loads.

CP 153. Windows and rooflights:

Part 2: 1970. Durability and maintenance.

Part 3: 1972. Sound insulation.

ISO 9050: 1990. Determination of light transmittance, solar direct transmittance, total solar energy transmittance and related glazing factors.

BUILDING RESEARCH ESTABLISHMENT PUBLICATIONS

BRE Digests

BRE Digest 108: 1991. Standard U-values.

BRE Digest 309: 1986. Estimating daylight in buildings Part 1.

BRE Digest 310: 1986. Estimating daylight in buildings Part 2.

BRE Digest 332: 1988. Loads on roofs from snow drifting against vertical obstructions and in valleys.

BRE Digest 338: 1988. Insulation against external noise.

BRE Digest 346. The assessment of wind loads:

Part 1: 1992. Background and method.

Part 2: 1989. Classification of structures.

Part 3: 1992. Wind climate in the United Kingdom.

Part 4: 1992. Terrain and building factors and gust peak factors.

Part 5: 1989. Assessment of wind speed over topography.

Part 6: 1989. Loading coefficients for typical buildings.

Part 7: 1989. Wind speeds for serviceability and fatigue assessments.

Part 8: 1990. Internal pressures.

BRE Digest 377: 1992. Selecting windows by performance.

BRE Digest 379: 1993. Double glazing for heat and sound insulation.

BRE Information Paper

BRE IP 12/93. Heat loss through windows.

BRE Report

BR 280: 1995. Double-glazing units: A BRE guide to improved durability.

TRADE ASSOCIATIONS

British Glass Manufacturers Confederation, Northumberland Road, Sheffield, S. Yorks. S10 2UA (0114 268 6201).

Fire Resistant Glass and Glazed Systems Association, 20 Park Street, Princes Risborough, Bucks. HP17 9AH (01844 275500).

Flat Glass Manufacturers Association, Prescot House, St. Helens, Merseyside WA10 3TT (01744 28882).

Glass and Glazing Federation, 44–48 Borough High Street, London SE1 1XB (0171 403 7177).

Laminated Glass Information Centre, 299 Oxford Street, London W1R 1LA (0171 499 1720).

Plastic Window Federation, Federation House, 87 Wellington Street, Luton LU1 5AF (01582 456147).

Steel Window Association, The Building Centre, 26 Store Street, London WC1E 7BT (0171 637 3571).

8

CERAMIC MATERIALS

Introduction

Ceramic materials, manufactured from fired clay, have been used in construction since at least 4000 BC in Egypt, and represent the earliest manufactured building materials. While the strict definition of ceramics includes glass, stone and cement, this chapter deals only with the traditional ceramics based on clays. The variety of traditional ceramic products used within the building industry arises from the wide range of natural and blended clays used for their production.

CLAY TYPES

Clays are produced by the weathering of igneous rocks, typically granite, which is composed mainly of feldspar, an alumino-silicate mineral. Clays produced within the vicinity of the parent rock are known as primary clays. They tend to be purer materials, less plastic and more vulnerable to distortion and cracking on firing. Kaolin ($Al_2O_3.2SiO_2.2H_2O$), which is the purest clay, comes directly from the decomposition of the feldspar in granite. Secondary clays, which have been transported by water, have a higher degree of plasticity, and fire to a buff or brown colour depending upon the nature and content of the incorporated oxides. Generally, secondary clays, laid down by the process of sedimentation, have a narrower size distribution and their particulate structure is more ordered.

The most common clay minerals used in the manufacture of building materials are kaolin, illite (a micaceous clay) and montmorillonite, a more plastic clay of variable composition. Clay crystals are generally hexagonal in form, and in pure kaolin the crystals are built up of alternating layers of alumina and silica (Fig. 8.1). However, in illite and montmorillonite clays, the variable composition produced by sedimentation produces more complex crystal structures.

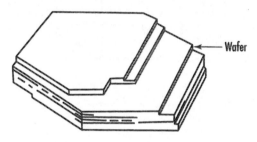

Typical clay crystal (magnified x 150 000)

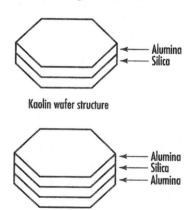

Kaolin wafer structure

Illite or montmorillonite wafer structure

Fig. 8.1 Structure of clays

Ball clays are secondary clays containing some organic matter which is burnt off during the firing process; they tend to have a fine grain size which makes them plastic. When fired alone they have a high shrinkage and produce a light grey or buff ceramic, but they are usually blended into other clays such as kaolin to make a workable clay. Terracotta clays contain significant proportions of iron oxide which gives rise to the characteristic red colour on firing. While the major clay materials used in the manufacture of ceramics are kaolin, illite, feldspar and ball clay; chalk, quartz and other minor constituents are frequently incorporated to produce the required ceramic properties on firing.

WATER IN CLAY

Moist clay contains both chemically and physically bonded water. The latter permeates between the clay particles, allowing them to slide over each other during the wet forming processes. As the formed clay slowly dries out before firing, a small proportion of the residual physically bonded water holds the clay in shape. On firing, the last of the physically bonded water is removed as the temperature exceeds 100°C.

MANUFACTURING PROCESSES

Clay products are formed either by dry or by wet processes. In the latter case the artefacts must be dried slowly prior to firing, allowing for shrinkage without cracking. Where a high level of dimensional accuracy is required, as in wall and floor tiles, a dry process is used in which powdered clay is compressed into the required form.

As the firing temperature is gradually increased, the majority of the chemically bonded water is removed when the temperature reaches 500°C. At 800°C, carbonaceous matter has been burnt off as carbon dioxide, and the sintering process commences, at first producing a highly porous material. As the temperature is further raised towards 1200°C, the alumina and silica components recrystallise to form mullite. With a further increase in firing temperature a more glassy ceramic is produced owing to further recrystallisation and if the firing temperature reaches 1300°C, any remaining free silica is recrystallised. In the presence of potassium or sodium salts vitrification occurs giving an impervious product (Fig. 8.2).

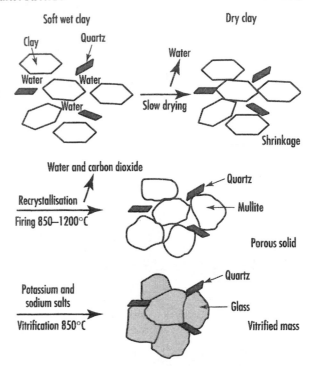

Fig. 8.2 Firing of clays

Ceramic products

FIRECLAY

A range of clays, predominantly blends of alumina and silica, high in silica (40–80%) and low in iron oxide (2–3%), produce fireclay refractory products which will withstand high temperatures without deformation. Dense products have high flame resistance, while the insulating lower-density products are suitable for flue linings. White glazed fireclay is typically used for urinals, floor channels, and industrial and laboratory sinks.

BRICKS AND ROOFING TILES

Bricks can be manufactured from a wide range of clays, the principal ones being Keuper marl, Etruria marl, Oxford clay, London clay, Coal Measure shale, Weald and Gault clays with some production from alluvial and fireclay deposits. The composition of the clay varies widely depending upon the type, but clay typically contains 40–65% silica, 10–25% alumina and 3–9% iron oxide. The loss on firing may reach 17% in the case of clay containing high levels of

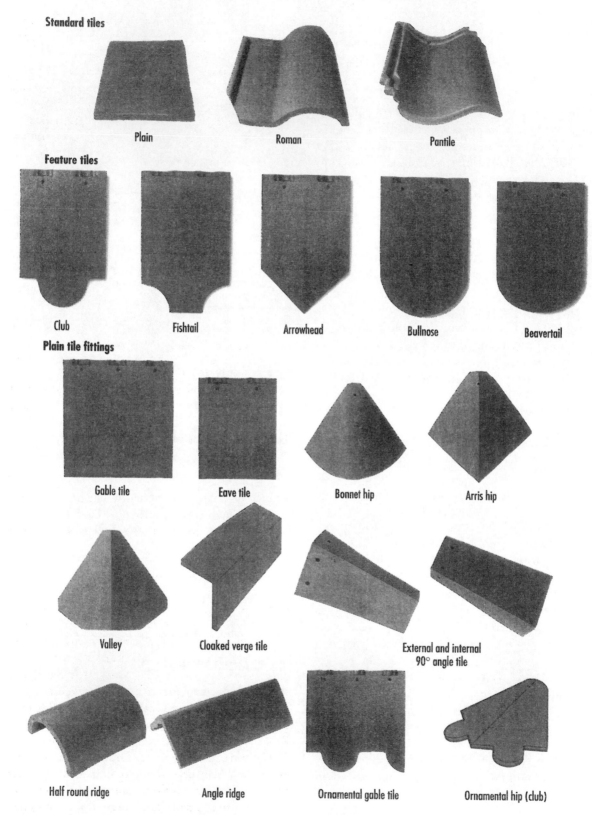

Standard tiles

Plain   Roman   Pantile

Feature tiles

Club   Fishtail   Arrowhead   Bullnose   Beavertail

Plain tile fittings

Gable tile   Eave tile   Bonnet hip   Arris hip

Valley   Cloaked verge tile   External and internal 90° angle tile

Half round ridge   Angle ridge   Ornamental gable tile   Ornamental hip (club)

Fig. 8.3 Roof tiles, feature tiles and plain tile fittings

organic matter. The production of bricks is described in detail in Chapter 1.

Glazed bricks are manufactured in a wide range of high-gloss, uniform or mottled colours. Colour-fast glazed bricks offer a low-maintenance, frost- and vandal-resistant material suitable for light-reflecting walls. Standard and purpose-made specials can be manufactured to order. Normal bricklaying techniques are appropriate but to reduce the visual effect of the mortar joints they may be decreased from the standard 10 to 6 mm. For conservation work, in order to match

new to existing, it may be necessary to fire the glazed bricks a second time at a reduced temperature to simulate the existing material colour.

Roofing tiles are made from similar clays to bricks, such as Etruria marl, but for both hand- and machine-made tiles, the raw materials have to be screened to a finer grade than for brick manufacture. Traditional red, brown, buff, brindled or 'antique' ceramic roofing tiles are unglazed with a plain or sanded finish. While most interlocking clay tiles can be used to a minimum pitch of 22.5°, one imported product with a double side interlock and a triple head/tail interlock may be used down to only 10°. This product is available in natural terracotta red or slip-coated brown or grey. Where bright colours are required, high- and low-gloss pantiles are available in a range of strong colours, or to individual specification. For plain tiles, ranges of standard fittings are produced for hips, valleys, eaves, ridges, verges, internal and external angles, as shown in Fig. 8.3. Tiles are usually shrink-wrapped for protection and ease of handling on site.

Certain floor tiles are also manufactured from Etruria marl. Firing to 1130°C produces sufficient vitrification to limit water absorption to less than 3%, thus giving a highly durable chemical- and frost-resistant product. Where high slip resistance is required, a studded profile or carborundum (silicon carbide) grit may be incorporated into the surface (Fig. 8.4).

TERRACOTTA

In order to produce intricately detailed terracotta building components, the clay has to be more finely divided than is necessary for bricks and roof tiles. The presence of iron oxide within the clay causes the buff, brown or red colouration of the fired product. During the latter part of the nineteenth century many civic buildings were constructed with highly decorative terracotta blocks. The material was used because it was cheaper than stone, durable and could be readily moulded. The blocks, which were usually partly hollowed out to facilitate drying and firing, were filled with concrete during construction.

Modern terracotta blocks may still be supplied for new work or refurbishment as plain ashlar, profiled or with sculptural embellishments. Terracotta may be used as the outer skin of cavity wall construction or as 25–40 mm thick cladding hung with stainless

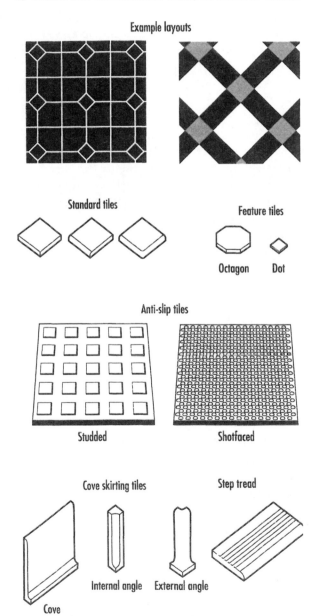

Fig. 8.4 Floor tiles – textured, smooth and specials

steel mechanical fixings. The production of terracotta blocks requires the manufacture of an oversize model (to allow for shrinkage), from which plaster moulds are made. Prepared clay is then pushed into the plaster mould, dried under controlled conditions and finally fired. Traditional colours together with greens and blues and various textures are produced. For refurbishment work existing terracotta can, subject to natural variations, usually be colour matched. In addition to cladding units, terracotta clay is also used in the manufacture of terracotta floor tiles and an extensive range of decorative ridge tiles and finials (Fig. 8.5).

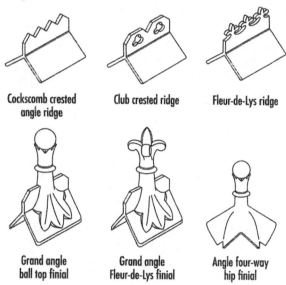

Cockscomb crested
angle ridge

Club crested ridge

Fleur-de-Lys ridge

Grand angle
ball top finial

Grand angle
Fleur-de-Lys finial

Angle four-way
hip finial

Fig. 8.5 Terracotta ridge tiles and finials

FAIENCE

Faience is glazed terracotta, used either as structural units or in the form of decorative slabs applied as cladding. It was popular in the nineteenth century and was frequently used in conjunction with polychrome brickwork on the facades of buildings such as public houses. Either terracotta may be glazed after an initial firing to the *biscuit* condition or the *slip* glaze may be applied prior to a single firing. The latter has the advantage that it reduces the risk of the glaze crazing although it also restricts the colour range. Faience, with an orange-peel texture, is available with either a matt or gloss finish and in plain or mottled colours. It is a highly durable material, being unaffected by weathering, frost or ultraviolet light,

but strong impacts can chip the surface causing unsightly damage.

STONEWARE

Stoneware is manufactured from secondary plastic clays, typically fireclays blended with an added flux such as feldspar. On firing to a temperature of between 1200°C and 1300°C, the material vitrifies, producing an impermeable ceramic product with high chemical resistance. The majority of unglazed vitrified clay pipes are stoneware. For most purposes push-fit polypropylene couplings are used which allow flexibility to accommodate ground movement; however, if required, traditional jointed socket/spigot drainage goods are also available in stoneware.

Large stoneware ceramic panels up to 1.2 m square and 8 mm in thickness are manufactured as cladding units for facades. The units, which are colour-fast and frost- and fire-resistant, may be uniform in colour or flecked and glazed or unglazed. Fixing systems are exposed or hidden; the open-joint system offers rear ventilation allowing any moisture diffusing from the supporting wall to be dissipated by natural air movement.

Stoneware is also used in the manufacture of some floor tiles. The high firing temperature gives a product of low porosity, typically less than 3%. In one manufacturing process a granular glaze is applied to the tiles within the kiln to produce an impervious vitreous finish.

EARTHENWARE

Earthenware is produced from a mixture of kaolin, ball clay and flint, with, in some cases, feldspar as a flux. The material when fired at a temperature of 1100°C is porous and requires a glaze to prevent water absorption. In the manufacture of traditional glazed drainage goods, the salt glaze is produced by adding damp common salt to the kiln during the firing process. The salt decomposes to form sodium oxide, which then reacts with silica and alumina on the surface of the clay component to produce the salt glaze, which is impermeable to moisture.

WALL TILES

Wall tiles are generally manufactured from earthenware clay to which talc (magnesium silicate) or limestone (calcium carbonate) is added to ensure a white burning clay. To prepare the clay for manufacturing wall tiles by the dry process, the components, typically a blend of china clay (kaolin), ball clay and silica sand together with some ground recycled tiles, are mixed with water to form a slip. This is sieved, concentrated to a higher-density slip, then dried to a powder by passage down a heated tower at a temperature of 500°C. The clay dust, which emerges with a moisture content of approximately 8%, is then pressed into tiles. A glaze is required both to decorate and to produce an impermeable product and this may be applied before a single firing process or after the tiles have been fired at a temperature of 1150°C to the biscuit stage in a tunnel kiln. Either the unfired or the biscuit tiles are coated with a slip glaze followed by firing under radiant heat for approximately 16 hours. Damaged tiles are rejected for recycling; the quality-checked tiles are packaged for dispatch. Standard sizes are 108 × 108 mm, 150 × 150 mm, 200 × 150 mm, 200 × 200 mm and 250 × 200 mm.

VITREOUS CHINA

Vitreous china, used for the manufacture of sanitary ware, has a glass-like body which limits water absorption through any cracks or damage in the glaze to only 0.5%. It is typically manufactured from a blend of kaolin (25%), ball clay (20%), feldspar (30%) and quartz (25%). For large units such as WCs and wash basins, a controlled drying-out period is required before firing to prevent cracking. Glaze containing metallic oxides for colouration is applied before firing to all visually exposed areas of the components.

Vitreous china is also used in the manufacture of some floor tiles owing to its impermeable nature. Unglazed floor tiles may be smooth, or alternatively studded or ribbed to give additional non-slip properties. Standard sizes are 100 × 100 mm, 150 × 150 mm, 200 × 200 mm and 300 × 300 mm with thickness usually in the range 8–13 mm. For lining swimming pools, additional protection against water penetration is given by the application of a glaze.

REPRODUCTION DECORATIVE TILES

Reproduction moulded ceramic wall tiles, encaustic tiles with strong colours burnt into the surface, and geometrical floor tiles can be manufactured to match existing units with respect to form, colour and texture for restoration work. Some manufacturers retain both the necessary practical skills and appropriate detailed drawings to ensure high-quality conservation products, which may be used to replace lost or seriously damaged units.

MOSAICS

Mosaics in glazed or unglazed porcelain are hard wearing, frost-proof and resistant to chemicals. Unglazed mosaics may be used for exterior use and other wet areas such as swimming pools, where good slip resistance is important. Mosaics are usually supplied attached to paper sheets for ease of application.

References

FURTHER READING

Ashurst, J. and Ashurst, N. 1988: *Brick, terracotta and earth*. Practical Building Conservation 2. Aldershot: Gower Technical Press.
Grimshaw, R.W. 1971: *The chemistry and physics of clays and allied ceramic materials*, 4th ed. London: Ernest Benn.
Hamer, F. and Hamer, J. 1977: *Clays* – Ceramic Skillbooks series. London: Pitman Publishing.
Hamilton, D. 1978: *The Thames & Hudson manual of architectural ceramics*. London: Thames & Hudson.
Worrall, W.E. 1975: *Clays and ceramic raw materials*. London: Applied Science Publishers.

STANDARDS

BS 65: 1992. Specification for vitrified clay pipes, fittings, and ducts, also flexible mechanical joints for use solely with surface water pipes and fittings.
BS 402. Clay roofing tiles and fittings:
    Part 1: 1990. Specification for plain tiles and fittings.
BS 493: 1970. Airbricks and gratings for wall-ventilation.
BS 1181: 1989. Clay flue linings and flue terminals.
BS 1188: 1974. Ceramic washbasins and pedestals.
BS 1196: 1989. Clayware field drain pipes and junctions.
BS 1206: 1974. Fireclay sinks: dimensions and workmanship.
BS 1289. Flue blocks as masonry terminals for gas appliances:
    Part 2: 1989. Specification for clay flue blocks and terminals.
BS 3402: 1969. Quality of vitreous china sanitary appliances.

BS 3921: 1985. Specification for clay bricks.

BS 5385. Wall and floor tiling:

Part 1: 1990. Code of practice for the design and installation of internal ceramic wall tiling and mosaics in normal conditions.

Part 2: 1991. Code of practice for the design and installation of external ceramic wall tiling and mosaics (including terra cotta and faience tiles).

Part 3: 1989. Code of practice for design and installation of ceramic floor tiles and mosaics.

Part 4: 1992. Code of practice for tiling and mosaics in specific conditions.

Part 5: 1994. Code of practice for the design and installation of terrazzo tile and slab, natural stone and composition block flooring.

BS 5503. Specification for vitreous china washdown WC pans with horizontal outlet:

Part 2: 1977. Materials, quality, performance and dimensions other than connecting dimensions.

BS 5504. Specification for wall hung WC pans:

Part 3: 1977. Materials, quality and functional dimensions other than connecting dimensions.

BS 5505. Specification for bidets:

Part 3: 1977. Quality, performance and functional dimensions other than connecting dimensions.

BS 5506. Specification for wash basins:

Part 3: 1977. Wash basins (one or three tap holes), materials, quality, design and construction.

BS 5534. Code of practice for slating and tiling:

Part 1: 1990. Design.

Part 2: 1986. Design charts for fixing slating and tiling against wind uplift.

BS 6431 Parts 1–23. Ceramic wall and floor tiles.

BS 8000. Workmanship on building sites:

Part 11: 1989. Code of practice for wall and floor tiling.

BS EN 295. Vitrified clay pipes and fittings and pipe joints for drains and sewers:

Part 1: 1991. Requirements.

Part 2: 1991. Quality control and samples.

Part 3: 1991. Test methods.

Part 4: 1995. Requirements for special fittings, adaptors and compatible accessories.

Part 6: 1996. Requirements for vitrified clay manholes.

Part 7: 1996. Requirements for vitrified clay, pipes and joints for pipe jacking.

BS EN 538: 1994. Clay roofing tiles for discontinuous laying – flexural strength test.

BS EN 539: Clay roofing tiles for discontinuous laying – determination of physical characteristics:

Part 1: 1994. Impermeability test.

BS EN 1304. Clay roof tiles.

TRADE ASSOCIATIONS

CERAM Research, Queens Road, Penkhull, Stoke-on-Trent ST4 7QL (01782 45431).

British Ceramic Tile Council, Federation House, Station Road, Stoke-on-Trent ST4 2RT (01782 747147).

Clay Pipe Development Association Ltd., Copsham House, 53 Broad Street, Chesham, Bucks. HP5 3EA (01494 791456).

Clay Roofing Tile Council, Federation House, Station Road, Stoke-on-Trent ST4 2SA (01782 744631).

Plate 1 De Montfort University, Queens Building, School of Engineering and Manufacture, Leicester, 1993

Architects: Short Ford and Associates

Photographs: Lens-based media – De Montfort University

Plate 2 Independent Television News
Headquarters, London, 1990
Architects: Sir Norman Foster and Partners
Photographs: Richard Davies

Plate 3 Darwin College Study Centre, Cambridge, 1994
Architects: Jeremy Dixon • Edward Jones
Photographs: Dennis Gilbert

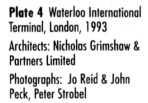

Plate 4 Waterloo International
Terminal, London, 1993

Architects: Nicholas Grimshaw &
Partners Limited

Photographs: Jo Reid & John
Peck, Peter Strobel

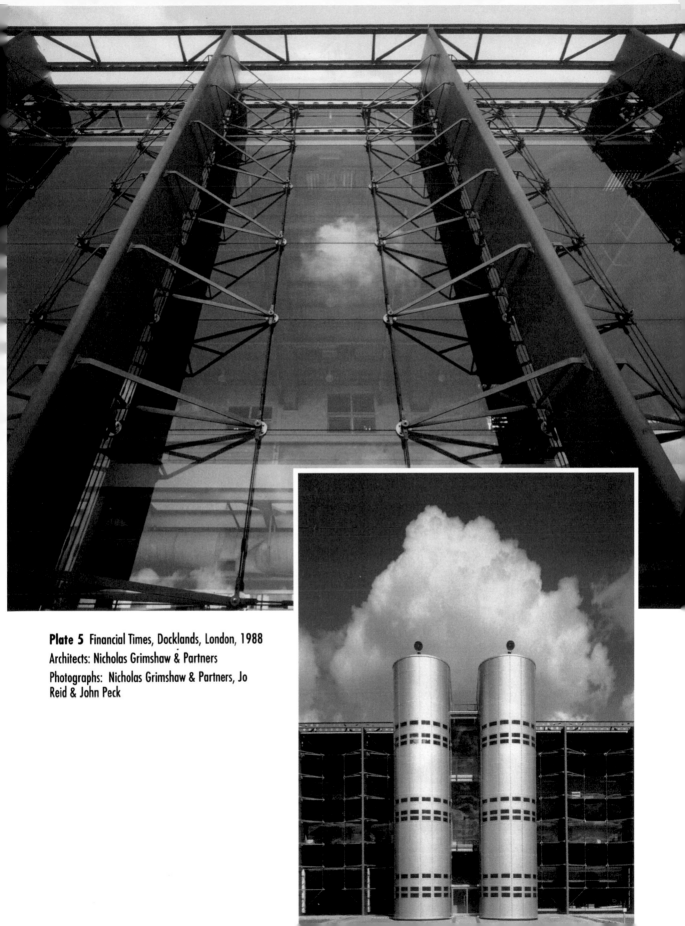

Plate 5 Financial Times, Docklands, London, 1988
Architects: Nicholas Grimshaw & Partners
Photographs: Nicholas Grimshaw & Partners, Jo
Reid & John Peck

Plate 6 David Mellor Cutlery Factory, Hathersage, Derbyshire, 1988

Architects: Michael Hopkins & Partners

Photographs: Arthur Lyons

Plate 7 Inland Revenue Amenity Building, Nottingham, 1995
Architects: Michael Hopkins & Partners
Photographs: Martine Hamilton Knight

Plate 8 Colour Dimensions System
Copyright: Colour Dimensions Association

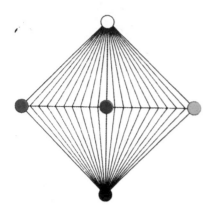

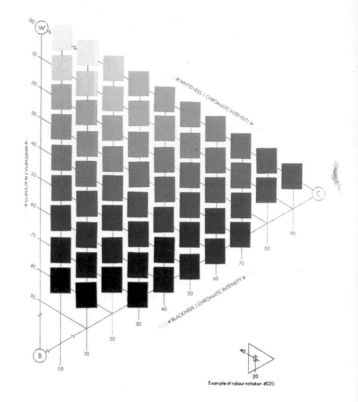

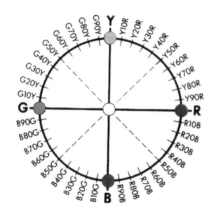

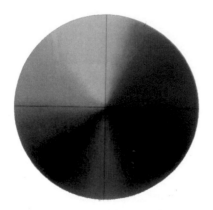

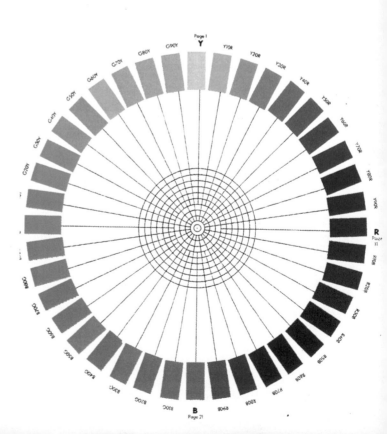

9

STONE AND CAST STONE

Introduction

The term stone refers to natural rocks after their removal from the earth's crust. The significance of stone as a building material is illustrated by widespread prehistoric evidence and its sophisticated use in the early civilisations of the world, including the Egyptians, the Incas of Peru, and the Mayans of Central America.

Geologically, all rocks can be classified into one of three groups: igneous, sedimentary or metamorphic, according to the natural processes by which they were produced within or on the earth's surface.

IGNEOUS ROCKS

Igneous rocks are the oldest, having been formed by the solidification of the molten core of the earth or *magma*. They form about 95% of the earth's crust, which is up to 16 km thick. Depending whether solidification occurred slowly within the earth's crust or rapidly at the surface, the igneous rocks are defined as plutonic or volcanic respectively. In the plutonic rocks, slow cooling from the molten state allowed large crystals to grow which are characteristic of the granites. Volcanic rocks such as pumice and basalt are fine grained and individual crystals cannot be distinguished by eye, thus the stones are visually less interesting. Dolerites, formed by an intermediate rate of cooling, exhibit a medium-grained structure.

Apart from crystal size, igneous rocks also vary in composition according to the nature of the original magma, which is essentially a mixture of silicates. A high silica content magma produces acid rocks (e.g. granite) while one with low silica content forms basic rocks (e.g. basalt and dolerite). Granites are mainly composed of feldspar (white, grey or pink), which determines the overall colour of the stone, but they are modified by the presence of quartz (colourless to grey or purple), mica (silver to brown), or horneblende (dark coloured). The basic rocks such as dolerite and basalt in addition to feldspar contain augite (dark green to black) and sometimes olivine (green). Although basalt and dolerite have not been used widely as building stones they are frequently used as aggregates.

Granites

Most granites are hard and dense, and thus form highly durable building materials, virtually impermeable to water, resistant to impact damage and stable within industrial environments. The appearance of granite is significantly affected by the surface finish, which may be sawn, rough punched, picked, fine tooled, honed or polished. It is, however, the highly polished form of granite which is most effective at displaying the intensity of the colours and reflectivity of the crystals. Additionally, granites may be flamed to a spalled surface, produced by the differential expansion of the various crystalline constituents. Many recent buildings have combined the polished and flamed material to create interesting contrasts in depth of colour and texture. Grey and pink granites are quarried in Scotland, the North of England, Devon and Cornwall, but a wide variety of colours including black, blue, green, red, yellow and brown are imported from other countries (Table 9.1). Because of the high cost of quarrying and finishing granite, it is frequently used as a cladding material (40 mm externally or 20 mm internally) or alternatively cast directly onto concrete cladding units. Granite is available for flooring and for hard landscaping including pavings, setts and kerbs.

SEDIMENTARY ROCKS

Sedimentary rocks are produced by the weathering and erosion of older rocks. In the earliest geological time these would have been the original igneous rocks, but subsequently other sedimentary and metamorphic rocks too will have been reworked. Weathering action by water, ice and wind, breaks the rocks down into small fragments which are then carried by rivers and sorted into size and nature by further water action. Most deposits are laid down in the oceans as sedimentary beds of mud or sand, which build up in layers, become compressed and

eventually are cemented together by minerals such as calcium carbonate (calcite), quartz (silica), iron oxide or dolomite (magnesium and calcium carbonate) remaining in the groundwater. The natural bedding planes associated with the formation of the deposits may be thick or thin but are potentially weak; this is used to advantage in the quarrying process. In masonry, to obtain maximum strength

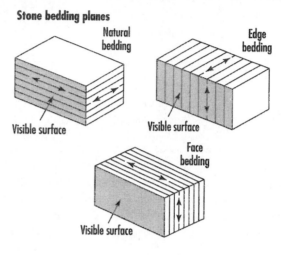

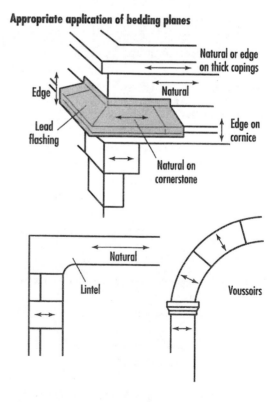

Fig. 9.1 Natural stone bedding planes

Table 9.1 UK and imported granites

Colour	Name	Country of origin
UK		
Light grey	Merrivale, Devon	England
Silver grey	De Lank and Hantergantick, Cornwall	England
Light and dark pink to brownish red	Shap	England
Pink	Peterhead	Scotland *
Pale to deep red	Ross of Mull	Scotland
Grey	Aberdeen	Scotland *
Black	Hillend	Scotland *
Black	Beltmoss	Scotland *
*available only in limited quantities		
Imported		
Red with black	Balmoral Red	Finland
Red	Bon Accord Red	Sweden
Black	Bon Accord Black	Sweden
Red	Virgo Granite	Sweden
Dark red with blue to purple quartz	Rose Swede	Sweden
Grey	Grey Royal	Norway
Grey	Sardinian Grey	Sardinia
Yellow	Nero Tijuca	Brazil
Beige/brown	Juparana	Brazil
Blue	Blue Pearl	Norway
Green/black	Emerald Pearl	Norway
Pink to red	Torcicoda	Brazil
Beige/brown	Giallio Veneziano	Brazil

and durability, stones should be laid to their natural bed except for cornices, cills and string courses, which should be edge-bedded. Stones which are face-bedded will tend to delaminate (Fig. 9.1). When quarried, stones contain *quarry sap* and may be worked and carved more easily than after exposure to the atmosphere.

Sandstones

Deposits of sand cemented together by calcium carbonate, silica, iron oxide and dolomite produce calcareous, siliceous, ferruginous and dolomitic sandstones respectively. Depending upon the nature of the original sand deposit, the sandstones may be fine or coarse in texture. Sandstones range in colour from white, buff and grey through to brown and shades of red depending upon the natural cement; they are generally frost-resistant. Some common UK sandstones are listed in Table 9.2. Typical finishes are sawn, split faced and clean rubbed, although a range of tooled finishes, including broached and droved, can also be selected (Fig. 9.2). For cladding, sandstone is normally 75 mm to 100 mm thick and fixed with non-ferrous cramps and corbels. Sandstones are quarried in Scotland, the North of England, Yorkshire and Derbyshire; they include the old and new red sandstones, York stone and millstone grit.

Table 9.2 Typical UK sandstones and their characteristics

Name	Colour	Source	Characteristics
Doddington	purple/pink	Northumberland	fine- to medium-grained
Darley Dale — Stancliffe	buff	Derbyshire	fine-grained
Birchover gritstone	pink to buff	Derbyshire	medium- to coarse-grained
York Stone	buff, fawn, grey, light brown	Yorkshire	fine-grained
Mansfield Stone	buff to white	Nottinghamshire	fine-grained
Hollington	pale pink, dull red, pink with darker stripe	Staffordshire	fine- to medium-grained
St. Bees	dark red	Cumbria	fine-grained
Blue Pennant	dark grey/ blue	Mid-Glamorgan	fine-grained

Broached with draughted margin

Stugged or punched face

Droved

Herringbone

Bats

Fig. 9.2 Typical tooled-stone finishes

Calcareous sandstone

Calcareous sandstones are not durable in acid environments, which may cause the slow dissolution of the natural calcium carbonate cement of the stone. Pure calcite is white, so these sandstones are generally white in colour.

Siliceous sandstone

Siliceous sandstones are predominantly grains of silica (sand) cemented with further natural silica, and are therefore durable even in acid environments. Siliceous sandstones are generally grey in colour.

Ferruginous sandstone

Ferruginous sandstones are bound with oxides of iron which may be brown, ochre or red. They are generally durable.

Dolomitic sandstone

Dolomitic sandstones are bound with a mixture of magnesium and calcium carbonates, and therefore do not weather well in urban environments. They are generally off-white and buff in colour.

Limestones

Limestones consist mainly of calcium carbonate, either crystallised from solution as calcite or formed from accumulations of fossilised shells deposited by various sea organisms. They are generally classified according to their mode of formation. Many colours are available including off-white, buff, cream, grey and blue. Limestones are found in England in a belt from Dorset, the Cotswolds, Oxfordshire, and Lincolnshire to Yorkshire. Some common UK limestones are listed in Table 9.3. The standard finishes are fine rubbed, fine dragged and split faced, although tooled finishes are also appropriate. Externally, limestones must not be mixed with or located above sandstones as this may cause rapid deterioration of the sandstone.

Oölitic limestone

Oölitic limestones are formed by crystallisation of calcium carbonate in concentric layers around small fragments of shell or sand, producing spheroidal grains or oöliths (Fig. 9.3). The oöliths become cemented together by further deposition of calcite to produce the rock. Typically the oöliths are up to 1 mm in diameter, giving a granular texture to the stone, which may also incorporate other fossils. Oölitic limestones are very workable and include Bath stone and Portland stone. Clipsham and Ketton stone have been widely used at Oxford and Cambridge respectively.

Table 9.3 Typical UK limestones and their characteristics

Name	Colour	Source	Characteristics
Ancaster	cream to buff	Lincolnshire	oölitic limestone – variable shell content; freestone available
Bath Stone	pale brown to light cream	Avon	oölitic limestone
– Westwood Ground			coarse-grained – buff coloured;
– Monks Park			fine-grained – buff coloured
Clipsham	buff to cream	Rutland	medium-grained oölitic limestone with shells; some blue stone; best quality stone is durable
Doulting	pale brown	Somerset	coarse textured; fossils uncommon
Hopton Wood	cream or grey	Derbyshire	carboniferous limestone containing many attractive fossils; may be polished
Ketton	pale cream to buff and pink	Lincolnshire	medium-grained oölitic limestone; even-textured; durable stone
Portland Stone	white	Dorset	exposed faces weather white, protected faces turn black
– Roach			coarse open-textured shelly stone; weathers very well
– Whitbed			fine-grained – some shell fragments; durable stone
– Basebed			fine-grained with few shells; suitable for carving
Purbeck	blue/grey to buff	Dorset	some shells; durable stone.

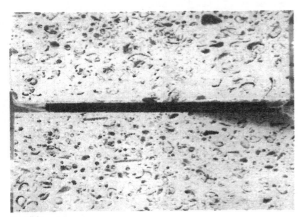

Roach limestone

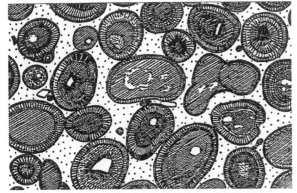

Oölitic limestone (x 20) (after Arkwell W.J. 1946: *Oxford stone*, Faber & Faber)

Fig. 9.3 Roach limestone and oölitic limestone (× 20)

Organic limestone

Organic limestones are produced in bedded layers from the broken shells and skeletal remains of a wide variety of sea animals and corals. Frequently clay is incorporated into organic limestones and this adversely affects the polish which can otherwise be achieved on the cut stone.

Crystallised limestone

When water containing calcium bicarbonate evaporates, it leaves a deposit of calcium carbonate. In the case of hot springs the material produced is travertine, and in caves, stalactites and stalagmites or *onyx-marble* result.

Dolomitic limestone

Dolomitic limestones have had the original calcium carbonate content partially replaced by magnesium carbonate. In general this produces a more durable limestone, although it is not resistant to heavily polluted atmospheres.

METAMORPHIC ROCKS

Metamorphic rocks are formed by the recrystallisation of older rocks, when subjected to intense heat or pressure or both, within the earth's crust. Clay is metamorphosed to slate, limestone to marble and sandstone to quartzite.

Slate

Slate is derived from fine-grained sand-free clay sediments. The characteristic cleavage planes of slate were produced when the clay was metamorphosed and frequently they do not relate to the original bedding planes. Slate can be split into thin sections (typically 4–10 mm for roofing slates) giving a natural riven finish, or it may be sawn, sanded, fine rubbed, honed, polished, flame textured or bush hammered. A range of distinctive colours is available: blue/grey, silver grey and green from the Lake District, blue, green, grey and plum red from North Wales and grey from Cornwall. Slate is also imported from Ireland (grey/green), Canada (blue/grey and purple), North American (red and green) France (blue/grey) and grey and blue/black from Spain, which is the world's largest producer of the material. Slate is strong, acid and frost-resistant, lasting up to 400 years as a roofing material. The minimum recommended pitch for slate roofing is 20° under sheltered or moderate exposure and 22.5° under severe exposure, and these situations require the use of the longest slates (460, 560 or 610 mm). Where thick slates (up to 20 mm in thickness) are used for a roof pitch of less than 25°, it should be noted that the slates lie at a significantly lower pitch than the rafters. Fixing nails should be of copper or aluminium. Slate is also used for flooring, cladding, copings, cills and stair treads. When used as a cladding material it should be fixed with non-ferrous fixings or cast directly onto concrete cladding units.

Reconstituted slate

Reconstituted slate for roofing is manufactured from slate granules and inert filler, mixed with a thermosetting resin and cast into moulds to give a natural riven slate finish. Certain products incorporate glass-fibre reinforcement, and offer a wider range of colours than are available in natural slate. Some interlocking slates may be used down to a pitch of 17.5°, while double-lap simulated natural slates can be used down to a pitch of 20° depending upon the degree of exposure. Reconstituted slate is also manufactured in glass-fibre reinforced cement (GRC) as described in Chapter 11.

Marble

Marble is metamorphosed limestone in which the calcium carbonate has been recrystallised into a mosaic of approximately equal-sized calcite crystals. The process, if complete, will remove all traces of fossils, the size of the crystals being largely dependent on the duration of the process. Some limestones which can be polished are sold as marble, but true marble will not contain any fossillised remains. Calcite itself is white, so a pure marble is white and translucent. The colours and veining characteristics of many marbles are associated with impurities within the original limestone; they range from red, pink, violet, brown, green, beige, cream and white to grey and black. Marble is attacked by acids; therefore honed, rather than highly polished surfaces, are recommended for external applications. Marbles are generally hard and dense, although fissures and veins sometimes require filling with epoxy resins. Most marbles used within Britain are imported from continental Europe, as indicated in Table 9.4.

Table 9.4 A selection of imported marbles

Colour	Name	Country of origin
White	White Carrara/Sicilian	Italy
White	White Pentelicon	Greece
Cream	Perlato	Sicily
Cream	Travertine	Italy
Beige	Botticino	Sicily
Pink	Rosa Aurora	Portugal
Red	Red Bilbao	Spain
Brown	Napoleon Brown	France
Green	Verde Alpi	Italy
Black	Belgian Black	Belgium
Black with white veins	Nero Marquina	Algeria

For external cladding above first-floor level 40 mm thick slabs are used, although 20 mm may be appropriate for internal linings and external cladding up to first-floor level. Fixing cramps and hooks should be in stainless steel, phosphor bronze or copper. Floor slabs, to a minimum thickness of 30 mm, should be laid on a minimum 25 mm bed. Marble wall and bathroom floor tiles are usually between 7 mm and 10 mm in thickness.

Reconstituted marble

Reconstituted marble is manufactured from marble chippings and resin into tiles and slabs for use as floor and wall finishes. The material has the typical colours of marble but without the veining associated with the natural material.

Quartzite

Quartzite is metamorphosed sandstone. The grains of quartz are recrystallised into a matrix of quartz, producing a durable and very hard wearing stone used mainly as a flooring material. The presence of mica allows the material to be split along smooth cleavage planes, producing a riven finish. Quartzite is mainly imported from Norway and South Africa and is available in white, grey, grey/green, blue/grey and ochre.

ALABASTER

Alabaster is naturally occurring gypsum or calcium sulfate. Historically it has been used for building as in the Palace of Knossos, Crete, but in the UK its use has been mainly restricted to carved monuments and ornaments. The purest form is white and translucent, but traces of iron oxide impart light brown, orange or red colourations.

Stonework

TRADITIONAL WALLING

Dressed stone may be used as an alternative to brick or block in the external leaf of standard cavity construction. Limestone and sandstone are the most frequently used for walling, but slate is also used where it is available locally. Although random rubble and hand-dressed stone can be supplied by stone suppliers, sawn-bedded (top and bottom) stones are generally the most available. These are normally finished split faced, pitch faced, fine rubbed or sawn. The standard sizes are 100 or 105 mm on bed, with course heights typically 50, 75, 100, 110, 125, 150, 170, 225 and 300 mm (Fig. 9.4). Stones may be to a particular course length, e.g. 300 mm or 450 mm, although they are frequently to random lengths. Quoin blocks, window and door surrounds, cills and other components are

Roughly squared split faced random rubble

Polygonal random rubble

Sawn bedded pitched face random walling

Sawn bedded pitched face coursed walling

Fig. 9.4 Traditional stone walling

often available as standard. In ashlar masonry, the stones are carefully worked and finely jointed. Stones within horizontal courses are of the same height and are perfectly rectangular in elevation. Joints are generally under 6 mm in width.

The mortar for stone masonry should be weaker than the stone selected. For porous limestones and sandstones, crushed stone aggregate is frequently used as the aggregate in the mortar, typically in a 1 : 3 : 12 mix of Portland cement : lime putty : crushed stone. For ashlar Bath stone a typical mix would be 1 : 2 : 8 cement : lime : stone dust. Dense sandstones may be bonded with a stronger 1 : 1 : 6 mix, and granite a 1 : 2 or 1 : 3 Portland cement to fine aggregate mix. Jointing should generally be to a similar texture and colour to that of the dressed stone itself, and should be slightly recessed to emphasise the stones rather than the joints. In ashlar work, a matching 5 mm flush joint is appropriate.

The David Mellor Cutlery Factory, Hathersage, Derbyshire (Plate 6), illustrates the use of tradition-

ally detailed Derbyshire stone as loadbearing masonry worked in conjunction with precast concrete quoins and padstones. The building takes its form from the base of an old gasholder which provides its foundations.

STONE CLADDING

For the majority of large commercial buildings, stone is used as a cladding material mechanically fixed to the structural system. The strength of the stone largely determines the appropriate cladding panel thickness. For granites, marbles and slate 40 mm slabs are usual for external elevations above ground floor level, but for the softer limestones and sandstones a minimum thickness of 75 mm is frequently recommended. Fixings (Fig. 9.5) must be manufactured from stainless steel or non-ferrous metal and must be sized to sustain the dead load of the cladding together with applied loads from wind and maintenance equipment. Movement joints are required to accept the differential structural movements of the frame and the thermal and moisture movements of the cladding. Horizontal compression joints of 15 mm minimum should be located at each floor level; vertical movement joints of 10 mm should be at approximately 6 m centres. Polysulfides, polyurethanes and silicones are used as joint sealants, although non-staining silicones should be used on stones which darken by absorption of silicone fluid. An alternative approach to stone cladding is the use of an integral stone veneer on concrete cladding panels. Stone cladding systems ideally should be protected from impact damage at ground level by the design detailing.

Deterioration of stone

The main agencies causing the deterioration of stone are soluble-salt action, atmospheric pollution, frost, the corrosion of metal components and poor design or workmanship.

SOLUBLE-SALT ACTION

If moisture containing soluble salts evaporates from the surface of stonework, then the salts will be left either on the surface as white efflorescence or as crystals within the porous surface layer. If the wetting and drying cycles continue, the crystalline material builds up within the pores to the point at which the pressure produced may exceed the tensile strength of the stone, causing it to crumble. The actual pore size significantly influences the durability of individual stones, but generally the more porous stones, such as limestone and sandstone, are susceptible to soluble-salt action.

ATMOSPHERIC POLLUTION

Stones based on calcium carbonate are particularly vulnerable to attack by acid, atmospheric pollutants. Sulfur dioxide in the presence of water and oxygen from the air produces sulfuric acid, which attacks calcium carbonate to produce calcium sulfate. Limestones and calcareous sandstones are vulnerable to attack. In the case of limestone, the gypsum (calcium sulfate) produced at the surface is slightly soluble and on exposed surfaces gradually

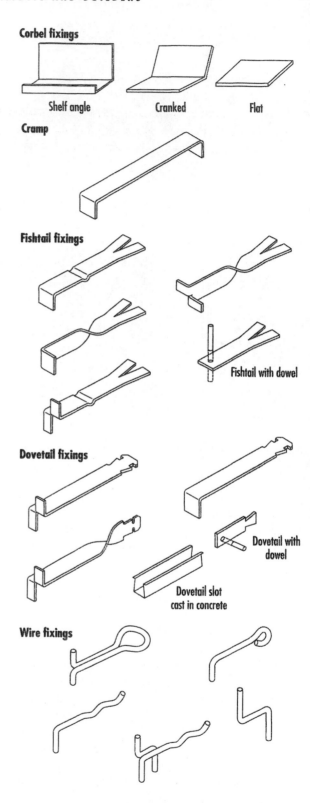

Fig. 9.5 Typical fixings for stone cladding

washes away leaving the eroded limestone clean. In unwashed areas, the surface becomes blackened with soot, producing a hard crust which eventually blisters, exposing powdered limestone. Magnesian limestones react similarly, except that in some cases the recrystallisation of magnesium sulfate under the blackened crust causes a more serious cavernous decay of the stone. Calcareous sandstones, when rain-washed, gradually decay to powder; however, in unwashed areas they produce a hard crust in which the pores are blocked with gypsum. The crust eventually fails owing to differential thermal expansion. Dolomitic sandstones are less vulnerable to acid attack, unless they contain a significant proportion of vulnerable calcite. Silicious sandstones, which are not attacked directly by atmospheric acids, can be damaged by the calcium sulfate washings from limestone, which then cause crystallisation damage to the sandstone surface. Marble, which is essentially calcium carbonate, is also affected by atmospheric acids. Any polished surface is gradually eroded; however, as marble is generally non-porous, crystallisation damage is unusual, and limited to *sugaring* in some cases.

FROST ACTION

Frost damage occurs in the parts of a building which become frozen when very wet, such as copings, cornices, string courses, window hoods and cills. Frost causes the separation of pieces of stone, but it does not produce powder as in a crystallisation attack. Generally, limestones and magnesian limestones are more vulnerable to frost damage than sandstones. Marble, slate and granite used in building are normally unaffected by frost owing to their low porosities.

CORROSION OF METALS

Rainwater run-off from copper and its alloys can cause green colour staining on limestones. Iron and steel produce rust staining which is difficult to remove from porous stones. Considerable damage is caused by the expansion of iron and steel in stonework caused by corrosion. All new and replacement fixings should normally be manufactured from stainless steel or non-ferrous metals.

FIRE

Fire rarely causes the complete destruction of stonework. In the case of granite, marble and most sandstones, the surfaces may be blackened or may spall. Limestones are generally unaffected by fire, although the paler colours may turn permanently pink owing to the oxidation of iron oxides within the stone. Reigate stone, a calcareous sandstone, is also resistant to heat, but it is not a durable stone for exterior use.

PLANTS

Generally, large plants including ivy should be removed from old stonework; however, Virginia creeper and similar species are not considered harmful. Lichens may contribute to deterioration of limestones and affected stonework should be treated. Damp north-facing walls and sloping sandstone surfaces are vulnerable to developing algae and lichen growth.

Maintenance of stonework

CLEANING

External granite, marble and slate claddings require regular washing with a mild detergent solution. Particularly, highly polished external marble should be washed at least twice per year to prevent permanent dulling of the surface. Limestone, where it is not self cleaned by rainwater, should be cleaned with a fine water spray and brushing, removing only deposit and not the gypsum-encrusted surface. However, the washing of limestone may cause a *ginger* staining or efflorescence as the stone dries out, with the risk of possible corrosion of embedded ferrous cramps, so water quantities should be adequately controlled. Sandstone is usually cleaned mechanically by abrasive blasting or chemical cleaning. Abrasive blasting with sand or grit is satisfactory for hard stones but can seriously damage soft stone and moulded surfaces. Hydrofluoric acid and sodium hydroxide (caustic soda) are used in the chemical cleaning of sandstones, but both are hazardous materials which need handling with extreme care by specialist contractors.

STONE PRESERVATION

Generally, coatings such as silicone water repellents should be applied to stonework only following expert advice and testing. Silicone treatment may in certain cases cause a build-up of salt deposits behind the treated layer, eventually causing failure. Silicone treatment should not be applied to already decayed stone surfaces. Polymeric silanes such as *Brethane* (alkyl-alkoxy-silane) can be used to consolidate decaying stone. The silane is absorbed up to 50 mm into the stone, where it polymerises, stabilising the stone but without changing its external appearance. Generally such treatment is appropriate for small artefacts which are in immediate danger of loss if left untreated.

Cast stone

The appearance of natural stones such as Bath, Cotswold, Portland and York can be recreated using a mixture of stone dust and natural aggregates with cement. In certain cases, iron oxide pigments may also be added to match existing stonework as required. Many architectural components such as classical columns, capitals, balustrades and porticos are stock items (Fig. 9.6), but custom-made products may be cast to designers' specifications. High-quality finishes are achieved by the specialist manufacturers, and cast stone often surpasses natural stone in terms of strength and resistance to moisture penetration. Cast stone may be homogeneous, or for reasons of economy may have the facing material intimately bonded to a backing of concrete, in which case the facing material should be at least 20 mm thick. Untreated and galvanised steel reinforcement should have at least 40 mm cover on exposed faces and corrosion resistant metals at least 10 mm cover. Most masonry units are designed to be installed with 5 or 6 mm joints, and locating holes for dowel joints should be completely filled. Mortars containing lime are recommended rather than plain sand and cement (Table 9.5). Careful workmanship is required to prevent staining of the cast stone surfaces with mortar as it is difficult to remove. Cast stone should weather in a similar manner to the equivalent natural stone.

Fig. 9.6 Typical cast stone units

Table 9.5 Recommended grades of mortar for cast stonework

Exposure	Masonry cement : sand	Plasticised cement : sand	Cement : lime : sand
Severe	1 : 4½	1 : 6	1 : 1 : 6
Moderate	1 : 6	1 : 8	1 : 2 : 9

References

FURTHER READING

Ashurst, N. 1994: *Cleaning historic buidings*, vol. 1: *Substrates, soiling and investigation*. London: Donhead.

Ashurst, N. 1994: *Cleaning historic buidings*, vol. 2: *Cleaning materials and processes*. London: Donhead.

Ashurst, J. and Ashurst, N. 1988: *Stone masonry*. Practical Building Conservation Series 1. Aldershot: Gower Technical Press.

Ashurst, J. and Ashurst, N. 1991: *Cleaning stone and brick*. Society for the Protection of Ancient Buildings, Technical Pamphlet 4. London: SPAB.

Ashurst, J. and Dimes, F.G. 1984: *Stone in building – Its use and potential today.* London: Stone Federation Great Britain.

Ashurst, J. and Dimes, F.G. 1990: *Conservation of building and decorative stone,* vols. 1 and 2. London: Butterworth-Heinemann.

Brereton, C. 1991: *The repair of historic buildings – Advice on principles and methods.* London: English Heritage.

Cathedral Communications. 1994: *The building conservation directory.* London: Cathedral Communications Ltd.

Kincaid, P. 1991: *Building with stone, traditional and modern.* Sydney: Hale & Iremonger.

Shadmon, A. 1989: *Stone – An introduction.* London: Intermediate Technology Publications.

Stone Federation. 1994: *Members' indigenous stone quarries – Specifiers guide.* London: Stone Federation Great Britain.

Stone Federation. 1990–93: *Information sheets.* London: Stone Federation Great Britain.

Torraca, G. 1988: *Porous building materials – Materials science for architectural conservation,* 3rd ed. Rome: ICCROM.

Webster, R.G.M. (ed.) 1992: *Stone cleaning and the nature, soiling and decay mechanisms of stone.* London: Donhead.

Williams, G.B.A. 1991: *Pointing stone and brick walling.* Society for the Protection of Ancient Buildings, Technical Pamphlet 5. London: SPAB.

STANDARDS

BS 435: 1975. Dressed natural stone, kerbs, channels, quadrants and setts.

BS 680. Roofing slates:
　　Part 2: 1971. Metric units.

BS 1217: 1986. Specification for cast stone.

BS 5080. Structural fixings in concrete masonry.
　　Part 1: 1993. Method of test for tensile loading.
　　Part 2: 1986. Method for determination of resistance to loading in shear.

BS 5385. Wall and floor tiling:
　　Part 5: 1990. Code of practice for the design and installation of terrazzo tile and slab, natural stone and composition block flooring.

BS 5390: 1976. Code of practice for stone masonry.

BS 5534. Slating and tiling:
　　Part 1: 1990. Design.
　　Part 2: 1986. Design charts for fixing roof slating and tiling against wind uplift.

BS 5628. Code of practice for use of masonry:
　　Part 3: 1985. Materials and components, design and workmanship.

BS 5642. Sills and copings:
　　Part 1: 1978. Specification for window sills of precast concrete, cast stone, clayware, slate and natural stone.

BS 6093: 1993. Code of practice for design of joints and jointing in building construction.

BS 6100. Building and civil engineering terms:
　　Part 5: 1992. Masonry.

BS 6270. Code of practice for cleaning and surface repair of buildings:
　　Part 1: 1982. Natural stone, cast stone and clay and calcium silicate brick masonry.

BS 6457: 1984. Specification for reconstituted stone masonry units.

BS 6477: 1992. Specification for water repellents for masonry surfaces.

BS 8000. Workmanship on building sites:
　　Part 3: 1989. Masonry.
　　Part 11. Code of practice for wall and floor tiling.
　　Sec.11.2: 1990. Natural stone tiles.

BS 8298: 1994. Code of practice for design and installation of natural stone cladding and lining.

CP 111: 1970. Structural recommendations for loadbearing walls.

CP 297: 1972. Precast concrete cladding (non-loadbearing).

CP 298: 1972. Natural stone cladding (non-loadbearing).

BUILDING RESEARCH ESTABLISHMENT PUBLICATIONS

BRE Digests

BRE Digest 177: 1990. Decay and conservation of stone masonry.

BRE Digest 269: 1989. The selection of natural building stone.

BRE Digest 280: 1983. Cleaning external surfaces of buildings.

BRE Digest 370: 1992. Control of lichens, moulds and similar growths.

BRE Digest 418: 1996 Bird, bee and plant damage to buildings.

BRE Current Paper

BRE CP 1/81. Brethane stone preservative.

BRE Information Papers

BRE IP 17/88. Ties for masonry cladding.

BRE IP 11/95. Control of biological growths on stone.

BRE Reports

SO 36: 1989. The building limestones of the British Isles, E. Leary.

BR 62: 1985. The weathering of natural building stones, R.J. Schaffer.

BR 84: 1986. The building sandstones of the British Isles, E. Leary.

BR 134: 1988. The building magnesian limestones of the British Isles, D. Hart.

BR 141: 1989. Durability tests for building stone, K.D. Ross and R.N. Butlin.

BR 195: 1991. The building slates of the British Isles, D. Hart.

TRADE ASSOCIATIONS

Cast Stone Association, Write Lines, 28 Manor Road, Wokingham, Berks. RG11 4AH (01734 788533).

Men of the Stones, 25 Cromarty Road, Stamford, Lincs. PE9 2TQ (01780 53527).

National Federation of Terrazzo, Marble and Mosaic Specialists, PO Box 50, Banstead, Surrey SM7 2RD (01737 360673).

Natural Slate Quarries Association, 26 Store Street, London WC1E 7BT (0171 323 3770).

Stone Federation Great Britain, 18 Mansfield Street, London W1M 9FG (0171 580 5404).

10

PLASTICS

—

Introduction

The plastics used in the construction industry are generally low-density non-loadbearing materials. Unlike metals, they are not subject to corrosion but they may be degraded by the action of direct sunlight, with a corresponding reduction in mechanical strength. Many plastics are flammable unless treated; the majority emit noxious fumes in fires. Approximately 20% of plastics production within the UK is used by the building industry. PVC (polyvinyl chloride), which has a high embodied energy content, accounts for 40% of this market share, predominantly in pipes, but also in cladding, electrical cable insulation, windows, doors and flooring applications. Foamed plastics for thermal and acoustic insulation are formulated either as open- or closed-cell materials, the latter being resistant to the passage of air and water.

In terms of their chemical composition plastics form a diverse group of materials which have chain-like molecular structures composed of a large number of small repeat units. While some materials such as rubber and cellulose derivatives are based on natural products, the majority of plastics are produced from petrochemical products. The manufacture of polythene, which dates back to 1933, involves the polymerisation of ethylene monomer, a colourless gas, which under high pressure at a temperature of 200°C is converted into the clear polymer polyethylene or polythene (Fig. 10.1).

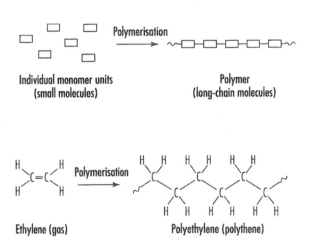

Fig. 10.1 Polymerisation of ethylene to polyethylene (polythene)

Polymerisation

In the production of polythene the small molecular units of ethylene are joined end to end by an addition polymerisation process to produce the long-chain macromolecules. A similar process converts vinyl chloride into polyvinyl chloride (PVC) (Fig. 10.2), styrene monomer into polystyrene and tetrafluoroethylene into polytetrafluoroethylene (PTFE).

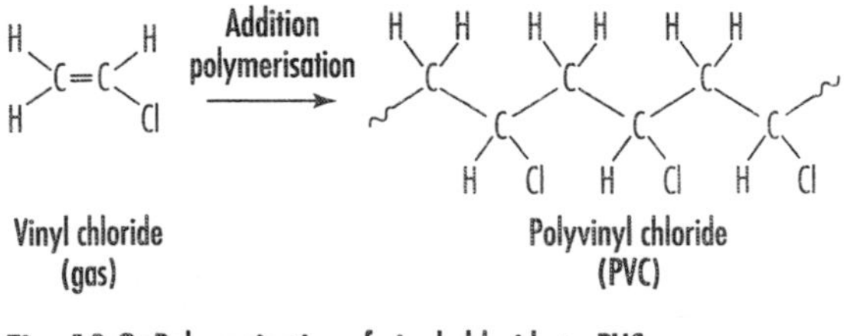

Fig. 10.2 Polymerisation of vinyl chloride to PVC

Condensation polymerisation

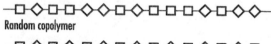

Fig. 10.3 Condensation polymerisation

While the molecular backbones of plastics are predominantly composed of chains of carbon atoms, variations occur, particularly when the polymerisation process involves the elimination of water between adjacent monomer units. Thus in the case of condensation polymerisation (Fig. 10.3), oxygen or nitrogen atoms are incorporated into the backbone of the macromolecular chains, as in the polyesters (resins) and polyamides (nylons).

BRANCHED CHAINS

Depending upon the conditions during the polymerisation process, the polymer chains produced may be linear or branched. In the case of polythene, this affects the closeness of packing of the chains and therefore the bulk density of the material. Thus high-density polythene (HDPE) (s.g. 0.97), which is relatively stiff, has few branched chains compared to low-density polythene (LDPE) (s.g. 0.92), which is softer and waxy (Fig. 10.4).

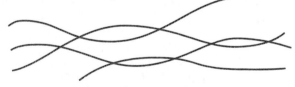

High-density polythene – straight chained

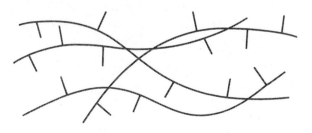

Low-density polythene – branched chained

Fig. 10.4 Straight- and branched-chain polymers

COPOLYMERS

Where two or more different monomers are polymerised together, the product will be a copolymer. The properties of the copolymer will be significantly dependent upon whether the two components have joined together in alternating, random or block sequences (Fig. 10.5).

Random copolymer

Alternate copolymer

Block copolymer

(☐ and ◇ represent two different monomer units)

Fig. 10.5 Random, alternate and block copolymers

More complex plastics can be produced for their specific physical properties by combining several components. Thus acrylonitrile butadiene styrene (ABS) is produced by the copolymerisation of the two precursor copolymers: styrene-acrylonitrile and butadiene-styrene rubber.

CRYSTALLINITY

In the initial manufactured state, most polymers consist of amorphous randomly-orientated molecular chains. However, if the plastic material is stretched in one direction, such as during the drawing of spun fibres, this causes an alignment of the molecular chains leading to partial formation of crystalline regions and an associated anisotropy (Fig. 10.6). Crystalline regions may also be produced during the solidification of simple polymers such as polyethylene, but they will be limited in their extents owing to the general entanglement of the molecular chains.

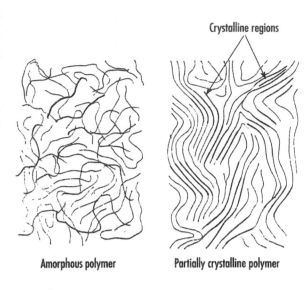

Crystalline regions

Amorphous polymer Partially crystalline polymer

Fig. 10.6 Crystallinity in polymers

GLASS TRANSITION TEMPERATURE

In the molten state, the individual molecular chains of a plastic material move freely relative to each other, allowing the material to be moulded within the various forming processes used for the manufacture of components. As the temperature of melted plastic material is lowered, the freedom of movement of the molecular chains is reduced; gradually the plastic becomes more viscous, until eventually it solidifies at its characteristic melting point temperature. However, even when solid, most plastics remain rubbery or flexible, owing to rotations within the individual molecular chains. As the temperature is lowered further, the material will eventually become rigid and brittle, since movement can no longer take place within the individual molecular units. The temperature at which a particular plastic changes from flexible to rigid is defined as its characteristic *glass transition temperature*. Depending upon the nature of the particular plastic material this may be above or below normal ambient temperatures. Further, the glass transition temperature for a par ticular plastic can be significantly changed by, for example, the addition of plasticisers, characterised by the differences in physical properties between PVC-U (unplasticised) and PVC (plasticised polyvinyl chloride).

Polymer types

Polymers are normally categorised in respect of their physical properties as either thermoplastic, thermosetting or elastomeric.

THERMOPLASTICS

Thermoplastics soften upon heating, and reset on cooling. The process is reversible and the material is unaffected by repeating the cycle, provided that excessive temperatures, which would cause polymer degradation, are not applied. Many thermoplastics are soluble in organic solvents, while others swell by solvent absorption. Thermoplastics are usually produced initially in the form of small granules for subsequent fabrication into components.

THERMOSETTING PLASTICS

Thermosetting plastics have a three-dimensional cross-linked structure, formed by the linkage of adjacent macromolecular chains (Fig. 10.7). Thermosets are not softened by heating, and will only char and degrade if heated to high temperatures. Thermosets are usually produced from a partially polymerised powder or by mixing two components, such as a resin and a hardener. The resin is essentially the macromolecular component and the hardener cross-links the liquid resin into

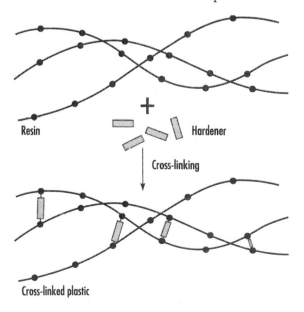

Resin Hardener

Cross-linking

Cross-linked plastic

Fig. 10.7 Cross-linking in thermosetting plastics

the thermoset plastic. Curing for epoxy resin adhesives and polyesters as in GRP (glass-fibre reinforced polyester) occurs at room temperature, while for phenolic and formaldehyde-based resins, a raised temperature and pressure are required. Thermosets, because of their three-dimensional structure, are usually solvent resistant and harder than thermoplastics.

ELASTOMERS

Elastomers are long-chain polymers in which the naturally helical or zig-zag molecular chains are free to straighten when the material is stretched, and recover when the load is removed. The degree of elasticity depends upon the extensibility of the polymeric chains. Thus natural rubber is highly extensible, but when sulfur is added, the vulcanisation process increasingly restricts movement by locking together adjacent polymer chains (Fig. 10.8). For most uses some cross-linking is required to ensure that an elastomeric material returns to its original form when the applied stress is removed.

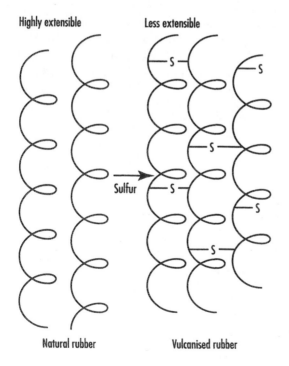

Fig. 10.8 Elastomers and the effect of cross-linking

Additives

PLASTICISERS

Plasticisers are frequently incorporated into plastics to increase their flexibility. The addition of the plasticiser separates the molecular chains, decreasing their mutual attraction. Thus unplasticised PVC (PVC-U) is suitable for the manufacture of rainwater goods, window units and glazing, whereas plasticised PVC is used for flexible single-layer roof membranes, tile and sheet floor coverings and electrical cable insulation. Loss of plasticiser by migration can cause eventual embrittlement of plasticised PVC components.

FILLERS

Chalk, sand, china clay or carbon black are often added to plastics to reduce costs or improve fire resistance or opacity. Titanium dioxide is added to PVC-U to produce a good shiny surface. Glass fibres are added to polyester resins to give strength to the composite material, glass-fibre reinforced polyester (GRP), as described in Chapter 11.

PIGMENTS AND STABILISERS

Dyes and pigments may be added to the monomer or polymer. Stabilisers are added to absorb ultraviolet light which otherwise would cause degradation. For example, organotin compounds are used in clear PVC sheet to preferentially absorb incident ultraviolet light, in order to prevent degradation by the elimination of hydrogen chloride.

Degradation of plastics

The degradation of plastics is most frequently attributed to the breakdown of the long molecular chains (Fig. 10.9) or, in the case of PVC, the loss of plasticiser. Polymeric molecular chains may be broken by the effect of either heat, ultraviolet light or ozone, or by a combination of any of these factors, thus reducing their average molecular chain length. Discolouration occurs through the production of molecular units with double bonds, usually causing a yellowing of the plastic. Surface crazing and stress cracks may develop where degradation has caused cross-linking, resulting in embrittlement of the surface.

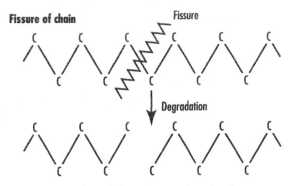

Fissure of chain   Fissure

Degradation

Breaking of polymer chain into shorter lengths

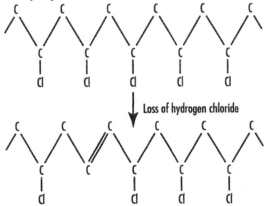

Loss of hydrogen chloride

Loss of hydrogen chloride

Production of double bonds – yellow degraded polymer

Fig. 10.9 Degradation of plastics

Where plasticiser is lost by migration from PVC, the glass transition temperature is gradually raised, so eventually the material becomes brittle at ambient temperatures. Typically, high-boiling-point oils such as dibutyl phthalate and dioctyl phthalate are incorporated into the original PVC, but these gradually evaporate, leaving the surface vulnerable to cracking and shrinkage.

Properties of plastics

FIRE

All plastics are combustible, producing noxious fumes and smoke (Table 10.1). Carbon monoxide is produced by most organic materials, but in addition, plastics containing nitrogen, such as polyurethane foam, generate hydrogen cyanide, and PVC produces hydrochloric acid. Some plastics, particularly acrylics and expanded polystyrene, have a high surface spread of flame and produce burning droplets; however, others when treated with fire retardant are difficult to ignite and some are self-extinguishing.

STRENGTH

Although plastics have a good tensile strength to weight ratio, they also have a low modulus of

Table 10.1 Behaviour of common building plastics in fire

Material	Behaviour in fire
Thermoplastics	
Polythene Polypropylene	} Melts and burns readily
Polyvinyl chloride	Melts, does not burn easily, but emits smoke and hydrogen chloride
PTFE	Does not burn, but at high temperatures evolves toxic fumes
Polymethyl methacrylate	Melts and burns rapidly, producing droplets of flaming material
Polystyrene	Melts and burns readily, producing dense black smoke and droplets of flaming material
ABS copolymer	Burns readily
Polyurethane	The foam burns readily, producing highly toxic fumes including cyanides and isocyanates
Thermosetting plastics	
Phenol formaldehyde Melamine formaldehyde Urea formaldehyde	} Resistant to ignition, but produces noxious fumes including ammonia
Glass-reinforced polyester (GRP)	Burns producing smoke, but flame-retarded grades are available
Elastomers	
Rubber	Burns readily, producing black smoke and sulfur dioxide
Neoprene	Better fire resistance than natural rubber

elasticity which renders them unsuitable for most loadbearing situations; the only exception is glass-fibre reinforced polyester (GRP), which has been used for some very limited loadbearing applications. Generally, thermoplastics soften at moderate temperatures and are subject to creep under ambient conditions.

THERMAL AND MOISTURE MOVEMENT

The thermal expansion of most plastics is high. The expansion of GRP is similar to that of aluminium, but most other plastics have larger coefficients of linear expansion. For this reason, attention must be paid to careful detailing to allow for adequate thermal movement, particularly where weather exclusion is involved. Most plastics are resistant to water absorption, and therefore do not exhibit moisture movement. (Typical coefficients of linear expansion are polythene (HD) 110–130, polypropylene 110, ABS 83–95, PVC 40–80, GRP 20–35 $\times 10^{-6}$deg C^{-1}.)

Plastics forming processes

Depending upon the nature of the product, plastics may be formed by either continuous or batch processes. With thermoplastics, frequently a two-stage process is most appropriate in which the raw materials, supplied by the primary manufacturer as powder or granules, are formed into an extrusion or sheet which is then reformed into the finished product. However, thermosetting plastics must be produced either from a partially polymerised material or directly from the resin and hardener mix in a single stage process. Foamed plastics are either blown with internally generated gas, or produced by a vacuum process which reduces reliance on environmentally damaging CFCs and HCFCs.

CONTINUOUS PROCESSES

Extrusion

Plastic granules are fed continuously into the heated barrel of a screw extruder, which forces the molten thermoplastic through an appropriately shaped die to produce rod, tube or the required section Fig. 10.10. Products include pipes, rainwater goods and fibres.

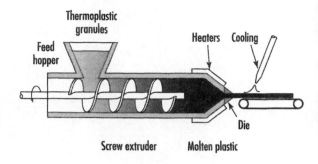

Fig. 10.10 Formation of plastics by extrusion

Film blowing

As a molten thermoplastic tube is produced in the extrusion process, air is blown in to form a continuous cylindrical plastic sheet, which is then rolled flat and trimmed to produce a folded sheet. Adjustment of the applied air pressure controls the sheet thickness.

Calendering

Sheet thermoplastic materials may be produced from plastics granules by compression and fusion between a series of heated rollers. Laminates may be produced by heating together two or more thermoplastic sheets, and during this process, sheet reinforcement material may be incorporated.

BATCH PROCESSES

Injection moulding

Thermoplastic granules are melted in a screw extruder to fill a ram which injects the plastic into an appropriate mould. After cooling, the components are removed from the mould and trimmed as necessary. The process is low cost and rapid. A series of moulds can be attached to the injection moulding machine to ensure continuity of production (Fig. 10.11). Thermosetting polymers can be injection moulded by initial forming at a low temperature followed by heating of the mould to cross-link the liquid plastic.

Compression moulding

In the compression moulding process for thermosetting resins, the appropriate quantity of uncross-linked resin powder is subjected to pressure and heat within the mould. When the polymer has melted and cross-linked, the mould can be opened and the component removed.

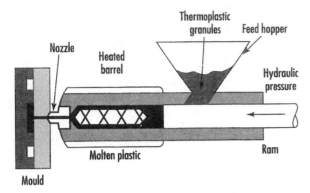

Fig. 10.11 Formation of plastics by injection moulding

Pressing

Pressing is used to form thermoplastic sheet into components. The sheet plastic is initially heated to softening point and then pressed between an appropriately shaped pair of dies.

Vacuum forming and blow moulding

During vacuum forming, thermoplastic sheet is heated over a mould which is then evacuated through a series of fine holes, drawing the soft plastic into the appropriate form. In a similar process, blow moulding, positive air pressure is applied inside a molten polymer tube which is expanded into the shape of the mould.

Plastics in construction

The broad range of thermoplastic, thermosetting and elastomeric plastics are collated into families in Fig. 10.12. Typical uses in construction are listed in Table 10.2. (Glass-fibre reinforced polyester is described in Chapter 11, foamed plastics as insulation materials in Chapter 13, and plastics used primarily as adhesives in Chapter 14.)

THERMOPLASTICS

Polythene (polyethylene)

Polythene (PE) is one of the cheapest plastics and is available both in the low-density (LD) (softening

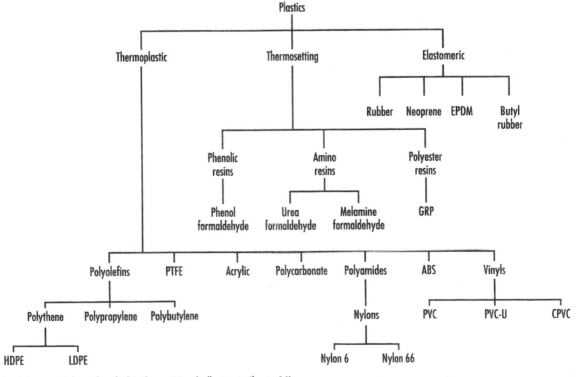

(Insulation materials are described in Chapter 13 and adhesives in Chapter 14)

Fig. 10.12 Plastics used in construction

Table 10.2 Typical uses of plastics in construction

Material		Examples of plastics in construction
Thermoplastics		
Polythene	(Low density)	DPC, DPM, vapour checks, roof sarking
	(High density)	Cold-water tanks, cold-water plumbing
Polypropylene		Pipework and fittings, drainage systems, water tanks, WC cisterns, DPCs, fibres in fibre-reinforced concrete
Polybutylene		Hot- and cold-water pipework and fittings
Polyvinyl chloride	(PVC-U)	Rainwater goods, drainage systems, pipes and fittings, underground services, window and door frames, conservatories, garage doors, cladding, translucent roofing sheets
	(PVC)	Tile and sheet floor coverings, single-ply roofing, cable insulation, electrical trunking systems, sarking, tensile membrane structures, glazing to flexible doors, door seals, handrail coatings, vinyl-film finishes to timber products
	(CPVC)	Hot-water systems, window and door frames
PTFE		Sealing tape for plumbing, tensile membrane structures, low-friction movement joints
Polymethyl methacrylate		Baths, shower trays, kitchen sinks, glazing, roof lights, luminaires
Polycarbonate		Vandal-resistant glazing, spa baths, kitchen sinks
Polystyrene		Bath and shower panels, decorative expanded polystyrene tiles
ABS copolymer		Pipes and fittings, rainwater goods, drainage systems, shower trays
Nylons		Electrical conduit and trunking, low-friction components – hinges, brush strips for sealing doors and windows, carpet tiles, carpets and shower curtains
Thermosetting plastics		
Phenol formaldehyde		Decorative laminates
Melamine formaldehyde		Laminates for working surfaces and doors, moulded electrical components, WC seats
Urea formaldehyde		Decorative laminates, decorative door furniture
Glass-reinforced polyester (GRP)		Cladding and roofing panels, simulated cast-iron rainwater goods, cold-water tanks, spa baths, garage doors, decorative tiles and panels
Elastomers		
Rubber		Flooring, door seals, anti-vibration bearings
Neoprene		Glazing seals, gaskets
EPDM		Glazing seals, gaskets, single-ply roofing systems
Butyl rubber		Sheet liners to water features and land-fill sites
Nitrile rubber		Tile and sheet flooring

point 90°C) and high-density (HD) (softening point 125°C) forms. Polythene is resistant to chemicals and tough at low temperatures, but is rapidly embrittled by ultraviolet light unless carbon black is incorporated. Polythene burns and has a relatively high coefficient of thermal expansion. Low-density polythene is used widely for damp-proof membranes, damp-proof courses and vapour barriers. High-density polythene, which is stiffer than the low-density material, is used for tanking membranes to basements. Polythene is used for the production of cold-water cisterns, but is only suitable for cold-water plumbing applications owing to its high thermal expansion; also, for mains water pressure it requires a significant wall thickness owing to its relatively low tensile strength.

Polypropylene

Polypropylene (PP), with a softening point of 150°C, is slightly stiffer than polythene, to which it is closely related chemically. Like polythene, it is resistant to chemicals and susceptible to ultraviolet light, but unlike polythene becomes brittle below 0°C. However, the block copolymer with ethylene does have improved low-temperature impact resistance. Polypropylene is used for pipes, drainage systems, water tanks, DPCs, connecting sleeves for clay pipes and WC cisterns. Polypropylene fibres are used in fibre-reinforced cement to produce an increase in impact resistance over the equivalent unreinforced material.

Polybutylene

Polybutylene is used for pipe-work as an alternative to copper. It has the advantage of flexibility and the very smooth internal surface is resistant to the build-up of scale and deposits. Pipes may be connected by fusion or compression jointing.

Polyvinyl chloride

Polyvinyl chloride (PVC) is the most widely used plastic material in the construction industry. It is available both in the unplasticised form (PVC-U) and as the plasticised product (PVC). In both forms polyvinyl chloride is combustible, giving off noxious hydrogen chloride fumes; however, the unplasticised form tends to burn only with difficulty. PVC begins to soften at 75°C, and therefore cannot be used for hot water systems, although chlorinated PVC (CPVC) can be used at higher temperatures. PVC is soluble in certain organic solvents which, therefore, can be used for the solvent welding of joints, but PVC is unaffected by acids and alkalis.

PVC-U is widely used for rainwater goods, usually in white, grey, black or brown and similarly for soil and waste pipes. It is also used colour-coded for underground water, gas, electrical and telecommunications systems. PVC-U is used extensively for the manufacture of extruded window frames, door frames and conservatories, usually incorporating sealed double-glazing units. Where insufficient rigidity is achieved with the PVC-U alone, steel inserts within the extruded sections give strength and provide additional protection against forced entry. Cellular PVC-U, co-extruded with a cellular centre and solid facing, is used to produce extrusions such as window boards, skirtings and architraves. PVC-U is used in the manufacture of translucent, transparent and coloured profiled sheeting for domestic structures such as carports and conservatories, where an economical product is required, although eventually the products discolour and craze owing to the effects of direct ultraviolet light.

Plasticised PVC is extensively used in the manufacture of floor coverings, either as individual tile units or as continuously jointed sheet. It is also the most widely used material for single-layer roofing systems, owing to its durability, colour range and ease of application. It also offers an alternative to bitumen felt for sarking. Plasticised PVC is the standard for electrical cable insulation, and many small building components are made from injection moulded PVC.

PVC-coated polyester is used for tensile membrane roof structures. The durability depends directly upon the degree of translucency, although with 15% transmission 15 years can be reasonably expected. At greater levels of translucency, within the range 10–30%, the expected serviceable lifetime is considerably reduced. PVC-coated polyester membranes are a cheaper alternative to PTFE-coated fabrics, but are not non-combustible. The thermal insulation afforded by tensile membrane roofs is negligible, although pressurised multi-layer fluoropolymer foil cushion structures can achieve U-values within the range 1.5–2.5 W/m^{2}K. PVC is an ideal material for air-supported single or double skin structures.

Polytetrafluoroethylene

Polytetrafluoroethylene (PTFE) tape has a very low coefficient of friction and a high melting point. It is therefore ideal for use as a sealing tape for threaded joints in water and gas pipes. It is also used to form sliding joints in large structures. PTFE-coated polyester and glass-fibre woven fabrics are used for tensile membrane structures. In a fire, PTFE gives off toxic combustion products, but only at temperatures above which any fabric would have already failed and vented the heat and smoke. With a fire rating of Class 0, PTFE coated glass-fibre membranes are more expensive than the Class 1 rated PVC-coated polyesters, but are generally more durable, with an anticipated lifespan in excess of 20–25 years.

The Inland Revenue Amenity Building in Nottingham (Plate 7) is roofed with a PTFE (*Teflon*) coated glass-fibre fabric membrane spanning 24 m. The translucent fabric gives a well-lit internal space during the daytime, and a striking glowing surface at night. The membrane roof is suspended from four steel columns, and is linked to the fixed structure below by inflatable elements which absorb any movement.

Polymethyl methacrylate

Acrylic or polymethyl methacrylate (PMMA) is available in a wide variety of translucent or transparent, clear or brightly coloured sheets. It softens at a temperature of 90°C, and burns rapidly with falling droplets of burning material. Stress crazing may occur where acrylic has been shaped in manufacture and not fully annealed, but generally the material is resistant to degradation by ultraviolet light. Acrylic is frequently used for decorative signs, rooflights and light fittings. Baths and shower trays are manufactured from acrylic as a lighter alternative to cast iron and ceramics. Although not resistant to abrasion, scratches can usually be polished out with proprietary metal polish.

Polycarbonate

Polycarbonates (PC) are used as vandal-resistant glazing, owing to their high impact resistance, good optical transparency and low ignitability. Proprietary extruded cellular systems offer combined thermal insulation and vandal-resistant properties. The protective outer surface prevents ultraviolet degradation for ten years, and sections may be curved on site within the limits of the manufacturers' specifications.

Acrylonitrile butadiene styrene

Acrylonitrile butadiene styrene (ABS) plastics are a range of complex terpolymers manufactured by combining together the two copolymers, styrene-acrylonitrile and butadiene-styrene. ABS plastics are relatively expensive but tough and retain their strength at low temperatures. They are used to manufacture moulded components, rainwater and drainage goods. A special ABS solvent cement is required for solvent welding.

Nylons

Nylons, usually nylon 66 or nylon 6, are used for the manufacture of small components where low friction is required. Nylons are tough and strong but tend to be embrittled and become powdery on prolonged exposure to sunlight. Carpet tiles in nylon 66 are durable and hard wearing.

Kevlar

Kevlar (poly*para*benzamide) fibres are produced by extrusion of a cold solution of the polymer into a cylinder at a temperature of 200°C, which causes the solvent to evaporate. The resulting fibres are stretched by a drawing process that aligns the polymer molecules along the fibres to produce a very high modulus material, used in ropes and composite plastics.

THERMOSETTING PLASTICS

Phenol formaldehyde

Phenol formaldehyde (PF) was the original, and remains the cheapest, thermosetting resin. Currently, its main use is in the production of laminates by the hot pressing of layers of resin impregnated paper, fabric or glass fibre. The cured resin is brown, but heat-resistant laminates for working surfaces and wallboards are laminated with a decorative printed paper film and coated with a clear melamine formaldehyde finish. Phenol formaldehyde is resistant to ignition, but produces a phenolic smell on burning.

Urea formaldehyde

Urea formaldehyde (UF) is similar to phenol formaldehyde except that because it is clear, it can be produced to a range of colours including white. It is used in the manufacture of electrical components and other moulded components such as WC seats. Urea formaldehyde is resistant to ignition, but produces a fishy smell on burning. Urea formaldehyde foam is no longer used for cavity wall insulation.

Melamine formaldehyde

Melamine formaldehyde (MF) is available clear and in a wide range of colours. When heat cured it is hard wearing, durable and resistant to heat, and is therefore used as the surface laminate over the cheaper brown phenol formaldehyde layers in the production of working surface and wallboard laminates. Melamine formaldehyde is resistant to ignition, but produces a fishy smell on burning.

ELASTOMERS

Natural rubber

Natural rubber is harvested from the species *Hevea brasiliensis* in Africa, South America and Malaysia. The white latex is predominantly *cis*-polyisoprene, a macromolecule containing some double bonds within the carbon chain. It is these double bonds which permit cross-linking with sulfur when natural rubber is heated under pressure in the vulcanisation process. Natural rubber is usually reinforced with carbon and treated with antioxidants to prevent degradation; it is used for flooring and in antivibration bearings for buildings and large structures.

Neoprene

Neoprene (polychloroprene), unlike natural rubber, is resistant to chemical attack, and is therefore used for glazing seals and gasket systems. It is available only in black.

EPDM

Unlike neoprene, EPDM (ethylene propylene diene monomer) can be obtained in any colour, and it is characterised by high elongation and good weathering resistance to ultraviolet light and ozone. It is therefore taking over from neoprene as the key material for gaskets and is extensively used in single-ply roofing systems.

Butyl rubber

A copolymer of isobutylene and isoprene, butyl rubber has good chemical and weathering resistance. It is used as liners to land-fill sites and decorative water features.

References

FURTHER READING

Johansson, C.M.A. 1991: *Plastics in building.* RAPRA Technology Ltd., Review Report No. 48, **4**(12). Shrewsbury: Rapra Technology Ltd.

Hollaway, L. 1993: *Polymer and polymer composites for civil and structural engineering.* London: Blackie Academic and Professional.

STANDARDS

BS 476. Fire tests on building materials and structures.
    Part 4: 1970. Non-combustibility test for materials.
    Part 6: 1989. Method of test for fire propogation for products.
    Part 7: 1987. Method for classification of the surface spread of flame of products.
BS 743: 1970. Materials for damp-proof courses.
BS 864. Capillary and compression tube fittings of copper and copper alloy pipe:
    Part 3: 1975. Compression fittings for polyethylene pipes.
    Part 5: 1990. Specification for compression fittings for polyethylene pipes with outside diameters to BS 5556.
BS 1254: 1981. Specification for WC seats (plastics).
BS 1763: 1975. Thin PVC sheeting (calendered, flexible, unsupported).

BS 2572: 1990. Specification for phenolic laminated sheet and epoxide cotton fabric laminated sheet.
BS 2592: 1973. Thermoplastic flooring tiles.
BS 2739: 1975. Thick PVC sheeting (calendered, flexible, unsupported).
BS 3012: 1970. Low and intermediate density polythene sheet for general purposes.
BS 3260: 1969. Specification for semi-flexible PVC floor tiles.
BS 3261. Unbacked flexible PVC flooring:
    Part 1: 1973. Homogeneous flooring.
BS 3284: 1967. Polythene pipes (Type 50) for cold water services.
BS 3379: 1991. Specification for flexible polyurethane cellular materials for loadbearing applications.
BS 3505: 1986. Specification for unplasticized polyvinyl chloride (PVC-U) pressure pipes for cold potable water.
BS 3757: 1978. Specification for rigid PVC sheet.
BS 3837. Expanded polystyrene boards:
    Part 1: 1986. Specification for board manufactured from expandable beads.
    Part 2: 1980. Specification for extruded boards.
BS 3869: 1965. Rigid expanded polyvinyl chloride for thermal insulation purposes and building applications.
BS 3927: 1986. Specification for rigid phenolic foam (PF) for thermal insulation in the form of slabs and profiled sections.
BS 3943: 1979. Specification for plastic waste traps.
BS 3953: 1990. Synthetic resin bonded woven glass fabric laminated sheet.
BS 4023: 1975. Flexible cellular PVC sheeting.
BS 4154. Corrugated plastic translucent sheets made from thermosetting polyester resins (glass fibre reinforced):
    Part 1: 1985. Specification for material and performance requirements.
    Part 2: 1985. Specification for profiles and dimensions.
BS 4203. Extruded rigid PVC corrugated sheeting:
    Part 1: 1980. Specification for performance requirements.
    Part 2: 1980. Specification for profiles and dimensions.
BS 4213: 1991. Specification for cold water storage and combined feed and expansion cisterns (polyolefin or olefin copolymer) up to 500 L capacity used for domestic purposes.
BS 4305. Baths for domestic purposes made from acrylic material:
    Part 1: 1989. Specification for finished baths.
BS 4346. Joints and fittings for use with unplasticized PVC pressure pipes:
    Part 1: 1969. Injection moulded unplasticized PVC fittings for solvent welding.
    Part 2: 1970. Mechanical joints and fittings, principally of unplasticized PVC.
    Part 3: 1982. Specification for solvent cement.

BS 4375: 1968. Unsintered PTFE tape for thread sealing applications.

BS 4514: 1983. Specification for unplasticized PVC soil and ventilating pipes, fittings and accessories.

BS 4576. Unplasticised polyvinyl chloride (PVC-U) rainwater goods and accessories:

Part 1: 1989. Half-round gutter and pipes of circular cross-section.

BS 4607. Non-metallic conduit fittings for electrical installations:

Part 2: 1970. Rigid PVC conduits and conduit fittings.

BS 4646: 1970. High density polythene sheet for general purposes.

BS 4660: 1989. Unplasticised polyvinyl chloride (PVC-U) pipes and plastics fittings for below ground gravity drainage and sewerage.

BS 4841. Rigid urethane foam for building applications:

Part 1: 1985. Laminated board for general purposes.

Part 2: 1975. Laminated board for use as a wall and ceiling insulation.

Part 3: 1987. Specification for two types of laminated board (roofboards).

BS 4901: 1976. Plastics colours for building purposes.

BS 4962: 1989. Specification for plastic pipes and fittings for use as subsoil field drains.

BS 4965: 1991. Specification for decorative laminated plastics sheet veneered boards and panels.

BS 4991: 1974. Specification for polypropylene copolymer pressure pipe.

BS 5085. Backed flexible PVC flooring:

Part 1: 1974. Needle-loom felt backed flooring.

Part 2: 1976. Cellular PVC backing.

BS 5241. Rigid polyurethane (PUR) and polyisocyanurate (PIR) foam when dispensed or sprayed on a construction site:

Part 1: 1994. Specification for sprayed foam thermal insulation applied externally.

Part 2: 1991. Specification for dispensed foam for thermal insulation or buoyancy applications.

BS 5254: 1976. Polypropylene waste pipe and fittings.

BS 5255: 1989. Thermoplastics waste pipe and fittings.

BS 5391. Specification for acrylonitrile-butadiene-styrene (ABS) pressure pipe:

Part 1: 1976. Pipe for industrial uses.

BS 5480: 1990. Glass reinforced plastics (GRP) pipes, joints and fittings for use for water supply or sewerage.

BS 5481: 1977. Specification for unplasticized PVC pipes and fittings for gravity sewers.

BS 5608: 1986. Specification for preformed rigid urethane (PUR) and polyisocyanurate (PIR) foams for thermal insulation of pipework and equipment.

BS 5617: 1985. Specification for urea-formaldehyde (UF) foam systems suitable for thermal insulation of cavity walls with masonry or concrete inner and outer leaves.

BS 5618: 1985. Code of practice for thermal insulation of cavity walls by filling with urea-formaldehyde (UF) foam systems.

BS 5955. Plastics pipework:

Part 8: 1980. Specification for the installation of thermoplastics pipes and associated fittings for use in domestic hot and cold water services and heating systems.

BS 6203: 1991. Guide to the fire characteristics and performances of expanded polystyrene (EP) materials used in building applications.

BS 6206: 1981. Specification for impact performance requirements for flat safety glass and safety plastics for use in building.

BS 6437: 1984. Specification for polyethylene pipes in metric diameters for general purposes.

BS 6515: 1984. Specification for polyethylene dampproof courses for masonry.

BS 6572: 1985. Specification for blue polyethylene pipes up to nominal size 63 for below ground use for potable water.

BS 6661: 1986. Guide for design, construction and maintenance of single-skin air supported structures.

BS 6730: 1986. Specification for black polythene pipes up to nominal size 63 for above ground use for cold potable water.

BS 7412: 1991. Plastics windows made from PVC-U extruded hollow profiles.

BS 7413: 1991. White PVC-U extruded hollow profiles with heat welded corner joints for plastics windows: materials type A.

BS 7414: 1991. White PVC-U extruded hollow profiles with heat welded corner joints for plastics windows: materials type B.

BS 7619: 1993. Specification for extruded cellular unplasticized PVC (PVC–ME) profiles.

BS 7722: 1994. Specification for surface covered PVC-U extruded hollow profiles with heat welded corner joints for plastics windows.

BS 7746: 1994. Generic identification and marking of plastics products.

BS 8203: 1987. Code of practice for installation of sheet and tile flooring.

BS EN 438. Decorative high-pressure laminates – sheets based on thermosetting resins:

Part 1: 1991. Specifications.

Part 2: 1991. Determination of properties.

BS EN 607: 1996. Eaves gutters and fittings made of PVC-U: definitions, requirements and testing.

BS EN 1054: 1996. Plastics piping systems – thermoplastics piping systems for soil waste discharge – test method for airtightness of joints.

BUILDING RESEARCH ESTABLISHMENT PUBLICATIONS

BRE Digests

BRE Digest 161: 1974. Reinforced plastics cladding panels.
BRE Digest 294: 1985. Fire risk from combustible cavity insulation.
BRE Digest 404: 1995. PVC-U windows.

BRE Report

BR 274: 1994. Fire safety of PTFE-based materials used in building.

TRADE ASSOCIATIONS

British Laminated Plastics Fabricators Association, 6 Bath Place, Rivington Street, London EC2A 3JE (0171 457 5000).
British Plastics Federation, 6 Bath Place, Rivington Street, London EC2A 3JE.
British Rubber Manufacturers Association Ltd., 90 Tottenham Court Road, London W1P 0BR (0171 580 2794).

11

GLASS-FIBRE REINFORCED PLASTICS, CEMENT AND GYPSUM

Introduction

Composite materials such as the glass-fibre reinforced materials GRP (glass-fibre reinforced polyester), GRC (glass-fibre reinforced cement) and GRG (glass-fibre reinforced gypsum) rely for their utility upon the advantageous combination of the disparate physical properties associated with the individual component materials. This is possible when a strong bond between the glass fibres and the matrix material ensures that the two materials within the composite act in unison. Thus polyester, which alone has a very low modulus of elasticity, when reinforced with glass fibres produces a material which is rigid enough for use as cladding. Cement, which alone would be brittle, when reinforced with glass fibres can be manufactured into thin, impact-resistant sheets. Similarly, glass-fibre reinforcement in gypsum considerably increases its impact and fire resistance.

Glass fibres

The glass fibres for GRP and GRG are manufactured from standard E-glass, as shown in Fig. 11.1. Molten glass runs from the furnace into a forehearth and through a spinneret of fine holes, from which it is drawn at high speed down to approximately 9 microns in thickness. The glass fibres are coated in size and bundled before winding up on a collet. Subsequently the glass fibre is used either as continuous rovings, as 20–50 mm chopped strand or as woven mats.

Glass-fibre reinforced plastics

The standard matrix material for glass-fibre reinforced plastics is polyester resin, although other thermosetting resins, including phenolic, epoxy and polyurethane, may be used. Glass fibres as continuous rovings or chopped strand are used for most purposes; however, the highest-strength products are obtained with woven glass fabrics and unidirectionally aligned fibres. The proportion of glass fibres ranges widely from 20% to 80% by weight depending upon the strength required. Alternative higher tensile strength fibres include the polyaramids such as *Kevlar* and carbon fibres, but these are more expensive than glass.

FABRICATION PROCESS

A major investment in the manufacture of GRP cladding panels lies within the production of the high-quality moulds. These are usually made from timber, but steel or GRP itself may also be used. Moulds are reused, sometimes with minor variations (e.g. the insertion of a window void within a wall unit), as many times as possible to minimise production costs. The number of different mould designs for any one building is therefore kept to a minimum, and this may be reflected in the repetitiveness of the design.

In the fabrication process, the mould is coated with a release agent to prevent bonding and associated damage to the finished panel surface. A gel coat, which ultimately will be the weathering surface, is applied to a finished thickness of 0.25–0.4 mm. Early examples of GRP without sufficient gel coat

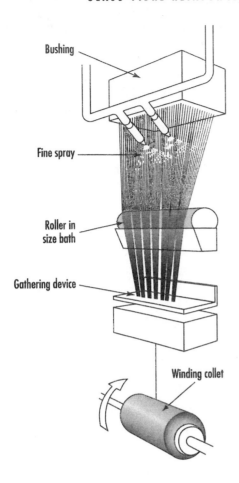

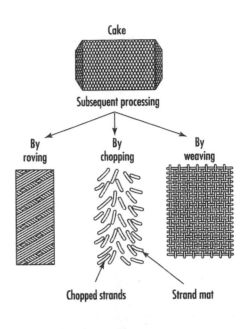

Fig. 11.1 Glass fibre production – rovings, chopped strand and mat

have weathered to a rough surface with consequent exposure of the glass fibres; however, modern gel coats, when applied to the correct thickness, are durable. The subsequent fabrication involves the *laying-up* of layers of glass fibres and polyester resin to the required thickness, usually with either sprayed rovings or chopped strand mat. Reinforcement and fixings, normally in aluminium owing to similarities in coefficients of expansion, may be incorporated and areas requiring additional strength can be thickened as appropriate by the laying-up process. Plastic foam insulation may be encapsulated to give the required thermal properties. Curing may take up to two weeks, after which the unit is stripped from the mould, trimmed around the edges and fitted out.

PHYSICAL PROPERTIES AND DESIGN CONSIDERATIONS

The choice of GRP, for example as a cladding panel, imparts its own aesthetic on a building design. The high strength to weight ratio of GRP allows for the use

of large panel units, but cost constraints in the mould-making reduce the number of panel variations to a minimum. Curved edges to panels and openings are preferred to reduce stress-raising points at very sharp corners. The high thermal expansion coefficient of GRP demands careful detailing of movement joints and their appropriate sealing where necessary with components that retain their flexibility. In some cases the high expansion can be resolved by the use of pro-filed forms, which also impart strength. Colour fading and yellowing of GRP panels has been a problem; however, recent products with ultraviolet light protection are more colour fast. Slightly textured finishes are generally more durable than smooth for exposure to full direct sunlight. GRP can be manufactured with fire-resistant additives; the phenolic resins have the advantage of lower flammability and smoke emissions. Long-term creep precludes the use of GRP as a significant loadbearing material, although single-storey structures, two-storey mobile units and structural overhead walkways are frequently constructed from the material. GRP is vandal resistant and can be laminated sufficiently to be bullet resistant. Where both surfaces are to be exposed, the material can be pressed between the two halves of a die.

USES OF GLASS-FIBRE REINFORCED PLASTICS

The lightweight properties of GRP make it eminently suitable for the manufacture of large cladding panels and custom-moulded structures (Fig. 11.2). Finishes may be self-coloured or incorporate a natural stone aggregate finish. In addition, GRP is frequently used for the production of architectural features such as barge boards, dormer windows, classical columns, entrance canopies and roof towers (Fig. 11.3). GRP may be pigmented to simulate various timbers, slate, Portland or Cotswold stone and lead or copper. It is also used to produce a wide range of small building components including baths, valley troughs, flat roof

edge trim and water drainage systems. In addition, a wide range of composite cladding panels are manufactured from glass-fibre reinforced resins incorporating stone granules within the core of the material. These products, which are impact and fire resistant, are available with either a granular stone, painted or gel-coat finish.

Glass-fibre reinforced cement

Glass-fibre reinforced cement is a relatively new material, having been developed in the early 1970s by the Building Research Establishment. The standard material is produced from a mixture of alkali-resistant glass fibres with Portland cement, sand aggregate and water. Admixtures such as pozzolanas, superplasticisers and polymers are usually incorporated into the mix to give the required fabrication or casting properties. The

Restaurant and Coffee shop, Blackpool
Architect: Building Design Partnership
Fig. 11.2 Typical GRP designs

Manchester City Football Ground Stand
Consulting Engineer: Brian Moorehead & Partners

nium oxide. Alkali-resistant glass fibres, which have been improved by progressive development, are manufactured under the trade name *Cem-FIL*. The addition to GRC mixes of metakaolin, a pozzolanic material produced by calcining china clay at a temperature of 750–800°C, prevents the development of lime crystals around the glass fibres. In the unblended GRC this leads to some gradual loss of strength. Standard grey GRC has the appearance of sheet cement and is non-combustible.

MANUFACTURE OF ALKALI-RESISTANT GLASS FIBRES

Silica, limestone and zircon are melted in a furnace; the alkali-resistant glass produced is drawn into fibres of 14 or 20 microns diameter and rolled into cakes for subsequent use as continuous rovings or for conversion into chopped strand. The process is comparable to that for standard E-glass fibres. *Cem-FIL* glass tissue with a fine texture is also available.

CEMENT MATRIX

Portland cement, strength class either 42.5 or 42.5R (rapid early strength), is normally used. Portland cement will produce a grey finish, but white Portland cement or added pigments may be used to give different effects. However, care must be taken with the use of pigments to ensure uniformity of colour. Washed sand and fly ash (pulverised fuel ash) are the usual aggregates, but crushed marble, limestone or granite may be used when a particular exposed aggregate finish is required.

FABRICATION PROCESSES

Fibre-reinforced cement components may be formed either by using a spray-gun, which mixes the glass fibres with a slurry of cement as it sprays directly into the mould, or by premixing a blend of cement, sand, water, admixtures and glass fibres before casting. Moulds similar to those required for the production of GRP components are used. Extrusion and injection moulding techniques are applicable for linear or small components, and bagged pre-blended mixes can be used for on site applications.

Sprayed glass-fibre reinforced cement

Spray techniques, which may be manual or robotic, are used to build up the required thickness, usually between 10 and 20 mm. During spraying, the gun

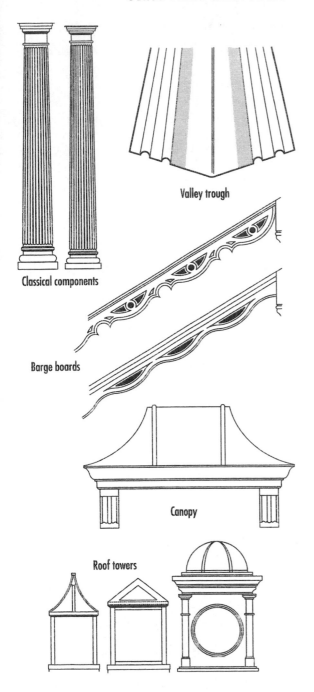

Fig. 11.3 Typical GRP components

Valley trough

Classical components

Barge boards

Canopy

Roof towers

breakthrough in the development of the material was the production of the alkali-resistant (AR) glass fibres, since the standard E-glass fibres, which are used in GRP and GRG, corrode rapidly in the highly alkaline environment of hydrated cement. Alkali-resistant glass, in addition to the sodium, silicon and calcium oxide components of standard E-glass, contains zirco-

chops the fibres into 25–40 mm lengths, depositing a uniform felt of fibres and mortar into the mould. A typical sprayed mix would contain 5% glass fibres, 36% Portland cement, 36% washed sand, 11% additives/polymer and 12% water. The curing of GRC is relatively slow, with 95% strength developed after seven days.

Premixed glass-fibre reinforced cement

It is normal to premix the cement, sand, water and admixtures then add the chopped fibres. A typical mix would contain up to 3.5% of 12 mm fibres in a sand : cement mix of 0.5 : 1 with a water : cement ratio of 0.35. The mix is then cast and vibrated, or pressed into form for smaller components. For renderings, a glass fibre content of between 1% and 2% is appropriate. A recent development involves the direct spraying of the premixed material.

PROPERTIES OF GLASS-FIBRE REINFORCED CEMENT

Appearance

While standard GRC has the appearance of cement, a wide diversity of colours, textures and simulated materials can be manufactured. A gloss finish should be avoided as it tends to craze and show any defects or variations. The use of specific aggregates followed by grinding can simulate marble, granite, terracotta, etc., while reconstructed stone with either a smooth or a tooled effect can be produced by the action of acid etching. An exposed aggregate finish is achieved by the use of retardants within the mould, followed by washing and brushing. Applied finishes, which are usually water-based synthetic latex emulsions, can be applied to clean, dust-free surfaces.

Moisture and thermal movement

GRC exhibits an initial irreversible shrinkage followed by a reversible moisture movement of approximately 0.2%. The coefficient of thermal expansion is within the range $7–20 \times 10^{-6}$ deg C^{-1}, typical for cementitious materials.

Thermal conductivity

The thermal conductivity of GRC is within the range 0.21–1.0 W/m K. Double-skin GRC cladding panel units usually incorporate expanded polystyrene, mineral wool or foamed plastic insulation. Cold bridging should be avoided where it may cause shadowing effects.

Durability

GRC is less permeable to moisture than normal concrete, so it has good resistance to chemical attack; however, unless manufactured from sulfate-resisting cement, it is attacked by soluble sulfates. GRC is unaffected by freeze/thaw cycling.

Impact resistance

GRC exhibits a high impact resistance but toughness and strength does decrease over long periods of time. However, the incorporation of metakaolin ($2SiO_2.Al_2O_3$) into the mix appears to improve the long-term performance of the material.

USES OF GLASS-FIBRE REINFORCED CEMENT

GRC is used extensively for the manufacture of cladding panels because it is lightweight and easily moulded. It is used in conservation work as a replacement for natural stone and in architectural features, including sophisticated decorative mouldings within countries of the Middle East (Fig. 11.4). It is used as permanent formwork for concrete, fire-resistant partitioning and in the manufacture of small components including slates, tiles and decorative ridge tiles. Glass-fibre reinforced cement slates

Fig. 11.4 Typical GRC components

are manufactured to simulate the texture and colour of natural slate. Some manufacturers incorporate blends of other non-asbestos natural and synthetic fibres together with pigments and fillers to produce a range of coloured products with glossy, matt or simulated riven finishes.

Glass-fibre reinforced gypsum (GRG)

Glass-fibre reinforced gypsum combines the non-combustibility of gypsum plaster with the reinforcing strength of glass fibres. Products contain typically 5% of the standard E-glass fibres, which considerably improve impact as well as fire resistance. Commercial GRG products are available as standard panels, encasement systems for the fire protection of steel and decorative wall panels. As with all gypsum products, GRG should not be used in damp conditions or at temperatures regularly over 50°C.

GLASS-FIBRE REINFORCED GYPSUM BOARDS

The standard boards, available in a range of thicknesses from 4 mm to 12.5 mm, are manufactured with a glass-fibre reinforced gypsum core and glass-fibre tissue immediately below the gypsum faces. The material is suitable for a wide range of applications including wall linings, ceilings and protected external positions such as roof soffits. The material can be easily cut on site and fixed with nails or screws; in addition, owing to the effect of the glass-fibre reinforcement, it can be curved to fit, for example, barrel-vault ceilings. The minimum radius of curvature depends upon the board thickness. The material has a smooth off-white finish; joints should be taped before finishing board plaster is applied.

For steelwork, protection thicknesses of 15, 20 and 25 mm are available. Depending upon the steel section factor (Hp/A m^{-1}), with double layers and staggered joints, up to 120 minutes' fire resistance can be achieved (Fig. 11.5).

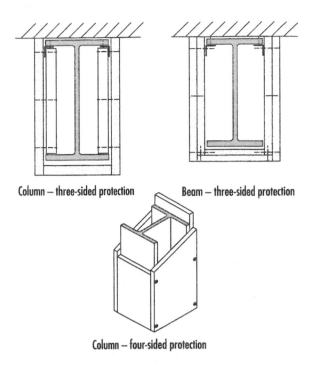

Column – three-sided protection   Beam – three-sided protection

Column – four-sided protection

Fig. 11.5 Fire protection with GRG panels

Decorative glass-fibre reinforced gypsum boards and ceiling tiles

Decorative boards manufactured with a range of motifs can be used as dado or wall panels (Fig. 11.6). Dabs of sealant are used initially to fix panels to existing walls and to allow adjustment to a flush finish. Panels may be painted after jointing.

Ceiling tiles manufactured from GRG are available to a wide range of designs, including plain, textured, patterned, open- or closed-cell surface and with square, tapered or bevelled edges. The standard size is usually 600 × 600 mm, although some manufacturers produce units at 300 × 600 or 1200 and 600 × 1200 mm. GRG has good fire-resistant properties; it is non-combustible to BS 476 Part 4: 1970, Class 1 surface spread of flame to BS 476 Part 6: 1989, Class 0 to Building Regulations Section E15, and does not emit smoke or noxious fumes in fire. Acoustic tiles with enhanced sound absorption and attenuation properties are normally part of the standard range, which may also include Imperial sizes for refurbishment work.

Decorative panels

![Georgian panels and Victorian panels]

Georgian

Victorian

Chinois

Gothic

Decorative mouldings

Centrepiece

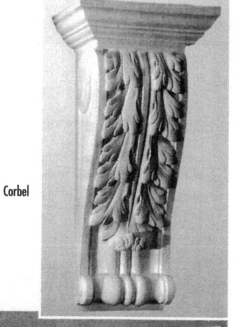

Corbel

Cornice

Fig. 11.6 Decorative GRG plaster components

References

FURTHER READING

British Gypsum. 1993: *The white book*. Loughborough: British Gypsum Ltd.

British Gypsum. 1995: *Glasroc fire book*. Loughborough: British Gypsum Ltd.

Fordyce, M.W. and Wodehouse, R.G. 1983: *GRC and buildings*. London: Butterworth.

Glassfibre Reinforced Cement Association. 1986: *This is GRC*. Newport: The Glassfibre Reinforced Cement Association.

Hollaway, L. 1976: *The use of plastics for load bearing and infill panels*. Croydon: Manning Rapley Publishing Ltd.

Hollaway, L. (ed.) 1978: *The design and specification of GRP cladding*. Croydon: Manning Rapley Publishing Ltd.

Hollaway, L. 1994: *Handbook of polymer composites for engineers*. Cambridge: Woodhead Publishing Ltd.

Leggatt, A.J. 1984: *GRP and buildings*. London: Butterworth.

Majumdar, A.J. and Laws, V. 1990: *Glass fibre reinforced cement*. Oxford: BSP Professional.

Pilkington. *CEM-FIL GRC technical data*. Merseyside: Cem-FIL International Ltd.

Swamy, R.N. (ed.) 1992: *Fibre reinforced cement and concrete*. London: E. & F. N. Spon.

Young, J. 1978: *Designing with GRC*. London: Architectural Press.

STANDARDS

BS 476. Fire tests on building materials and structures.
    Part 6: 1989. Methods of test for fire propogation for products.
    Part 7: 1987. Method for classification of the surface spread of flame of products.

BS 5544: 1978. Specification for anti-bandit glazing (glazing resistant to manual attack).

BS 6206: 1981. Specification for impact requirements for flat safety glass and safety plastics for use in buildings.

BS 6432: 1984. Methods for determining properties of glass reinforced cement material.

BS 7491. Glass fibre reinforced plastic cisterns for cold water storage:
    Part 1: 1991. Specifications for one piece cisterns of capacity up to 500 L.
    Part 2: 1992. Specification for one piece cisterns of nominal capacity from 500 L to 25 000 L.
    Part 3: 1994. Specification for sectional tanks.

BS EN 492: 1994. Fibre-cement slates and their fittings for roofing – product specification and test methods.

BS EN 494: 1994. Fibre-cement profiled sheets and fittings for roofing – product specification and test methods.

BUILDING RESEARCH ESTABLISHMENT PUBLICATIONS

BRE Digests

BRE Digest 161: 1974. Reinforced plastics cladding panels.
BRE Digest 331: 1988. GRC.

BRE Information Papers

BRE IP 5/84. The use of glass-reinforced cement in cladding panels.
BRE IP 10/87. Polymer modified grc.
BRE IP 1/91. Durability of non-asbestos fibre-reinforced cement.

BRE Report

BR 49: 1984. The use of glass-reinforced cement in cladding panels.

TRADE ASSOCIATIONS

British Plastics Federation, 6 Bath Place, Rivington Street, London EC2A 3JE.

Fibre Cement Manufacturers Association Ltd., PO Box 117, Hexham, Northd. NE46 3LQ (01434 601393).

Glassfibre Reinforced Cement Association, The Wigan Investment Centre, Waterside Drive, Wigan, Lancs. WN3 5BA (01942 705550).

12

PLASTER AND BOARD MATERIALS

—

Introduction

Plastering, based on lime, was brought to Britain by the Romans. In Britain it was originally used to strengthen and seal surfaces and in the case of combustible materials to afford some fire protection, but by the eighteenth century its value as a decorative finish had been appreciated. The use of gypsum plaster both as a sealant and as a decorative material by the Minoan civilisation is well documented, and current UK practice is now based on gypsum (hydrated calcium sulfate), rather than lime. Gypsum is mined from geological deposits produced by the gradual evaporation of lakes containing the mineral; there are extensive reserves within the UK, mainly in the North of England, but also in the East Midlands.

Historically, fibrous materials have been used to reinforce plaster. Traditionally ox, horse and goat hair were the standard materials; however, straw, hemp and jute have also been used. The earliest lightweight support for plasters was interwoven hazel twigs, but by the fifteenth century split timber laths were common. The modern equivalent is the use of galvanised and stainless steel expanded metal.

Gypsum plaster

MANUFACTURE OF GYPSUM PLASTER

Rock gypsum is mined, crushed and ground to a fine powder. The natural mineral may be white or coloured pale pink, grey or brown owing to small quantities of impurities which do not otherwise

affect the product. On heating to temperatures in the range of 130°–160°C, water is driven off the hydrated gypsum; the type of plaster produced is largely dependent upon the extent of this dehydration process.

$$CaSO_4.2H_2O \xrightarrow{130°C} CaSO_4.\tfrac{1}{2}H_2O \xrightarrow{160°C} CaSO_4$$

hydrated gypsum → hemi-hydrate → anhydrous gypsum

The classes of plaster are defined in the British Standard BS 1191: 1973.

CLASSES OF PLASTER

Class A – Plaster of Paris

Plaster of Paris is produced by driving off three quarters of the water content from natural hydrated gypsum. Plaster of Paris sets very quickly on the addition of water, and is therefore often used as a moulding material.

Class B – retarded hemi-hydrate gypsum plaster

The majority of plasters in current use within construction are based on retarded hemi-hydrate gypsum. The addition of different quantities of a retarding agent, usually keratin, is used to adjust the setting time for different products.

Undercoat and one-coat plasters
The main constituents of undercoat and one-coat plasters are retarded hemi-hydrate gypsum, with expanded perlite or exfoliated vermiculite for the lightweight products, together with small quantities of limestone, anhydrite (anhydrous gypsum), clay and sand. In addition, other materials are incorpor-

ated to adjust the product specification and setting time, which normally ranges between one and two hours. Thus, lime is added to undercoat plaster, and for backgrounds of high suction, a water retention agent is also required. For example, *browning* is suitable for use on backgrounds with moderate or high suction and a good mechanical key. For higher impact resistance, cement and granulated blastfurnace slag are incorporated, and for a one-coat plaster, limestone is added. Typical applications would be 11 mm for undercoats with a finish coat of 2 mm, or a single one-coat application of 13 mm.

Finish-coat plasters

For finish-coat plasters, like undercoat plasters, the main constituent is retarded hemi-hydrate gypsum, but with a small addition of lime to accelerate the set. The lightweight products contain exfoliated vermiculite. Finish coats on masonry substrates are usually 2 mm in thickness, and board-finish plaster is normally applied to 2–3 mm.

Class C – Anhydrous gypsum plaster

When natural gypsum is heated at a temperature of 160°C, most of the water is driven off leaving anhydrous calcium sulfate or anhydrite. The proportion of the hemi-hydrate remaining is dependent upon the heating time and temperature. Anhydrous gypsum plaster sets very slowly, so an accelerator such as alum is added. The plaster has an initial set, after which it can be smoothed with the addition of more water to the surface. The material has been superseded by the Class B plasters.

Class D – Keene's plaster

Anhydrous gypsum with an accelerator sets slowly to a very hard surface, which can be worked to a high-quality, glass-like finish. It is difficult to paint owing to its glassy surface and therefore requires a special primer to provide a key. The material has been superseded by cement-based products.

BACKGROUNDS FOR PLASTER

Plaster bonds to the background by a combination of mechanical key and adhesion. Backgrounds should be clean, dry and free from other contamination and the specification of the plaster should be appropriate to the suction of the background surface. Where possible, as in the case of brickwork, a good mechanical

key should be obtained by raking out the joints. On hard, low-suction materials such as smooth concrete and ceramic tiles, a PVA (polyvinyl acetate) bonding agent should be applied. Similarly, to control the high suction in substrates such as aerated concrete blocks, a PVA bonding agent can be applied or the substrate wetted prior to the application of plaster. Plaster can, however, be applied directly to dense aggregate concrete blocks without prior wetting. Where two or more coats of plaster are used, the undercoats should be scratched to ensure good subsequent bonding. Gypsum plasters, if put on correctly, do not shrink or crack on drying out and subsequent coats can be applied in quick succession.

PLASTERBOARD

Plasterboard consists of an aerated gypsum core bonded to strong paper liners. Most wallboards have one light surface for direct decoration and one grey surface which may be plastered with a skim of board plaster. The decorative surface may be tapered at its edge, while the grey surface is square for plastering. Plasterboard may be cut with a saw or scored and snapped. Nail fixings should be driven in straight, leaving a shallow depression but without fracturing the paper surface. Alternatively, boards may be screwed. Standard thicknesses are 9.5, 12.5, 15 and 19 mm. Only the moisture-resistant grades of plasterboard normally require the application of a PVA bonding agent before plastering. These have a water-resistant core and treated liners, so may be used behind external finishes such as vertical tiling and weatherboarding or in external sheltered positions protected from direct rain. Boards are available finished with PVC, backed with aluminium foil or laminated to insulation (expanded polystyrene, extruded polystyrene, rigid polyurethane foam or mineral wool) for increased thermal properties. (The thermal conductivity of standard plasterboard is 0.16 W/m K.)

Fibre-reinforced gypsum boards

Fibre-reinforced gypsum boards are manufactured with either natural or glass fibres. Glass-fibre reinforced gypsum (GRG) is described in Chapter 11.

Natural fibre-reinforced gypsum boards are manufactured from cellulose fibres, frequently from recycled paper, within a matrix of gypsum. The panel boards are either uniform or laminated with a perlite and gypsum core, encased in a hard layer of fibre-reinforced gypsum. Boards are impact- and fire-resistant and easily fixed by nails, screws, staples or adhesive as a dry-lining system to timber, metal framing or masonry. Standard boards are 1200 × 2400 mm with thicknesses in the range 9.5–18 mm. Joints are filled or taped and corners beaded as for standard plasterboard products. A composite board of fibre-reinforced gypsum and expanded polystyrene offers enhanced insulation properties. (The thermal conductivity of fibre-reinforced gypsum board is typically 0.36 W/m K.)

ACCESSORIES FOR PLASTERING

Beads

Angle and stop beads are manufactured from galvanised or stainless perforated steel strip or expanded metal. They provide a protected, true straight arris or edge for traditional plastering to masonry or for thin-coat plasterboard. Proprietary systems are manufactured similarly from perforated galvanised or stainless steel to form movement joints in dry lining systems (Fig. 12.1).

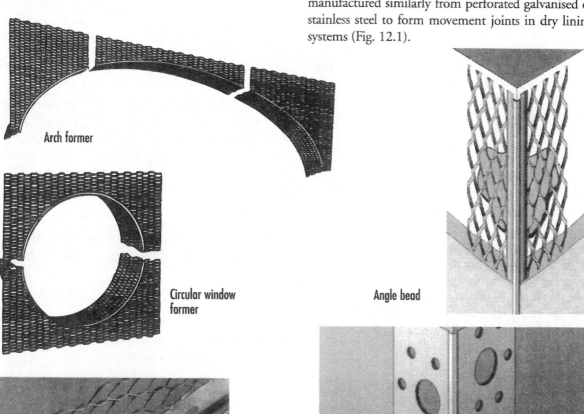

Arch former

Circular window former

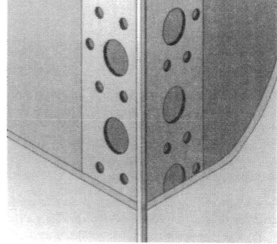

Angle bead

Stop bead

Thin coat bead

Fig. 12.1 Plastering beads and arch formers

Scrim

Scrim, an open-weave material, is used across joints between plaster boards and in junctions between plaster and plasterboard. Both self-adhesive glass-fibre mesh and traditional jute scrim are available. For the prevention of thermal movement cracking at plasterboard butt joints, paper tape bedded into the plaster skim is often more effective than the use of self-adhesive scrim.

Coves and cornices

Decorative coves and cornices are manufactured from gypsum plaster encased in a paper liner. In some cases the gypsum is reinforced with glass fibres. The components (Fig. 12.2) may be cut to size with a saw, and are normally fixed with proprietary adhesives.

SPECIAL PLASTERS

Renovating plaster

Renovating plaster is used where walls have been stripped of existing plaster, during the successful installation of a new damp-proof course. Renovating plasters contain aggregates which promote surface drying when they are applied to structures with residual moisture, but they should not be used in permanently damp locations below ground level. Renovating plaster should also not be used where masonry is heavily contaminated with salts, such as in buildings not originally built with damp-proof courses, and on the brickwork of chimney breasts.

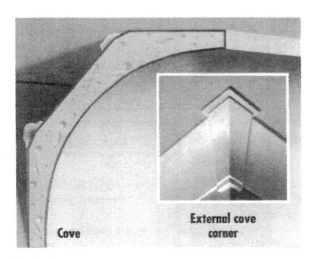

Cove

External cove corner

Fig. 12.2 Preformed plaster coves

Renovating plasters contain a fungicide to inhibit mould growth during the drying out process.

Projection plaster

Projection plaster is sprayed onto the background from a plaster projection machine. The plaster should be built up to the required thickness, ruled to an even surface then flattened and trowelled to a flat surface. As with all plastering, the process should not be carried out under freezing, excessively hot or dry conditions.

Acoustic plaster

Acoustic plaster has a higher level of sound absorption than standard gypsum plasters owing to its porosity and surface texture. Aluminium powder is added to the wet plaster mix to produce fine bubbles of hydrogen gas which remain trapped as the plaster sets, giving it a honeycomb structure. One form of acoustic plasterboard consists of a perforated gypsum plasterboard which may be backed with a 100 mm glass wool sound-absorbing felt.

X-ray plaster

X-ray plaster is retarded hemi-hydrate plaster containing barium sulfate (barytes) aggregate. It is used as an undercoat plaster in hospitals etc. where protection from X-rays is required. Typically, a 20 mm layer of X-ray plaster affords the same level of protection as a 2 mm sheet of lead, provided that it is free of cracks.

Textured plaster

Textured plaster is frequently applied to plasterboard ceilings. A variety of different patterns and textures can be achieved. The textured surface may be left as a natural white finish or painted as required.

Fibrous plaster

Fibrous plaster is plaster of Paris reinforced with hessian, wire mesh or wood laths. It is used for casting in moulds, ornate plasterwork such as fire surrounds, decorative cornices, dados, friezes, panel mouldings, corbels and centrepieces for ceilings in both restoration and new work.

GYPSUM FLOOR SCREED

Gypsum interior floor screed, manufactured from a mixture of hemi-hydrate gypsum, limestone and less than 2% cement, may be used as an alternative to a traditional sand and cement screed, provided that a floor covering is to be used. The material is self smoothing and may be pumped. It is laid on a polythene membrane to a minimum thickness of 35 mm for floating screeds, and may be used over underfloor heating systems. When set, the hard plaster has a minimum 28 day compressive strength of 30 N/mm^2.

FIRE RESISTANCE OF PLASTER MATERIALS

Gypsum products afford good fire protection within buildings owing to their basic chemical composition. Gypsum, hydrated calcium sulfate ($CaSO_4.2H_2O$), as present in plaster and plasterboard, contains nearly 21% water of crystallisation. When exposed to a fire this chemically combined water is gradually expelled in the form of vapour. It is this process which absorbs the incident heat energy from the fire, considerably reducing the transmission of heat through the plaster, thus protecting the underlying materials. The process of dehydrating the gypsum commences on the face adjacent to the fire, and immediately the dehydrated material, because it adheres to the unaffected gypsum, acts as an insulating layer slowing down further dehydration. Even when all the water of crystallisation has been expelled, the remaining anhydrous gypsum continues to act as an insulating layer while it retains its integrity. The inclusion of glass fibres into gypsum plasterboards increases the cohesiveness of the material within fires.

Calcium silicate boards

Calcium silicate boards are manufactured from silica with lime and/or cement, usually incorporating cellulose fibres or softwood pulp and mica or exfoliated vermiculite filler, to produce a range of densities. The high-density material is laminated under steam and pressure, while the lower-density material is produced by rolling followed by curing in an autoclave. Calcium silicate boards, like gypsum boards, are non-combustible. The material is grey or off-white in colour, easily worked and nailed. Calcium silicate boards are durable, moisture, chemical and impact resistant with dimensional stability and a good strength to weight ratio. They are available with a range of smooth or textured factory finishes for interior or exterior use and also laminated to extruded polystyrene for enhanced insulation properties. Standard thicknesses include 4.5, 6.0, 9.0 and 12.0 mm, although thicknesses up to 60 mm are available in the vermiculite lightweight boards used for fire protection, giving up to 4 hours' resistance. Typical applications include wall, roof and partition linings, suspended ceilings, fasciae, soffits, weatherboarding and fire protection to structural steelwork. External cladding boards may be finished with a sprayed or trowelled render to produce a seamless finish. (The thermal conductivities of calcium silicate boards are usually within the range 0.13 to 0.29 W/m K depending upon their composition.)

References

FURTHER READING

Ashurst, J. and Ashurst, N. 1988: *Practical building conservation vol. 3: Mortars, plasters and renders*. Aldershot: Gower Technical Press.
British Gypsum. 1993: *The white book*. Loughborough: British Gypsum.
Cape Boards. 1995: *The fire protection handbook*. Uxbridge: Cape Boards Ltd.

STANDARDS

BS 1191. Gypsum building plasters:
    Part 1: 1973. Excluding premixed lightweight plasters.
    Part 2: 1973. Premixed lightweight plasters.
BS 1230. Gypsum plasterboard:
    Part 1: 1985. Specification for plasterboard excluding materials submitted to secondary operations.
BS 1369. Steel lathing for internal plastering and external rendering:
    Part 1: 1987. Specification for expanded metal and ribbed lathing.
BS 4022: 1970. Prefabricated gypsum wallboard panels.
BS 5270. Bonding agents for use with gypsum plasters and cement:
    Part 1: 1989. Specification for polyvinyl acetate (PVAC) emulsion bonding agents for indoor use with gypsum building plasters.
BS 5492: 1990. Code of practice for internal plastering.

BS 6100. Glossary of building and civil engineering terms:
  Part 6. Concrete and plaster.
  Subsec. 6.6.2: 1990. Plaster.
BS 6452. Beads for internal plastering and dry lining:
  Part 1: 1983. Specification for galvanized steel beads.
BS 7364: 1990. Galvanized steel studs and channels for stud and sheet partitions and linings using screw fixed gypsum wallboards.
BS 8000. Workmanship on building sites:
  Part 8: 1994. Code of practice for plasterboard partitions and dry linings.
  Part 10: 1995. Code of practice for plastering and rendering.
BS 8212: 1995. Code of practice for dry lining and partitioning using gypsum plasterboard.

BUILDING RESEARCH ESTABLISHMENT PUBLICATIONS

BRE Defect Action Sheets

BRE DAS 81: 1986. Plasterboard ceiling for direct decoration: nogging and fixing – specification.
BRE DAS 82: 1986. Plasterboard ceiling for direct decoration: nogging and fixing – site work.
BRE DAS 86: 1986. Brick walls: replastering following dpc injection.

BRE Good Building Guide

BRE GBG 7: 1991. Replacing failed plasterwork.

TRADE ASSOCIATIONS

Gypsum Products Development Association, c/o KPMG, 165 Queen Victoria Street, London EC4V 4DD (0171 311 2942).

13

INSULATION MATERIALS

—

Introduction

With increasing emphasis being placed upon energy-conscious design and the broader environmental impact of buildings, greater attention is necessarily being focused upon the appropriate use of thermal and sound insulation materials.

Thermal and sound insulation materials

The Approved Document of the Building Regulations gives guidance on minimum thermal performance criteria for buildings, based on standards for their individual elements, or the overall energy efficiency of the whole building. To consider the relative efficiency of insulating materials, the thermal conductivities (W/m K) are quoted at the standard 10°C to allow direct comparisons. U-values would not illustrate direct comparability owing to the varying thicknesses used, and the wide variety of combinations of materials typically used in construction.

In considering acoustic control, distinction is made between the reduction of sound transmitted directly through the building components and the attenuation of reflected sound by the surfaces within a particular enclosure. Furthermore, transmitted sound is considered in terms of both impact and air-borne sound. Impact sound is caused by direct impact onto the building fabric which then vibrates, transmitting the sound through the structure; it is particularly significant in the case of intermediate floors. Air-borne sound waves, from the human voice and sound-generating equipment, cause the building fabric to vibrate, thus transmitting the sound. Air-borne sound is particularly critical in relation to separating walls and is significantly increased by leakage at discontinuities within the building fabric, particularly around unsealed openings. The reduction in sound energy passing through a building element is expressed in decibels (dB). The doubling of the mass of a building component reduces the sound transmission by approximately 5 dB; thus sound-insulating materials are generally heavy structural elements. However, the judicious use of dissipative absorbers within walls can reduce the reliance for sound absorption on mass alone. Noise may be transmitted through services installations, so consideration should be given to the use of acoustic sleeves and linings as appropriate.

The absorption of sound at surfaces is related to the porosity of the material. Generally, light materials with fibrous or open surfaces are good absorbers, reducing ambient noise levels and reverberation times, whereas smooth, hard surfaces are highly reflective to sound (Table 13.1). Sound absorption is measured on a 0 to 1 scale with 1 representing total absorption of the sound.

FORMS OF INSULATION MATERIALS

Insulation materials may be categorised variously according to their appropriate uses in construction, their physical forms or their material origin. Many insulating materials are available in different physical forms each with their appropriate uses in building. Broadly, the key forms of material could be divided

Table 13.1 Typical sound absorption coefficients at 125, 500 and 2000 Hz for various building materials

Material	Absorption coefficient		
	125 Hz	500 Hz	2000 Hz
Concrete	0.02	0.02	0.05
Brickwork	0.05	0.02	0.05
Plastered solid wall	0.03	0.02	0.04
Glass 6 mm	0.1	0.04	0.02
Timber boarding, 19 mm over air space against solid backing	0.3	0.1	0.1
Wood wool slabs, 25 mm, on solid backing, unplastered	0.1	0.4	0.6
Fibreboard, 12 mm on solid backing	0.05	0.15	0.3
Fibreboard, 12 mm over 25 mm air space	0.3	0.3	0.3
Mineral wool, 25 mm with 5% perforated hardboard over	0.1	0.85	0.35
Expanded polystyrene board, 25 mm over 50 mm air space	0.1	0.55	0.1
Flexible polyurethane foam, 50 mm on solid backing	0.25	0.85	0.9

into:

- structural insulation materials;
- rigid and semi-rigid sheets and slabs;
- loose fill, blanket materials and applied finishes;
- aluminium foil.

However, within this grouping, it is clear that certain materials spread over two or three categories. Insulation materials are therefore categorised according to their composition, with descriptions of their various forms, typical uses in construction and, where appropriate, fire protection properties. Materials are initially divided into those of inorganic and organic origin respectively.

The broad range of non-combustible insulating materials are manufactured from ceramics and inorganic minerals including natural rock, glass, calcium silicate and cements. Some organic products are manufactured from natural cork or wood fibres but materials developed by the plastics industry predominate. In some cases these organic materials offer the higher thermal insulation properties but many are either flammable or decompose within fire. Cellular plastics include open- and closed-cell materials. Generally the closed-cell products are more rigid and have better thermal insulation properties and resistance to moisture, whereas the open-cell materials are more flexible and permeable. Aluminium foil is considered as a particular case since its thermal insulation properties relate to the transmission of radiant, rather than conducted, heat. Typical thermal conductivity values are indicated in Table 13.2.

Table 13.2 Typical thermal conductivity values for various building materials

Material	Thermal conductivity (W/m K)
Phenolic foam	0.018–0.031
Polyurethane foam (rigid)	0.019–0.023
Foil-faced foam	0.020
Polyisocyanurate foam	0.023–0.025
Extruded polystyrene	0.025–0.027
Expanded PVC	0.030
Mineral wool	0.031–0.040
Glass wool	0.031–0.040
Expanded polystyrene	0.033–0.040
Urea-formaldehyde foam	0.038
Rigid foamed glass	0.037–0.048
Corkboard	0.042
Fibre insulation board	0.050
Perlite board	0.050
Exfoliated vermiculite	0.062
Wood wool slabs	0.077
Foamed concrete (low density)	0.10
Lightweight to dense concrete	0.10–1.5
Compressed straw slabs	0.101
Softwood	0.13
Particleboard/plywood	0.14
Gypsum plasterboard	0.16
Bituminous felt	0.19
Calcium silicate boards	0.13–0.29
GRC – lightweight	0.21–0.5
GRC – standard density	0.5–1.0
Mastic asphalt	0.5
Calcium silicate brickwork	0.67–1.24
Clay brickwork	0.65–1.95
Glass	1.05

Inorganic insulation materials

FOAMED CONCRETE

The manufacture of foamed concrete is described in Chapter 3. Foamed concrete with an air content in the range 30–80% is a fire- and frost-resistant material. Foamed concrete can be easily placed without the need for compaction but it does exhibit a higher drying shrinkage than dense concrete. It is suitable for insulation under floors and on flat roofs where it may be laid to a fall of up to 1 in 100. (Thermal conductivity ranges from 0.10 W/m K at a density of 400 kg/m³ to 0.63 W/m K at a density of 1600 kg/m³).

LIGHTWEIGHT AGGREGATE CONCRETE

Lightweight concrete blocks and *in situ* concrete are discussed in Chapters 2 and 3 respectively. Lightweight concrete materials offer a range of insulating and loadbearing properties, starting from 0.10 W/m K at a crushing strength of 2.8 N/m². Resistance to air-borne sound in masonry walls is closely related to the mass of the wall. However, any unfilled mortar joints which create air paths will allow significant leakage of sound. In cavity walls mass is significant, but to reduce sound transmissions the two leaves should also be physically isolated, with the exception of the necessary wall ties, to comply with the Building Regulations.

GYPSUM PLASTER

Plasterboard thermal linings will increase the thermal response in infrequently heated accommodation; the effect can be enhanced with metallised polyester-backed boards which reduce radiant as well as transmitted heat loss. The addition of such linings for either new or upgrading existing buildings reduces the risk of thermal bridging at lintels etc. (The thermal conductivity of gypsum plaster is typically 0.16 W/m K.)

Sound transmission through lightweight walls can be reduced by the use of two layers of differing thicknesses of gypsum plasterboard (e.g. 12.5 and 19 mm) as these resonate at different frequencies. The addition of an extra layer of plasterboard attached to existing ceilings with resilient fixings can reduce sound transmission from upper floors, particularly if an acoustic quilt can also be incorporated.

WOOD WOOL SLABS

Wood wool slabs manufactured from wood fibres and cement (Chapter 4) are both fire and rot resistant. With their combined loadbearing and insulating properties, wood wool slabs are suitable as a roof decking material, which may be exposed, painted or plastered to the exposed lower face. Wood wool slabs offer good sound absorption properties owing to their open-textured surface, and this is largely unaffected by the application of sprayed emulsion paint. Acoustic insulation for a pre-screeded 50 mm slab is typically 30 dB. (The thermal conductivity of wood wool is typically 0.077 W/m K.)

MINERAL WOOL

Mineral wool is manufactured from volcanic rock (predominantly silica, with alumina and magnesium oxide) which is blended with coke and limestone and fused at a temperature of 1500°C in a furnace. The melt runs onto a series of rotating wheels which spin the droplets into fibres; they are then coated with resin binder and water-repellent mineral oil. The fibres fall onto a conveyor belt, where the loose mat is compressed to the required thickness and density, then passed into an oven where the binder is cured; finally, the product is cut into rolls or slabs. Mineral wool is non-combustible, water-repellent, rot proof and contains no CFCs or HCFCs.

Mineral wool is available in a range of forms dependent on its degree of compression during manufacture and its required use:

- loose for blown cavity insulation;
- mats for insulating lofts, lightweight structures and within timber-framed construction;
- batts (slabs) for complete cavity fill of new masonry;
- semi-rigid slabs for partial cavity fill of new masonry;
- rigid slabs for warm pitched roof and flat-roof insulation;
- rigid resin-bonded slabs for floor insulation;
- weather-resistant boards for inverted roofing systems;
- dense pre-painted boards for exterior cladding;
- ceiling tiles.

The mats and board materials may be faced with aluminium foil to enhance their thermal properties. Roof slabs may be factory cut to falls or bitumen faced for torch-on roofing felt systems. Floor units are coated with paper when they are to be directly screeded. A resilient floor can be constructed with floor units manufactured from mineral wool slabs, with the fibres oriented vertically rather than horizontally, bonded directly to tongued and grooved flooring-grade particleboard.

The thermal conductivity of mineral wool products for internal use ranges typically between 0.031 and 0.040 W/m K at 10°C, although products for external use have higher conductivities.

Mineral wool can be used effectively to attenuate transmitted sound. In lightweight construction, acoustic absorbent quilts are effective for reducing transmitted sound through separating walls when combined with double plasterboard surfaces and a wide air space, as well as in traditional timber joist floors when combined with a resilient layer between joists and floor finish. Pelletised mineral wool can be used for *pugging* between floor joists to reduce sound transmission, and is particularly appropriate for upgrading acoustic insulation during refurbishment.

Mineral wool, owing to its non-combustibility, is used for manufacture of fire stops to prevent fire spread through voids and cavities, giving fire resistance ratings of between 30 and 120 minutes. Mineral wool slabs give typically between 60 minutes' and 4 hours' fire protection to steel. Similar levels of protection can be achieved with sprayed-on mineral wool, which may then be coated with a decorative finish.

Ceiling tiles for suspended ceilings manufactured from mineral wool typically provide Class 1 spread of flame to BS 476 Part 7: 1987 and Class 0 to Part 6: 1989 on both their decorative and back surfaces. The thermal conductivity of mineral wool suspended ceiling tiles is typically within the range 0.052–0.057 W/m K. Sound attenuation of mineral wool ceiling tiles usually lies within the range 34–36 dB, but depending upon the openness of the tile surface, the sound absorption coefficient may range from 0.1 for smooth tiles, through 0.5 for fissured finishes to 0.95 for open-cell tiles overlaid with 20 mm mineral wool.

GLASS WOOL

Glass wool is made by the Crown process (Fig. 13.1), which is similar to that used for mineral wool. A thick stream of glass flows from a furnace into a forehearth and by gravity into a rapidly rotating steel alloy dish, punctured by hundreds of fine holes around its perimeter. The centrifugal force expels the filaments, which are further extended into fine fibres by a blast of hot air. The fibres are sprayed with a bonding agent and then sucked onto a conveyor to produce a mat of the appropriate thickness. This is cured in an oven to set the bonding agent, then finally cut, trimmed and packaged.

Glass wool is non-combustible, water-repellent, rot proof and contains no CFCs or HCFCs and is available in a range of product forms:

■ loose for blown cavity wall insulation;
■ rolls, either unfaced or laminated between kraft

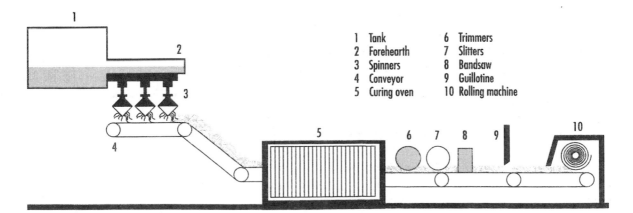

1	Tank	6	Trimmers
2	Forehearth	7	Slitters
3	Spinners	8	Bandsaw
4	Conveyor	9	Guillotine
5	Curing oven	10	Rolling machine

Fig. 13.1 Crown process for the manufacture of glass wool

paper and polythene, for roofs, within timber-frame construction, internal walls and within floors;

- semi-rigid batts with water-repellent silicone for complete cavity fill of new masonry;
- rigid batts for partial cavity fill within new masonry;
- compression-resistant slabs for solid concrete or beam and slab floors;
- a laminate of rigid glass wool and plasterboard for dry linings;
- PVC-coated rigid panels for exposed factory roof linings.

(The thermal conductivity of glass wool products ranges typically between 0.031 and 0.040 W/m K at 10°C.)

The sound and fire-resistant properties of glass wool are similar to those of mineral wool. Glass wool sound-deadening quilts, which have overlaps to seal between adjacent units, are used to reduce impact sound in concrete and timber floating floors. Standard quilts are appropriate for use in lightweight partitions and over suspended ceilings.

Resin-bonded glass wool treated with water repellent is used to manufacture some ceiling tiles which meet the Class 0 fire spread requirements of the Building Regulations (BS 476: Parts 6 and 7) and also offer sound absorption to reduce reverberant noise levels.

FOAMED GLASS BLOCKS

Foamed glass is manufactured from a mixture of crushed glass and fine carbon powder which, on heating to a temperature of 1000°C, causes the carbon to oxidise creating bubbles within the molten glass. The glass is annealed, cooled and finally cut to size. The black material is durable, non-combustible, easily worked and has a high compressive strength. It is water-resistant owing to its non-interconnecting cellular structure, impervious to water vapour and contains no CFCs.

Foamed glass slabs are appropriate for roof insulation, including roof-top car parks, owing to their high compressive strength. The slabs are usually bonded in hot bitumen to either concrete screeds, profile metal decking or bitumen-felt coated timber roofing. Foamed glass is suitable for floor insulation under the screed and may be used internally, externally or with

in the cavity of external walls. Externally it may be rendered or tile hung and internally finished with plasterboard or expanded metal and conventional plaster. (The thermal conductivity of foamed glass is within the range 0.037–0.048 W/m K at 10°C, depending upon the grade.)

EXFOLIATED VERMICULITE

Exfoliated vermiculite, which contains up to 90% air by volume, is used as a loose fill for loft insulation and within a cementitious spray produces a hard fire-protective coating for exposed structural steelwork. Where thicknesses over 30 mm are required, application should be in two coats. The product has a textured surface finish which may be exposed internally or painted in external applications. Depending upon the thickness of application and the ratio (Hp/A) between exposed surface area and steel cross-section (Chapter 5), up to 4 hours' fire protection may be obtained. Vermiculite is used for certain demountable fire stop seals where services penetrate through fire compartment walls. (The thermal conductivity of exfoliated vermiculite is 0.062 W/m K. Within lightweight aggregate concrete a thermal conductivity of typically 0.11 W/m K can be achieved.)

GLASS AND MULTIPLE GLAZING

The thermal and sound insulation effects of double and triple glazing and the use of low-emissivity glass are described in Chapter 7.

CALCIUM SILICATE

Calcium silicate, which is described in Chapter 12, has the advantage of good impact resistance and is very durable. A range of wallboards are manufactured with calcium silicate boards laminated to extruded polystyrene. (Calcium silicate typically has a thermal conductivity of 0.29 W/m K.)

Organic insulation materials

CORK PRODUCTS

Cork is harvested from the cork oak (*Quercus suber*) on a nine-year (or more) cycle and is therefore considered to be an environmentally friendly material. For conversion into boards, typically used for roof insulation, cork granules are expanded, then formed under heat and pressure into blocks using the natural resin within the cork. The blocks are trimmed to standard thicknesses or to a taper to produce falls for flat roofs (Fig. 13.2). For increased thermal insulation properties, the cork may be bonded to closed-cell polyurethane or polyisocyanurate foam. In this case the laminate should be laid with the cork uppermost. Cork products are unaffected by the application of hot bitumen in flat roofing systems. (The thermal conductivity of corkboard is 0.042 W/m K.)

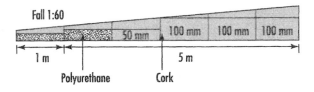

Fig. 13.2 Cork insulation to falls for flat roofs

FIBRE INSULATION BOARD

The manufacture of insulation board or softboard, which is a low-density fibre building board, is described in Chapter 4. Standard grades of insulation board should only be used in situations where they are not in contact with moisture, or at risk from the effects of condensation. Insulation board is used for wall linings and may be backed with aluminium foil for increased thermal insulation. Insulation board may be impregnated with inorganic fire retardants to give a Class 1 surface spread of flame to BS 476 Part 7: 1987 or finished with plasterboard to give a smooth Class 0 fire rated surface.

Exposed insulation board has good sound absorbing properties owing to its surface characteristics. Standard 12 mm lining softboard has a noise reduction coefficient of 0.42, although this is increased to 0.60 for the 24 mm board.

Bitumen-impregnated insulation board, with its enhanced water-resistant properties, is used as a thermal insulation layer on concrete floors. The concrete floor slab is overlaid with polythene, followed by bitumen-impregnated insulation board and the required floor finish such as particleboard. In the upgrading of existing suspended timber floors, a loose-laid layer of bitumen-impregnated insulation board under a new floor finish can typically reduce both impact and air-borne sound transmission by 10 dB. Bitumen-impregnated insulation board is frequently used in flat roofing systems as a heat protective layer to polyurethane, polystyrene or phenolic foams prior to the application of the hot bitumen waterproof membrane. It is also used for sarking in pitched roofs. (The thermal conductivity of insulation board is typically 0.050 W/m K.)

EXPANDED POLYSTYRENE

Expanded polystyrene is a combustible material, which, in fire, produces large quantities of noxious black smoke although Type A, with a flame retardant additive, is not easily ignitable. Expanded polystyrene, a closed-cell product, is unaffected by water, dilute acids and alkalis but is readily dissolved by most organic solvents. It is rot and vermin proof, and CFC and HCFC free.

Polystyrene beads

Expanded polystyrene beads are used as loose fill for cavity insulation. To prevent subsequent slippage and escape through voids, one system bonds the polystyrene beads by spraying them with atomised PVA adhesive during the injection process, although other processes leave the material loose. Walls up to 12 m in height can be insulated by this type of system. Polystyrene bead insulation should not be used where electrical wiring is present in the cavity, as the polystyrene gradually leaches the plasticiser out from plastic cables causing their embrittlement, which could lead to problems later if the cables are subsequently moved. Polystyrene bead aggregate cement is used to form an insulating sandwich core in concrete cladding panel systems.

Expanded polystyrene boards

Expanded polystyrene rigid lightweight boards are used for thermal insulation and for impact sound insulation. There are five grades available, each of which may be normal (Type N) or with fire-retardant additive (Type A) (Table 13.3).

The boards, which are manufactured by fusing together pre-foamed beads under heat and pressure,

Table 13.3 Thermal conductivity values for various grades of polystyrene

Grade		Thermal conductivity (W/m K)
UHD	Ultra high duty	0.033
EHD	Extra high duty	0.033
HD	High duty	0.034
SD	Standard duty	0.037
ISD	Impact sound duty	0.040

can easily be cut, sawn or melted with a hot wire. Polystyrene boards provide thermal insulation for walls, roofs and floors. In addition, polystyrene may be cast into reinforced concrete, from which it is easily removed to create voids for fixings.

In cavity wall insulation, a 25 mm cavity may be retained to prevent the risk of water penetration, with proprietary wall ties fixing the boards against the inner leaf. Alternatively, with a full-fill cavity system the boards may be slightly moulded on the outer surface to shed any water back onto the inside of the external masonry leaf. Interlocking joints prevent cold bridging, air leakage and water penetration at the board joints. In upgrading existing walls, external expanded polystyrene insulation should be protected by suitably supported rendering or tile hanging. For internal wall insulation, expanded polystyrene can be used in conjunction with 12.5 mm plasterboard either separately or as a laminate. Expanded polystyrene is used to give thermal insulation in ground floors. It may be laid below or above the oversite slab; if the latter, it may be screeded or finished with chipboard. Composite floor panels manufactured from expanded polystyrene and oriented strand board are suitable for beam and block floors while proprietary systems offer thermal insulation to prestressed concrete beam and reinforced concrete screed floors. Expanded polystyrene boards reduce impact and airborne sound transmission through intermediate floors.

Expanded polystyrene is suitable for thermal insulation in flat and pitched roofs. For flat roofs it may be cut to falls. Where hot bitumen products are to be applied, the expanded polystyrene boards must be protected by an appropriate layer of bitumen-impregnated fibreboard, perlite board or corkboard. In metal deck applications the insulating layer may be above or below the purlins, whereas in traditional pitched roofs expanded polystyrene panels are normally installed over the rafters. Expanded

polystyrene, although a closed-cell material, acts as a sound absorber, provided it is installed with an air gap between it and the backing surface. It particularly absorbs sound at low frequencies and may be used in floors and ceilings. It is, however, less effective than the open-cell materials such as flexible polyurethane foam. (The thermal conductivity of expanded polystyrene is in the range 0.033–0.040 W/m K depending upon the grade.)

EXTRUDED POLYSTYRENE

Extruded polystyrene is normally manufactured by a vacuum process although some is blown with CFCs. It is slightly denser and therefore slightly stronger in compression than expanded polystyrene but has a lower thermal conductivity. It has a closed-cell structure with very low water-absorption and vapour-transmission properties. Extruded polystyrene is available with densities and associated compressive strengths ranging from 20–40 kg/m^3, and 120–500 kPa respectively. Extruded polystyrene is widely used for cavity wall and pitched roof insulation. Because of its high resistance to water absorption, extruded polystyrene may be used for floor insulation below the concrete slab and on inverted roofs where its resistance to mechanical damage from foot traffic is advantageous. Extruded polystyrene is also available laminated to tongued and grooved moisture-resistant flooring-grade chipboard for direct application to concrete floor slabs, and laminated to plasterboard as a wallboard. (The thermal conductivity of extruded polystyrene is typically 0.025–0.027 W/m K.)

EXPANDED PVC

Plasticised PVC open, partially open and closed-cell foams are manufactured as flexible or rigid products within the density range of 24–72 kg/m^3. BS 3869: 1965 specifies two grades: 24–48 kg/m^3 and over 48 kg/m^3. The rigid closed-cell products provide low water permeability and are self-extinguishing in fire. Expanded PVC boards are used in sandwich panels and for wall linings. The low-density open-cell material has particularly good acoustic absorbency and can be used to reduce sound transmission through unbridged cavities and floating floors. (The thermal conductivity of expanded PVC is typically 0.030 W/m K.)

POLYISOCYANURATE FOAM

Polyisocyanurate foam (PIR), blown with HCFCs, is available in two grades: PIR1 and PIR2. It is used as a roof insulation material since it is more heat resistant than other organic insulation foams, which cannot be directly hot-bitumen bonded. PIR is combustible (BS 476 Part 4) with a Class 1 surface spread of flame (BS 476 Part 7) but is more fire resistant than polyurethane foam. Polyisocyanurate tends to be rather friable and brittle. Certain proprietary systems for insulated cavity closers use PVC-U coated polyisocyanurate insulation. Such systems offer a damp-proof barrier and can assist in the elimination of cold bridging, which sometimes causes condensation and mould growth around door and window openings. (The thermal conductivity of polyisocyanurate foam is usually in the range 0.023–0.025 W/m K).

POLYURETHANE FOAM

Rigid polyurethane (PUR) is closed-cell foam currently manufactured using CFCs (chlorofluorocarbons) or HCFCs (hydrochlorofluorocarbons), the latter being slightly less damaging to the atmospheric ozone layer. The CFCs and HCFCs remain trapped in the closed cells, enhancing the thermal performance. Certain polyurethanes are modified with polyisocyanurates.

Rigid polyurethane is a combustible material producing copious noxious fumes and smoke in fire, although a flame-resistant material is available. It is used to enhance the thermal insulation properties of concrete blocks either by filling the void spaces in hollow blocks or by direct bonding onto the cavity face. Roofboards, in certain systems pre-bonded to bitumen roofing felt, are suitable for mastic asphalt and built-up roofing systems. Owing to the temperature stability of polyurethane no additional protection from the effects of hot bitumen application is required; the durability of the material also makes it suitable for use in inverted roofs. Laminates with foil or kraft paper are available. Factory-manufactured double-layer profiled-metal sheeting units are frequently filled with rigid polyurethane foam owing to its good adhesive and thermal insulation properties. Polyurethane laminated to plasterboard is used as a wallboard. When injected as a premixed two-component system into cavity walls polyurethane adheres well to the masonry, foaming and expanding *in situ* to completely fill the void space. It has been used in situations where the cavity ties have suffered serious corrosion, and where additional bonding between the two leaves of masonry is required. However, polyurethane foam is not now widely available as a cavity insulation material.

Flexible polyurethane foam is an open-cell material offering good noise absorption properties. It is therefore used in unbridged timber-frame partitions, floating floors and duct linings to reduce noise transmission. Polyurethane foams are resistant to fungal growth, aqueous solutions and oils, but not to organic solvents. (The thermal conductivity of rigid polyurethane foam is usually in the range 0.019–0.023 W/m K at a nominal density of 32 kg/m^3. Flexible polyurethane foam typically has a thermal conductivity of 0.048 W/m K.)

UREA-FORMALDEHYDE FOAM

Urea-formaldehyde (UF) foam was used extensively in the 1980s for cavity wall insulation, but it can shrink after installation, creating fissures which link the outer and inner leaves. Occasionally, in conditions of high exposure, this has led to rainwater penetration. After installation, the urea-formaldehyde foam emits formaldehyde fumes which have, in certain cases, entered buildings causing occupants to suffer from eye and nose irritation. The problem normally arises only if the inner leaf is permeable and a cavity greater than 100 mm is being filled. Recent advances claim to have reduced formaldehyde emissions but all installations must be undertaken to the stringent British Standard BS 5618: 1985. (The thermal conductivity of urea-formaldehyde foam is typically 0.038 W/m K.)

PHENOLIC FOAM

Phenolic foams, which have very low thermal conductivities, are used as alternatives to rigid polyurethane and polyisocyanurate foams, where a self-extinguishing, low smoke emission material is required. Phenolic foams are produced with densities in the range 35 kg/m^3 to 200 kg/m^3, but some material is still blown with CFCs or HCFCs. Wallboard laminates with plasterboard offer good thermal insulation properties owing to the very low thermal conductivity of phenolic foam, compared to polyurethane or extruded polystyrene. Phenolic foams are stable up to a continuous temperature of 120°C. (The thermal conductivity of phenolic foam in the density range 35 to 60 kg/m^3 is typically 0.020 W/m K, although the open-cell material has a thermal conductivity of 0.031 W/m K.)

Aluminium foil

Aluminium foil is frequently used as an insulation material in conjunction with organic foam or insulating gypsum products. It acts by a combination of two physical effects. First, it reflects back incident heat owing to its highly reflecting surface. Second, owing to its low emissivity, the re-radiation of any heat that is absorbed is reduced. Proprietary quilt systems incorporating multilayers of aluminium foil, fibrous materials and cellular plastics act as insulation by reducing conduction, convection and radiation. (The thermal conductivity of foil-faced foam is typically 0.020 W/m K.)

Chlorofluorocarbons in foamed plastics

Until recently, rigid polyurethane and polyisocyanurate foams were blown with chlorofluorocarbons (CFCs). However, owing to the worldwide concern over the effects of these gases on the ozone layer, the use of CFCs is being rapidly phased out in favour of reduced ozone depletion potential (ODP) blowing agents such as the partially halogenated alkanes (PHAs), usually hydrochlorofluorocarbons (HCFCs). HCFCs themselves are due to be phased out early in the next century, and it is likely that hydrofluorocarbons (HFCs) with zero ozone depletion potential will quickly become the standard blowing agents. Carbon dioxide can be used as a blowing agent, but it produces less dimensionally stable products with higher thermal conductivities. Generally, CFC blown polyurethane foam has better insulating properties (thermal conductivity 0.019 W/m K) than the equivalent foam blown by non-CFCs (thermal conductivity 0.022 W/m K).

References

FURTHER READING

CIRIA. 1986: *Sound control for homes – A design manual.* CIRIA Report No.114. London: Construction Industry Research and Information Association.

Johnson, S. 1993: *Greener buildings – Environmental impact of property.* Basingstoke: Macmillan.

Kefford, V.L. 1993: *Plastics in thermal and acoustic building insulation.* Review Report No. 67, **6**(7): Shrewsbury: RAPRA Technology Ltd.

Parkin, P.H. and Humphreys, H.R. 1969: *Acoustics, noise and buildings.* London: Faber.

TIMSA. 1994: *Handbook – The specifiers insulation guide.* Aldershot: Thermal Insulation Manufacturers and Suppliers Association.

STANDARDS

BS 476. Fire tests on building materials and structures.
    Part 6: 1989. Method of test for fire propagation of materials.
    Part 7: 1987. Method for classification of the surface spread of flame of products.
BS 661: 1969. Glossary of acoustical terms.
BS 874: 1973. Methods for determining thermal insulating properties with definitions of thermal insulating terms.
BS 1142: 1989. Fibre building boards.
BS 2750. Methods of measurement of sound insulation in buildings and of building elements:
    Part 1: 1980, Part 3: 1995, Parts 4–8: 1990, Part 9: 1987.
BS 3379: 1991. Flexible polyurethane foam materials for loadbearing applications.
BS 3533: 1981. Glossary of thermal insulation terms.
BS 3837. Expanded polystyrene boards:
    Part 1: 1986. Specification for boards manufactured from expandable beads.
    Part 2: 1990. Specification for extruded boards.
BS 3869: 1965. Rigid expanded polyvinyl chloride for thermal insulation purposes and building applications.
BS 3927: 1986. Specification for rigid phenolic foam (PF) for thermal insulation in the form of slabs and sections.
BS 4023: 1975. Flexible cellular PVC sheeting.
BS 4840. Rigid polyurethane (PUR) foam in slab form.
    Part 2: 1994. Specification for PUR foam for use in refrigerator cabinets, cold rooms and stores.
BS 4841. Rigid polyurethane (PUR) foam for building applications:
    Part 1: 1975. Laminated board for general purposes.
    Part 2: 1975. Laminated board for use as a wall and ceiling insulation.

Part 3: 1994. Specification for two types of laminated board (roofboards).

BS 5241. Rigid polyurethane (PUR) and polyisocyanurate (PIR) foam when dispensed or sprayed on a construction site:

Part 1: 1994. Specification for sprayed foam thermal insulation applied externally.

Part 2: 1991. Specification for dispensed foam for thermal insulation or buoyancy applications.

BS 5250: 1989. Code of practice for control of condensation in buildings.

BS 5363: 1976. Method for measurement of reverberation time in auditoria.

BS 5422: 1990. Thermal insulating materials on pipes, ductwork and equipment.

BS 5608: 1986. Specification for preformed rigid polyurethane (PUR) and polyisocyanurate (PIR) foams for thermal insulation of pipework and equipment.

BS 5617: 1985. Specification for urea-formaldehyde (UF) foam systems suitable for thermal insulation of cavity walls with masonry or concrete inner and outer leaves.

BS 5618: 1985. Code of practice for thermal insulation of cavity walls by filling with urea-formaldehyde (UF) foam systems.

BS 5803. Thermal insulation for use in pitched roof spaces in dwellings:

Part 1: 1985. Specification for man-made mineral fibre thermal insulation mats.

Part 2: 1985. Specification for man-made mineral fibre thermal insulation in pelleted or granular form for application by blowing.

Part 3: 1985. Specification for cellulose fibre thermal insulation for application by blowing.

Part 4: 1985. Methods for determining flammability and resistance to smouldering.

Part 5: 1985. Specifications for installations of man-made mineral fibre and cellulose fibre insulation.

BS 5821: 1984. Methods for rating the sound insulation in buildings and of building elements.

BS 6203: 1991. Guide to the fire characteristics and fire performance of expanded polystyrene materials used in building applications.

BS 6676. Thermal insulation of cavity walls using man-made mineral fibre batts (slabs):

Part 1: 1986. Specification for man-made mineral fibre batts.

Part 2: 1986. Code of practice for installation of batts (slabs) filling the cavity.

BS 7021: 1989. Code of practice for thermal insulation of roofs externally by means of sprayed rigid polyurethane (PUR) or polyisocyanurate (PIR) foam.

BS 7456: 1991. Code of practice for stabilisation and insulation of cavity walls by filling with polyurethane (PUR) foam systems.

BS 7457: 1994. Specification for polyurethane (PUR) foam systems suitable for stabilisation and thermal insulation of cavity walls with masonry or concrete inner and outer leaves.

BS 8207: 1985. Code of practice for energy efficiency in buildings.

BS 8216: 1991. Code of practice for use of sprayed lightweight mineral coatings used for thermal insulation and sound absorption in buildings.

BS 8233: 1987. Sound insulation and noise reduction for buildings.

BS EN ISO 140. Acoustics – measurement of sound insulation in buildings and of building elements:

Part 2: 1993. Determination, verification and application of precision data.

Part 3: 1995 Laboratory measurement of airborne sound insulation of building elements.

Part 9: 1994. Laboratory measurement of room-to-room airborne sound insulation of a suspended ceiling with a plenum above.

Part 10: 1992. Laboratory measurements of airborne sound insulation of small building elements.

DD 156: 1987. Method of test for bond strength of sprayed mineral coatings.

BUILDING RESEARCH ESTABLISHMENT PUBLICATIONS

BRE Digests

BRE Digest 236: 1984. Cavity insulation.

BRE Digest 293: 1985. Improving the sound insulation of separating walls and floors.

BRE Digest 294: 1985. Fire risk from combustible cavity insulation.

BRE Digest 324: 1987. Flat roof design: thermal insulation.

BRE Digest 333: 1988. Sound insulation of separating walls and floors. Part 1: Walls.

BRE Digest 334: 1988. Sound insulation of separating walls and floor, Part 2: Floors.

BRE Digest 337: 1988. Sound insulation: basic principles.

BRE Digest 338: 1988. Insulation against external noise.

BRE Digest 347: 1989. Sound insulation of lightweight buildings.

BRE Digest 358: 1992. CFCs in buildings.

BRE Digest 379: 1993. Double glazing for heat and sound insulation.

BRE Information Papers

BRE IP 6/88. Methods for improving the sound insulation between converted flats.

BRE IP 12/91. Fibre building boards: types and uses.

BRE IP 18/92. Sound insulation and the 1992 edition of Approved Document E.
BRE IP 6/94. The sound insulation provided by windows.
BRE IP 12/94. Assessing condensation risk and heat loss at thermal bridges around openings.

BRE Defect Action Sheets

BRE DAS 77: 1986. Cavity external walls: cold bridges around windows and doors.
BRE DAS 79: 1986. External masonry walls: partial cavity fill insulation – resisting rain penetration.
BRE DAS 104: 1987. Masonry separating walls: airborne sound insulation in new-build housing.
BRE DAS 105: 1987. Masonry separating walls: improving airborne sound insulation between existing dwellings.
BRE DAS 119: 1988. Slated or tiled pitched roofs – conversion to accommodate rooms: installing quilted insulation at rafter level.
BRE DAS 131: 1989. External walls: combustible external plastics insulation – horizontal fire barriers.
BRE DAS 132: 1989. External walls: external combustible plastics insulation – fixings.
BRE DAS 133: 1989. Solid external walls: internal dry-lining – preventing summer condensation.

BRE Good Building Guide

BRE GBG 5: 1990. Choosing between cavity, internal and external wall insulation.

BRE Reports

BR 238: 1993. Sound control for homes.
BR 262: 1994. Thermal insulation: avoiding risks.

TRADE ASSOCIATIONS

Association of Insulation Manufacturers, 38 Bridlesmith Gate, Nottingham NG1 2GQ (0115 941 5269).
British Rigid Urethane Foam Manufacturers Association Ltd., Third Floor, Central Buildings, 11 Peter Street, Manchester M2 5QR (0161 835 1031).
British Urethane Foam Contractors Association, PO Box 23, Kenilworth, Warwickshire CV8 2YZ (01926 513187).
Cork Industry Federation, 62 Leavesden Road, Weybridge, Surrey KT13 9BX (01932 848416).
Eurisol-UK Mineral Wool Association, 39 High Street, Redbourn, Herts. AL3 7LW (01582 794624).
Expanded Polystyrene Bead Board Information Service, The British Plastics Federation, 6 Bath Place, Rivington Street, London EC2A 3JE (0171 457 5000).
Expanded Polystyrene Cavity Insulation Association, 284 High Road, North Weald, Essex CM16 6ED (0137 882 2026).
External Wall Insulation Association, PO Box 12, Haslemere, Surrey GU27 3AH (01428 654011).
National Cavity Insulation Association, PO Box 12, Haslemere, Surrey GU27 3AH (01428 654011).
Polyethylene Foam Insulation Association, Association House, 235 Ash Road, Aldershot, Hants. GU12 4DD (01252 336318).
Thermal Insulation Manufacturers and Suppliers Association, PO Box 111, Aldershot, Hants. GU11 1YW (01252 336318).

14

SEALANTS, GASKETS AND ADHESIVES

—

Introduction

Although used in relatively small quantities compared with the loadbearing construction materials sealants, gaskets and adhesives play a significant role in the the perceived success or failure of buildings. A combination of correct detailing and appropriate use of these materials is necessary to prevent the need for expensive remedial work.

Sealants

Sealants are designed to seal the joints between adjacent building components while remaining sufficiently flexible to accommodate any relative movement. They may be required to exclude wind, rain and air-borne sound. A wide range of products is available matching the performance characteristics of the sealant to the requirements of the joint. Incorrect specification or application, or poor joint design or preparation is likely to lead to premature failure of the sealant.

Key factors in specifying the appropriate sealant are:

- understanding the cause and nature of the relative movement;
- matching the nature and extent of movement to an appropriate sealant;
- appropriate joint design, surface preparation and sealant application;
- the service life of the sealant.

Relative movement within buildings

The most common causes of movement in buildings are associated with settlement, dead and live load effects including wind loading, fluctuations in temperature, changes in moisture content and, in some cases, the deteriorative effects of chemical or electrolytic action. Depending upon the prevailing conditions, the various effects may be additive or compensatory.

SETTLEMENT

Settlement is primarily associated with changes in loadings on the foundations during the construction process although it may continue for some time, frequently up to five years, after the construction is complete. Subsequent modifications to a building or its contents may cause further relative movement. Settlement is usually slow and in one direction, creating a shearing effect on sealants used across the boundaries.

THERMAL MOVEMENT

All building materials expand and contract to some degree with changes in temperature. For timber the movement is low, but is moderate for glass, steel, brick, stone and concrete, and relatively high for plastics and aluminium. Such thermal movements are accentuated by the effects of colour, insulation and the thickness of the material. Dark materials absorb solar radiation and heat more quickly than light reflective materials. Also, well insulated claddings respond quickly to changes in solar radiation, producing rapid cyclical expansion movements, whereas heavy construction materials respond more slowly but will still exhibit considerable movements over an annual cycle. Typical thermal movements are shown in Table 14.1.

Table 14.1 Thermal movements of building materials

Typical thermal movements of building materials in use calculated for a temperature variation of 85°C (e.g. −15 to + 70°C) (measured in mm per metre)

Material	Typical thermal movement (mm/m for 85°C change)	Coefficient of linear expansion per °C $\times 10^{-6}$
Masonry		
Concrete – standard aggregates	1.2	10–14
Calcium silicate brickwork	1.2	8–14
Concrete blockwork	1.0	6–12
Concrete – aerated	0.7	8
Concrete – limestone aggregate	0.6	7–8
Clay brickwork	0.5–0.7	5–8
GRC	0.8–1.7	10–20
Metals		
Zinc (along roll)	2.7	32 (23 across roll)
Lead	2.5	29
Aluminium	2.0	23
Titanium zinc	1.8	20–22
Copper	1.4	17
Stainless steel	1.4	17
Terne coated stainless steel	1.4	17
Structural steel	1.0	12
Stone and glass		
Glass	0.9	9–11
Slate	0.9	9–11
Granite	0.8	8–10
Sandstone	0.8	7–12
Marble	0.4	4–6
Limestone	0.3	3–4
Plastics		
ABS	8.0	83–95
PVC	6.0	40–80
GRP	3.0	20–35
Timber		
Wood (along grain)	0.5	4–6

MOISTURE MOVEMENT

Moisture movement falls into two categories: irreversible movements as new materials acclimatise to the environment, and reversible cyclical movements due to climatic variations. Many building materials, especially concrete and mortars, exhibit an initial contraction during the drying-out process. Incorrectly seasoned timber will also shrink but new bricks used too quickly after manufacture will expand. After these initial effects, all materials which absorb moisture will expand and contract to varying degrees in response to changes in their moisture content. Depending upon climatic conditions, moisture and thermal movements may oppose or reinforce each other. Typical irreversible and reversible moisture movements are shown in Table 14.2.

LOADING AND DETERIORATION

Movements associated with live loads such as machinery, traffic and wind can cause rapid cyclical movements within building components. The deterioration of materials, such as the corrosion of steel or sulfate attack on concrete, is often associated with irreversible expansion, causing movement of adjacent components. Concrete structures may exhibit creep, which is gradual permanent deformation under load, over many years.

Types of sealant

There are three distinct types of sealant, plastic, elastoplastic and elastic, each of which exhibit significantly different properties which must be matched to the appropriate application.

PLASTIC SEALANTS

Plastic sealants, which include general-purpose mastics, allow only a limited amount of movement, but when held in a deformed state they stress-relax. Plastic sealants dry by the formation of a surface skin, leaving liquid material encased to retain flexibility. However, with time, the plastic core continues to harden; thus durability is related to the thickness of the material used.

Table 14.2 Moisture movements of typical building materials

Typical reversible and irreversible moisture movements of building materials in use (measured in mm per metre)

Material	Reversible (mm/m)		Irreversible (mm/m)	
Concrete	0.2–0.6		0.3–0.8	(shrinkage)
Aerated concrete	0.2–0.3		0.7–0.9	(shrinkage)
Brickwork – clay	0.2		0.2–1.0	(expansion)
Brickwork – calcium silicate	0.1–0.5		0.1–0.4	(shrinkage)
Blockwork – dense	0.2–0.4		0.2–0.6	(shrinkage)
Blockwork – aerated	0.2–0.3		0.5–0.9	(shrinkage)
Glass-fibre reinforced cement	1.5		0.7	(shrinkage)
Softwood	5–25	(60–90% relative humidity)		
Hardwood	7–32	(60–90% relative humidity)		
Plywood	2–3	(60–90% relative humidity)		
(timber has no irreversible movement)				

Oil-based mastics

For oil-based mastics a 10 mm depth is required for optimum durability with a typical life expectancy of 2 to 10 years. The effects of ultraviolet degradation are reduced by painting. Typical uses include sealing around window and door frames in traditional low-rise building. (The typical movement accommodation for oil-based mastics is 10%.)

Butyl sealants

Butyl sealants are plastic but with a slightly rubbery texture. They are used in small joints as a gap filler and general-purpose sealant where oil-based mastics would dry too rapidly. Life expectancy is between 10 and 20 years if they are protected from sunlight by painting, but only up to 5 years in exposed situations. (The typical movement accommodation for butyl sealants is 10%.)

Acrylic sealants

Water-based acrylic sealants are frequently used for internal sealing such as between plaster and new windows. The solvent-based acrylic sealants are durable for up to 20 years, with good adhesion to slightly contaminated surfaces. They accommodate only limited movement but produce a good external seal around windows, for both new and remedial work. (The typical movement accommodation for water-based and solvent-based acrylic sealants is 15% and 20% respectively.)

Polymer/bitumen sealants

Solvent-based bitumen sealants are generally suitable for low-movement joints in gutters and flashings. Hot-poured bitumen is used for sealing movement joints in asphalt and concrete floor slabs, although compatibility with any subsequent floor coverings should be verified.

Linseed oil putty

Traditional putty contains a mixture of linseed oil and inorganic fillers (BS 544: 1969) which sets by a combination of aerial oxidation of the oil and some absorption into the timber. A skin is produced initially, but the mass ultimately sets to a semi-rigid material. Application is with a putty knife onto primed timber. For application to steel window frames, non-absorbent hardwoods and water-repellent preservative-treated softwoods, non-linseed oil putty is appropriate. Linseed oil putty should be painted within two weeks, whereas metal casement putty may be left three months before painting.

ELASTOPLASTIC SEALANTS

Elastoplastic sealants will accommodate both slow cyclical movements and permanent deformations. A range of products offer appropriately balanced strength, plastic flow and elastic properties for various applications.

Polysulfide sealants

Polysulfide sealants are available as one- or two-component systems. The one-component systems have the advantage that they are ready for immediate use. They cure relatively slowly by absorption of moisture from the atmosphere, forming a skin initially and fully curing within 2–5 weeks. One-component systems are limited in their application to joints up to 25 mm in width, but their ultimate performance is comparable to that of the two-component materials. Typical uses include structural movement joints in masonry, joints between precast concrete or stone cladding panels and sealing around windows. The two-component polysulfide sealants require mixing immediately before use and fully cure within 24–48 hours. They are more suitable than one-component systems for sealing joints which are wider than 25 mm, have large movements or are subject to vandalism during setting. Uses include sealing joints within concrete and brickwork cladding systems and also within poorly insulated lightweight cladding panels. Polysulfides have a life expectancy of 20–25 years. (The typical movement accommodation for polysulfide sealants is up to 25% for one-part systems and up to 30% for two-part systems.)

ELASTIC SEALANTS

Elastic sealants are appropriate for sealing dynamic joints where rapid cyclic movement occurs.

Polyurethane sealants

Polyurethane sealants are available as one- or two-component systems. The products are highly elastic but surfaces should be carefully prepared and usually primed to ensure good adhesion. Durability is good, ranging from 20 to 25 years. Typical applications are joints within glazing, curtain walling and lightweight cladding panels. (The typical movement accommodation for polyurethane sealants is between 10% and 30% depending on the modulus.)

Silicone sealants

Silicone sealants are usually one-component systems which cure relatively quickly in air, frequently with the evolution of characteristic smells such as acetic acid. Generally, silicone sealants adhere well to metals and glass, but primers may be necessary on friable or porous surfaces such as concrete or stone. High-modulus silicone sealants are resilient. Typical applications include glazing and curtain-wall systems, movement joints in ceramic tiling and around sanitary ware. Low-modulus silicone sealants are very extensible and are appropriate for use in joints subject to substantial thermal or moisture movement. Typical applications are the perimeter sealing of PVC-U and aluminium windows and also cladding systems. Silicone sealants are durable, with life expectancies within the range 25 to 30 years. (The typical movement accommodation for silicone sealants ranges from 20% to 70% depending upon the modulus.)

Epoxy sealants

Epoxy sealants are appropriate for stress-relieving joints where larger movements in compression than tension are anticipated. Typical applications include floor joints and the water-sealing of tiling joints within swimming pools. Epoxy sealants have a life expectancy of 10 to 20 years. (The typical movement accommodation of epoxy sealants is within the range 5% to 15%.)

Joint design

There are three forms of joint: butt, lap and fillet (Fig. 14.1); however, only butt and lap joints will accommodate movement. Generally, lap joints, in which the sealant is stressed in shear, will accommodate double the movement of butt joints in which the sealant is under tension or compression. Furthermore, lap joints tend to be more durable as the sealant is partially protected from the effects of weathering. However, lap joints are generally more difficult to seal than butt joints. Frequently, joints are made too narrow, either for aesthetic reasons or owing to miscalculation of component tolerances. The effect is that the extent of movement is excessive in proportion to the width of sealant, causing rapid failure.

To control correctly the depth of the sealant and to prevent it adhering to the back of the joint, a compressible back-up material, usually rectangular or round closed-cell polyethylene, is inserted (Fig. 14.2). The polyethylene acts as a bond-breaker by not adhering to the sealant. Where the joint is filled with a filler board, such as impregnated fibreboard or

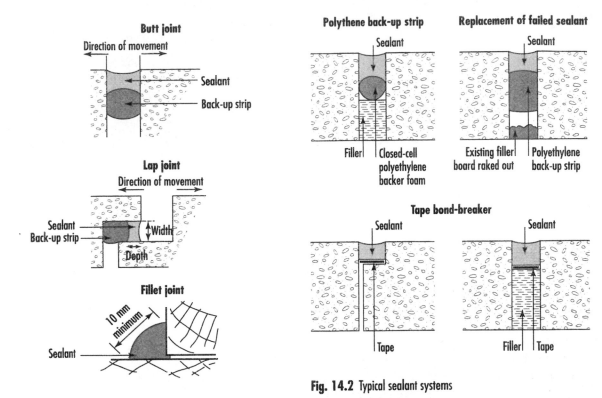

Fig. 14.1 Butt, lap and fillet joints

Fig. 14.2 Typical sealant systems

corkboard, a plastic bond-breaker tape or closed-cell polyethylene strip should be inserted. Normally the depth of the sealant should be half the width of the joint for elastic and elastoplastic sealants and equal to the width of the joint for plastic sealants, the minimum width of the joint being calculated from the maximum movement to be accommodated and the movement accommodation factor (MAF), that is, the extensibility of the sealant. Where insufficient depth is available to insert a polyethylene foam strip, a tape bond-breaker should be inserted at the back of the joint.

Minimum joint width calculation:

Total movement	=	5 mm
Movement accommodation factor (MAF)	=	70%
Width of sealant to accommodate movement	=	5/0.7 = 7.2 mm
Minimum joint width = 5 + 7.2 mm	=	12.2 mm

In order to obtain good adhesion, the joint surfaces should be prepared by the removal of contaminants, loose material or grease and by the application of a primer if specified by the sealant manufacturer. Most sealants are applied directly by gun application, although tooled, poured and tape/strip sealants are also used. Tooling helps to remove air bubbles entrained in two-component mixes; if left, air bubbles would reduce the durability of the seal. Externally, recessed cladding joints show less staining than flush joints, although the usual finish is a slightly concave surface. Where stonework is being sealed, non-staining silicone sealants must be used to prevent the migration of plasticiser into the stone which could cause discolouration. Sealants to floor joints need to be tough, therefore wider to accommodate the necessary movements and recessed to prevent mechanical damage. Alternatively, proprietary mechanical jointing systems should be used.

COLOUR MATCHING

While most sealants, except the black bituminous products, are available in white, translucent, greys and browns, the silicone sealants appropriate for use around kitchen and bathroom units are available in a wide range of colours. For these purposes, fungicides are often included within the formulation.

Fire-resistant sealants

Intumescent oil-based mastics and acrylic sealants are suitable for sealing low-movement joints around fire-check doors. For the fire-resistant sealing of structural movement joints, fire-resistant grades of low-modulus silicone, two-part polysulfide and acrylic sealants are available. Maximum fire resistance is obtained if the sealant is applied to both faces of the joint, with mineral wool or glass-fibre insulation in the void space. Four hours fire resistance with respect to both integrity and insulation can be achieved for a 20 mm wide movement joint within 150 mm concrete (BS 476 Part 20: 1987). The low-modulus silicone is appropriate for sealing fire-resisting screens, curtain walls, claddings and masonry subject to movement. The two-part polysulfide is designed for use in concrete and masonry fire-resisting joints. Acrylic sealants are appropriate over a wide range of materials but where timber is involved an allowance must be made for its loss by charring.

Intumescent fillers manufactured from acrylic emulsions with inert fillers and fire-retardant additives can be applied by either gun or trowel to fill voids created around service ducts within fire-resistant walls. Four hours of fire resistance can be achieved with these materials. Intumescent tapes are appropriate for application within structural movement joints. Most intumescent sealants are now *low-smoke* and evolve no halogenated products of combustion in fire situations. (The typical movement accommodation for intumescent acrylic sealants is 15%.)

Foam sealants

Compressible strips of closed-cell PVC and polyethylene, or open-cell polyurethane foams, coated on one or both edges with pressure-sensitive adhesive, are used to seal thermal movement and differential settlement joints, gaps around window and door frames, and in air-conditioning ductwork. Strips may be uniform in section or profiled for particular applications. Aerosol-dispensed polyurethane foam is widely used as an all-purpose filler. It is available either as foam or as expanding foam, and acts as an adhesive, sealant, filler and insulator.

Gaskets

Gaskets are preformed elastomeric components which are held in place either by compression or by encapsulation into the adjacent building materials (Fig. 14.3). Typical applications include the weather sealing of precast cladding units and facade systems. Within precast concrete, GRP (glass-fibre reinforced polyester) or GRC (glass-fibre reinforced cement) cladding units the gaskets are typically inserted into recessed open-drained joints. The gaskets therefore act as a rain barrier, but because they do not necessarily fit tightly along their full length, they may be backed up by compressed cellular foam wind penetration seals. In facade glazing systems, gaskets may be applied as capping seals, retained by appropriate profiles within the mullions and transoms; alternatively, the gaskets may be recessed within the joints of the glazing system to give a narrower visual effect to the joint. Some glazing gaskets of H or U-sections are sealed with a zipper or filler strip which is inserted in the profile, compressing the material into an air- and watertight seal.

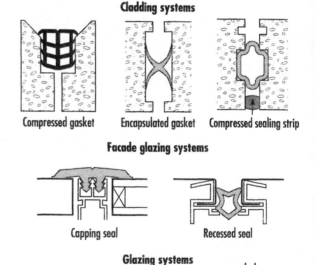

Cladding systems

Compressed gasket   Encapsulated gasket   Compressed sealing strip

Facade glazing systems

Capping seal   Recessed seal

Glazing systems

U-gasket   Zipper H-gasket   Zipper U-gasket

Fig. 14.3 Typical gaskets for cladding and glazing systems

The standard materials for gaskets used in construction are neoprene, which is highly elastic, EPDM (ethylene propylene diene monomer), which has better weathering characteristics than neoprene, and silicone rubbers, which are highly resistant to ultraviolet light, operate over a wide range of temperatures, and are available in almost any colour.

Waterstops for embedding into *in situ* concrete for sealing movement and construction joints are manufactured in PVC or rubber according to the required movement (Fig. 14.4). Sections are available in long extruded lengths and factory-produced intersections. Applications include water-containing structures and water exclusion from basements. Waterstops placed centrally within concrete will resist water pressure from either side, but externally positioned waterstops, not encased below the concrete slab or within permanent concrete shuttering, will only resist water pressure from the outer face.

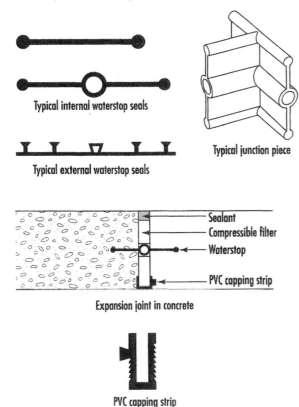

Typical internal waterstop seals

Typical external waterstop seals

Typical junction piece

Expansion joint in concrete

Sealant
Compressible filter
Waterstop
PVC capping strip

PVC capping strip

Fig. 14.4 Concrete waterstop seals

Proprietary systems offer watertight expansion jointing for horizontal surfaces such as roof car parks and pedestrian areas. Systems usually combine

complex aluminium or stainless steel profiles with extruded synthetic rubber inserts. Materials can withstand high loads, with good resistance to bitumen and salt water.

Dry glazing strips are based on elastomeric polymers, typically EPDM or butyl rubber. Usually the synthetic rubber strip has a self-adhesive backing which adheres to the rebate upstand. With external beading, the dry glazing strip can also be applied to each bead, which is then fixed with suitable compression to ensure a good seal to the glass.

Adhesives

TYPES OF ADHESIVE

The traditional adhesives based on animal and vegetable products have largely been superseded by synthetic products manufactured by the polymer industry. The range of adhesives is under constant development and particular applications should always be matched to manufacturers' specifications. Special notice should be taken of exclusions where materials and adhesives are incompatible, also safety warnings relating to handling and the evolution of noxious fumes or flammable vapours. Adhesives are more efficient when used for the bonding of components subject to shear forces rather than direct tension. They are least efficient against peeling stresses. Most adhesives have a *shelf life* of 12 months when stored unopened under appropriate conditions. The *pot life* after mixing the two-component systems ranges from a few minutes to several hours.

Ceramic wall tile adhesives

Wall tile adhesives are usually PVA (polyvinyl acetate), acrylic or cement based compositions. The British Standard BS 5980: 1980 classifies the products according to their composition and degree of resistance to water (Table 14.3).

The PVA thin bed adhesives, typically to 3 mm, (Type 2 Class B) will only tolerate moisture, whereas the thin bed water-resistant acrylic based adhesives (Type 2 Class AA) are suitable for fixing wall tiles and mosaics in damp and wet conditions associated for example with domestic showers. Some acrylic-based products evolve ammonia on setting. The water-resistant cements and polymer-modified

Table 14.3 Classification of wall tile adhesives by composition and water resistance

Classification	Composition and water resistance
Type 1	hydraulically hardening mortar
Type 2	dispersion adhesive
Type 3	dispersion/cement adhesive
Type 4	dissolved resin adhesive
Type 5	reaction resin adhesive
Class AA	faster development of water resistance
Class A	slower development of water resistance
Class B	no requirement for water resistance

cement products (Type 1 Class AA) are appropriate both for internal and external use and can usually be applied with either thin or thick bedding. The polymer-modified cement adhesives are also suitable for fixing marble, granite and slate tiles up to 15 mm thick. For chemical resistance thin bed epoxy-resin-based adhesives are available. In all cases the substrate must be sound with new plaster, brickwork or concrete, fully dried out for 2–6 weeks. Plasterboard and timber products must be adequately fixed at 300 mm centres horizontally and vertically to ensure rigidity. In refurbishment work, flaking or multi-layered paint should be removed and glazed surfaces made good. Where the tile adhesive is classified as waterproof, either acrylic- (Type 2 Class AA) or cement-based (Type 1 Class AA), it may be used as the grouting medium. Alternatively, equivalent waterproof grouting is available in a wide range of colours to blend or contrast with the wall tiles. Epoxy-resin tile grout is available for very wet conditions.

Ceramic floor tile adhesives

The majority of ceramic floor tile adhesives are cement based, used either as thick bed (up to 25 mm) or thin bed according to the quality of the substrate. Standard products are suitable for fixing ceramic tiles, quarries, brick slips, stone and terrazzo to well dried out concrete or cement/sand screed. Where suspended timber floors are to be tiled, they must be well ventilated and strong enough to support the additional dead load. An overlay of 12 mm exterior grade plywood, primed with bonding agent and screwed at 200 mm centres, may be necessary. In refurbishment work, it is better to remove all old floor finishes, but ceramic floor tiles may be fixed

over cleaned ceramic or possibly primed vinyl tiles, provided all loose material is first removed.

Cement-based grouting can be pigmented to the required colour, but care must be taken to ensure that excess grout is removed from the surface of the tiles before staining occurs. Thin-bed two-component epoxy-based adhesives (Type 5 Class AA) are more water and chemical resistant than the standard cement-based products and are appropriate for use where repeated spillage is likely from industrial processes. Where there is likely movement of the substrate, two-component rubber-based adhesives (Type 3 Class AA) are generally appropriate.

Contact adhesives

Contact adhesives based on polychloroprene rubber, in either organic solvents or aqueous emulsions, are normally suitable for bonding decorative laminates, and other rigid plastics such as PVC and ABS, to timber, timber products and metals. The adhesive is usually applied to both surfaces and, the solvent or emulsion allowed to become touch dry, prior to bringing the two surfaces into contact, when an immediate strong bond is produced. The aqueous emulsion products can also be suitable for fixing sealed cork and expanded polystyrene and have the advantage that no fumes are evolved. Expanded polystyrene tiles may be adversely affected by solvent-based formulations.

Vinyl floor tile and wood block adhesives

Most vinyl floor tile and wood block adhesives are based on either rubber/bitumen, rubber/resin or modified bitumen emulsions. In all cases it is essential that the subfloor is dry, sound, smooth and free from any contamination which would affect the adhesion. Where necessary cement/acrylic or cement/latex floor levelling compound should be applied to concrete, asphalt or old ceramic tiled floors. Some cement/latex materials evolve ammonia during application.

Wood adhesives

Wood joints generally should be close contact with a gap of less than 0.15 mm, but so-called *gap-filling* adhesives (BS 1204: 1993) satisfactorily bond up to 1.3 mm. Polyvinyl acetate (PVA) wood glues are widely used for most on site work and in the factory assembly of mortice and tenon joints for doors, windows and furniture. The white emulsion sets to a colourless translucent thermoplastic film, giving a bond of similar strength to that of the timber itself, but insufficient for bonding loadbearing structural members. Components should be clamped in position for up to 12 hours to ensure maximum bonding, although this may be reduced by increasing the temperature. Waterproof PVA adhesives which partially cross-link on curing are suitable for protected external use but not immersion in water. PVA adhesives generally retain their strength up to a temperature of 60°C and do not discolour the timber, except by contact with ferrous metals.

The thermosetting wood resins are mainly two-component systems based on phenolic compounds such as urea, melamine, resorcinol or phenol which cure with formaldehyde to produce loadbearing adhesives. Most formulations require the mixing of the resin and hardener, but a premixed dry powder to which water is added is also available. Resin adhesives based on phenol-formaldehyde, resorcinol-formaldehyde or a blend of the two give high-strength waterproof bonding, categorised as Type WBP (weather and boil proof) according to BS 1204: 1993. Melamine formaldehyde adhesives are generally classified as boil resistant (Type BR) but will not resist prolonged exposure to weathering. Urea formaldehyde adhesives are generally moisture resistant (MR) or for interior use only (INT). Certain timber fire-retardant and preservative treatments reduce the efficiency of timber adhesives, although generally those based on phenol formaldehyde or resorcinol formaldehyde are unaffected.

Wallpaper adhesives

Standard wallpaper adhesives are based on methyl cellulose, a white powder which is water soluble giving a colourless solution. For fixing the heavier papers and decorative dado strips, polyvinyl acetate (PVA) is an added component. Cold water starch is also available both as a wall sizing agent and a wallpaper adhesive. Most wallpaper pastes contain fungicide to inhibit mould growth. The British Standard BS 3046: 1981 describes five types of adhesive ranging from low solids to high wet and dry strength with added fungicide.

Epoxy resin adhesives

Epoxy resins are two-component, cold-curing adhesives which produce high-strength, durable bonds.

Most require equal quantities of the resin and hardener to be mixed and various formulations are available giving curing times ranging from minutes to hours. Strong bonds can be obtained to timber, metal, glass, concrete, ceramics and rigid plastics. Epoxy resins may be used internally or externally and they are resistant to oils, water, dilute acids, alkalis, and most solvents except chlorinated hydrocarbons. Epoxy resins are frequently used for attaching stainless steel fixings into stone and brick slips prior to their casting into concrete cladding panels. Epoxy flooring adhesives may be used for bonding vinyl floor finishes in wet service areas and to metal surfaces.

Cyanoacrylate adhesives

Cyanoacrylates are single-component adhesives which bond components held in tight contact within seconds. A high tensile bond is produced between metals, ceramics, most plastics and rubber. The curing is activated by adsorbed moisture on the material surfaces, and only small quantities of the clear adhesive are required. The bond is resistant to oil, water, solvents, acid and alkalis but does not exhibit high impact resistance. A range of adhesive viscosities are manufactured to match to particular applications.

Hot-melt adhesives

Hot-melt adhesives for application by glue-gun are usually based on the thermoplastic copolymer, ethylene vinyl acetate (EVA). Formulations are available for joining materials to either flexible or rigid substrates. Generally, the adhesive should be applied to the less easily bonded surface first (e.g. the harder or smoother surface) and then the two components should be pressed together for at least one minute. Where metals are to be bonded they should be pre-warmed to prevent rapid dissipation of the heat. Similar adhesives are used in iron-on edging veneers for plastic- and wood-faced particleboard.

Bitumen roofing felt adhesives

Bitumen adhesives are available for hot application, emulsion or in hydrocarbon solvent for cold-bonding bituminous roofing felt. The adhesives should be poured and spread by trowel to avoid air pockets, which may cause premature delamination of the felt from the substrate. Excess bitumen should be removed as it may stain adjacent materials.

Plastic pipe adhesives

Solvent-based vinyl resin adhesives are used for bonding PVC-U and ABS pipes and fittings. The adhesive is brush-applied to both components, which are then united and slightly rotated to complete the seal. Curing is rapid, but in cold water supply systems, water pressure should not be applied for several hours.

Gap-filling adhesives

Gun grade gap-filling adhesives, usually based on solvent-borne rubber or synthetic rubber resins with filler reinforcement, are versatile in their applications. They are generally formulated to bond timber, timber products, decorative laminates, sheet metals, PVC-U and rigid insulating materials (except polystyrene), to themselves and also to brickwork, blockwork, concrete, plaster and GRP. Typical applications include the fixing of decorative wall panels, dado rails, architraves and skirting boards without nailing or screwing. Surfaces to be bonded must be sound and clean, but the gap-filling properties of the products can allow fixing to uneven surfaces. The materials have good immediate adhesion, and can allow the components to be adjusted into position.

PVA bonding agent and sealant

PVA (polyvinyl acetate) is a versatile material which will act not only as an adhesive as described but also as a bonding agent or surface sealant. As a bonding agent it will bond cement screeds, rendering and plaster to suitable sound surfaces without the requirement for a good mechanical key. PVA will seal porous concrete surfaces to prevent dusting.

References

FURTHER READING

CIRIA. 1991: *Manual of good practice in sealant application*. Special Publication 80. London: Construction Industry Research and Information Association/British Adhesives and Sealants Association.

Panek, J.R. 1991: *Construction sealants and adhesives*, 3rd ed. New York: John Wiley & Sons Inc.

Woolman, R. and Hutchinson, A. (ed.) 1994: *Resealing of buildings: A guide to good practice*. Oxford: Butterworth-Heinemann.

STANDARDS

BS 476. Fire tests on building materials and structures.
Part 6: 1989. Method of test for fire propagation for products.
Part 7: 1987. Method for classification of the surface spread of flame of products.
BS 544: 1969. Linseed oil putty for use in wooden frames.
BS 745: 1969. Animal glue for wood (joiner's glue) (dry glue; jelly or liquid glue).
BS 1203: 1979. Specification for synthetic resin adhesives (phenolic and aminoplastic) for plywood.
BS 1204: 1993. Specification for type MR phenolic and aminoplastic synthetic resin adhesives for wood.
BS 2499. Hot-applied joint sealant systems for concrete pavements:
Part 1: 1993. Specification for joint sealants.
Part 2: 1992. Code of practice for application and use of joint sealants.
Part 3: 1993. Methods of test.
BS 3046: 1981. Specification for adhesives for hanging flexible wallcoverings.
BS 3712. Building and construction sealants:
Part 1: 1991. Method of test of homogeneity, relative density and penetration.
Part 2: 1973. Methods of test for seepage, staining, shrinkage, shelf-life and paintability.
Part 3: 1974. Methods of test for application life, skinning properties and tack-free time.
Part 4: 1991. Methods of test for adhesion in peel.
BS 4071: 1966. Polyvinyl acetate (PVA) emulsion adhesives for wood.
BS 4169: 1988. Specification for manufacture of glue-laminated timber structural members.
BS 4255. Rubber used in preformed gaskets for weather exclusion from buildings:
Part 1: 1986. Specification for non-cellular gaskets.
BS 4346. Joints and fittings for use with unplasticized PVC pressure pipes:
Part 3: 1982. Specification for solvent cement.
BS 4375: 1968. Unsintered PTFE tape for thread sealing applications.
BS 5212. Cold applied joint sealants for concrete pavements:
Part 1: 1990. Specification for joint sealants.
Part 2: 1990. Code of practice for application and use of joint sealants.
Part 3: 1990. Methods of test.
BS 5270. Bonding agents for use with gypsum plaster and cement:
Part 1: 1989. Specification for polyvinyl acetate (PVAC) emulsion bonding agents for indoor use with gypsum building plasters.

BS 5291: 1984. Specification for manufacture of finger joints in structural softwood.

BS 5385. Wall and floor tiling:

Part 1: 1990. Code of practice for the design and installation of internal ceramic wall tiling and mosaics in normal conditions.

Part 2: 1991. Code of practice for the design and installation of external ceramic wall tiling and mosaics (including terra cotta and faience tiles).

Part 3: 1989. Code of practice for the design and installation of ceramic floor tiles and mosaics.

Part 4: 1992. Code of practice for tiling and mosaics in specific conditions.

Part 5: 1990. Code of practice for the design and installation of terrazzo tile and slab, natural stone and composition block flooring.

BS 5442. Adhesives for construction:

Part 1: 1989. Classification of adhesives for use with flooring materials.

Part 2: 1989. Classification of adhesives for use with interior wall and ceiling coverings (excluding decorative flexible material in roll form).

Part 3: 1979. Adhesives for use with wood.

BS 5980: 1980. Specification for adhesives for use with ceramic tiles and mosaics.

BS 6093: 1993. Code of practice for design of joints and jointing in building construction.

BS 6209: 1982. Specification for solvent-cement for non-pressure thermoplastics pipe systems.

BS 6213: 1982. Guide to selection of constructional sealants.

BS 6446: 1984. Specification for manufacture of glued structural components of timber and wood based panel products.

BS 6576: 1985. Code of practice for installation of chemical damp-proof courses.

BS 8000. Workmanship on building sites:

Part 11: 1989. Code of practice for wall and floor tiling.

Part 12: 1989. Code of practice for decorative wall coverings and painting.

BS 8203: 1987. Code of practice for installation of sheet and tile flooring.

BS EN 204: 1991. Classification of non-structural adhesives for joining wood and derived timber products.

BS EN 205: 1991. Test methods for wood adhesives for non-structural applications – determination of tensile shear strength of lap joints.

BS EN 259: 1992. Specification for heavy duty wall coverings.

BS EN 301: 1992. Adhesives, phenolic and aminoplastic, for load-bearing timber structures: classification and performance requirements.

BS EN 302: 1992. Adhesives for loadbearing timber structures.

BS EN 542: 1995. Adhesives – determination of density.

BS EN 26927: 1991. Building construction – jointing products – sealants vocabulary.

BS EN 27389: 1991. Building construction – jointing products – determination of elastic recovery.

BS EN 27390: 1991. Building construction – jointing products – determination of resistance to flow.

BS EN 28339: 1991. Building construction – jointing products – sealants – determination of tensile properties.

BS EN 28340: 1991. Building construction – jointing products – sealants – determination of tensile properties or maintained extension.

BS EN 28394: 1991. Building construction – jointing products – determination of extrudability of one-component sealants.

BS EN 29046: 1991. Building construction – determination of adhesion/cohesion properties at constant temperature.

BS EN 29048: 1991. Building construction – jointing products – determination of extrudability of sealants under standardized apparatus.

BS EN ISO 9664: 1995. Adhesives – test methods for fatigue properties of structural adhesives in tensile shear.

DIN 4102: 1981. Fire behaviour of building materials and building components.

BUILDING RESEARCH ESTABLISHMENT PUBLICATIONS

BRE Digests

BRE Digest 33: 1971. Sheet and tile flooring made from thermoplastic binders.

BRE Digest 227: 1979. Estimation of thermal and moisture movements and stresses: Part 1.

BRE Digest 228: 1979. Estimation of thermal and moisture movements and stresses: Part 2.

BRE Digest 229: 1979. Estimation of thermal and moisture movements and stresses: Part 3.

BRE Digest 245: 1986. Rising damp in walls: diagnosis and treatment.

BRE Digest 314: 1986. Gluing wood successfully.

BRE Digest 340: 1989. Choosing wood adhesives.

BRE Digest 346: 1992. The assessment of wind loads.

BRE Information Paper

BRE IP 25/81. The selection and performance of sealants.

TRADE ASSOCIATION

British Adhesives and Sealants Association, 33 Fellowes Way, Stevenage, Herts. SG2 8BW (01438 358514).

15

PAINTS, WOOD STAINS, VARNISHES AND COLOUR

Introduction

As colour is an important factor in the description of paints, wood stains and varnishes, the key elements of the British Standards BS 4800: 1989, Colour Dimensions and the RAL systems are described, although other colour systems including Munsell and *Pantone* are also used within the construction industry.

Colour

BRITISH STANDARDS SYSTEM

The British Standards BS 5252: 1976 and BS 4800: 1989 define colour for building purposes and paints respectively. A specific colour is defined by the framework with a three-part code consisting of hue (two digits, 00–24), greyness (letter, A to E) and weight (two further digits) (Fig. 15.1). Hue is the attribute of redness, yellowness, blueness, etc., and the framework consists of 12 rows of hue in spectral sequence plus one neutral row. Greyness is a measure of the grey content of the colour at five levels from the maximum-greyness Group A, to clear Group E. The third attribute, weight, is a subjective term which incorporates both lightness (reflectivity to incident light) and greyness. Within a given column, colours have the same weight, but comparisons between columns in different greyness groups should only be made in respect of lightness. The framework has up to eight columns of equal lightness in each greyness group commencing with the highest light-

ness. Thus any colour is defined through the system by its three-part code, e.g. Magnolia is yellow-red 08, nearly grey B, and low weight 15 (i.e. 08 B 15), Midnight 20 C 40 and Plum 02 C 39.

COLOUR DIMENSIONS

The Natural Colour System (NCS), frequently referred to in the UK as Colour Dimensions, was developed by the Scandinavian Colour Institute in the 1980s. It is a colour language system which can describe any colour by a notation, communicable in words without the need for visual matching. Increasingly it has been adopted by architects, builders and designers who need to coordinate colour specification across a broad range of building products. An extensive range of materials can now be colour referenced using the system; these include wall, floor and ceiling tiles, carpets, fabrics, wall coverings, flexible floor finishes, paints, architectural ironmongery and metalwork, sanitary fittings, laminates and furniture.

The Colour Dimensions System is based on the assumption that for people with normal vision there are six pure colours: yellow, red, blue, green, white and black. The four colours yellow, red, blue and green are arranged around the *colour circle*, which is then subdivided into 10% steps. For example, yellow changes to red through orange, which could be described as Y50R (yellow with 50% red) (Fig. 15.2). In order to superimpose the black/white variation and also intensity of colour, each of the forty 10% steps around the colour circle may be represented by colour triangles, with the pure colour at the perimeter apex and the vertical axis illustrating blackness/whiteness. A colour

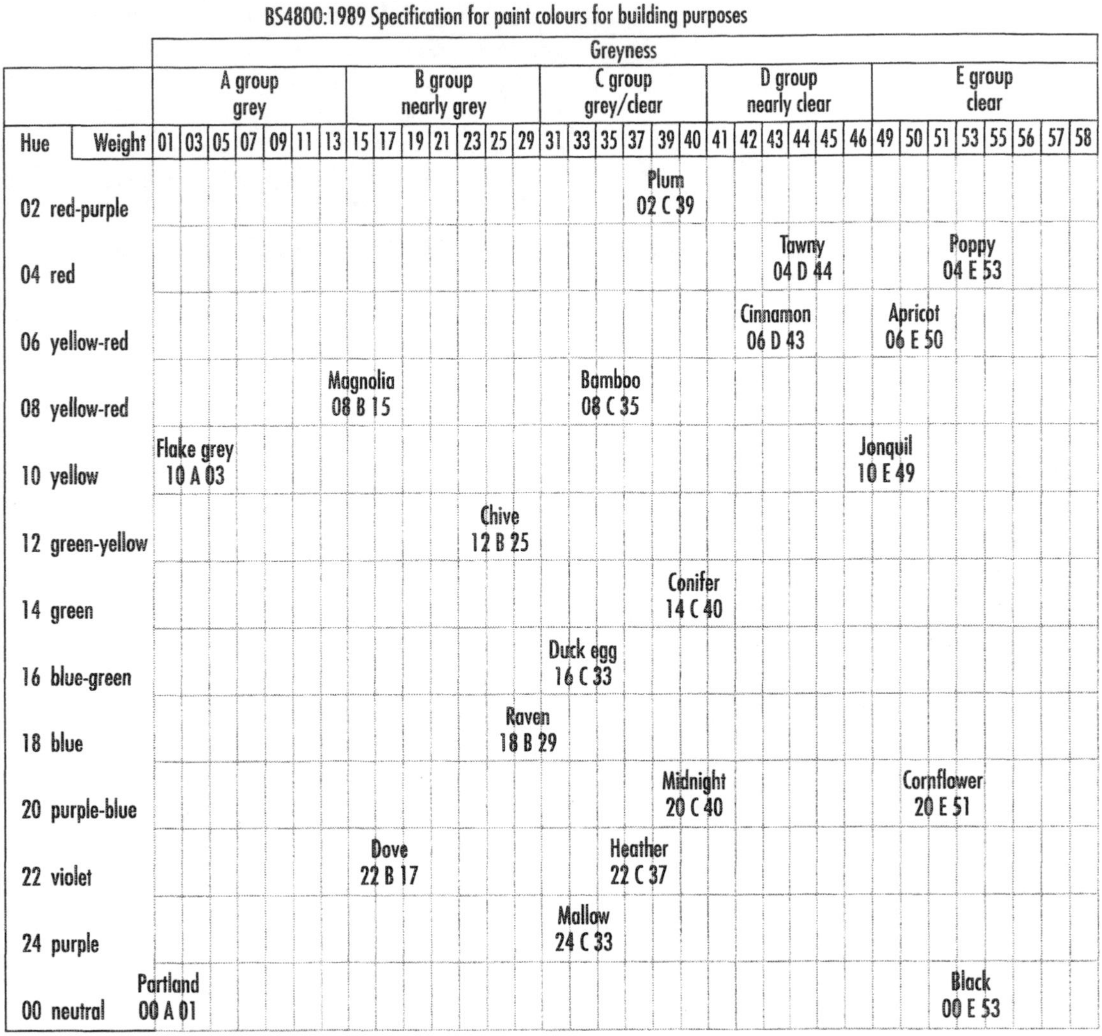

BS4800:1989 Specification for paint colours for building purposes

Hue	Weight: A group grey (01 03 05 07 09 11 13)	B group nearly grey (15 17 19 21 23 25 29)	C group grey/clear (31 33 35 37 39 40)	D group nearly clear (41 42 43 44 45 46)	E group clear (49 50 51 53 55 56 57 58)
02 red-purple			Plum 02 C 39		
04 red				Tawny 04 D 44	Poppy 04 E 53
06 yellow-red				Cinnamon 06 D 43	Apricot 06 E 50
08 yellow-red		Magnolia 08 B 15	Bamboo 08 C 35		
10 yellow	Flake grey 10 A 03				Jonquil 10 E 49
12 green-yellow		Chive 12 B 25			
14 green			Conifer 14 C 40		
16 blue-green			Duck egg 16 C 33		
18 blue		Raven 18 B 29			
20 purple-blue			Midnight 20 C 40		Cornflower 20 E 51
22 violet		Dove 22 B 17	Heather 22 C 37		
24 purple			Mallow 24 C 33		
00 neutral	Portland 00 A 01				Black 00 E 53

Fig. 15.1 British Standards Colour System with some illustrative examples

may be therefore described as having 10% blackness and 80% chromatic intensity. The full colour specification thus reads 1080-Y50R for an orange with 10% blackness, 80% chromatic intensity at yellow with 50% red. Colour Plate 8 illustrates the colour circle and the colour chart representing the diversity of orange colours at the Y50R point.

The system allows for a finer subdivision of the colour circle, and this is necessary to define any colour and to make direct comparisons with colours defined within the British Standards system. Thus Magnolia (BS 08 B 15) is 0606-Y41R (6% blackness, 6% chromatic intensity on a yellow with 41% red), Plum (BS 02 C 39) becomes 5331-R21B in Colour Dimensions and Midnight (BS 20 C 40) becomes 7415-R82B.

RAL COLOUR COLLECTION

The RAL colour collection is used significantly within the building industry for defining the colours of finishes, particularly to plastics and metals, but also materials such as glazed bricks. Typical applied finishes include acrylics, polyesters and polyurethane as well as some paints and lacquers. The RAL system, established in Germany in 1925, has developed through several phases. It commenced with 40 colours; subsequently many were added and others removed, leaving 170 standard colour shades. Because of its development, the RAL system (designated RAL 840-HR) does not have a systematic order of colours with equal steps between shades.

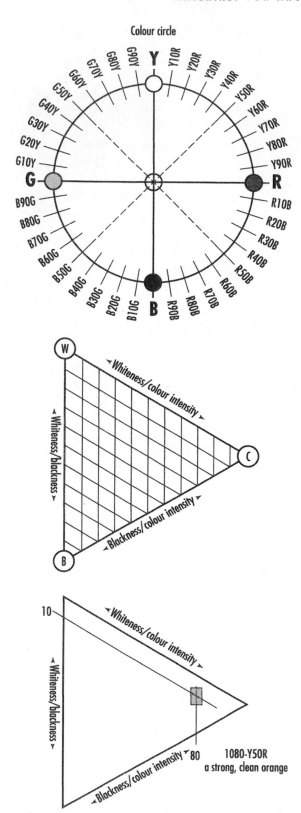

Fig. 15.2 Natural Colour System (Colour Dimensions)

Colours are defined by four digits, the first being the colour class (1 yellow, 2 orange, 3 red, 4 violet, 5 blue, 6 green, 7 grey, 8 brown and 9 black/white), and the further three digits relate only to the sequence in which the colours were filed. An official name is also applied to each standard RAL colour (e.g. RAL 1017 Saffron Yellow, RAL 5010 Gentian Blue, RAL 6003 Olive Green). Some additional colours have been added to the original RAL 840-HR listing, giving 194 colours, most of which can be matched to gloss or matt finishes.

RAL DESIGN SYSTEM

Unlike the RAL colour collection, which only has a limited selection of standard colours, the RAL design system has 1688 colours arranged in a colour atlas based on a three-dimensional colourspace defined by the coordinates of Hue, Lightness and Chroma. Hue is the attribute of colour, e.g. red, blue or yellow. Lightness ranges from black to white and chroma is the saturation or intensity of the colour. The system is equivalent to the HLS (Hue, Lightness, Saturation) system, which is used alongside RGB (Red, Green, Blue) in many computer colour systems. The RAL design system is similar to the Natural Colour System, except that it is based on a mathematical division of the whole visible wavelength spectrum, rather than the visually assessed four standard colours, yellow, red, blue and green.

The colour spectrum is therefore divided into mostly 10° steps around a circle. Each step, illustrated on a page of the associated colour atlas, represents a particular hue. For each hue on the colour atlas page, samples illustrate lightness decreasing from top to bottom and intensity or saturation increasing from the inside to the outside. Any colour is therefore coded with the three numbers relating to hue, lightness and chroma, e.g. 70 75 55. The standard RAL colour collection numbers do not fit neatly to the RAL design system coding but any colour can be defined; thus Saffron Yellow (RAL 1017) becomes 69.9 75.6 56.5. However, as the number defining the hue is not exactly 70, the colour Saffron Yellow will not appear on the atlas page. Computer programs generating colour through the attributes of hue, lightness and chroma can immediately formulate colours according to this system.

Paints

COMPONENTS OF PAINTS

Paints consist of a blend of components, each with their specific function. Commonly these include the binder (or medium), solvent, base, extenders, pigments and driers, although other additives may be incorporated into specialist paints.

The binder solidifies to produce the paint film. Traditionally, the binder was natural linseed oil, which set by gradual oxidation on exposure to air. However, linseed oil has now largely been replaced by alkyd resins which oxidise in air, or vinyl and acrylic resins which solidify by drying. To ensure adequate fluidity of the paint during application by brushing or spraying, either water or organic solvents (hydrocarbons, ketones or esters) are incorporated; paint thinners have the same effect. The base material, usually white titanium dioxide, produces the required opacity, although the *body* of the paint may be increased by the incorporation of inert extenders such as silica, calcium carbonate or barytes. Colouring materials are frequently a mixture of organic and inorganic dyes and pigments. Driers which induce the polymerisation of the binder ensure a rapid drying process. Because of the immediate health risks and long-term environmental effects associated with the widespread use of organic solvents, water-based paint products are increasingly used for many applications.

PAINT SYSTEMS

Coats within a paint system perform specific tasks. Usually a complete system would require primer, undercoat and finishing coat, although in the case of new external materials, four coats may be appropriate.

Primers

The primer must adhere well to the substrate, offer protection from deterioration or corrosion and provide a good base for the undercoat. To ensure adhesion, the substrate surface must be free of loose or degraded material. Appropriate systems are indicated in Table 15.1. For use on timber, primers may be oils, alkyd resins or acrylic emulsions, frequently with titanium oxide. Aluminium wood primer is recommended for resinous woods and to seal aged creosoted and bitumen-coated surfaces. For the corrosion protection of ferrous metals, primers incorporate zinc- or lead-rich compounds within oils or alkyd resins. While lead-based paints such as red lead and calcium plumbate are considered environmentally less acceptable than the alternatives, they remain very efficient in the inhibition of steel corrosion. Alternatively, acrylated rubber paints which form a physical barrier over steel may be used as primers. For non-ferrous metals, zinc phosphate primers are frequently used. The application of primers suitable to ferrous metals may cause increased corrosion on non-ferrous substrates, particularly aluminium. Masonry paints are usually based on alkyd or acrylic resins with titanium oxide; where surfaces are likely to be alkaline, such as new plaster, brickwork or concrete, alkali-resisting primer should be used.

Undercoats

Undercoats provide cover and a good base for the finishing coat. Most undercoats are based on alkyd resins or acrylic emulsions.

Table 15.1 Recommended primers for various substrates

Primer	Suitable substrates and conditions
Timber	
Preservative primer	Exterior use, contains fungicides
Wood primer	Softwoods and hardwoods, interior and exterior
Aluminium wood primer	Resinous softwoods and hardwoods
Acrylic primer	Softwoods and hardwoods
Plaster and masonry	
Alkali resisting primer	Plaster, cement and concrete
Acrylic primer sealer	Loose, friable surfaces
Ferrous metals	
Zinc phosphate	Steel, iron, galvanised steel. Good rust inhibitor
Red lead	Steel. Contains lead but excellent rust inhibitor
Metal primer	Steel and iron. Non-toxic alternative to red lead. Grey
Calcium plumbate	Galvanised steel. Contains lead but excellent rust inhibitor
Acrylated rubber	Steel, iron, galvanised steel. Must be a full acrylated rubber system
Zinc-rich primer	Steel. Two-component system
Non-ferrous metals	
Zinc phosphate	Aluminium
Acrylated rubber	Aluminium. Must be a full acrylated rubber system
Acrylic metal primer	Aluminium, copper, lead, brass. Quick-drying water-based primer

Finishing coats

Finishing coats provide a durable and decorative surface. Typically the gloss, eggshell and satin finishes are based on oils and alkyd resins, although waterborne products are increasingly becoming available. The waterborne gloss finishes tend to be visually softer and are more moisture permeable than the traditional solvent-borne hard glosses. However, they have the advantage of quick drying without the evolution of solvent odour and generally they do not yellow on ageing. Matt and silk finishes are usually vinyl or acrylic emulsions.

Special paints

MULTICOLOUR PAINTS

Multicolour paints incorporating flecks give a hard-wearing surface which may be glazed over to ease the removal of graffiti. Application is with a spray gun, which can be adjusted to change the pattern and texture of the fleck. This type of paint system may be applied to most dust- and grease-free internal surfaces. Alternative systems use a base coat, applied by brush or roller, overpainted, with a clear glazecoat bearing coloured flecks, or with a different colour for a multicolour effect. A proprietary system produces a two-tone broken colour by the action of a special roller, which flails the wet finish coat giving random partial exposure of the darker first coat.

ACRYLATED RUBBER PAINTS

Acrylated rubber paints are suitable for internal and external applications exposed to chemical attack or wet and humid atmospheric conditions. They are tending to replace chlorinated rubber coatings which rely on carbon tetrachloride solvent, now considered environmentally damaging. Acrylated rubber paints may be applied to metal or masonry by either brushing or spraying. Usually a film of dry thickness 100 microns is applied compared to 25–30 microns for most standard paint products.

HEAT-RESISTING PAINT

Aluminium paint, which has a lustrous metallic finish, is resistant to temperatures up to 230–260°C. A dry film thickness of 15 microns is typical. Acrylated rubber paints can usually be used satisfactorily to 100°C.

FLAME-RETARDANT PAINTS

Flame-retardant paints emit non-combustible gases when subject to fire, the usual active ingredient being antimony oxide. Combustible substrates such as plywood and particleboard can be raised to Class 1 BS 476 Part 7 – surface spread of flame. Products include matt, semi-gloss and gloss finishes, and may be applied by brush, roller or spray.

INTUMESCENT COATINGS

Thin-film intumescent coatings, typically 1 or 2 mm in thickness, offer fire protection to structural steel without noticeable visual effect. In the event of fire, the thin coating expands up to 50 times to form a layer of insulating foam. The carbonaceous material in the coating, typically starch, is charred, while the heat also causes the release of acids. These act to produce large volumes of non-inflammable gases which blow up the charring starch within the softened binder into an insulating cellular carbon layer. Coatings may be applied to give 30, 60 or 120 minutes' fire protection. Intumescent emulsion paints or clear varnishes are appropriate for use on timber, although, where timber has been factory impregnated with a flame-retardant salt, the compatibility of the intumescent coating and flame retardant must be verified.

FUNGICIDE PAINTS

Fungicide paints for application in areas where mould growth is a recurrent problem usually contain a blend of fungicides to give high initial activity and steady long-term performance. The latter can be achieved with fungicide constituents of low solubility which are gradually released to the surface during the lifetime of the paint. Matt acrylic finishes are available in a range of colours.

ENAMEL PAINTS

Enamel paints based on polyurethane or alkyd resins give highly durable, impact-resistant, easily cleaned, hard gloss surfaces. Colours tend to be strong and bright, suitable for machinery and plant in interior and exterior locations.

MICACEOUS IRON OXIDE PAINTS

Micaceous iron oxide paints have good resistance to moisture on structural steelwork, iron railings, etc. owing to the mica plates, which reduce permeability to moisture vapour. A dry film thickness of 45–50 microns is typical, and therefore these paints require longer drying times than standard paint products. Micaceous iron oxide paints should be applied over an appropriate metal primer.

MASONRY PAINTS

Smooth and sand textured masonry paints are suitable for application to exterior walls of brick, block, concrete, stone or renderings. Where fine cracks are present, these can often be hidden using the sand textured material. Usually masonry paints contain fungicides to prevent discolouration by moulds and algae. Acrylic resin-based products are predominantly water-based; however, fast-drying solvent-based systems are also produced. Mineral silicate paints form a crystalline protective layer over the masonry surface, which tends to be more durable than the organic finishes from synthetic resins.

WATER-REPELLENT AND WATERPROOFING PAINTS

Silicone water-repellent paints can be applied to porous surfaces including brick, concrete, stone and renderings to prevent damp penetration. Such treatment does not prevent rising damp, but will allow the continued evaporation of moisture within the masonry. Two-pack epoxy waterproofing systems may be applied to sound masonry surfaces to provide an impervious coating. Typical applications are to rooms where condensation causes the blistering of normal paint films; also in basements and solid external walls where penetrating water is a problem, provided that a good bond can be achieved between substrate and epoxy resin. Bituminous paints provide a waterproof finish to metals and masonry, and may be used as a top dressing to asphalt or for renovating bitumen roofing felt. Aqueous bitumen coatings, if fully protected against physical damage, can provide a vertical membrane where the external ground level is higher than the internal floor level.

EPOXY PAINTS

Epoxy ester paint coatings are highly resistant to abrasion and spillages of oils, detergents or dilute aqueous chemicals. They are therefore frequently used as finishes to concrete, stone, metal or wood in heavily trafficked workshops and factories. Many are produced as two-pack systems requiring mixing immediately before application.

Natural wood finishes

Natural wood finishes include wood stains, varnishes and oils. Wood stains are pigmented resin solutions which penetrate into the surface and may then build up a sheen finish. Varnishes are unpigmented resin solutions which are intended to create a surface film. Timber preservatives are described in Chapter 4.

WOOD STAINS

Most wood stain systems for exterior use include a water- or solvent-based preservative basecoat which controls rot and mould growth. Typical formulations include zinc or copper naphthenate, dichlorofluanid, tri-(hexylene glycol) biborate and disodium octaborate tetrahydrate. Wood stain finishes are either low-, medium- or high-build systems, according to the particular application; they usually contain iron oxide pigments to absorb the ultraviolet light, which otherwise causes the surface degradation of unprotected timber. Generally, for rough-sawn timber, deeply penetrating wood stains are appropriate, whereas for smooth-planed timber a medium- or high-build system gives the best protection from weathering. Products are based on acrylic and/or alkyd resins.

For sawn timber, both organic solvent-based and water-based materials are available, usually in a limited range of colours. Solvent-based low-build products which are low in solids penetrate deeply, leaving a water-repellent matt finish, enhance the natural timber grain and are suitable for timber cladding. Deep penetration should eliminate the risk of flaking or blistering on the surface. Medium- and high-build products for exterior joinery offer the choice of semi-transparency to allow the grain to be partially visible, or opaque colours for uniformity. Solvent- and water-based products are available in a wide range of colours with matt or gloss finishes. The first coat both penetrates and adheres to the surface, while the second coat provides a continuous micro-porous film which is both permeable to moisture vapour and water-repellent, thus reducing the moisture movement of the timber. The coating, typically 30–40 microns thick, should remain sufficiently flexible to accept natural timber movements.

VARNISHES

Polyurethane varnishes are available in matt, satin or gloss finishes, based on either water- or solvent-based systems. The solvent-based systems produce the harder and more durable coatings, up to 80 microns thick, suitable for exterior woodwork. Products either retain the natural wood colour, enhance it, or add colour. Screening agents to protect timber from the effects of ultraviolet light are normally included in the formulations. Urethane-modified alkyd resins are suitable for interior use, and have the advantage of high resistance to scuffing and hot liquids. External weathering causes eventual failure by flaking and peeling as light passing through the varnish gradually degrades the underlying wood surface. For example, hardwood doors decorated with polyurethane varnish, protected from rain and direct sunlight by a porch, should have extended periods between maintenance.

OILS

Oils such as teak oil are used mainly for internal applications. Formulations based on natural oils for exterior use are high in solids, producing an ultraviolet resistant, microporous finish which may be transparent or opaque. The finish, which should not flake or crack, may be renovated by the application of a further coat.

References

FURTHER READING

CDA. 1994: *Colour Dimensions Association Directory*, London: Colour Dimensions Association.
Graystone, J. 1985: *The care and protection of wood*. Slough: ICI Paints Division.

ICI. 1986: *Colour Dimensions – Colour Atlas*. Imperial Chemical Industries plc.
ICI Paints. 1993: *Dulux trade paint specifier*. Version Four. Imperial Chemical Industries plc.
Wilkinson, J.G. 1979: *Industrial timber preservation*. London: Associated Business Press.

STANDARDS

BS 217: 1961. Red lead for paints and jointing compounds.
BS 476. Fire tests on building materials and structures.
    Part 6: 1989. Method of test for fire propagation for products.
    Part 7: 1987. Method for classification of the surface spread of flame products.
BS 1070: 1993. Black paint (tar-based).
BS 2015: 1992. Glossary of paint and related terms.
BS 2523: 1966. Specification for lead-based priming paints.
BS 3416: 1991. Specification for bitumen-based coatings for cold applications, suitable for use in contact with potable water.
BS 3698: 1964. Calcium plumbate priming paints.
BS 3761: 1995. Specification for solvent-based paint remover.
BS 4147: 1980. Specification for bitumen-based hot-applied coating materials for protecting iron and steel, including a suitable primer.
BS 4310: 1968. Specification for permissible limits of lead in low-lead paints and similar materials.
BS 4652: 1971. Metallic zinc-rich priming paint (organic media).
BS 4756: 1971. Ready-mixed aluminium priming paints for woodwork.
BS 4764: 1986. Specification for powder cement paints.
BS 4800: 1989. Specification for paint colours for building purposes.
BS 4900: 1976. Vitreous enamel colours for building purposes.
BS 5082: 1974. Specification for water-borne priming paints for woodwork.
BS 5252: 1976. Framework for colour co-ordination for building purposes.
BS 5358: 1993. Specification for solvent-borne priming paints for woodwork.
BS 5589: 1989. Code of practice for preservation of timber.
BS 5707. Solutions of wood preservatives in organic solvents:
    Part 1: 1979. Specification for solutions for general purpose applications, including timber that is to be painted.
    Part 2: 1979. Specification for pentachlorophenol wood preservative solution for use on timber that is not required to be painted.

Part 3: 1980. Methods of treatment.

BS 6150: 1991. Code of practice for painting of buildings.

BS 6477: 1992. Specification for water repellents for masonry surfaces.

BS 6900: 1987. Specification for raw, refined and boiled linseed oils for paints and varnishes.

BS 6949: 1991. Specification for bitumen-based coatings for cold application, excluding use in contact with potable water.

BS 6952. Exterior wood coating systems:

Part 1: 1988. Guide to classification and selection.

BS 7079. Preparation of sheet steel substrates before application of paints and related products:

Parts 0 and A–F.

BS 7664: 1993. Specification for undercoat and finishing paint.

BS 7719: 1994. Specification for water-borne emulsion paints for interior use.

BS 8000. Workmanship on building sites:

Part 12: 1989. Code of practice for decorative wallcoverings and painting.

BS 8202. Coatings for fire protection of building elements:

Part 1: 1987. Code of practice for the selection and installation of sprayed mineral coatings.

Part 2: 1992. Code of practice for the use of intumescent coating systems to metallic substrates for providing fire resistance.

BS EN 971. Paints and varnishes – terms and definitions for coating materials:

Part 1: 1996. General terms.

BS EN 21512: 1994. Paints and varnishes – sampling of products in liquid or paste form.

BUILDING RESEARCH ESTABLISHMENT PUBLICATIONS

BRE Digests

BRE Digest 54: 1971. Damp-proofing solid floors.

BRE Digest 197: 1982. Painting walls Part 1: Choice of paint.

BRE Digest 198: 1984. Painting walls Part 2: Failures and remedies.

BRE Digest 354: 1990. Painting exterior wood.

BRE Digest 387: 1993. Natural finishes for exterior wood.

BRE Good Building Guide

BRE GBG 22: 1995. Maintaining exterior wood finishes.

BRE Information Papers

BRE IP 16/87. Maintaining paintwork on exterior timber.

BRE IP 17/87. Factory applied priming paints for exterior joinery.

BRE IP 20/87. External joinery: end grain sealers and moisture control.

BRE IP 5/90. Preservation of hem-fir timber.

BRE IP 5/91. Exterior wood stains.

BRE IP 2/92. Factory-applied stain basecoats for exterior joinery.

BRE IP 3/92. Solvent vapour hazards during painting with white-spirit-borne eggshell paints.

BRE IP 4/94. Water-borne coatings for exterior wood.

BRE IP 8/95. Interior painting of trim with solvent-borne paints.

BRE IP 12/95. Controlling mould growth by using fungicidal paints.

BRE IP 5/96. Progress in European standardisation for exterior wood coatings.

BRE Defect Action Sheet

BRE DAS 135: 1989. External masonry painting.

TRADE ASSOCIATIONS

British Wood Preserving and Damp Proofing Association, 6 Office Village, 4 Romford Road, Stratford, London E15 4EA (0181 519 2588).

Colour Dimensions Association, 44 Rockley Road, London W14 0BT (0171 602 3456).

Paint Research Association, 8 Waldegrave Road, Teddington, Middx. TW11 8LD (0181 977 4427).

INDEX

—